Better Homes and Gardens®

ANNUAL

Recipes

2006

Baked Mediterranean Eggs
page 60

Meredith® Books
Des Moines, Iowa

Coffee Coffee Cake
page 64

Good food is near and dear to our hearts. During the week we whip together quick, nutrient-packed meals for our families. On weekends many of us savor the chance to create recipes we didn't have time for during the week. Holidays, celebrations, and parties revolve around delicious food, whether it's our favorite time-honored dishes or fun new meal ideas we've been waiting to try. From a quick snack before dinner to a barbecue for 50 guests, there's no better resource than the collection of trusted recipes from *Better Homes and Gardens*® magazine.

As the new Editor in Chief, I am delighted to share this year's collection of recipes. As you page through the book you'll discover hundreds of recipes that have graced the pages of *Better Homes and Gardens*® magazine during the past year. You'll find meal ideas for busy nights when dinner must be prepared and eaten after work and before soccer practice, as well as recipes that pull out all the stops. Turn to the back of this book for inspiring special-event menus: a milestone birthday, a casual summer lunch on the deck, or a meal of ethnic foods. Each recipe in the menus section comes from our Prize Tested Recipes® contest, a monthly feature in the magazine since 1937, in which readers share their recipes.

Expert food editors and home economists on our staff are constantly on the watch for the latest trends in food, wine, cookware, and just about anything that helps the home cook. Look for special sections highlighting their finds, as well as tips on celebrating with food. We offer advice on efficiency in the kitchen and healthful eating, as well as simple ideas for entertaining. You'll also find dozens of other helpful cooking tips and hints. Every recipe is backed by the Better Homes and Gardens® Test Kitchen seal, meaning it meets our high standards of taste, practicality, and reliability. Every recipe is guaranteed to work every time you make it. From our kitchen to yours—enjoy!

Gayle Butler

GAYLE BUTLER, EDITOR IN CHIEF
Better Homes and Gardens® magazine

Better Homes and Gardens® Annual Recipes 2006
Editor: Jessica Saari
Contributing Recipe Editor: Janet Figg
Contributing Writer: Carrie Holcomb
Contributing Designer: Diana Van Winkle
Associate Design Director: Som Inthalangsy
Copy Chief: Terri Fredrickson
Publishing Operations Manager: Karen Schirm
Senior Editor, Asset & Information Management: Phillip Morgan
Edit and Design Production Coordinator: Mary Lee Gavin
Editorial Assistant: Cheryl Eckert
Book Production Managers: Pam Kvitne, Marjorie J. Schenkelberg,
    Rick von Holdt, Mark Weaver
Contributing Copy Editor: Amanda Knief
Contributing Proofreaders: Maria Duryée, Gretchen Kauffman, Susan J. Kling
Contributing Indexer: Elizabeth Parson
Test Kitchen Director: Lynn Blanchard
Test Kitchen Product Supervisor: Maryellyn Krantz

Meredith® Books
Executive Director, Editorial: Gregory H. Kayko
Executive Director, Design: Matt Strelecki
Managing Editor: Amy Tincher-Durik
Executive Editor: Jennifer Darling
Senior Editor/Group Manager: Jan Miller
Senior Associate Design Director: Ken Carlson

Publisher and Editor in Chief: James D. Blume
Editorial Director: Linda Raglan Cunningham
Executive Director, New Business Development: Todd M. Davis
Executive Director, Sales: Ken Zagor
Director, Operations: George A. Susral
Director, Production: Douglas M. Johnston
Director, Marketing: Amy Nichols
Business Director: Jim Leonard

Vice President and General Manager: Douglas J. Guendel

Better Homes and Gardens® Magazine
Editor in Chief: Gayle Goodson Butler
Executive Editor: Kitty Morgan
Creative Director: Bradford W.S. Hong
Managing Editor: Lamont D. Olson
Art Director: Michael D. Belknap
Associate Art Director: Jessica Thomas
Deputy Editor, Food and Entertaining: Nancy Wall Hopkins
Associate Editors: Richard Swearinger, Stephen J. Exel
Editorial Assistants: Karen Pollock, Anna Anderson

Meredith Publishing Group
President: Jack Griffin
Senior Vice President: Karla Jeffries
Vice President, Corporate Solutions: Michael Brownstein
Vice President, Creative Services: Ellen de Lathouder
Vice President, Manufacturing: Bruce Heston
Vice President, Consumer Marketing: David Ball
Consumer Product Associate Marketing Director: Steve Swanson
Consumer Product Marketing Manager: Wendy Merical
Business Manager: Darren Tollefson

Meredith Corporation
Chairman of the Board: William T. Kerr
President and Chief Executive Officer: Stephen M. Lacy

In Memoriam: E. T. Meredith III (1933–2003)

Our seal assures you that every recipe in *Better Homes and Gardens® Annual Recipes 2006* has been tested in the Better Homes and Gardens® Test Kitchen. This means that each recipe is practical and reliable, and meets our high standards of taste appeal. We guarantee your satisfaction with this book for as long as you own it.

All of us at Meredith® Books are dedicated to providing you with information and ideas to enhance your home. We welcome your comments and suggestions. Write to us at: Meredith Books Editorial Department, 1716 Locust St., Des Moines, IA 50309-3023. Title is available by mail. To order editions from past years, call 800/439-4119.

Pictured on the front cover: Chocolate Harvest Cake (page 229)
Pictured on the back cover (clockwise from the top left): Roasted Chicken with Rosemary and Garlic Herb Potatoes (page 82); Zesty Lemon-Chicken Salad Sandwiches (page 171); Grilled Garden Pasta (page 41); Grilled Bananas and Pudding (page 47); Pork Chops with Gorgonzola and Pears (page 147); Quick-Change Chowder (page 200); Smoky Double Cheeseburger (page 40); Red, White, and Blueberry Shortcake (page 134).

Puffed Heart Lemon Cookies
page 27

Banana Breakfast Sundaes
page 117

Good friends, good times, and, of course, good food—that's what *Better Homes and Gardens®* *Annual Recipes 2006* is all about. Every meal you prepare is a chance to celebrate with family and friends. And we want you to celebrate! Whether you gather the family over make-ahead food during a weekend at the lake (see page 166), round up the kids for slumber party snacks (see page 10), or grill up some grub for 50 of your closest friends (see page 124), great times, fun, and laughs will abound. Or celebrate on a smaller scale by curling up on the couch with a heartwarming chowder (see page 200) or reconnecting with family over classic comfort food like pot roast (see page 188). No matter how you choose to celebrate your life, you'll find great recipes throughout this book to get the job done. Also look for:

Recipe Icons: Throughout the book, you'll find certain recipes are marked with one (or more) of three icons: "Kid Friendly," "Fast," and/or "Low Fat." These icons are quick indicators for you to recognize certain recipes you're searching for. Looking for something the kids will be sure to eat? Target the "Kid Friendly" icons. Need a meal on the table in under 30 minutes? You'll find dozens when looking for the "Fast" icon. And if you want dishes that are lighter for the waistline, search for the "Low Fat" icons (for more information, see page 334).

Home front section: At the end of most chapters, we included food-related stories from the "Home front" section of the magazine. Here you'll find fun tips and hints, as well as food ideas, restaurants to visit, and where certain brand-name items can be found.

Prizewinning Recipes: Every month we feature the Prize Tested Recipes® contest. Readers submit their creative recipes based on the topic of that month. You'll find the $400 and $200 winners of the contest beginning on page 252. In addition, you'll find the honor roll recipes from the contest—those that didn't make it into the magazine but were too delectable to keep out of this book.

Menu Ideas: For those special (or everyday) occasions when you need several recipes and serve-along ideas, look to the menu pages for inspiration! Starting on page 302 you'll find 28 menu ideas of all sorts ranging from informal to special occasion. All of the recipes here come from our Prize Tested Recipes® contest with serve-along ideas and beverage selections to round out the menus.

Ingredient Substitution Guide: Before you run off to the store for that one ingredient you forgot, check out the practical guide on page 335. It's designed to help you find realistic substitutions for common ingredients you may have forgotten to pick up when shopping.

2006 CONTENTS

Corn Bread Pineapple Sundae
page 46

Roasted Chicken with Rosemary and Garlic Herbed Potatoes
page 82

JANUARY

Catch-A-Dream Sleepover

Sausage Muffin Cups
page 13

Good Morning Oatmeal
page 12

Mini Ice Cream Dippers with Double-Dip Fondue
page 14

Cinnamon Grapes and Peanut Butter Dip
page 14

Catch-A-Dream Sleepover

GOOD TIMES, GOOD FRIENDS, AND GOOD SNACKS—THE PERFECT INGREDIENTS FOR HAPPY CHILDHOOD MEMORIES!

> When there's catching up to do or DVDs to watch, a big bowl of this salty-sweet snack mix will stave off hunger pangs.

Dream-Catcher Snack Mix

START TO FINISH: 10 MINUTES

- 1 10-oz. pkg. bear-shape cinnamon-flavored graham snack cookies (4 cups)
- 1 3.5-oz. pkg. unpopped white cheddar or cheddar microwave popcorn, microwaved according to package directions, or 9 cups packaged white cheddar popcorn
- 1 cup chocolate-covered raisins
- ¼ cup butter, melted
- ½ tsp. garlic salt
- 1½ cups red candy twist bites, or red candy twists, coarsely chopped

1. In a bowl combine cookies, popcorn, and raisins. Combine butter and garlic salt. Drizzle over popcorn mixture; toss. Add candy; toss. Store in an airtight container up to 24 hours. Makes 12 servings.

EACH SERVING: 367 cal., 13 g total fat (5 g sat. fat), 11 mg chol., 320 mg sodium, 61 g carbo., 2 g fiber, 3 g pro. Daily Values: 3% vit. A, 9% calcium, 8% iron.

Dream-Catcher Snack Mix

What's more fun than a magical night for giggles galore and spooky stories, when some best friends get together for a sleepover!

With a bit of mom-and-daughter planning, a fun sleepover is easy to arrange. The setting is an enchanting indoor campsite—complete with tents, pillows, and snacks aplenty.

A few days before the sleepover, let your young hostess print cards, address envelopes, and deliver or mail the invitations. If needed, let guests know to bring pillows, blankets, or sleeping bags. For the sleepover campsite, clear space in the family or TV room. Set up tents (or make some from sheets) around the middle of the room, leaving an area open for a late-night talkfest.

Party food, the center of attention of many sleepovers, keeps the campsite theme going. The girls will be so impressed with these scrumptious snacks that they'll never miss ordering in pizza. When the camping crew arrives to spend the night, settle everyone in with Cinnamon Grapes and Peanut Butter Dip, a treat that transforms PB&J into a kid's appetizer. A big bowl of Dream-Catcher Snack Mix—cheddar popcorn, chocolate-covered raisins, bear-shape graham crackers, and red candy twists—provides good munching from craft time until it's time to snuggle in for movies or talking.

At suppertime serve kid-size Sausage Muffin Cups with a sausage-and-barbecue sauce filling as tasty as any pizza. Ham and Peas Macaroni 'n' Cheese brims with wagon wheel pasta and chunks of deli ham to make the creamy mac 'n' cheese extra special. For dessert, everyone is served her own tray of Mini Ice Cream Dippers with Double-Dip Fondue—scoops of ice cream with pretzel handles—all in a muffin pan that's filled with toppers for dipping. For a bedtime snack, serve maple syrup stirred into milk and a stack of gingerbread cookies for dunking.

In the morning, tummies will likely be grumbling for breakfast. Watch the rush to the table when you serve Sunrise Sparklers and Eggheads, drinks made with peach nectar, white grape juice, and cranberry juice. Let the campers make edible art by decorating peeled hard-cooked eggs with food-safe markers.

Warming Good Morning Oatmeal, topped with vanilla yogurt and pear and dried fruit compote, ensures that everyone is sent out the door ready to greet civilization.

Good Morning Oatmeal

For a healthful start to the day, top quick-cooking oats with vanilla yogurt, granola, and a compote of dried fruits, pears, and cinnamon simmered in apple juice.

Good Morning Oatmeal
PREP: 10 MINUTES   **COOK:** 30 MINUTES

- 1¾   cups apple juice
- 1   7-oz. pkg. mixed dried fruit bits
- ⅓   cup packed brown sugar
- 3   inches stick cinnamon or ½ tsp. ground cinnamon
- 2   medium pears, cored and chopped
- 5   cups water (or 2½ cups water and 2½ cups milk)
- ½   tsp. salt
- 3   cups quick-cooking oats
- 2   6-oz. containers vanilla yogurt
- 1   cup granola

1. In saucepan combine juice, fruit bits, sugar, and cinnamon. Bring to boiling. Reduce heat; simmer, covered, 20 minutes. Add pears. Cook, covered, 10 minutes. Cool; remove cinnamon stick. Drain; discard liquid. In saucepan bring water and salt to boiling. Add oats. Reduce heat to medium; cook about 1 minute, stirring occasionally. To serve, top with fruit mixture, yogurt, and granola. Makes 8 servings.

 EACH SERVING: 357 cal., 5 g total fat (2 g sat. fat), 2 mg chol., 204 mg sodium, 74 g carbo., 5 g fiber, 8 g pro. Daily Values: 1% vit. A, 11% calcium, 13% iron.

Skewers of melon, kumquat, pineapple, and orange stir up these sparkly early morning drinks.

Sunrise Sparklers and Eggheads
For Eggheads, let the children color peeled hard-cooked eggs with food-safe markers as an art activity with breakfast.
START TO FINISH: 25 MINUTES

- Kumquats (optional)
- Melon chunks (optional)
- Pineapple chunks (optional)
- Halved orange slices or orange wedges (optional)
- 8   hard plastic drinking straws or wooden skewers (optional)
- 2⅔   cups peach or apricot nectar, chilled
- 2⅔   cups sparkling white grape juice, chilled
- 2⅔   cups cranberry juice, chilled

1. If desired, thread a kumquat, melon chunk, pineapple chunk, and orange slice on each straw. (Remove any pieces that block opening.) Stir together chilled nectar and grape and cranberry juices. Pour into glasses. Insert fruit straws. Makes 8 servings.

EACH SERVING: 145 cal., 0 g total fat, 0 mg chol., 13 mg sodium, 36 g carbo., 0 g fiber, 0 g pro. Daily Values: 4% vit. A, 111% vit. C, 5% calcium, 5% iron.

Mac 'n' cheese gets new life with the additions of ham, peas, and cream cheese.

Ham and Peas Macaroni 'n' Cheese

START TO FINISH: 25 MINUTES

- 8 oz. dried large wagon wheel pasta or elbow macaroni
- 2 cups frozen peas or cut green beans
- ¾ cup milk
- 2 6½-oz. containers or four 4-oz. containers light semisoft cheese with garlic and herb
- 12 oz. cooked ham or cooked chicken, cut into chunks
- ½ cup shredded cheddar cheese

1. In a Dutch oven or large pot cook pasta according to package directions. Stir in peas for last minute of cooking (or stir in green beans last 3 minutes). Drain pasta mixture; return to pot. Add milk, semisoft cheese, ham, and cheddar cheese. Cook and stir until heated through. Makes 8 servings.

EACH SERVING: 413 cal., 22 g fat, 76 mg chol., 651 mg sodium, 31 g carbo., 3 g fiber, 18 g pro. Daily Values: 16% vit. A, 12% vit. C, 13% calcium, 10% iron.

Ham and Peas Macaroni 'n' Cheese
Sausage Muffin Cups

Barbecue sauce adds tang to this pizza-in-a-cup. These simple and quick dinners are just right for kid-size appetites.

Sausage Muffin Cups

PREP: 25 MINUTES **BAKE:** 12 MINUTES

Nonstick cooking spray
- 1 11.5-oz. pkg. (8) refrigerated cornbread twists
- 4 oz. cooked sausage (such as smoked Polish sausage links or chicken sausage links), cut into ½-inch pieces
- ⅔ cup shredded cheddar, mozzarella, or pizza cheese
Scant ¼ cup bottled barbecue sauce

1. Preheat oven to 375°F. Coat eight 2½-inch muffin cups with cooking spray. Unroll cornbread dough into 16 pieces; do not twist. Cut each piece in half crosswise to equal 32 pieces. Press 3 halves into each cup, cutting and pressing to line cup.
2. Divide sausage among dough-lined cups. Top with cheese. Spoon sauce into cups. Cut remaining 8 dough halves lengthwise into halves. Arrange strips on top of each muffin in a pattern.
3. Bake 12 minutes until golden. Cool 2 minutes. Makes 8 servings.

EACH SERVING: 237 cal., 14 g total fat (5 g sat. fat), 22 mg chol., 586 mg sodium, 19 g carbo., 8 g pro. Daily Values: 2% vit. A, 1% vit. C, 8% calcium, 8% iron.

Welcome everyone to the party with this fresh fruit and dip treat. A scattering of nuts and a dusting of cinnamon enliven the flavors.

Cinnamon Grapes and Peanut Butter Dip

START TO FINISH: 10 MINUTES **FAST!**

- ⅓ cup plain yogurt
- ⅔ cup creamy peanut butter
- ½ a 7-oz. jar marshmallow crème
- 1 Tbsp. chopped peanuts
- 1 1-lb. bunch red seedless grapes
  Ground cinnamon or cinnamon-sugar

1. In a bowl beat yogurt and peanut butter with mixer. Beat in marshmallow crème. Transfer to a serving bowl; sprinkle with peanuts. Cut grapes into bunches; rinse. Dust with cinnamon. Makes 8 servings.

EACH SERVING (2 OUNCES GRAPES+2 TABLESPOONS DIP): 219 cal., 12 g total fat (2 g sat. fat), 1 mg chol., 129 mg sodium, 25 g carbo., 2 g fiber, 7 g pro. Daily Values: 1% vit. A, 10% vit. C, 4% calcium, 4% iron.

Cinnamon Grapes and Peanut Butter Dip

Double-dipping is allowed when each guest has her own muffin cup fondue pot.

Mini Ice Cream Dippers with Double-Dip Fondue

PREP: 30 MINUTES **FREEZE:** 30 MINUTES

- 2 pints cinnamon, butter pecan, or other desired flavor ice cream
  Tiny pretzel twists or pretzel sticks
  Orange or blue coarse sugar
  Crushed sugar cookies or shortbread cookies
  Shaved white chocolate or flaked coconut, toasted
  Peanuts, chopped
  Chocolate- and/or caramel-flavor hard shell-style
    ice cream coating

1. Place a baking sheet in the freezer 30 minutes. Use a 1-tablespoon scoop to make 24 ice cream balls; place on sheet. Press pretzel into each ball. Cover; freeze until firm. Using eight 6-cup muffin tins,* fill five cups in each with toppings. Add ice cream balls to sixth cup. Makes 8 servings.

*NOTE: Small bowls or cups can be substituted for the muffin tins.

EACH SERVING: 150 cal., 7 g total fat (5 g sat. fat), 30 mg chol., 146 mg sodium, 20 g carbo., 1 g fiber, 2 g pro. Daily Values: 6% vit. A, 6% calcium, 1% iron.

Mini Ice Cream Dippers with Double-Dip Fondue

New Yorkers Dave Arnold and Jennifer Carpenter, far left, share a traditional homemade Sunday night supper with family, including their infant son, Dax, and friends.

Recipe for Comfort

"So many of our friends leave the city when they have children, but we wanted to stay," says Jennifer Carpenter. She and husband Dave Arnold, along with their two little boys, Booker and Dax, make their home in a remodeled 800-square-foot space on Manhattan's Lower East Side. It's there the family embraces city living in an apartment that is cozy but, by national standards, small.

"It's a place where the boys can play with toy cars, a place where Dave can make biscuits on Saturday morning, and a place where we can have my sisters and friends over for Sunday night supper," Jennifer says.

Those Sunday night suppers have been a long-standing tradition for Jennifer and Dave as a primary way of staying connected to their extended family. Cooking and gathering people around the table is a natural inclination for Dave. He's a sculptor turned food consultant who has applied his expertise to the city's new Museum of Food and Drink.

With cooking a major part of the family's life, it was important to create a strong connection between the kitchen and living area in their small home. The kitchen was expanded in two directions to give Dave more space to work. A solid wall separating the kitchen from the living room was replaced with a long kitchen island that juts farther into the living area. Space once devoted to a hallway and eating area was folded into the kitchen, allowing room for more cabinets and countertop work area.

"I love that I can be in the kitchen cooking and Jennifer and her sisters can be in the living room, but we're all together," Dave says. "That's the strength of the apartment. It's comfortable for the four of us or for 10 for Sunday night supper. And it's very easy to live here."

On this Sunday evening, Dave carries on his mother's cooking tradition, serving her Pumpkin Lasagna. And just as comforting to them is knowing that the thoughtful design of their home makes spending time together with family and friends relaxed and joyful.

Pumpkin Lasagna
PREP: 1 HOUR **BAKE:** 40 MINUTES **STAND:** 15 MINUTES

- 12 dried lasagna noodles
- 8 oz. shiitake or porcini mushrooms, stemmed and sliced
- 8 oz. cremini or button mushrooms, sliced
- ¾ tsp. kosher salt or ½ tsp. salt
- 2 Tbsp. olive oil
- 12 slices bacon, cut crossways into ¼-inch strips
- 1½ cups chopped onion
- 3 Tbsp. snipped fresh sage or 2 tsp. dried leaf sage, crushed
- 2 15-oz. cans pumpkin
- ¾ cup whole milk or half-and-half
- 1 tsp. ground black pepper
- 1 tsp. cider vinegar
- 1 tsp. kosher salt or ¾ tsp. salt
- 1 15-oz. carton ricotta cheese
- 1 lb. fresh mozzarella cheese, cut in thin slices
- 6 oz. Parmigiano-Reggiano or Grana Padano cheese, finely shredded (1½ cups)

1. Preheat oven to 400°F. Cook noodles according to package directions. Drain; set aside. In skillet cook mushrooms and the ¾ teaspoon salt in hot olive oil over medium heat until tender and no liquid remains. Remove; set aside. Add bacon to skillet; cook until crisp. Remove; set aside. Discard all but 1 tablespoon drippings in skillet. Add onion; cook in drippings until tender. Add sage; cook 30 seconds. Add pumpkin, milk, pepper, vinegar, and the 1 teaspoon salt. Heat through.

2. In a greased 3-quart oval baking dish spread ½ cup pumpkin sauce. Cover bottom of dish with 4 noodles, trimming to fit. Spread one-third of sauce over noodles. Layer with one-third each of mushrooms, bacon, ricotta, mozzarella, and Parmigiano-Reggiano. Repeat layers twice. Bake, uncovered, for 40 to 45 minutes. Let stand for 15 minutes. Makes 12 servings.

EACH SERVING: 435 cal., 25 g total fat (13 g sat. fat), 64 mg chol., 806 mg sodium, 27 g carbo., 3 g fiber, 24 g pro. Daily Values: 231% vit. A, 7% vit. C, 55% calcium, 13% iron.

Pumpkin Lasagna

In good taste
FOOD AND ENTERTAINING

Teamwork: Beer, Blue Cheese, and Cheddar

Complete the list of football-watching necessities—a comfortable sofa, chunky chili, and frosty beer—by pairing several beer styles with robust blue cheeses and tangy cheddars. David Gremmels, president/cheesemaker of Rogue Creamery in Central Point, Oregon, suggests matching Pilsner and sharp cheddar, ale and mild cheddar, India pale ale with aged blue-veined blues, porter with smoked blue, and chocolate stout with chocolate stout cheddar. "Beer can be crisp, sharp, malty, or anything in between. Cheese is the same; they work in creamy contrast as well as crisp, complementary flavors," Gremmels says. "Regardless, when you're done, you're happy." Rogue Creamery; 866/665-1155; roguecreamery.com.

Rogue Creamery has won several awards for velvety-textured, sharply flavored Oregonzola cheese. Aged for at least 120 days, it pairs well with firm, bitter ales.

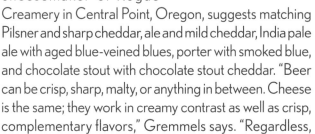

Double-Dip Fun

Assemble a gift of snacks for cozy afternoon get-togethers with friends. Package two flavors of potato chips. Tuck in a packet containing a tablespoon of a spice blend, such as Montreal steak or Cajun, to add to an 8-ounce carton of sour cream—instant chips and dip. Include a whisk, bowl, and napkins. Place it all in a baking dish with a cover that your hostess can keep to use later.

Oh My Darling

Be on the lookout for tangy-sweet clementines, which have a short season in winter. Because they're seedless and easy to peel, this citrusy blast of summer is convenient for kids to handle. Enjoy clementine slices dipped in melted chocolate, cut up in chicken salad, set atop cheesecake, added to beef stir-fry, mixed in salsa, and chopped and stirred into strawberry sauce and served over waffles.

FEBRUARY

SWEETS, TREATS, AND A LITTLE SOMETHING SPECIAL...

Puffed Heart Lemon Cookies
page 27

Paper, Glue, and I Love You

Beef Tenderloin with Three Spreads
page 25

**Ruby Red Winter Iced Tea,
Valentine's Snack Mix**
page 26

Braised Hunter-Style Chicken
page 29

Paper,
glue, and
I LOVE YOU

TURN THE ANNUAL TASK OF
MAKING VALENTINE'S DAY
CARDS INTO A REASON TO
CELEBRATE. THROW A PARTY
WITH GOOD FOOD AND ALL
THE CARD-MAKING SUPPLIES
THE KIDS WILL NEED.

No-Stir Oven Risotto and Heart-Shape Beets

PREP: 15 MINUTES **COOK (FOR BEET ONLY):** 35 MINUTES
BAKE: 45 MINUTES

1   large fresh beet (about 8 oz.) or one 14½-oz. can
       sliced beets, drained
2   14-oz. cans reduced-sodium chicken broth
1   cup water
1½   cups Arborio rice or medium grain white rice
1   medium onion, finely chopped (½ cup)
2   Tbsp. snipped fresh oregano or 2 tsp. dried oregano, crushed
1   Tbsp. olive oil
½   tsp. salt
1   cup finely shredded Gruyère cheese or Swiss cheese (4 oz.)

1. Wash and trim beet (do not peel). Cook, covered, in lightly salted boiling water for 35 to 45 minutes or until tender. Drain and cool slightly. Slip skin off beet and slice into ¼-inch slices. If desired, using a 1½-inch heart-shape cookie cutter, cut beet slices into hearts.

2. Meanwhile, preheat oven to 350°F. In a medium saucepan combine broth and water. Bring to boiling. In a 2-quart soufflé or casserole dish combine broth mixture, rice, onion, oregano, oil, and salt. Bake, covered, about 40 minutes or until rice is tender. Stir in cheese.

3. Top risotto with beets. Return to oven and bake, uncovered, 5 minutes more. Makes 8 side-dish servings.

EACH SERVING: 177 cal., 6 g total fat, (3 g sat. fat), 16 mg chol., 444 mg sodium, 23 g carbo., 1 g fiber, 8 g pro. Daily Values: 3% vit. A, 3% vit. C, 15% calcium, 10% iron.

No-Stir Oven Risotto and Heart-Shape Beets

T

he patient snip, snip, snip of scissors shaping construction paper into hearts, the scratching of pens writing poetry, the chain reaction as giggles make their way around the room—these are the sounds that fill the house when you throw a card-making party for Valentine's Day.

Creating a party like this is easy because the food uses make-ahead ingredients. For a snack while crafting, serve a Valentine-pretty trail mix of freeze-dried strawberries and raspberries, nuts, and pretzels prepared up to a week before party day.

Dividing party activities, with crafts and eating separate, doubles the fun and lets guests enjoy the meal while the glue dries on the cards.

Stacks of roasted beef tenderloin slices can be eaten with knife and fork or piled on crusty white bread. Top the beef slices with Blue Cheese-Parsley Crumble, Black Pepper-Olive Relish, or Horseradish Mayo. All three toppers are no-cook and made with five or fewer ingredients.

No-Stir Oven Risotto is a rice side dish that needs none of the stirring that the stovetop version requires. Because it wouldn't be a Valentine menu without hearts, top the risotto with beet slices cut into heart shapes with a cookie cutter. Another flash of red comes to the meal via four-ingredient Tomato Vinaigrette. The dressing is made by blending tomatoes with olive oil, vinegar, and just a hint of brown sugar; pour it over a salad of radishes, spinach, and spicy greens, such as arugula.

Finish the meal with a dessert that features sweet valentine colors. Heap raspberries—delicately coated in a butter and brown sugar syrup—over vanilla ice cream. For double the berry flavor, trade raspberry sorbet for the ice cream.

Valentine's Day without chocolate is unthinkable. Tiny coconut-dusted truffles take only an hour to make. To cut prep time even more, we explain how to create square truffles. Triple Chocolate Truffles have a traditional truffle center that's draped in melted chocolate.

As guests pack their treasures, that's your cue to bring out one more treat: Puffed Heart Lemon Cookies. These cakelike confections are a little tart with citrus and slightly sweet from a pink glaze.

Tuck one or two cookies in cellophane bags for each guest, then seal the bags with heart stickers so guests can tote them home in style.

Pink Coconut, Triple Chocolate, and Square Truffles

You have options with this recipe; make one or make them all.

PREP: 45 MINUTES **CHILL:** 1½ HOURS
FREEZE: 10 MINUTES **STAND:** 15 MINUTES

- 10 oz. semisweet chocolate, chopped
- ½ cup whipping cream
- ¼ cup butter, cut up

1. In a medium microwave-safe bowl combine semisweet chocolate, whipping cream, and butter. Microwave, uncovered, on 100% power (high) for 1 minute. Remove from microwave and stir until smooth. If necessary, return chocolate mixture to microwave and cook on high for 30 seconds more; stir until smooth. Use to make Pink Coconut Truffles, Triple Chocolate Truffles, or Square Truffles. Let all truffles stand at room temperature for 15 minutes before serving.

PINK COCONUT TRUFFLES: After melting chocolate mixture, stir ⅔ cup shredded coconut into the chocolate mixture. Cover bowl and refrigerate for 1½ hours. Line two baking sheets with nonstick foil or lightly greased foil. Drop chocolate mixture from rounded teaspoons onto prepared sheets. Cover with waxed paper; freeze for 10 minutes. Meanwhile, if desired, tint 1⅓ cups shredded coconut by combining coconut and 1 to 2 drops of pink gel food coloring; toss until coconut is tinted. Roll the chocolates between the palms of your hands into round balls, wetting hands if necessary. Roll the chocolate balls in tinted coconut; cover and refrigerate. Makes 35 truffles.

TRIPLE CHOCOLATE TRUFFLES: After melting chocolate mixture in Step 1, above, cover bowl and chill for 1½ hours. Line two baking sheets with nonstick foil or lightly greased foil. Drop chocolate mixture from rounded teaspoons onto prepared sheets. Cover with waxed paper; freeze for 10 minutes. In a small microwave-safe bowl microwave 6 ounces chocolate-flavor candy coating on 100% power (high) for 1 minute. Stir until smooth. If necessary, return to microwave and cook on 100% power (high) for 30 seconds more; stir until smooth. Using a fork, quickly dip the chocolate balls, one at a time, into coating. Draw the fork across the rim of the bowl to remove excess coating. Return to baking sheet. Let stand about 30 minutes or until coating is set.

In another small bowl combine ¼ cup white chocolate baking pieces and 1 teaspoon shortening. Microwave on 100% power (high) for 30 seconds; stir until melted. If necessary, microwave on high for 15 seconds more; stir until smooth. Drizzle over tops of chocolate-covered truffles. Let stand until set. Refrigerate truffles, tightly covered, up to 2 weeks. Makes 35 truffles.

SQUARE TRUFFLES: Line an 8-inch-square baking pan with nonstick foil or lightly greased foil, extending foil over edges of pan; set aside. After melting chocolate mixture in Step 1, pour ¾ cup chocolate mixture in prepared pan. Spread evenly. Sprinkle 1 cup shredded coconut evenly over chocolate layer. Pour remaining chocolate mixture over coconut; spread evenly. Freeze 1 to 48 hours. Use edges of foil to lift chocolate from pan. Cut chocolate into 36 squares. Place ⅓ cup cocoa powder in a small bowl. Dredge truffles in cocoa powder. Refrigerate until 15 minutes before serving. Makes 36 truffles.

EACH TRUFFLE COCONUT, CHOCOLATE, AND SQUARE VARIATIONS: 150 cal., 11 g total fat, (8 g sat. fat), 12 mg chol., 17 mg sodium, 12 g carbo., 1 g fiber, 1 g pro. Daily Values: 3% vit. A, 1% calcium, 4% iron.

Raspberry-Nut Sundaes

If fresh raspberries aren't available, substitute frozen strawberries, thawed according to package directions.

START TO FINISH: 20 MINUTES

- ½ cup butter
- ½ cup packed light brown sugar
- 1½ cups fresh raspberries
- ⅔ cup honey-roasted cashews or honey-roasted almonds, coarsely chopped
- 1 tsp. finely shredded lemon peel
- 2 pints vanilla ice cream and/or raspberry sorbet

1. In a large skillet melt butter; stir in brown sugar until melted. Cook, stirring frequently, over medium heat until boiling. Reduce heat to medium-low. Cook and stir for 1 minute. Remove from heat. Add raspberries, nuts, and lemon peel; stir gently to coat.

2. Scoop ice cream and/or sorbet into eight small dessert cups. Top with raspberry mixture. Serve immediately. Makes 8 servings.

EACH SERVING: 401 cal., 28 g total fat, (16 g sat. fat), 99 mg chol., 164 mg sodium, 35 g carbo., 2 g fiber, 4 g pro. Daily Values: 17% vit. A, 9% vit. C, 11% calcium, 7% iron.

Pink Coconut Truffles, Triple Chocolate Truffles, and Raspberry-Nut Sundaes

Tomato Vinaigrette with Mixed Green Salad and
Beef Tenderloin with Three Spreads

Beef Tenderloin with Three Spreads
PREP: 10 MINUTES   **ROAST:** 35 MINUTES   **STAND:** 10 MINUTES

- 2   2-lb. beef tenderloin roasts or four 12-oz. pork tenderloins
- 1   Tbsp. olive oil
- 1   tsp. dried rosemary, crushed
- ½   tsp. coarse sea salt or kosher salt
- 1   recipe Horseradish Mayo
- 1   recipe Black Pepper-Olive Relish
- 1   recipe Blue Cheese-Parsley Crumble
- 12   slices firm-texture white bread
  Sliced radishes (optional)

1. Preheat oven to 425°F. Brush roasts with olive oil; sprinkle with rosemary and salt. Insert oven-safe meat thermometer into center of one of the roasts. For beef, roast, uncovered, for 35 to 45 minutes or until thermometer registers 140°F. For pork, roast, uncovered 25 to 35 minutes or until thermometer registers 160°F.

2. Allow roasts to stand, covered loosely with foil, about 10 minutes (this allows juices to reabsorb and roast to firm for easier slicing). Cut into ¼- to ½-inch-thick slices. Serve with Horseradish Mayo, Black Pepper-Olive Relish, Blue Cheese-Parsley Crumble, bread, and, if desired, sliced radishes. Makes 12 to 16 servings.

EACH SERVING OF BEEF (WITHOUT SPREADS): 315 cal., 14 g total fat, (4 g sat. fat), 93 mg chol., 271 mg sodium, 13 g carbo., 0 g fiber, 33 g pro. Daily Values: 3% calcium, 26% iron.

HORSERADISH MAYO: In a bowl stir together ½ cup mayonnaise, 1 tablespoon prepared horseradish, 1 tablespoon snipped fresh flat-leaf parsley, and ⅛ teaspoon cayenne pepper. Makes ⅔ cup.

EACH TABLESPOON HORSERADISH MAYO: 80 cal., 8 g total fat, (2 g sat. fat), 4 mg chol., 65 mg sodium, 0 g carbo., 0 g fiber, 0 g pro. Daily Values: 1% vit. A, 1% vit. C.

BLACK PEPPER-OLIVE RELISH: In a bowl stir together 1 cup pitted and chopped kalamata or niçoise olives; 1 small red sweet pepper, chopped; 1 tablespoon olive oil; 1 tablespoon balsamic vinegar or red wine vinegar; and 1 teaspoon cracked black pepper. Makes about 1⅔ cups.

EACH TABLESPOON BLACK PEPPER-OLIVE RELISH: 14 cal., 1 g total fat, (0 g sat. fat), 0 mg chol., 2 mg sodium, 0 g carbo., 0 g fiber, 0 g pro. Daily Values: 2% vit. A, 8% vit. C.

BLUE CHEESE-PARSLEY CRUMBLE: In a small bowl lightly toss together 2 ounces blue cheese, crumbled; ½ cup chopped fresh flat-leaf parsley; 1 tablespoon lemon juice; and ⅛ teaspoon coarse sea salt or kosher salt. Makes about ¾ cup.

EACH TABLESPOON BLUE CHEESE-PARSLEY CRUMBLE: 17 cal., 1 g total fat, (1 g sat. fat), 4 mg chol., 84 mg sodium, 0 g carbo., 0 g fiber, 0 g pro. Daily Values: 5% vit. A, 7% vit. C, 3% calcium, 1% iron.

Tomato Vinaigrette with Mixed Green Salad
PREP: 20 MINUTES   **STAND:** 20 MINUTES

- 1   14½-oz. can diced tomatoes with onion and garlic
- ¼   cup red wine vinegar or white wine vinegar
- ½   to 1 tsp. packed brown sugar
- 2   Tbsp. olive oil or salad oil
- 6   cups baby spinach leaves
- 2   cups torn arugula
- 2   cups torn red endive or red cabbage
- ½   cup sliced radishes (optional)
- ¼   cup snipped fresh basil
  Shards of fresh Parmesan cheese

1. In a blender combine undrained tomatoes, vinegar, and brown sugar. Cover and blend until smooth. With blender running, gradually add oil in a steady stream. Cover and let stand 20 minutes to blend flavors or chill up to 4 days. If chilled, let stand at room temperature for 30 minutes before serving. Stir before serving.

2. Meanwhile, in a salad bowl toss together spinach, arugula, endive, radishes (if desired), and basil. Add ¼ cup dressing; toss to coat. Top with Parmesan cheese; pass remaining vinaigrette. Makes 8 servings.

EACH SERVING: 63 cal., 4 g total fat, (1 g sat. fat), 1 mg chol., 301 mg sodium, 5 g carbo., 1 g fiber, 2 g pro. Daily Values: 50% vit. A, 19% vit. C, 7% calcium, 8% iron.

Ruby Red Winter Iced Tea

White tea is slightly sweeter than green or black tea, either of which can be substituted to make this drink.

PREP: 10 MINUTES **STAND:** 10 MINUTES **CHILL:** 4 HOURS

- ½ cup sugar
- ½ cup water
- 8 bags hibiscus flower herb tea (such as Red Zinger)
- 1 recipe Brewed White Tea
  - Ice cubes
- 12 fresh rosemary sprigs (optional)

1. For syrup, in a small saucepan stir together the sugar and water; add tea bags. Cook and stir over medium heat until sugar is dissolved and mixture just comes to boiling. Remove from heat. Cover and let stand for 10 minutes. Carefully remove tea bags, gently squeezing to remove liquid.

2. Divide Brewed White Tea between two 2-quart pitchers. Divide syrup between pitchers. Cover and chill at least 4 hours or up to 24 hours. Serve over ice. If desired, add a rosemary sprig as a stirring stick. Makes about 12 (8-ounce) servings.

BREWED WHITE TEA: If using loose tea, divide ½ cup (about 1½ ounces) tea between two large tea balls. Place tea balls or 12 tea bags in a large heatproof bowl or pitcher. Cover with 12 cups boiling water. Allow to stand 4 minutes. Remove tea ball or bags. Cool before refrigerating.

LOW FAT **EACH SERVING:** 33 cal., 0 g total fat (0 g sat. fat) , 0 mg chol., 0 mg sodium, 9 g carbo., 0 g fiber, 0 g pro.

Ruby Red Winter Iced Tea and Valentine's Snack Mix

Valentine's Snack Mix

Find dried or freeze-dried raspberries and strawberries in the produce section.

START TO FINISH: 30 MINUTES

- Butter or nonstick cooking spray
- 1¼ cups pecan halves
- 1¼ cups lightly salted shelled pistachio nuts
- ⅓ cup sugar
- 2 Tbsp. butter
- ¼ tsp. kosher salt or ⅛ tsp. salt
- 1½ cups small pretzels (assorted shapes) or chocolate-covered raisins
- 1¼ cups dried raspberries
- 1 cup dried strawberries
- 1 Tbsp. slivers of fresh orange peel

1. Preheat oven to 325°F. Line a baking sheet with foil or nonstick foil. Butter regular foil or lightly coat with nonstick cooking spray; set aside. In a shallow baking pan evenly spread the nuts; keep warm in oven while you make the glaze.

2. For glaze, place sugar in a large heavy skillet. Heat over medium-high heat, shaking skillet several times to heat sugar evenly (do not stir). Heat until the sugar begins to melt (it should look syrupy). Stir only the melted sugar to prevent it from overbrowning; shake pan and stir gently to incorporate remaining unmelted sugar as it begins to melt. Reduce heat to medium-low. Continue to cook until all the sugar is melted and golden, about 5 minutes more. Add the 2 tablespoons butter to skillet; stir until butter is melted and mixture is combined. Remove from heat. Stir in salt. Add the warm nuts to skillet; stir to coat. Pour nut mixture onto prepared baking sheet. Cool completely. Break into clusters.

3. Store nut mixture in airtight container at room temperature up to 1 week. Before serving, transfer to a bowl; add pretzels, raspberries, strawberries, and orange peel; stir to mix. Makes about 8 cups (sixteen ½-cup servings).

EACH SERVING: 186 cal., 11 g total fat, (2 g sat. fat), 4 mg chol., 123 mg sodium, 19 g carbo., 3 g fiber, 3 g pro. Daily Values: 2% vit. A, 3% vit. C, 2% calcium, 5% iron.

Puffed Heart Lemon Cookies

Lemon Glaze was used for the cookies in the photo (right). To create the Marbled Puffed Heart Cookies (see photo, below), use Royal Icing.

PREP: 30 MINUTES **BAKE:** 8 MINUTES PER BATCH

  Nonstick cooking spray
1 cup all-purpose flour
¼ tsp. baking powder
1 cup butter, softened
¾ cup granulated sugar
2 eggs
1 egg yolk
¼ tsp. vanilla
2 tsp. finely shredded lemon peel
1 recipe Lemon Glaze or Royal Icing

1. Preheat oven to 375°F. Lightly coat 3-inch heart-shape pans* or 3½-inch muffin top pans with nonstick cooking spray; set aside.
2. In a small bowl stir together flour and baking powder; set aside.
3. In a large mixing bowl beat butter with an electric mixer on low speed for 30 seconds. Add sugar. Beat until combined, scraping sides of bowl occasionally. Beat in eggs, egg yolk, and vanilla. Beat in flour mixture. Stir in lemon peel.
4. Using about 2 tablespoons batter, spread into the prepared heart-shape pans or muffin top pans. Bake for 8 to 10 minutes or until edges are golden. Carefully transfer to a cooling rack; cool completely.
5. Spread half of each cookie top with white Lemon Glaze and the other half with pink Lemon Glaze or frost all one color. Let stand on wire rack until icing is dry. Transfer some of the icing to a pastry bag fitted with a writing tip or a small resealable plastic bag with a small corner snipped off to pipe initials, if desired. Makes about 20 cookies.

*TEST KITCHEN TIP: These cookies were made in Heart Cookie Treat Pans from www. wilton.com. The pans have a slot for inserting lollipop sticks, but the batter is thick enough that it will not run out of these grooves. If you do not have this pan or a madeleine or muffin top pan, add 1½ cups all-purpose flour and 1 teaspoon finely shredded lemon peel to the dough. Cover and refrigerate dough for 3 hours or until easy to handle. On a lightly floured surface, roll dough to ⅛- to ¼-inch thickness. Cut out dough with 3-inch heart-shape cookie cutters. Bake as above.

Puffed Heart Lemon Cookies

LEMON GLAZE: In a large bowl stir together 3 to 4 tablespoons lemon juice and 2½ cups powdered sugar. Spoon half the mixture into another bowl. One drop at a time, add red food coloring to one bowl; stir thoroughly between each addition to reach desired shade of pink.

ROYAL ICING: In a large mixing bowl combine one 16-ounce package powdered sugar (4¼ cups), 2 tablespoons meringue powder (with cake decorating supplies at crafts stores), and ½ teaspoon cream of tartar. Add ½ cup warm water. Beat with an electric mixer on low speed until combined; beat on high speed for 7 to 10 minutes or until sugar mixture is stiff. Add 1 teaspoon finely shredded lemon peel. Cover bowl with a damp paper towel and plastic wrap; refrigerate up to 2 days. Makes about 5 cups.

EACH COOKIE WITH LEMON GLAZE: 199 cal., 10 g total fat (6 g sat. fat), 56 mg chol., 76 mg sodium, 27 g carbo., 0 g fiber, 2 g pro. Daily Values: 6% vit. A, 2% vit. C, 1% calcium, 2% iron.

TO MAKE THE MARBLED PUFFED HEART

Prepare Royal Icing; divide among three bowls. Tint light pink, orange, and bright pink.

Spread cookie halves with light pink and bright pink. To create marbling, pipe orange and bright pink icing in parallel lines on light pink icing; draw the tip of a toothpick or skewer through icing. To outline, pipe orange icing around cookie edges and along center; dot with icing on edges. If desired, press a silver dragée in icing; remove dragée before eating.

FLAVOR IT HEALTHFULLY

BY **RICHARD SWEARINGER** PHOTOGRAPHS BY **JAMES CARRIER** FOOD STYLING BY **SUSAN BROWN DRAUDT**

Getting kids to eat sensibly is a

goal that's easy to set but sometimes hard to reach. For every kid who loves squash and carrots, there are 10 who'll only eat plain spaghetti.

The issue isn't stubborn kids, says Connie Guttersen, nutritionist and author of *The Sonoma Diet* (www.sonomadiet.com), published in 2005 by Meredith Books. Connie, mother of William, 5, and GiGi, 8, says the challenge is finding a way to unlock the good flavors in healthful foods, such as vegetables and whole grains, that appeal to the whole family.

"People always come back from Europe saying 'Why don't our vegetables taste as good as the ones over there?' As a matter of fact they do," says Connie. "We have the best produce in the world. People just need to change the way they cook it."

For example, to get the most flavor from broccoli, broccoli raab, spinach, and other greens, she recommends sauteing them in a little olive oil and adding a sprinkle of salt and splash of lemon—then sweetening them with a light drizzle of honey. Roasting vegetables at high heat, then drizzling them with balsamic vinegar, is another trick that works well, she says. (For a recipe and a guide to roasting vegetables, see page 29.)

Connie has gathered cooking ideas from widely different sources: memories of childhood meals at her grandparents' home in Italy, her work as an obesity researcher, years in the kitchen cooking for family and friends, and, most recently, creating recipes for *The Sonoma Diet*.

Besides highlighting vegetables, Connie also encourages kids to eat healthfully by ensuring they choose their food in right-size portions. The secret is in learning to judge correct proportions by eye.

She considers a "healthy plate" about half vegetables, a quarter carbohydrates like potatoes or pasta, and one-quarter protein. This visual approach is easy for kids to understand and it teaches them a skill they can use for a lifetime.

Braised Hunter-Style Chicken (see photo, right) illustrates how healthful eating and great taste go hand in hand. The chicken gets a nutritional boost from generous amounts of onions and tomatoes, and the ingredients also provide a significant amount of flavor.

Braised Hunter-Style Chicken

When using the chicken broth option, increase the tomato paste to 3 tablespoons.

PREP: 40 MINUTES **BAKE:** 25 MINUTES

- 3 lb. meaty chicken pieces (such as breasts, thighs, and legs), skinned
  Kosher salt or salt and freshly ground black pepper
- 1 Tbsp. olive oil
- 8 oz. button mushrooms, sliced
- 1½ cups chopped onions
- 2 cloves garlic, minced
- ½ cup dry red wine or chicken broth
- 2 Tbsp. tomato paste
- 1 14-oz. can stewed tomatoes
- 1 Tbsp. finely chopped fresh thyme or 1 tsp. dried thyme, crushed
- 1 bay leaf
- 1 Tbsp. chopped fresh flat-leaf parsley
- 1 to 2 Tbsp. lemon juice

1. Preheat oven to 350°F. Season chicken with salt and pepper. In a 12-inch ovenproof skillet with lid cook chicken in hot oil for 10 minutes or until light brown, turning to brown evenly. Drain off the drippings, reserving 1 tablespoon. Remove chicken and set aside.

2. In the same skillet cook mushrooms, onions, and garlic in reserved drippings until tender. Stir in wine and tomato paste. Cook and stir for 1 to 2 minutes or until most of the liquid has evaporated. Stir in stewed tomatoes, thyme, and bay leaf. Arrange chicken pieces on the tomato mixture. Season chicken with additional salt and black pepper. Bring mixture to boiling over medium heat.

3. Cover and bake for 25 to 30 minutes or until chicken is no longer pink (170°F for breasts; 180°F for legs and thighs).

4. To serve, arrange chicken on a platter; spoon sauce over top. Sprinkle with parsley and drizzle with lemon juice. Makes 6 servings.

LOW FAT EACH SERVING: 281 cal., 10 g total fat (2 g sat. fat), 92 mg chol., 278 mg sodium, 11 g carbo., 2 g fiber, 32 g pro. Daily Values: 4% vit. A, 19% vit. C, 5% calcium, 16% iron.

Braised Hunter-Style Chicken

Roasted Asparagus

Roasted Asparagus

PREP: 10 MINUTES **ROAST:** 10 MINUTES

- 1½ lb. fresh asparagus, trimmed, or other vegetables (see chart, below)
- 2 Tbsp. chopped fresh herbs or 2 tsp. dried herbs,* crushed (optional)
- 2 Tbsp. extra virgin olive oil
  Kosher salt and freshly ground black pepper
- 1 oz. Parmesan cheese, shaved

1. Preheat oven to 450°F. Heat a heavy shallow baking pan in the oven for 5 minutes.

2. Meanwhile, in a large bowl toss asparagus with herbs, oil, salt, and pepper.

3. In the hot baking pan spread asparagus in a single layer. Return to oven. Roast, uncovered, until spears are tender when pierced with the tip of a knife, about 10 to 12 minutes, depending on spear thickness, stirring once during roasting.

4. Remove baking pan from oven. Transfer asparagus to a platter. Sprinkle with shaved Parmesan cheese. Makes 4 to 6 servings.

***TEST KITCHEN TIP:** Use dried Italian seasoning or a combination of dried herbs, such as thyme, oregano, or rosemary.

EACH SERVING: 107 cal., 9 g total fat (2 g sat. fat), 5 mg chol., 243 mg sodium, 4 g carbo., 2 g fiber, 5 g pro. Daily Values: 14% vit. A, 7% vit. C, 11% calcium, 11% iron.

VEGETABLE ROASTING TIMES

VEGETABLE	MINUTES
1 lb. carrots, peeled and cut in 1-inch pieces	35 to 40
1 lb. green beans, trimmed and precooked in boiling water for 2 minutes, then drained	8 to 10
1½ lb. sweet potatoes, thinly sliced	16 to 18
1½ lb. fingerling potatoes, or new potatoes, cut in half lengthwise	25 to 30

NOTE: All roasting times are at 450°F. For vegetables roasted longer than 15 minutes, stir occasionally until they are tender.

Pastry Cream Danish

PASTRY CREAM DANISH

PREP: 45 MINUTES **RISE:** 2³⁄₄ HOURS
CHILL: 6 HOURS **BAKE:** 10 MINUTES

- 1 pkg. active dry yeast
- ¼ cup warm water (105°F to 115°F)
- ¼ cup butter, softened
- ¼ cup granulated sugar
- ½ tsp. salt
- 2 cups all-purpose flour
- 1 tsp. ground cardamom
- ⅓ cup milk
- 1 egg
- 1 egg yolk
- ¾ cup raisins
- 6 Tbsp. cold butter, thinly sliced
- 1 Tbsp. butter, melted
- 1 recipe Cream Filling
- 1 recipe Powdered Sugar Icing

GREAT DANISH

BY **STEPHEN EXEL** PHOTOGRAPHS BY **JOYCE OUDKERK POOL** AND **GREG SCHEIDEMANN**

Danish ranks high on our list of

companions for morning coffee at the diner. If you're hoping to be the hit with your breakfast set, serve the rich, buttery taste and tender, flaky pastry that these homemade Danish offer. But be prepared: You'll have to earn your accolades with time and muscle.

Yummy cream filling substitutes for the usual jam center, a secret to the goodness of these sweet pastries. Rolling out the dough, layering it with butter, folding it over, and repeating the process is another. This process creates a multilayer pastry dough similar to puff pastry and gives this Danish its light-as-air quality. Double-rising is the third secret, but you can shorten that step by making the dough one day ahead and refrigerating it.

If you've wondered whether Danish really are Danish, they are; but in Denmark they're called Vienna Bread. The reason for the name involves a bit of labor history. During a baker's strike in Denmark in the late 1800s, Viennese bakers were enlisted to staff pastry shops. They brought with them their "roll-and-fold" method, which was later adopted by the Danes when they returned to work.

1. In a mixing bowl stir yeast into warm water to soften. In a second mixing bowl beat the ¼ cup butter, the sugar, and salt until creamy. Add ½ cup of the flour, the cardamom, and milk. Add egg and egg yolk. Add softened yeast; beat until well combined. Stir in remaining flour and the raisins until dough is smooth and comes together. Cover bowl; let rise in a warm place until double (about 2 hours). Chill dough 6 hours. (Or omit 2-hour rising time and chill dough 12 to 24 hours.)
2. Grease a baking sheet; set aside. Turn dough out onto a well-floured surface.
3. Roll dough into a 15×10-inch rectangle. Place half the butter slices evenly on dough; lightly press butter into dough. Fold dough crosswise into thirds. Rotate dough a quarter turn to the right. Repeat rolling and folding using remaining butter slices. Roll again to 15×10-inch rectangle; fold crosswise into thirds. Give dough a quarter turn to the right.
4. Roll folded dough into a 12×9-inch rectangle. Cut dough into twelve 3-inch squares. Fold corners of square into center, pressing lightly to seal. Place each on prepared baking sheet. Using the rounded side of a floured tablespoon, press firmly to make an indentation in the center of each dough square. Cover; let rise in a warm place until double (45 to 55 minutes). (You may see the butter slices soften and begin to melt out of rolls.) Press indentation again, if necessary.

5. Bake in a 375°F oven for 10 to 12 minutes or until golden brown. Remove from pan. Brush with melted butter; cool on wire racks. Meanwhile, prepare Cream Filling and Powdered Sugar Icing. Spoon cream filling into the center of each Danish. Drizzle each with icing. Makes 12 pastries.

CREAM FILLING: In a medium saucepan combine ½ cup milk and 5 teaspoons all-purpose flour using a whisk. Cook and stir over medium heat until thickened and bubbly. Reduce heat; cook and stir 2 minutes more. Remove from heat. Cover surface with plastic wrap. Cool to room temperature (do not stir). In a mixing bowl beat ½ cup softened butter, ½ cup granulated sugar, and ½ teaspoon vanilla with an electric mixer on medium speed until light and fluffy. Add half the cooled cooked mixture at a time, beating on low speed after each addition until smooth. Makes about 1½ cups.

POWDERED SUGAR ICING: In a small bowl combine 1 cup sifted powdered sugar, ½ teaspoon vanilla, and 1 tablespoon milk. Stir in additional milk, 1 teaspoon at a time, until icing reaches drizzling consistency.

EACH PASTRY: 374 cal., 21 g total fat (13 g sat. fat), 89 mg chol., 310 mg sodium, 44 g carbo., 1 g fiber, 4 g pro. Daily Values: 16% vit. A, 1% vit. C, 4% calcium, 8% iron.

1. After lightly pressing the butter slices into the dough, carefully fold the dough into thirds as you would a letter. Repeat the process to incorporate the butter into the dough.

2. You may want to use a little water to moisten the dough when you press the corners into the center of the cut pastry square.

3. The back of a rounded tablespoon measure is an effective way to make an indentation for the pastry cream filling. After the second rising, it may be necessary to repeat the indentation.

4. The Powdered Sugar Icing should run easily off a spoon but not be watery. If icing is too thick, add up to 1 teaspoon of milk a splash at a time to the powdered sugar mixture to reach the desired consistency.

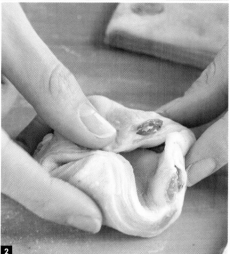

POT ROAST TWO WAYS

BY **RICHARD SWEARINGER** PHOTOGRAPHS BY **GREG SCHEIDEMANN**

Dressed up for company with

spices and distinctive ingredients or served as a homey meat-and-potatoes supper, pot roast never fails to please everyone at the table.

Budget Pot Roast, the comfort-food version, sticks to classic flavors: thyme, onions, carrots, and a little red wine vinegar to give zing to the gravy. Company Pot Roast adds apples; parsnips; dried plums; and a savory rub of garlic, sage, and cayenne pepper.

Tumble these into a Dutch oven, turn the heat to low, and savor the aromas filling the house.

Both recipes begin with one of the least-expensive meat selections in the grocery store—beef chuck. Chuck is ideal for these recipes because it has a robust meaty flavor that stands up to long, slow cooking.

Budget Pot Roast

PREP: 30 MINUTES **COOK:** 1¾ HOURS

- 1 2½- to 3-lb. boneless beef chuck pot roast
   Salt and ground black pepper
- ¼ cup cooking oil
- 2 large onions, cut into ¾-inch slices
- ¾ cup water
- ¼ cup red wine vinegar
- 1 tsp. dried thyme, crushed
- ¼ tsp. salt
- 1 lb. potatoes
- 1 lb. carrots cut in 2-inch pieces
- 2 stalks celery, bias-sliced in 1-inch pieces
- ½ cup cold water
- ¼ cup all-purpose flour

1. Trim fat from roast. Sprinkle with salt and pepper. In a 4½- to 6-quart Dutch oven over medium heat brown roast on all sides in hot oil. Remove roast. In same pan cook onions until browned. Remove onions. Carefully wipe excess oil from pan. Return roast and onions to pan. Combine the ¾ cup water, the vinegar, thyme, and ¼ teaspoon salt. Pour over roast and onions. Bring to boiling; reduce heat. Simmer, covered, for 1 hour.

2. Meanwhile, if using new potatoes, peel a strip of skin from the center of each. If using medium potatoes or sweet potatoes, peel and cut into eighths. Add potatoes, carrots, and celery to roast. Return to boiling; reduce heat. Simmer, covered, for 45 to 55 minutes more or until roast and vegetables are tender. Transfer meat and vegetables to a serving platter, reserving juices in Dutch oven. Keep warm.

3. For gravy, measure juices; skim off fat. If necessary, add enough water to juices to equal 1½ cups. Return to Dutch oven.

4. In a small bowl whisk together the ½ cup cold water and the flour until smooth. Stir into juices in pan. Cook and stir over medium heat until thickened and bubbly. Cook and stir for 1 minute more. If desired, season with pepper. Serve gravy with roast and vegetables. Makes 8 to 10 servings.

EACH SERVING: 342 cal., 13 g total fat (3 g sat. fat), 83 mg chol., 363 mg sodium, 22 g carbo., 4 g fiber, 33 g pro. Daily Values: 138% vit. A, 23% vit. C, 5% calcium, 25% iron.

Budget Pot Roast

Company Pot Roast

PREP: 30 MINUTES **COOK:** 1 HOUR 40 MINUTES

- 1   2½- to 3-lb. boneless beef chuck pot roast
- 2   cloves garlic, minced
- 1   tsp. dried sage, crushed
- ½   tsp. salt
- ½   tsp. ground black pepper
- 2   Tbsp. cooking oil
- ¼   tsp. cayenne pepper
- 1   cup of water
- 1   large onion, cut into thin wedges
- 1   cup dried pitted plums (prunes), halved
- 1   lb. apples, cored and cut in thick wedges
- 2   lb. parsnips and/or carrots, peeled and cut in 2-inch pieces
- ½   cup cold water
- ¼   cup all-purpose flour
      Salt and ground black pepper
- 1   Tbsp. balsamic vinegar or 1 tsp. red wine vinegar

Company Pot Roast

1. Trim fat from roast. In a small bowl stir together garlic, sage, salt, and black pepper. Pat garlic-spice mixture on the surface of the roast. In a 5½- to 6-quart Dutch oven over medium heat brown roast on all sides in hot oil. Drain off fat. Sprinkle cayenne pepper on roast. Pour water over roast; add onion. Bring to boiling; reduce heat. Simmer, tightly covered, for 1 hour and 20 minutes.

2. Add fruits and vegetables to roast. Return to boiling; reduce heat. Simmer, covered, for 20 to 25 minutes more or until parsnips and apples are tender, adding water if necessary. With a slotted spoon transfer all to a platter, reserving juices in Dutch oven. Keep warm.

3. For gravy, measure juices; skim off fat. If necessary, remove some of the juices or add enough water to juices to equal 1½ cups. Return to Dutch oven. In a small bowl whisk together the ½ cup cold water and the flour until smooth. Stir into juices in pan. Cook and stir over medium heat until thickened and bubbly. Cook and stir for 1 minute more. Season to taste with salt and pepper. Stir in balsamic vinegar. Serve gravy with roast, vegetables, and fruits. Makes 8 to 10 servings.

LOW FAT **EACH SERVING:** 361 cal., 10 g total fat (3 g sat. fat), 83 mg chol., 248 mg sodium, 37 g carbo., 6 g fiber, 32 g pro. Daily Values: 5% vit. A, 23% vit. C, 5% calcium, 24% iron.

Home front

X's and O's

Send edible kisses and hugs to your favorite valentine. Cut homemade or purchased sugar cookie dough with X and O cookie cutters and sprinkle with red and pink sugar. Pile them in a bowl for a Valentine's Day party or slip into waxed paper sandwich bags for kids to hand out as party favors.

Aprons: adult $14, child $18, notNeutral; 800/270-6511; www.notneutral.com.

The Way to Someone's Heart

Enlist the help of homemade or prepared sauces to serve dinner in valentine colors. These three can take you from appetizer to dessert. Your loved one will be tickled pink!

Grilled or sauteed shrimp appetizers get a sweet and savory Southwestern note with Guava Prickly Pear Cactus sauce. Brush on sauce after grilling or add to food at the end of cooking time. Guava Prickly Pear Cactus Sauce, $8; Earth & Vine Provisions; 888/723-8463; www.earthnvine.com.

Pesto lovers will be green with envy when you serve pasta or bruschetta topped with Pink Pesto. This sauce combines traditional pesto ingredients—basil, olive oil, pine nuts, and garlic—with a tomato base for pure pink pleasure. Or stir jarred pesto sauce into chopped tomatoes to top pasta. Pink Pesto, $7; Sauces 'n Love, Inc.; 866/772-8237; www.saucesnlove.com.

For dessert, fill a large bowl with strawberry or cherry ice cream and top it with Port 'Spiked' Cranberries dessert sauce or a puree of cooked fresh or frozen strawberries. Serve the bowl with two spoons and the intent to huddle close. Port 'Spiked' Sauce Cranberries, $5; Sable & Rosenfeld; 800/505-7839; www.gourmetathome.net.

MARCH

SPRING IS JUST BEGINNING TO BLOSSOM THIS MONTH,
BUT ON THOSE DAYS WHEN THERE'S A CHILL IN THE AIR,
GRILLED FOOD IS STILL POSSIBLE. OPT FOR THE INDOOR
VERSION OF YOUR SIZZLED AND SEARED FAVORITES.

Jalapeño Steak Sandwiches
page 49

Fire Up the Grill Indoors

Smoky Double Cheeseburger
page 40

Spiced Chicken Thighs and Bean Salad
page 45

Grilled Garden Pasta
page 41

Spicy Orange Pork and Bok Choy
page 42

Fire Up the Grill INDOORS

WHILE THE FLAVORS IMPARTED BY CHARCOAL AND GAS GRILLS MAY BE HARD TO BEAT, INDOOR GRILLS HAVE JUST AS MUCH TO OFFER—CONVENIENCE AND EASE BEING AT THE TOP OF THE LIST.

Prosciutto-Wrapped Roughy

Prosciutto-Wrapped Roughy

Rosemary sprigs add flavor to the fish, but the sprigs are not meant to be eaten. Be sure to remove them before serving.

PREP: 20 MINUTES **GRILL:** 10 MINUTES

- 2 orange roughy or cod fillets, ½ inch thick, or 4 skinless flounder, catfish, or trout fillets, about ¼ inch thick
- 4 2-inch sprigs fresh rosemary or 2 tsp. dried rosemary, crushed
- 4 slices prosciutto or thinly sliced cooked ham
- 3 Tbsp. lemon juice
  Freshly ground black pepper
- 2 medium roma tomatoes, halved
- 1 Tbsp. olive oil
- 1 19-oz. can cannellini beans, rinsed and drained
- 1 clove garlic, minced
- 2 tsp. snipped fresh rosemary or ½ tsp. dried rosemary, crushed
- ¼ tsp. smoked sea salt, crushed, or ⅛ tsp. salt

1. Thaw fish, if frozen. Rinse and pat dry with paper towels. Cut each fillet in half crosswise. If using roughy or cod, place a rosemary sprig on top of each fillet half or sprinkle with the 2 teaspoons dried rosemary. If using thinner fish fillets, place rosemary sprigs or dried rosemary on half of the pieces and top with remaining fish pieces to make 4 stacks. Wrap 1 slice of prosciutto around fish and rosemary. Sprinkle fish with 1 tablespoon of the lemon juice and the pepper. Set aside.

2. Heat a nonstick or well-seasoned grill pan on stovetop over medium heat until hot. Meanwhile, cut tomatoes in half lengthwise. Brush tomatoes lightly with olive oil. Add tomato halves to grill pan,* cut sides down. Grill 6 to 8 minutes or until tomatoes are very tender, turning once. Remove tomatoes from grill; set aside to cool slightly.

3. Place fish fillets on grill pan, rosemary sprig sides up if fillets are not stacked. Grill for 4 to 6 minutes or until fish flakes easily when tested with a fork, turning once halfway through cooking.

4. Coarsely chop grilled tomatoes. In a medium serving bowl gently toss together tomatoes, remaining lemon juice, the olive oil, beans, garlic, the 2 teaspoons snipped rosemary, and the salt. Place fish on bean mixture. Remove rosemary sprigs. Makes 4 servings.

FOR TABLETOP GRILL: Preheat grill according to manufacturer's directions. Place tomato halves on grill rack. If using a covered grill, close lid. Grill until tomatoes are tender. For covered grill, allow 3 to 4 minutes. (For open grill, allow 6 to 8 minutes, turning tomatoes once halfway through grilling.) Remove tomatoes from grill; set aside. Add fish fillets to grill, tucking under any thin edges if using whole fillets. If using a covered grill, close lid. Grill until fish flakes easily when tested with a fork. For covered grill, allow 2 to 3 minutes. (For open grill, allow 4 to 6 minutes, turning stacked fillets or halved fillets once halfway through grilling.) Continue as directed in Step 4 above.

*TEST KITCHEN TIP: If grill pan is large enough, tomatoes and fish may be grilled at the same time.

 EACH SERVING: 276 cal., 7 g total fat (1 g sat fat), 49 mg chol., 989 mg sodium, 21 g carbo., 7 g fiber, 39 g pro. Daily Values: 9% vit. A, 18% vit. C, 9% calcium, 12% iron.

Mmm ... the hiss and sputter of meat over the flames creates a matchless sultry, smoky taste. Nothing beats the barbecue for big flavor with little fuss—and you don't even have to leave your kitchen to get it.

Traditionally, the primal pleasures of the grill are the province of good weather. But today's tabletop grills and stovetop grill pans, thick on store shelves, are worthy pinch-hitters for the backyard variety. These beauties put that fresh-from-the-coals taste within reach even when it's 30°F and sleeting outside. It's summer on a plate all year.

Just like outdoor grills, indoor models have a built-in bonus: speed. High-heat searing seals in flavor and cooks food in a jiffy, so dinner will be on the table before the kids can finish their pickup basketball game. And nothing beats an indoor grill for simplicity—no waiting for coals to burn down, no reminders to refill the propane tank. Just preheat and cook!

The taste-enhancing tricks that fuel our fervor for outdoor cooking work just as well under your roof. Soak cuts of meat or fish in garlicky marinades, massage them with peppery spice rubs, or splash them with tangy finishing sauces. Best of all, kitchen mess is minimal—you can pull off a company-special meal, such as spicy orange-sauced pork chops accompanied by baby bok choy, using a single grill pan. Or keep things simple; it doesn't get much more satisfying than a luscious burger, rich with smoked cheese and onion slices.

You'll find three basic indoor grill types on the market. Freestanding tabletop grills are closest to outdoor gas or electric grills, with heating units under an open-face grate. Tabletop "contact" grills (à la George Foreman grills) have closable lids and work like waffle irons: Heat radiates from the top and bottom plates. Grill pans are heavy-duty skillets with ridged bottoms for creating those appetizing grill marks. Each of the quick-fix meals on these pages works with all three options, though cooking times will vary slightly. Most of the dishes go from start to finish in 30 minutes or less.

So if the snow is still flying when your family starts craving great grilled food, go ahead and indulge them by giving indoor grilling devices a try.

Smoky Double Cheeseburger

Smoky Double Cheeseburger
Burgers grilled indoors take on outdoor flavor from smoked cheese mixed into the patties. Watch the timing; cheese can burn quickly!
PREP: 25 MINUTES **GRILL:** 15 MINUTES

1	egg, lightly beaten
½	cup soft bread crumbs
3	oz. smoked cheddar cheese or cheddar cheese, finely shredded (¾ cup)
3	green onions, chopped
2	Tbsp. Worcestershire sauce
1	Tbsp. Dijon-style mustard
¼	tsp. ground black pepper
1¼	lb. ground beef round or ground sirloin
4	¼- to ½-inch onion slices (optional)
4	hamburger buns, split and toasted
¼	cup mango chutney or cranberry relish
½	cup arugula leaves * or watercress
1	to 2 oz. Asiago or Parmesan cheese, shaved

1. In a large bowl combine egg, bread crumbs, smoked cheddar, green onions, Worcestershire sauce, mustard, and pepper. Add ground beef and mix gently. Shape into four ½-inch-thick patties; set aside.

2. Heat a nonstick or well-seasoned grill pan on stovetop over medium-high heat until hot. Reduce heat to medium; if using, add onion slices to grill pan. Grill for 6 to 8 minutes or until tender and lightly browned, turning once. Remove from pan.

3. Add patties to pan. Grill for 9 to 12 minutes or until meat is done (160°F), turning once.

4. Spread bottoms of hamburger buns with chutney; top with arugula, patties, onion slices (if using), shaved cheese, and bun tops. Makes 4 servings.

FOR TABLETOP GRILL: Preheat grill according to manufacturer's directions. Add onions, if using, to grill. If using a covered grill, close lid. Grill until onions are lightly browned. For covered grill, allow 5 to 7 minutes. (For open grill, allow about 10 minutes.) Remove onions. Add patties to grill. If using a covered grill, close lid. Grill until meat is done (160°F). For a covered grill, allow 4 to 6 minutes. (For open grill, allow about 7 to 8 minutes per side.) Continue as directed in Step 4 above.

*TEST KITCHEN TIP: Rinse arugula thoroughly (it can be gritty). Dry in a salad spinner or pat dry with paper towels before laying on burgers.

EACH SERVING: 586 cal., 31 g total fat (14 g sat. fat), 172 mg chol., 777 mg sodium, 35 g carbo., 2 g fiber, 41 g pro. Daily Values: 11% vit. A, 11% vit. C, 32% calcium, 31% iron.

Grilled Garden Pasta

Grill vegetables in large pieces; then chop and toss with pasta.

PREP: 30 MINUTES   **GRILL:** 20 MINUTES

- ½ cup small fresh basil leaves or fresh Italian flat-leaf parsley leaves
- ½ cup crumbled feta cheese or finely shredded Parmesan cheese
- ¼ cup pine nuts, toasted, if desired
- 1 or 2 cloves garlic, minced
- 1 jalapeño chile pepper, seeded and minced (see tip, page 49)
- 2 tsp. finely shredded lemon peel
- 6 oz. dried spaghetti or fettuccine
- ¼ cup olive oil
- ¼ cup lemon juice
- ½ tsp. kosher salt or salt
- 2 leeks or baby Vidalia onions or 1 small onion
- 1 small eggplant (12 oz.) and/or 1 medium zucchini
- 2 medium tomatoes, sliced ¾ inch thick

1. In a bowl combine basil, feta cheese, pine nuts, garlic, jalapeño pepper, and lemon peel. Set aside.

2. Prepare pasta according to package directions. Drain. Toss pasta with olive oil, lemon juice, and salt. Cover and keep warm.

3. Meanwhile, prepare vegetables. If using leeks, trim root ends and tough green leaves; halve leeks lengthwise and wash thoroughly. If using onions, cut into ¾-inch slices. If using eggplant, peel if desired, and cut into ¾-inch slices. If using zucchini, halve lengthwise. Brush vegetables with additional olive oil.

4. Heat a nonstick or well-seasoned grill pan on stovetop over medium heat until hot. Add half the eggplant, leeks, and tomatoes to grill pan; grill about 5 minutes per side or until brown and tender. Repeat with remaining vegetables.

5. Cut vegetables into bite-size chunks. On a large platter swirl pasta with a fork to make a large nest, or divide pasta among 4 plates. Transfer vegetable mixture from cutting board to pasta nest(s). Sprinkle feta mixture over all. Makes 4 servings.

FOR TABLETOP GRILL: Preheat grill according to manufacturer's directions. Grill leeks, eggplant, and tomato slices on grill until eggplant and leeks are tender and tomatoes are heated through. If using a covered grill, close lid. For covered grill, allow 5 to 6 minutes for leeks, 4 to 5 minutes for eggplant and leeks, and 2 to 3 minutes for tomatoes. (For open grill, allow 12 to 14 minutes for leeks, 8 to 10 minutes for eggplant, and 4 to 5 minutes for tomatoes, turning once.)

EACH SERVING: 371 cal., 18 g total fat (5 g sat. fat), 16 mg chol., 458 mg sodium, 43 g carbo., 5 g fiber, 10 g pro. Daily Values: 23% vit. A, 37% vit. C, 13% calcium, 13% iron.

Grilled Garden Pasta

Spicy Orange Pork and Bok Choy

Spicy Orange Pork and Bok Choy
Bok choy looks like white celery with wide, dark green leaves.
PREP: 20 MINUTES **MARINATE:** 4 HOURS **GRILL:** 16 MINUTES

- 1 cup orange juice
- ½ cup bottled chili sauce
- 2 Tbsp. cooking oil
- 1 Tbsp. curry powder
- ½ tsp. crushed red pepper
- 4 ¾-inch-thick boneless center pork loin chops (1¼ to 1½ lb.)
- 2 baby bok choy (8 oz. total), halved lengthwise, or 1 small head bok choy (1 lb.), quartered lengthwise
- 2 Tbsp. cooking oil
  Hot cooked rice (optional)

1. For marinade, in a 2-cup glass measure combine orange juice, chili sauce, oil, curry powder, and crushed red pepper; stir well. Place half the marinade in a resealable plastic bag set in a shallow dish; cover and refrigerate remaining half. Add pork to marinade in plastic bag; seal. Marinate in refrigerator for 4 to 24 hours.

2. Remove pork from marinade; discard marinade. Heat a nonstick or well-seasoned grill pan on stovetop over medium-high heat until hot. Reduce heat to medium; place pork in pan. Grill pork for 8 to 10 minutes or until chops are slightly pink in the center and juices run clear (160°F), turning once. Remove pork from pan; cover and keep warm.

3. Brush bok choy with cooking oil. Add bok choy to grill pan, cut sides down; grill 8 minutes or until just tender, turning after 5 minutes.

4. Meanwhile, in a small saucepan bring reserved marinade to boiling. Reduce heat and simmer, uncovered, for 10 to 13 minutes or until liquid is reduced to ½ cup. Serve pork with bok choy, sauce, and, if desired, rice. Add *salt* to taste. Makes 4 servings.

FOR TABLETOP GRILL: Preheat grill according to manufacturer's directions. Place pork on the grill rack. If using a covered grill, close lid. Grill until chops are slightly pink in center and juices run clear (160°F). For covered grill, allow 6 to 8 minutes. (For open grill, allow 10 to 12 minutes, turning once halfway through grilling.) Remove chops and cover to keep warm. Brush bok choy with cooking oil; add to grill, cut sides down. Grill until just tender. For covered grill, allow 5 to 7 minutes. (For open grill, allow 10 to 12 minutes, turning once after 5 minutes of grilling.) Continue as directed in Step 4 above.

EACH SERVING: 399 cal., 22 g total fat (5 g sat. fat), 77 mg chol., 497 mg sodium, 16 g carbo., 3 g fiber, 33 g pro. Daily Values: 50% vit. A, 81% vit. C, 10% calcium, 13% iron.

Sausage and Pepper Salad

If you like, drizzle on additional dressing to soak up with the bread.
PREP: 20 MINUTES **GRILL:** ABOUT 34 MINUTES

Sausage and Pepper Salad

- 1 8- to 10-inch plain or herbed Italian flatbread (focaccia)
- 1 Tbsp. olive oil
- 2 large red, yellow, and/or green sweet peppers
- 4 seasoned, fully cooked sausages, such as chicken and sun-dried tomato sausages (8 to 10 oz.)
- 1 6-oz. pkg. fresh baby spinach
- ½ cup bottled balsamic vinaigrette salad dressing
   Thinly shaved or shredded Parmesan cheese

1. Heat a nonstick or well-seasoned grill pan on stovetop over medium heat until hot. Split focaccia bread in half horizontally. Brush cut side of one half with olive oil (save remaining half for another use). Add focaccia half to hot grill pan, cut side down. Grill 12 minutes or until browned and crisp, turning once. Remove from grill pan; set aside.

2. Cut peppers lengthwise in 1-inch strips, removing seeds, membranes, and stems. Add pepper strips to hot grill pan; grill for 12 minutes or until tender, turning once. Remove from pan; set aside.

3. Prick sausages with a fork in several places; cut sausages in half lengthwise. Place sausage halves in hot grill pan. Grill 10 minutes or until browned, turning once. Remove from grill pan; set aside.

4. In a large bowl combine pepper strips and spinach. Add ¼ cup of the salad dressing; toss to coat. Divide spinach mixture among 4 serving plates. Cut bread half into narrow wedges; add to plates along with sausage halves. Top with Parmesan. Pass remaining dressing. Serve immediately. Makes 4 servings.

FOR TABLETOP GRILL: Preheat grill according to manufacturer's directions. Split and brush focaccia as directed above. Add focaccia half to grill. If using a covered grill, close lid. Grill until bread is browned and crisp, about 6 to 8 minutes for covered grill. (For open grill, allow about 12 minutes, turning once.) Remove bread. Cut peppers as directed above; grill until pepper pieces are tender, about 10 minutes for covered grill. (For open grill, allow about 12 minutes, turning once.) Remove peppers. Prepare sausages as directed above. Add sausage halves to grill. Grill until browned, about 6 to 8 minutes for covered grill. (For open grill, allow 10 minutes, turning once.) Remove sausages. Continue as directed in Step 4 above.

EACH SERVING: 356 cal., 23 g total fat (5 g sat. fat), 21 mg chol., 992 mg sodium, 26 g carbo., 3 g fiber, 15 g pro. Daily Values: 111% vit. A, 177% vit. C, 17% calcium, 11% iron.

SPICE UP SUPPER WITH A DIFFERENT KIND OF CHICKEN SALAD. COMBINED WITH GREEN BEANS, AVOCADO, AND BLUE CHEESE, THESE CUMIN- AND CORIANDER-BRUSHED CHICKEN THIGHS ARE TOPS!

Spiced Chicken Thighs and Bean Salad

Spiced Chicken Thighs and Bean Salad

For an even quicker chicken dish, replace the green beans and edamame with 6 to 8 cups coarsely torn romaine lettuce.

START TO FINISH: 30 MINUTES

- 2 Tbsp. olive oil
- 1 tsp. ground coriander
- 1 tsp. ground cumin
- ½ tsp. salt
- ½ tsp. ground cinnamon
- ¼ tsp. cayenne pepper
- 1¼ lb. skinless, boneless chicken thighs
- 1 cup fresh or frozen green and/or wax beans
- 1 cup frozen edamame (green soy beans) or lima beans
- 1 avocado, halved, seeded, peeled, and sliced
- 3 oz. blue cheese, broken into chunks
- ¼ cup bottled creamy garlic, cucumber ranch, or Italian vinaigrette salad dressing

1. Heat a nonstick or well-seasoned grill pan on stovetop over medium heat until hot. In a small bowl combine oil, coriander, cumin, salt, cinnamon, and cayenne pepper. Trim fat from chicken. Brush oil mixture on both sides of chicken thighs.

2. Place chicken in hot grill pan. Cook about 12 minutes or until chicken is tender and no longer pink, turning once. Transfer chicken to a cutting board. Cut each chicken thigh into 3 pieces.

3. Meanwhile, in a large saucepan cook fresh beans, covered, in enough boiling water to cover for 10 to 15 minutes or until crisp-tender. If using frozen beans, cook for 5 to 10 minutes or until crisp-tender. Remove beans with a slotted spoon;* set aside. Add edamame to boiling water. Cover and cook for 4 to 6 minutes or until tender. Drain well. Arrange chicken, beans, edamame, avocado, and cheese on salad plates or a platter; drizzle with dressing. Serve immediately. Makes 4 servings.

FOR TABLETOP GRILL: Preheat grill according to manufacturer's directions. Brush chicken with oil mixture as above. Place chicken on the grill rack. If using a covered grill, close lid. Grill until chicken is tender and no longer pink. For covered grill, allow 4 to 6 minutes. (For open grill, allow 14 to 18 minutes, turning once halfway through grilling.) Cut each thigh into 3 pieces. Continue as directed in Step 3 above.

*TEST KITCHEN TIP: If you do not have a slotted spoon, place green beans in a heat-proof strainer. Lower strainer into boiling water and cook as directed above. Lift strainer out of water to drain. Cook edamame or lima beans as directed above.

EACH SERVING: 543 cal., 35 g total fat (9 g sat. fat), 129 mg chol., 880 mg sodium, 15 g carbo., 7 g fiber, 43 g pro. Daily Values: 11% vit. A, 51% vit. C, 28% calcium, 25% iron.

A LITTLE SOMETHING ON THE SIDE

While your main dish sizzles on the grill, whip up one of these speedy and tasty serve-alongs.

▪ Toss together a fruit salsa to pile on salad greens in lieu of conventional dressing. Chop one or two peaches or nectarines (or other fruit), add a bit of sliced green onion, chopped jalapeño chile pepper, snipped cilantro, and a squeeze of fresh lime juice.

▪ Make a batch of quick-cooking couscous or orzo, then stir in chopped fresh veggies, such as tomatoes and cucumbers. Drizzle with lemon juice and olive oil and add a sprinkle of freshly grated Parmesan cheese.

▪ Open a bag of slaw mix, add finely chopped banana peppers and onion, then splash with coleslaw dressing. Just before serving, stir in fresh mint.

▪ Pair grilled pineapple with chicken, grilled pears with pork, or grilled mangoes with salmon. (Lightly brush fruit with cooking oil before grilling.)

Corn Bread Pineapple Sundae
Crusty corn bread is a wonderful contrast to pineapple.
PREP: 20 MINUTES **GRILL:** 4 MINUTES

- 1 8½-oz. pkg. corn muffin mix, 1 recipe Homemade Corn Bread Muffins, or 6 purchased corn bread muffins
- ¼ cup butter, melted
- 2 Tbsp. sugar
- ½ tsp. ground cinnamon
- 1 fresh pineapple, peeled, cored, and cut crosswise in ½-inch slices, or one 20-oz. can pineapple slices (juice pack), drained
  Vanilla ice cream
- ½ cup caramel-flavor ice cream topping, warmed
- 1 recipe Toasted Walnuts

1. Prepare muffin mix according to package directions, making 6 muffins, or prepare Homemade Corn Bread Muffins. Using a serrated knife, cut each muffin in half. Brush cut sides of muffins with half the melted butter. In a small bowl combine sugar and cinnamon. Sprinkle cut sides of muffins with some of the cinnamon-sugar mixture. Heat a nonstick or well-seasoned grill pan on stovetop over medium heat until hot. Place muffin halves on grill, cut sides down, and grill for 1 to 2 minutes or until browned and crisp. Set aside.

2. Brush remaining melted butter on pineapple slices. Grill pineapple slices 3 to 5 minutes or until grill marks appear, turning once. Remove from grill. Sprinkle with remaining cinnamon-sugar mixture. For each serving, arrange 2 muffin halves and some of the fruit in a serving dish with a scoop of vanilla ice cream. Drizzle warm caramel-flavor topping over all. Sprinkle with Toasted Walnuts. Serve immediately. Makes 6 servings.

FOR TABLETOP GRILL: Preheat grill according to manufacturer's directions. Place muffin halves on grill, cut sides down. If using a covered grill, close lid. Allow 1 to 2 minutes for open and covered grill. Remove muffins. Add brushed fruit. For a covered grill, close lid. Allow 3 to 5 minutes, turning if necessary. (For open grill, allow 3 to 5 minutes for pineapple, turning once to brown evenly.) Serve as above.

HOMEMADE CORN BREAD MUFFINS: In a medium bowl stir together ½ cup all-purpose flour, ⅓ cup cornmeal, 1 to 2 tablespoons sugar, 1¼ teaspoons baking powder, and ¼ teaspoon salt; set aside. In a small bowl combine 1 beaten egg, ½ cup milk, and 2 tablespoons cooking oil or melted butter. Add egg mixture all at once to flour mixture. Stir just until moistened. Spoon batter into 6 greased 2½-inch muffin cups, filling cups two-thirds full. Bake in a 400°F oven about 15 minutes or until lightly browned and a wooden pick inserted near center comes out clean. Makes 6 muffins.

TOASTED WALNUTS: Preheat oven to 350°F; spread ½ cup chopped walnuts in a single layer in a shallow baking pan. Bake for 5 to 8 minutes or until light golden brown, stirring once after 3 minutes. Watch carefully to avoid burning.

EACH SERVING: 668 cal., 33 g total fat (12 g sat. fat), 116 mg chol., 489 mg sodium, 85 g carbo., 2 g fiber, 10 g pro. Daily Values: 15% vit. A, 27% vit. C, 22% calcium, 9% iron.

Corn Bread Pineapple Sundae

Grilled Bananas and Pudding

Layer instant pudding with shortbread cookies and grilled buttery, sweet bananas for this tempting Southern-style dessert.

PREP: 20 MINUTES **GRILL:** 2 MINUTES

- 1 4-serving size pkg. instant vanilla pudding mix
- 2 cups milk
- ⅓ cup dairy sour cream
- 1½ tsp. vanilla
- 4 medium-size firm bananas
- 2 Tbsp. butter, melted
- 1 to 2 Tbsp. sugar
- 12 shortbread cookies or gingersnaps, broken into 1-inch pieces
- 1 Tbsp. honey, such as wildflower, orange blossom, or clover
- ¼ tsp. ground nutmeg
-    Pecan halves, toasted

1. Prepare pudding mix according to package directions using the 2 cups milk. Whisk in sour cream and vanilla until smooth. Cover surface with plastic wrap. Once set up, set aside half the prepared pudding. Reserve the other half for another use.

2. Peel bananas. Cut each banana in half crosswise, then cut each half in half lengthwise (16 pieces). Brush banana quarters on both sides with butter; sprinkle with sugar. Heat a nonstick or well-seasoned grill pan on stovetop over medium heat. Grill bananas (half at a time, if necessary) about 2 minutes or until browned and softened, turning once.

3. To serve, place 2 banana quarters in each of 4 parfait or dessert dishes, cutting bananas as necessary to fit. Top with some of the cookies and pudding. Repeat layers. Combine honey and nutmeg; drizzle over pudding. Top with pecans. Makes 4 servings.

FOR TABLETOP GRILL: Preheat grill according to manufacturer's directions. Place bananas on grill. If using a covered grill, close lid. Grill bananas until browned and softened, about 1 to 2 minutes for a covered grill. (For open grill, allow 4 to 6 minutes, turning once.) Continue as directed in Step 3 above.

EACH SERVING: 450 cal., 20 g total fat (7 g sat. fat), 30 mg chol., 362 mg sodium, 66 g carbo., 4 g fiber, 6 g pro. Daily Values: 9% vit. A, 18% vit. C, 10% calcium, 7% iron.

Grilled Bananas and Pudding

Jalapeño Steak Sandwiches

A HINT OF JALAPEÑO MAKES ALMOST EVERYTHING TASTE BETTER! THIS STEAK'S MARINADE THROWS IN THREE TIMES THE CHILE PEPPER FOR A TASTE THAT IS UNDENIABLY (AND IRRESISTIBLY) SOUTHWESTERN.

Jalapeño Steak Sandwiches

Grill onions, if desired, for a milder, sweeter flavor.

PREP: 25 MINUTES **MARINATE**: 4 HOURS **GRILL**: 14 MINUTES

6	cloves garlic, minced
3	jalapeño chile peppers, finely chopped (don't seed) (see tip, below right)
⅓	cup olive oil
⅓	cup fresh lime juice
3	Tbsp. Dijon-style mustard
1	tsp. kosher salt or salt
1¼	to 1½ lb. beef flank steak or sirloin steak
12	slices Texas toast or other thick-cut white bread, toasted*
½	cup purchased chipotle mayonnaise or ½ cup mayonnaise with 1 tsp. chili powder
1	red onion, quartered and thinly sliced
4	oz. queso fresco or farmer cheese, crumbled
	Fresh cilantro sprigs
	Lime wedges

1. For marinade, in a bowl whisk together garlic, jalapeño peppers, olive oil, lime juice, mustard, and salt.

2. Trim fat from meat. With a sharp knife score meat on both sides at 1-inch intervals in diamond pattern. Place meat in a resealable plastic bag set in a shallow dish. Pour marinade over meat; seal bag. Marinate in refrigerator for 4 to 24 hours.

3. Heat a nonstick or well-seasoned grill pan on stovetop over medium heat. Drain meat; discard marinade. Place meat in hot pan. Grill for 14 to 16 minutes or until steak is medium, turning once halfway through grilling. Carve steak diagonally across the grain into thin slices.

4. Meanwhile, spread one side of each toast slice with mayonnaise. Place steak, onions, cheese, and cilantro on half the toast slices. Top with remaining slices. Serve with lime wedges. Makes 6 servings.

FOR TABLETOP GRILL: Preheat grill according to manufacturer's directions. Place steak on grill rack. If using a covered grill, close lid. Grill until steak is desired doneness. For covered grill, allow 7 to 9 minutes. (For open grill, allow 12 to 14 minutes for medium, turning once halfway through grilling.) Thinly slice steak diagonally across the grain. Continue as directed in Step 4 above.

*TEST KITCHEN TIP: To toast bread in a grill pan or an open grill, place on grill rack and allow 1 to 2 minutes per side.

EACH SERVING: 560 cal., 28 g total fat (6 g. sat. fat), 158 mg chol., 965 mg sodium, 46 g carbo., 0 g fiber, 36 g pro. Daily Values: 3% vit. A, 9% vit. C, 15% calcium, 26% iron.

TOO HOT TO HANDLE

Because hot chile peppers, such as jalapeños, contain volatile oils that can burn your skin and eyes, avoid direct contact with them as much as possible. When working with chile peppers, wear plastic or rubber gloves. If your bare hands do touch the chile peppers, wash your hands well with soap and water.

EAT AND GROW YOUNG

BY **SARAH LACAMOIRE** AND **BRIDGET NELSON** PHOTOGRAPHS BY **GREG SCHEIDEMANN**

Lasagna lovers and cats named

Garfield, take note: Eating the tomato sauce in dishes such as this may decrease the risk of breast and prostate cancer. Tomatoes are rich in lycopene, a compound that may inhibit the growth of some cancers. To get the most benefit, stock up on cooked and processed tomato products because the body absorbs more lycopene from them. Try pizza and pasta sauces, tomato juice, diced tomatoes, and even ketchup. Ten tablespoons per week is all it takes to make an impact.

Tomatoes aren't the only nutritional superpowers on grocery store shelves. A host of other foods (see chart, below) have the potential to fight disease, boost your immune system, and, ultimately, help you live a longer, healthier life.

By the same token, a diet poor in such foods can do the reverse, says Dr. David L. Katz, associate professor of public health at Yale University and author of *The Flavor Point Diet*. "Food has a profound influence on all aspects on health," he says. "We age much more slowly and more gracefully when we take good care of ourselves, and eating well plays an important part in that."

"Your biological age may already be older than your chronological age simply because of poor food choices you've made in the past," says Dr. Michael Roizen, chairman of the division of anesthesiology, critical care medicine, and comprehensive pain management at Cleveland Clinic, and author of *RealAge: Are You as Young as You Can Be?* (To calculate your current biological age, take Roizen's Kitchen IQ test at www.realage.com.) Roizen claims that with the proper diet, you can prevent up to 75 percent of arterial aging and even reverse some of the arterial damage already done. Even those with a preexisting cardiovascular condition, such as high blood pressure, high cholesterol, or a history of heart attacks, can slow the aging process just by modifying their diet.

This is particularly important because cardiovascular disease (CVD) remains the number one killer of both women and men in the United States. The American Heart Association reports that 40 percent of all female deaths are due to CVD, yet a recent study showed that only 13 percent of women considered heart disease to be their greatest health risk.

FOOD	BENEFITS	GOAL
Spinach	Excellent source of folate, which reduces the risk of heart and vascular disease.	400 mcg of folate (folic acid) a day
Oats	High fiber content aids digestion, stabilizes blood sugar, and lowers cholesterol.	25 grams of fiber a day or about 1½ cups of dry oats
Avocado	Rich in monounsaturated fat (which raises good HDL cholesterol), fiber, beta-carotene, potassium, magnesium, and vitamin C.	Replace saturated and trans fats in your diet with monounsaturated fat, such as that found in avocado
Fish (specifically oily fish like mackerel, tuna, salmon, sardines, and lake trout)	Contains omega-3 fatty acids, which increase good cholesterol and lower bad cholesterol. May help lower blood pressure, reduce the risk of breast cancer, and minimize symptoms of rheumatoid arthritis.	13 ounces of fish a week
Almonds	Good source of protein and healthy polyunsaturated fat. High in vitamin E, which helps prevent blood clots, heart attacks, and certain eye ailments, such as macular degeneration and cataracts.	One ounce of almonds, five times a week

Certain foods can reduce your biological age by strengthening your cardiovascular and immune systems. Add these foods to your diet.

One of the most important (and complicated) food choices you will have to make is which types of fat to include in your diet. While most of us could afford to eat less fat, the body does need a modest amount in order to metabolize many vitamins. "Healthful fats are definitely an important component of good nutrition," Katz says. "But they're only beneficial if they replace other calories, rather than add to them."

Instead of selecting foods high in saturated and trans fats, which age the arteries and immune system, choose those high in mono- and polyunsaturated fats, such as olive oil, avocados, nuts, and fish. Lowering bad cholesterol (LDL) and raising good cholesterol (HDL) will help keep your arteries young.

When changing your diet, bear in mind that it takes a few weeks to retrain the palate. What may taste unsatisfying at first will become pleasing. Stick with it and you'll come to prefer the new foods.

TWO-BEAN CHILI WITH AVOCADO

Loaded with protein, fiber, healthful fat, and lycopene, 1³⁄₄ cups of this chili makes your RealAge 8.3 days younger.

PREP: 15 MINUTES **COOK:** 28 MINUTES

Two-Bean Chili with Avocado

- 1 large onion, chopped
- 2 tsp. dried oregano, crushed
- 2 tsp. canola or olive oil
- 2 14.5-oz. cans diced tomatoes, undrained
- 1 15-oz. can black or kidney beans, rinsed and drained
- 1 15-oz. can pinto beans, rinsed and drained
- ½ cup salsa (preferably guajillo chile salsa)
- 1 medium ripe avocado, peeled, seeded, and diced
- ¼ cup snipped fresh cilantro

1. In a large saucepan cook onion and oregano in hot oil over medium-high heat for 3 minutes or until tender. Stir in undrained tomatoes, beans, and salsa. Bring to boiling; reduce heat. Simmer, uncovered, about 25 minutes. To serve, top with avocado and snipped cilantro. Makes 5½ cups (4 to 5 servings).

 EACH SERVING: 325 cal., 10 g total fat (1 g sat. fat), 0 mg chol., 985 mg sodium, 50 g carbo., 15 g fiber, 14 g pro. Daily Values: 10% vit. A, 60% vit. C, 20% calcium, 26% iron.

Home front

ASPARAGUS VINEGAR

The essence of spring's favorite crop has been distilled into delicately flavored vinegar. A small amount goes a long way, so use it as a finishing touch. Sprinkle it over tuna steak, greens, or an avocado and crabmeat salad. Stir into a chilled pea or potato soup or drizzle over roasted or fresh veggies. Gegenbauer Asparagus Vinegar, 720 ml, $36.99; www.dibruno.com.

CHUTNEY USES

Spice up soups, sandwiches, dips, pasta and rice dishes, and burgers with chutney, the condiment staple of Indian cooking. Nirmala Gupta, of Bombay Emerald Chutneys, began selling her homemade mint, plum, cranberry, and tomato chutneys at farmers' markets in 2004. "Flavors in chutney are both sweet and savory, so it's a versatile addition to any cupboard," she says. Royal Plum Chutney, $7; 571/333-4154; www.bombayemeraldchutneyco.com.

MORE THAN A S'MORE

A toasted marshmallow is a thing of beauty. Use toasted marshmallows to top pecan pie, almond torte, or bananas Foster; stir into coffee; top off roasted plums, pineapples, or other fruits; or cover a chocolate fudge sundae.

To toast marshmallows, use a long nonmetallic utensil, such as a bamboo skewer. Prevent scorching by holding the marshmallow about 2 inches above the flame, turning occasionally.

For really dynamic flavors, try homemade-style marshmallows like Chocolate Chipetta, Caramel Swirl, Orange Honey, or Toasted Coconut from Plush Puffs, 4 oz. bag, $7.99; www.plushpuffs.com.

APRIL

EGGS, SAUSAGES, AND PANCAKES MAKE THEIR EVENING DEBUT AT THE DINNER TABLE. TURNS OUT, BREAKFAST DISHES ARE JUST AS DELICIOUS AT NIGHT.

B.L.T. Pancake Club
page 63

Anytime Breakfast

Salmon-Potato Bake
page 58

Tuna Hash
page 58

Sausage and Squash Scrapple
page 61

Anytime Breakfast

FUN TWISTS ON OLD FAVORITES
MAKE BREAKFAST-FOR-DINNER
NEW AND EXCITING.

Breakfast in Bread

Breakfast in Bread

To toast nuts, place them in a shallow baking pan. Bake in preheated 350°F oven for 5 to 7 minutes, shaking pan once or twice.

PREP: 20 MINUTES **BAKE:** 12 MINUTES

- 2 English muffins, halved
- 4 eggs
- 3 Tbsp. orange juice
- 1 Tbsp. white wine vinegar
- 1 Tbsp. olive oil
- 1 Tbsp. Dijon-style mustard
- 1/8 tsp. salt
- 1/8 tsp. freshly ground black pepper
- 1/2 cup dairy sour cream
- 6 cups mesclun and/or arugula or other favorite salad mix
- 1/2 cup walnut pieces, toasted

1. Preheat oven to 400°F. Place split English muffin halves in a greased 13×9×2-inch baking pan. Use a 1½- or 2-inch cutter to cut a hole in the center of each muffin half. Place cutouts beside muffins in baking pan. Crack open eggs and carefully place one egg in the center of each muffin hole. Transfer pan to preheated oven. Bake for 12 to 15 minutes or until eggs are just set.

2. Meanwhile, for dressing, in a small bowl whisk together orange juice, vinegar, olive oil, mustard, salt, and pepper. Gradually whisk in sour cream. Divide mesclun among 4 dinner plates. Place 1 egg-filled muffin half on top of greens. Cut remaining rounds from muffin halves into wedges and sprinkle around eggs. Drizzle with dressing. Add walnuts. Makes 4 servings.

EACH SERVING: 342 cal., 24 g total fat (6 g sat. fat), 222 mg chol., 387 mg sodium, 21 g carbo., 3 g fiber, 13 g pro. Daily Values: 17% vit. A, 14% vit. C, 11% calcium, 14% iron.

BY RICHARD SWEARINGER PHOTOGRAPHS BY TINA RUPP FOOD STYLING BY ALISON ATTENBOROUGH

A healthful, hearty, quick dinner at the end of the day is at your fingertips; just open the fridge and reach for eggs, milk, and other morning-meal staples. A pinch of breakfast is an ideal ingredient for weeknight meals because it's fast, one of the most healthful ways to eat, and it's fun.

Start with simple ingredients, such as scrambled eggs and stuffed French toast, then give them a little more dinnertime appeal by bringing them to the table transformed with bold flavors and eye-catching shapes.

Unexpected combinations make the evening adventurous yet soothing. Ease the ache of a long day with a stack of fluffy golden flapjacks dinnered up with thick slices of red tomato and bacon still sizzling hot from the pan. Tuna Hash—corned beef hash adapted with tuna, potatoes, dill, and cumin—goes together in about 45 minutes.

If you haven't yet made breakfast for dinner, you're working too hard. Give yourself a night off now and then, which doesn't mean sacrificing healthful habits. Often dinner is the meal that people use to catch up on nutrition for the day. Many breakfast choices are full of good-for-you ingredients.

Baked Mediterranean Eggs features tomatoes, low-fat feta cheese, and cucumbers for protein and vitamins. In Savory French Toast, use the option of soymilk and soy cream cheese to provide calcium and protein with less fat. Eye-appealing flourishes—greens (rich in vitamin A) make a delicious bed for eggs cooked in English muffins.

Pancakes seem much more dinnerlike when you play down their sweet side by skipping the syrup. Try topping pancakes with blue cheese dressing; its creamy tang brings out the smoky side of bacon. Nevertheless, if your family's taste buds crave the sweetness of maple syrup, bring it out. It plays equally well with the bacon and tomato. The beauty is that everyone chooses favorites: Kids might want to pour syrup while the parents opt for dressing.

Best of all, the meal is a lark—an excuse to have fun at the end of the day. Let your decorating instincts run wild and use dinnertime tableware in fanciful ways: goblets for juice, soup bowls for salad. Bring out the gravy boat to serve syrup or dressing. Use the time to work in a cooking class—show kids how to crack eggs neatly and measure flour accurately. Or perhaps give them an introductory course in the art of making your kitchen the heart of your home.

Salmon-Potato Bake

The popular lox-and-bagels combo inspired this recipe. Sliced potatoes substituted for bagels create a warm and hearty dish.

PREP: 20 MINUTES **BAKE:** 30 MINUTES **STAND:** 10 MINUTES

Nonstick cooking spray
1 16-oz. pkg. refrigerated sliced potatoes
8 oz. Gouda or Monterey Jack cheese, shredded (2 cups)
6 oz. thinly sliced smoked salmon (lox style), cut in bite-size strips
6 eggs, beaten
2 cups milk
¼ tsp. salt
¼ tsp. ground black pepper

1. Preheat oven to 350°F. Lightly coat six 10- to 14-ounce casserole dishes or ramekins with nonstick cooking spray. Place dishes in a 15×10×1-inch baking pan; set aside. Place potatoes in a 2-quart square microwave-safe baking dish. Add 1 tablespoon *water* to dish. Cover with waxed paper. Microwave on 100% power (high) for 2 minutes. Arrange half the potatoes in prepared dishes. Layer with half the cheese and all the smoked salmon. Top with remaining potatoes and remaining cheese.

2. In a large bowl whisk together eggs, milk, salt, and pepper. Slowly pour over layers in dishes. Bake for 30 to 35 minutes or until puffed, set, and golden (press lightly in center of mixture; casseroles are done when no liquid appears).

3. Allow to stand 10 minutes before serving. Makes 6 servings.

MAKE-AHEAD DIRECTIONS: Cover and refrigerate unbaked casseroles up to 24 hours. Uncover and bake for 35 to 40 minutes or until done.

EACH SERVING: 352 cal., 18 g total fat (9 g sat. fat), 268 mg chol., 1,127 mg sodium, 21 carbo., 1 g fiber, 25 g pro. Daily Values: 13% vit. A, 8% vit. C, 39% calcium, 9% iron.

Salmon-Potato Bake

Tuna Hash

Potatoes are the base for most hash dishes, and any assortment of meat, vegetables, and herbs can be added to the crisp mixture.

START TO FINISH: 45 MINUTES

4 4-oz. fresh or frozen skinless tuna steaks or salmon fillets
3 cups refrigerated or frozen loose-pack diced hash brown potatoes
2 Tbsp. olive oil
½ cup chopped white or red onion
2 Tbsp. snipped fresh dill or thyme or 1 tsp. dried dillweed or thyme, crushed
¾ tsp. ground cumin or dry mustard
½ tsp. salt
¼ tsp. freshly ground black pepper
1 Tbsp. olive oil
Salt and freshly ground black pepper
8 cups torn fresh Swiss chard, spinach, or kale
1 recipe Caramelized Red Onions (optional)
Fresh dill sprigs (optional)
½ to 1 cup bottled honey Dijon salad dressing or Homemade Dressing

1. Thaw tuna and potatoes, if frozen. Set fish aside. In a large skillet heat the 2 tablespoons olive oil over medium heat. Add potatoes, onion, dill, cumin, ½ teaspoon salt, and ¼ teaspoon pepper. Spread evenly in skillet. Cook over medium-high heat for 20 to 25 minutes or until potatoes are golden brown and slightly crisp, stirring occasionally. Transfer to a medium bowl; cover and keep warm.

2. In the same skillet heat the 1 tablespoon olive oil over medium heat. Lightly sprinkle tuna with salt and pepper. Add tuna to skillet; cook for 4 minutes. Carefully turn tuna. Reduce heat to medium-low; cook for 2 to 4 minutes more or until fish flakes easily when tested with a fork (tuna should be slightly pink in the center). Remove tuna from skillet; keep warm. Add greens to skillet. Cook over medium-low heat, tossing frequently, for 5 to 7 minutes or until tender and beginning to wilt if using Swiss chard or kale, or 1 to 2 minutes or beginning to wilt if using spinach (add more oil to skillet during cooking, if necessary).

3. Divide wilted greens among 4 serving plates. Top with potato mixture, tuna steaks, and, if desired, Caramelized Red Onions. If desired, garnish with dill sprigs. Pass salad dressing. Makes 4 servings.

HOMEMADE DRESSING: In a small bowl stir together one 8-ounce carton light dairy sour cream, 2 tablespoons coarse brown mustard, 1 tablespoon honey, and ¼ teaspoon salt. Stir in ¼ cup milk until smooth. If necessary, add additional milk, 1 teaspoon at a time, to make desired consistency. Makes about 1¼ cups.

CARAMELIZED RED ONIONS: Heat 1 tablespoon olive oil in a medium skillet over medium heat. Add half a medium red onion, thinly sliced. Turn heat to medium-low. Cook onion for 8 to 10 minutes or until golden brown, stirring occasionally.

EACH SERVING WITH 2 TABLESPOONS SALAD DRESSING: 512 cal., 28 g total fat (4 g sat. fat), 43 mg chol., 748 mg sodium, 35 g carbo., 3 g fiber, 31 g pro. Daily Values: 133% vit. A, 50% vit. C, 6% calcium, 15% iron.

TURN ORDINARY BREAKFAST HASH BROWN POTATOES INTO A SENSATIONAL HIT BY ADDING SWISS CHARD, CARAMELIZED RED ONIONS, AND TUNA STEAKS.

Tuna Hash

Baked Mediterranean Eggs

Baked Mediterranean Eggs

To make breadsticks with leftover pizza dough, cut into ½-inch-wide strips, twist, and sprinkle with grated Parmesan cheese. Place on a baking sheet and bake for 8 to 10 minutes.

PREP: 30 MINUTES **BAKE:** 15 MINUTES

    Nonstick cooking spray
 8 eggs
 ¼ cup sliced, pitted kalamata or black olives
 1 13.8-oz. pkg. refrigerated pizza dough or 4 pita bread rounds
 4 roma tomatoes, chopped
 ½ a small cucumber, seeded and chopped
 2 Tbsp. snipped fresh flat-leaf parsley
 8 slices Canadian bacon or bacon
 4 oz. crumbled feta cheese with garlic and herb
 ¼ cup plain low-fat yogurt

1. Preheat oven to 400°F. Lightly coat the inside of four 10- to 12-ounce ramekins or custard cups with nonstick cooking spray. Break 2 eggs into each ramekin. Divide olives evenly among ramekins.

2. Unroll pizza dough. Cut 4 circles about 1 inch larger than the ramekins. Place dough rounds on baking sheet. Place ramekins in a 3-quart rectangular baking dish; add boiling water to dish to depth of 1 inch. Place baking dish with eggs on a lower oven rack. Place baking sheet with dough rounds on upper oven rack. Bake for 15 to 20 minutes or until eggs are set when lightly shaken and dough rounds are browned. (If using pita bread rounds, bake for 8 minutes or until warmed through.)

3. Meanwhile, in a bowl combine tomatoes, cucumber, parsley, ¼ teaspoon *salt*, and ⅛ teaspoon *ground black pepper*. Lightly coat a large skillet with cooking spray; cook Canadian bacon over medium heat until lightly browned, turning once; or cook bacon until crisp.

4. Transfer rounds to 4 plates. Sprinkle rounds with feta cheese. To serve, carefully remove ramekins from water bath; invert onto rounds. Top each serving with some of the tomato mixture and 1 tablespoon of yogurt. Serve immediately. Pass additional tomato-cucumber mixture. Makes 4 servings.

EACH SERVING: 536 cal., 24 g total fat (9 g sat. fat), 470 mg chol., 1,624 mg sodium, 45 carbo., 3 g fiber, 33 g pro. Daily Values: 30% vit. A, 24% vit. C, 36% calcium, 36% iron.

Savory French Toast

For a fresh fruit accompaniment, core and cut a large pear into 8 wedges. Wrap long strips of thinly sliced prosciutto or ham (about 2 ounces total) around pear wedges.

PREP: 30 MINUTES **CHILL:** 2 HOURS **BAKE:** 30 MINUTES

- 8 ¾-inch slices French bread
- 1 recipe Cream Cheese Filling
- 4 eggs
- 1 cup milk or soymilk
- 1 cup orange juice
  Maple or fruit syrup (optional)

1. Place half the bread slices in a 3-quart rectangular baking dish. Top each slice with some of the Cream Cheese Filling. Top with remaining bread slices.

2. In a medium bowl beat together eggs, milk, and orange juice. Slowly pour egg mixture over bread slices, covering all the tops. Cover and chill for 2 to 24 hours.

3. Preheat oven to 375°F. Line a 15×10×1-inch baking pan with parchment paper or nonstick foil. Arrange bread stacks in pan. Bake, uncovered, for 30 to 35 minutes or until golden, turning halfway through baking. If desired, serve with syrup. Makes 4 servings.

CREAM CHEESE FILLING: In a medium bowl combine one 8-ounce package of cream cheese or soy cream cheese, ½ cup chopped dried fruit (apricots or golden raisins), and 1 teaspoon ground cinnamon.

EACH SERVING: 520 cal., 21 g total fat (154 g sat. fat), 212 mg chol., 813 mg sodium, 66 g carbo., 7 g fiber, 18 g pro. Daily Values: 27% vit. A, 52% vit. C, 15% calcium, 24% iron.

Sausage and Squash Scrapple

Savory French Toast

Sausage and Squash Scrapple

Scrapple began as a Pennsylvania Dutch dish of leftover pork, cornmeal, and spices. As it became popular in other regions, ingredients were adapted to suit local tastes.

PREP: 25 MINUTES **COOK:** 30 MINUTES

- 3 cups peeled butternut squash, cut in 1-inch cubes
- 1 12- to 16-oz. pkg. turkey kielbasa, cut in ½-inch slices
- 2 Tbsp. olive oil
- 1 medium yellow sweet pepper, cut in bite-size strips
- 2 Tbsp. fresh sage or basil leaves cut into thin strips
- ⅓ cup balsamic vinegar
- 1 tsp. sugar
- 1 16-oz. tube refrigerated cooked polenta, cut in 12 slices
- ⅓ cup pure maple syrup
  Fresh sage or basil leaves (optional)

1. In a medium saucepan cook butternut squash, covered, in a small amount of boiling salted water for 10 minutes or until tender; drain and set aside.

2. In a large skillet cook turkey kielbasa in 1 tablespoon of the hot oil over medium heat until lightly browned and crisp on the edges. Add butternut squash, yellow sweet pepper, sage, vinegar, and sugar; bring to boiling. Reduce heat; simmer, uncovered, until vinegar has almost evaporated. Remove from skillet. Cover with foil to keep warm.

3. Rinse and wipe out skillet. Add remaining 1 tablespoon oil. Fry polenta slices in hot oil over medium-high heat until golden brown, about 5 minutes. Turn with pancake turner; fry 5 minutes more. Stack 3 polenta slices on each of 4 dinner plates. Top with sausage mixture; drizzle each serving with maple syrup. If desired, garnish with sage leaves. Makes 4 servings.

EACH SERVING: 432 cal., 14 g total fat (1 g sat. fat), 0 mg chol., 1,241 mg sodium, 58 g carbo., 5 g fiber, 19 g pro. Daily Values: 25% vit. A, 136% vit. C, 6% calcium, 7% iron.

BREAKFAST AND LUNCH COME TOGETHER IN A FUN SANDWICH—ALSO PERFECT FOR EARLY SUPPERS.

B.L.T. Pancake Club

B.L.T. Pancake Club
Trade in bread for whole wheat pancake slices in this B.L.T. twist.
PREP: 25 MINUTES **BAKE:** 12 MINUTES

	Butter
2	eggs, beaten
1½	cups buttermilk
1	Tbsp. butter, melted
1	cup white whole wheat or whole wheat flour
1	Tbsp. sugar
1	tsp. baking powder
½	tsp. baking soda
¼	tsp. salt
2	medium tomatoes, sliced
4	lettuce leaves
8	to 12 slices thick-cut bacon, cooked and drained
¼	to ½ cup bottled blue cheese salad dressing
4	cherry tomatoes (optional)

1. Preheat oven to 375°F. Generously butter a 15×10×1-inch baking pan; set aside. In a medium bowl combine eggs, buttermilk, and melted butter. In a large bowl combine flour, sugar, baking powder, baking soda, and salt. Make a well in the center of the flour mixture. Add buttermilk mixture; stir just until combined (do not overmix).
2. Pour batter into prepared pan, spreading evenly. Immediately place in oven. Bake 12 to 15 minutes or until set and lightly browned.
3. Loosen edges of pancake with a table knife or thin spatula. With a serrated knife carefully cut pancake into 12 equal-size portions.
4. For each serving, place a pancake portion on a plate. Top with 1 or 2 tomato slices, a second pancake, lettuce, 2 slices bacon, and 1 tablespoon salad dressing. Top with a third pancake. If desired, add a cherry tomato on a skewer. Pass additional dressing. Makes 4 servings.
EACH SERVING: 427 cal., 25 g total fat (9 g sat. fat), 147 mg chol., 1,163 mg sodium, 33 g carbo., 4 g fiber, 19 g pro. Daily Values: 18% vit. A, 15% vit. C, 17% calcium, 12% iron.

STACKING UP THE HOTCAKES
is a job that invites help from little hands.
Knowing that their efforts are essential
in getting dinner on the table goes a long
way to making kids eager to participate.

COOKING WITH COFFEE

BY **STEPHEN EXEL** PHOTOGRAPHS BY **GREG SCHEIDEMANN**

Whether you have a love affair

with the brew or just a nodding acquaintance, you'll find that coffee is a friendly partner in the kitchen, giving a deep, mellow boost to a variety of recipes—from soups to desserts.

Coffee adds smoky, roasted notes to beef, lamb, and pork. It's a good match with red chiles and tomato-based sauces. Meaty mushrooms, such as cremini, button, and portobello, soak up roasted flavor when coffee is added to the recipe.

In a recipe, replace up to one-third of the water or beef broth with coffee, or replace a small amount (up to one-fourth) of chicken broth when you cook dark meat fowl or chicken thighs and legs. Coffee also adds robust depth to a red wine-based dish; simply substitute it for some of the wine.

In desserts, let the coffee flavor stand on its own. Keep the recipe simple, using coffee in creams, puddings, mousse, frostings, cakes, and cookies. Soak dried fruits, such as raisins, plums, and apricots, in a blend of coffee with orange juice or brandy. Sweet spices—cinnamon, cloves, ginger, and nutmeg—pair well with coffee. (Does this inspire you to make a pumpkin-coffee pie?)

It's important to remember that coffee has a distinct flavor, so be sure you aren't substituting or adding too much. In addition, the strength of the brewed coffee makes a difference in the flavor. Try using a half cup the first time around, then experiment if you find you'd like more coffee flavor.

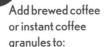

Add brewed coffee or instant coffee granules to:
- Dishes that use soy, hoisin, oyster, or plum sauce as an ingredient
- Meat stews, chili, and braises
- Glazed or mashed sweet potatoes
- Rye and whole wheat flour breads
- The liquid used in chocolate cakes or fudge
- Warmed maple syrup
- Whipped cream to top desserts

Coffee Coffee Cake

Coffee Coffee Cake

PREP: 30 MINUTES **BAKE:** 1 HOUR **COOL:** 50 MINUTES

- 1½ cups strong brewed coffee
- 1 cup granulated sugar
- ⅔ cup cooking oil
- ½ cup honey
- 2 Tbsp. vinegar
- 1 tsp. vanilla
- 2 eggs, slightly beaten
- 3 cups all-purpose flour
- ¼ cup unsweetened cocoa powder
- 2 tsp. baking powder
- ½ tsp. baking soda
- ½ tsp. salt
- ½ tsp. ground nutmeg
- 1 cup finely chopped hazelnuts, toasted
- 1 recipe Coffee-Hazelnut Syrup
- ¼ cup chopped hazelnuts, toasted (optional)

1. Preheat oven to 350°F. Grease and lightly flour a 10-inch fluted tube pan. In a mixing bowl whisk together coffee, sugar, oil, honey, vinegar, and vanilla. Add eggs; whisk until combined. In another bowl combine flour, cocoa powder, baking powder, soda, salt, and nutmeg. Whisk in coffee mixture until combined. Add the 1 cup hazelnuts; stir to combine. Pour batter into prepared pan.

2. Bake in preheated oven about 1 hour or until a wooden pick inserted near center comes out clean. Cool in pan on wire rack for 20 minutes. Remove from pan to a serving platter. Brush with some of the Coffee-Hazelnut Syrup. Cool for 30 minutes. Brush again with syrup. If desired, sprinkle with the ¼ cup toasted hazelnuts. Serve cake warm with remaining syrup. Makes 12 servings.

COFFEE-HAZELNUT SYRUP: In a saucepan combine 1 cup packed light brown sugar, 1 cup powdered sugar, 2 tablespoons butter, and 1 cup strong brewed coffee. Bring to boiling, stirring to dissolve sugar. Reduce heat. Boil gently, uncovered, for 25 to 30 minutes or until mixture thickens slightly and is reduced to about 1⅓ cups. Remove from heat. Stir in 2 tablespoons hazelnut-flavor liqueur. Makes about 1½ cups.

EACH SERVING: 541 cal., 22 g total fat (4 g sat. fat), 41 mg chol., 257 mg sodium, 81 g carbo., 2 g fiber, 6 g pro. Daily Values: 3% vit. A, 1% vit. C, 10% calcium, 15% iron.

Tomato-Joe Soup

Tomato-Joe Soup

PREP: 30 MINUTES **COOK:** 25 MINUTES

- 2 medium onions, chopped (1 cup)
- 2 stalks celery, chopped (1 cup)
- 2 medium carrots, chopped (1 cup)
- 2 Tbsp. butter
- 6 medium tomatoes, peeled and quartered (about 2 lb.), or two 14½-oz. cans diced tomatoes, drained
- 2 cups strong brewed coffee
- ½ cup water
- 1 6-oz. can tomato paste
- 2 tsp. sugar
- ½ tsp. salt
  Few dashes bottled hot pepper sauce
- ¾ cup whipping cream

1. In a saucepan cook onion, celery, and carrots in hot butter over medium heat about 5 minutes or until nearly tender, stirring occasionally. Add tomatoes, coffee, water, tomato paste, sugar, salt, and hot pepper sauce. Bring to boiling; reduce heat. Cover; simmer 20 to 25 minutes until vegetables are tender. Cool slightly.

2. Place half of the tomato mixture in a blender or food processor. Cover; blend until smooth. Repeat with remaining tomato mixture. Return all to saucepan. Stir in ¼ cup of the whipping cream; heat through. In a mixing bowl beat remaining whipping cream with an electric mixer on low speed just until soft peaks form. Spoon some of the whipped cream on each serving. Makes 6 to 8 side-dish servings.

EACH SERVING: 164 cal., 12 g total fat (7 g sat. fat), 39 mg chol., 378 mg sodium, 14 g carbo., 3 g fiber, 3 g pro. Daily Values: 109% vit. A, 48% vit. C, 4% calcium, 6% iron.

Steamed Spinach

GIVE SPINACH A NEW SPIN

BY **RICHARD SWEARINGER** PHOTOGRAPHS BY **GREG SCHEIDEMANN**
FOOD STYLING BY **CHARLES WORTHINGTON**

Taking a favorite recipe like

creamed spinach and paring it down to just the few ingredients that make it wonderful is the best way to enjoy a garden favorite that's at its peak of flavor. Our Creamed Spinach recipe includes just a handful of chopped onion and some garlic cooked with a little butter; then the spinach is tossed with cream and dusted with salt, pepper, and nutmeg—ideal served with T-bones. Steamed Spinach gets a similarly stripped-down approach: Toss with herbs, splash with vinegar, done. It's perfect for a meal with grilled fish or pasta. The heartiest version has just five elements: The spinach is cooked in butter and tossed with bacon, mustard, and red pepper. Try it with a poached egg on top or serve it alongside a roast pork or roasted chicken.

Spinach is available in a variety of forms: fresh in bunches, prewashed and bagged, and frozen. All require rinsing; fresh bunches require extra time in the colander with lots of running water to remove sand and dirt.

Steamed Spinach

This recipe is easy to prepare in a microwave oven; microwave spinach and herbs on 100% power (high) for 3 minutes.

START TO FINISH: 20 MINUTES

- 3 6-oz. bags prewashed fresh baby spinach or two 10-oz. bags prewashed spinach
- 1 cup snipped fresh parsley, basil, cilantro, or watercress
- ¼ cup sherry vinegar or herb vinegar
  Salt and freshly ground black pepper
  Lemon wedges (optional)

1. In a large Dutch oven or large skillet with steamer basket insert* bring 1 inch of water to boiling. Combine spinach and herbs in basket; place over boiling water. Cover and steam for 2 to 3 minutes or until wilted, stirring once. Remove basket carefully; drain. Transfer spinach to a serving bowl. Drizzle with some of the vinegar. Season to taste with salt and pepper.
2. Pass remaining vinegar. If desired, garnish with lemon wedges. Makes 4 servings.
*NOTE: If you don't have a Dutch oven or a large skillet with a steamer basket, use a small steamer basket set in a large skillet and cook the spinach in three batches.

 EACH SERVING: 40 cal., 1 g total fat (0 g sat. fat), 0 mg chol., 256 mg sodium, 6 g carbo., 3 g fiber, 4 g pro. Daily Values: 265% vit. A, 94% vit. C, 15% calcium, 25% iron.

Creamed Spinach

START TO FINISH: 30 MINUTES

- 2 10-oz. bags spinach (large stems removed) or two 10-oz. pkg. frozen chopped spinach, thawed
- ½ cup chopped onion
- 2 to 3 cloves garlic, minced
- 2 Tbsp. butter
- 1 cup whipping cream
- ½ tsp. freshly ground black pepper
- ¼ tsp. salt
- ¼ tsp. ground nutmeg

1. In a large pot of rapidly boiling salted water cook fresh spinach (if using) for 1 minute. Drain well, squeezing out excess liquid. Pat dry with paper towels. Snip spinach with kitchen shears to coarsely chop; set aside. If using frozen spinach, drain well, squeezing out excess liquid.
2. In a large skillet cook onion and garlic in hot butter about 5 minutes. Stir in cream, pepper, salt, and nutmeg. Bring onion mixture to boiling; cook, uncovered, until cream begins to thicken. Add spinach. Simmer, uncovered, about 2 minutes or until thickened. Season to taste with additional salt and pepper. Makes 4 servings.
EACH SERVING: 312 cal., 29 g total fat (17 g sat. fat), 98 mg chol., 347 mg sodium, 11 g carbo., 4 g fiber, 6 g pro. Daily Values: 340% vit. A, 83% vit. C, 22% calcium, 27% iron.

Creamed Spinach

Sauteed Spinach with Bacon and Mustard

Sauteed Spinach with Bacon and Mustard

Splurge on a specialty bacon, such as applewood smoked or honey-basted hickory smoked.

START TO FINISH: 15 MINUTES

- 4 slices bacon, cut into 1-inch pieces
- 2 10-oz. bags prewashed spinach
- 1 Tbsp. butter
- 1 Tbsp. Dijon-style mustard
- ¼ tsp. crushed red pepper

1. In a large skillet cook bacon over medium heat until crisp. Remove bacon to drain on paper towels, reserving 1 tablespoon drippings in skillet. Gradually add spinach to skillet, stirring frequently with metal tongs. Cook for 2 to 3 minutes or until spinach is just wilted. Remove spinach from skillet to a colander; hold over sink and press lightly to drain. (If using large leaf spinach, use kitchen scissors to snip.)
2. In the same skillet melt butter over medium heat; stir in mustard and crushed red pepper. Add drained spinach; toss to coat and reheat spinach, if necessary. Top with cooked bacon. Serve immediately. Makes 4 to 6 servings.
EACH SERVING: 135 cal., 11 g total fat (4 g sat. fat), 18 mg chol., 340 mg sodium, 5 g carbo., 3 g fiber, 7 g pro. Daily Values: 241% vit. A, 60% vit. C, 13% calcium, 20% iron.

PIZZA MAKES A SQUARE MEAL

BY **JEANNE AMBROSE** PHOTOGRAPHS BY **GREG SCHEIDEMANN**

Good news for pizza-loving families: The Italian pie is actually a heckuva square meal when made properly. In fact, eating healthfully prepared pizza twice a week may lower the risk of heart attack and digestive cancer, according to a study from—where else?—Italy.

Instead of the typical American extravaganza topped with gooey extra cheese and triple meat, think Italian. Go easy on the meat. Drizzle the crust with heart-healthy olive oil, add sliced fresh tomatoes, and sprinkle lightly with shredded mozzarella cheese. Top the pie with a handful of snipped fresh basil as you pull it from the oven. The aroma is divine. The flavor is heavenly. And the calorie content isn't bad.

Good-for-you variations provide plenty of options for everyone. For the most benefit, start with homemade whole wheat crust or use frozen whole wheat bread dough. Pile on your favorite veggies and add a bit of cheese or divvy up different toppings on one crust to personalize a portion for every family member.

SQUARE MEAL PIZZA
Each topping (below) covers an entire pizza. If dividing the pizza into four small squares, use only one-fourth topping in each portion. Bake as directed in Good-for-You Pizza, page 69.

CHICKEN, APPLE, CHEDDAR Spread partially baked crust with a mixture of 1/3 cup peanut butter and 1/3 cup sour cream. Top with 1 cup shredded rotisserie chicken, thinly sliced apples, and 2 cups shredded cheddar cheese. Bake as directed.

TACO-STYLE Spread partially baked crust with 1 cup refried beans (thin with salsa, if necessary), 1 cup soy crumbles or cooked ground beef, and 2 cups shredded Monterey Jack cheese. Bake. Top with shredded lettuce and salsa.

GARDEN-FRESH Spread partially baked crust with pesto. Top with 1 cup grape tomatoes, quartered, and 8 ounces fresh mozzarella cheese, cubed. Bake.

PINEAPPLE Spread partially baked crust with one 8-ounce can pizza sauce. Top with one 15 1/4-ounce can pineapple tidbits, drained; 1 cup chopped Canadian bacon; and 8 ounces shredded mozzarella cheese. Bake.

Good-for-You Pizza

As a substitute to making crust from scratch, use a 1-pound loaf of frozen whole wheat bread dough, thawed.

PREP: 40 MINUTES **RISE:** 30 MINUTES **REST:** 10 MINUTES
STAND: 15 MINUTES **BAKE:** 22 MINUTES

Good-For-You Pizza

1	pkg. active dry yeast
⅔	cup warm water (105°F to 115°F)
1	Tbsp. honey
1	Tbsp. extra virgin olive oil
¾	cups whole wheat flour
¼	cup cornmeal
½	tsp. sea salt
¾	to 1¼ cup all-purpose flour
1	cup packed spinach leaves
1	cup packed fresh basil leaves
3	cloves garlic, peeled
¼	cup grated Parmesan cheese
⅓	cup extra virgin olive oil
2	tsp. lemon juice
2	oz. turkey pepperoni or pepperoni
1½	cups reduced fat mozzarella cheese or shredded mozzarella cheese

1. In a small bowl combine yeast and warm water. Let stand for 5 minutes. Stir in honey and the 1 tablespoon olive oil. In a large bowl combine whole wheat flour, cornmeal, and salt. Stir in yeast mixture. Stir in as much of the all-purpose flour as you can.

2. Turn dough out onto a lightly floured surface. Knead in enough of the remaining flour to make a moderately stiff dough that is smooth and elastic (6 to 8 minutes total). Shape dough in a ball; cover and let rise until nearly double (30 to 45 minutes).

3. Meanwhile, prepare spinach pesto. In a food processor place spinach, basil, garlic, Parmesan cheese, the ⅓ cup olive oil, and the lemon juice. Cover and process to a smooth paste. Set aside.

4. Preheat oven to 425°F. Punch down dough; let rest for 10 minutes. On a lightly floured surface roll dough to a 12-inch round or 10-inch square. Transfer to greased baking sheet. Bake for 12 minutes or until browned. Top with pesto, pepperoni, and cheese. Bake for 10 to 15 minutes more or until bubbly. Makes 8 servings.

SQUARE MEAL PIZZA: Reserve a small portion of dough; shape in two 10-inch ropes. Brush one side of each rope with water; lay brushed side on unbaked crust to divide in quarters. Partially bake crust. Top each square with different toppings. Bake as directed in Step 4.

EACH SERVING: 261 cal., 15 g total fat (4 g sat. fat), 19 mg chol., 356 mg sodium, 24 g carbo., 2 g fiber, 9 g pro. Daily Values: 16% vit. A, 5% vit. C, 12% calcium, 9% iron.

HEALTHFUL TIPS

- Use whole wheat tortillas as a base for Mexican-style pizza.
- When making homemade pesto to top pizza, combine plenty of spinach with the basil. Popeye's favorite green is loaded with vitamins and fiber.
- Try meatless pepperoni from the organic produce section. It has a spicy flavor and is low in fat and high in protein.

THE ROYAL THISTLE

BY **BRIDGET NELSON** PHOTOGRAPHS BY **COLLEEN DUFFLEY**

Chances are, artichokes don't come to mind when you think of royalty. But this vegetable was popular with nobility throughout history, from the gods of Greek mythology to the 1948 crowning of Marilyn Monroe as California's first artichoke queen. And just like royalty, an artichoke can be intimidating—how to cook it isn't obvious; how to eat it is even more of a mystery.

Despite its lofty reputation, this edible thistle is remarkably easy to prepare and fun to eat once you know the basics. Look for artichokes with tightly packed leaves and a soft green color. They're available year-round, but you'll find the best quality during the peak season of mid-March to mid-May. Once home, they can be refrigerated up to two weeks before being prepared. Wait until you're ready to cook to wash the artichokes. While they're steaming, make a quick sauce with mayonnaise, mustard, and green onion tops.

Steaming is the easiest and quickest way to bring out an artichoke's flavor. Use a large saucepan or pot with about 1 inch of water. Place a steamer basket in the saucepan or pot, then bring the water to boiling. Add artichokes, stem ends down, to the steamer basket using tongs or a slotted spoon. Reduce heat; simmer, covered, for 20 to 25 minutes. Artichokes are done when you can easily pull out a leaf from the center. Be careful. The artichokes will be hot, so use tongs or a slotted spoon to remove them from the steamer. Spread paper towels on a countertop and drain the artichokes upside down. Steamed artichokes can be served warm or cold. If you want to serve them cold, steam them ahead of time, cover, and refrigerate for up to a day.

GOOD TO KNOW

Although there are as many as 50 varieties of artichokes, you're most likely to find the Green Globe variety in grocery stores. Green Globes are the main variety commercially produced in the United States. Other U.S. varieties include thornless artichokes, available in some grocery stores.

Serve steamed artichokes in a large bowl with flowers and lemons tucked in for spring flair. For dip, spoon a favorite sauce or dressing into a small bowl.

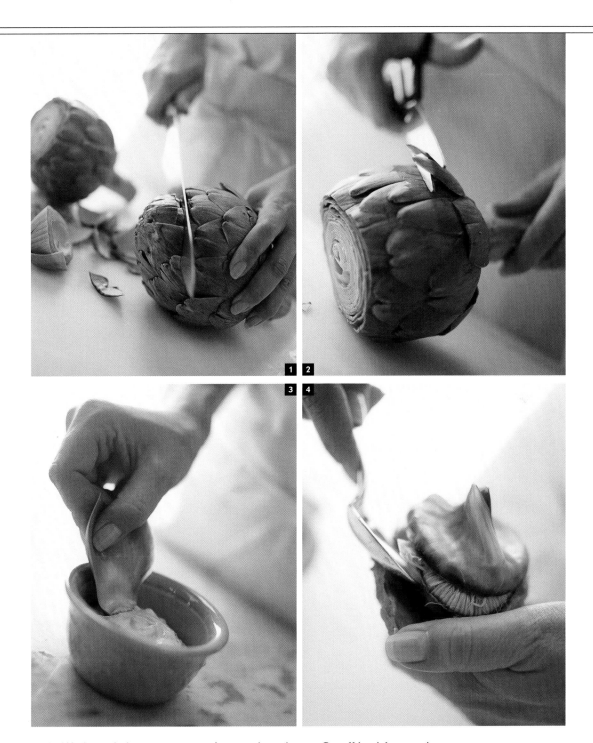

1. Wash artichokes; trim stems and remove loose leaves. Cut off 1 inch from each top.
2. Snip off the sharp leaf tips and brush the cut edges with a little lemon juice. Steam as directed on opposite page.
3. To eat steamed artichokes, pull off one leaf at a time. Dip the base of each leaf into a bit of sauce or melted butter. Draw the base of the leaf through your teeth, scraping off only the tender flesh. Discard remainder of the leaf.
4. Continue removing leaves until the fuzzy choke appears. Remove the choke by scooping it out with a spoon. If you have trouble getting it out with a spoon, try loosening it with a grapefruit knife. Eat the remaining heart with a fork, dipping each piece into sauce.

JEWELS OF THE TOMATO PATCH

BY **RICHARD SWEARINGER** PHOTOGRAPHS BY **BILL HOPKINS**

Intrigued by their small size and decorative possibilities, Elvin McDonald, garden editor for *Better Homes and Gardens*® magazine, spent the summer growing dozens of tomato varieties in pots. "I grow tomatoes in pots so I can give them ideal conditions and to avoid the back-breaking work of digging holes in terrible clay soil," McDonald says.

Few culinary delights compare

to the taste of a tomato fresh-picked off the vine, still warm from the sun. And few just-plucked flavors compare to a crop of sweet, easy-to-grow miniature tomatoes. They're succulent and sprightly, and it's easy to pop a handful in your mouth while strolling through the garden. For the cook, their small size and tender skins mean they need just a little cooking to bring out their best. (See recipes, pages 74–75.)

As if delightful flavors weren't enough, these littlest of tomatoes also bring visual impact to the garden. The plants are just the right size to form a row on both sides of an entry or lush green accents on the porch, patio, or deck. Many varieties of miniature tomatoes thrive when planted in pots, which allows gardeners to place them in the right spot for quick growth.

"We planted seeds on Memorial Day," says Elvin McDonald, garden editor for *Better Homes and Gardens*® magazine, "and by the Fourth of July, I was able to harvest the first ripe tomatoes." In his Zone 5 garden, he tested 38 varieties. By summer's end, just six tiny tomato varieties and six slightly larger bite-size types performed well in the garden and brought exceptionally good taste to the dinner table (see photos, opposite).

Because tomatoes are among the most forgiving of plants when it comes to where they're grown, gardeners can feel free to experiment with eye-catching containers. "I grew some tomatoes last summer in $4.99 purple plastic beach baskets from the supermarket," McDonald says. "I drilled some drainage holes in the bottom and then filled them with packaged potting soil. Generally, one to three tomato plants can be accommodated in a 14-inch pot, but 18 inches would be better."

Whether germinating tomato seeds or starting with seedlings from a garden center, plant tomatoes outdoors when nighttime temperatures stay above 50°F. Place pots where they'll get at least a half day of full sun, although more is better. For McDonald, the best spot was the path to the front door.

"One night, dinner guests started up the walk and stopped to sample first this tomato and then that one, so by the time they were at the door, hors d'oeuvres had already been consumed."

TINY

'Red Currant' (right): sweet/tart, all-tomato taste; vigorous plants

'Yellow Currant' (above): grapelike clusters, sweet taste

'Sweet Pea', a currant type (left): tiny bursts of pure tomato

'Sugar Snack' (right): high-yield hybrid, long season, tasty

'Cuban Yellow Grape' (left): showy clusters of low-acid, juicy, sweet fruit

'Rosalita' (right): A pink grape tomato; tiny, sweet, abundant

BITE-SIZE

'Galina's' (right): golden cherry from Siberia; sweet, prolific

'Isis Candy' (left): red-marbled yellow, fruity sweet

'Super Snow White' (right): pale ivory, exceptionally sweet tasting

'Florida Basket' (left): small plant and fruit, big tomato taste

'Black Cherry' (right): juicy, complex, sweet fruit, strong plant

'Sun Gold' (left): cherry shape, orange color, fruity sweet

TOMATOES SHOWN ACTUAL SIZE

Grilled Cherry Tomatoes with Garlic
PREP: 20 MINUTES **GRILL:** 4 MINUTES **FAST!**

- 24   cherry tomatoes, 1 to 1½ inches in diameter
- 4   cloves garlic, cut into slivers
- 1   Tbsp. olive oil
- 1   tsp. snipped fresh rosemary or parsley
- 1   tsp. sugar
- ¼   tsp. salt, coarse sea salt, or kosher salt

1. Remove stems, if necessary, from tomatoes. With the tip of a sharp knife, pierce tomatoes. Carefully insert a sliver of garlic into each one.
2. Place tomatoes in the center of an 18×12 sheet of foil. Drizzle tomatoes with olive oil; sprinkle with rosemary, sugar, and salt. Bring the two long sides of the foil together and seal with a double fold. Fold remaining edges together to completely enclose tomatoes.
3. Grill tomatoes on the rack of a grill directly over coals or gas burners for 4 to 5 minutes or until heated through. (Or bake in a preheated 350°F oven for 4 to 5 minutes or until heated through.)
4. To serve, carefully open foil packet (hot steam may escape from packet). Transfer tomatoes to serving plate or platter. Sprinkle with salt and serve immediately. Makes 12 servings.

LOW FAT **EACH 2-TOMATO SERVING:** 55 cal., 3 g total fat (1 g sat. fat), 5 mg chol., 103 mg sodium, 5 carbo., 0g fiber, 2 pro. Daily Values: 5% vit. A, 8% vit. C, 4% calcium, 2% iron.

Tomato-Squash Salad

Tomato-Squash Salad
START TO FINISH: 25 MINUTES **FAST!**

- 8   oz. baby patty pan squash and/or baby zucchini (about 2 cups)
- 2   pt. red and/or yellow currant tomatoes (about 4 cups)
- 1   to 2 cups fresh arugula or romaine lettuce, coarsely torn
- 2   Tbsp. snipped fresh basil, tarragon, and/or chives
- ¼   cup olive oil
- ¼   cup red wine vinegar or champagne vinegar
- 1   Tbsp. lime or lemon juice
- ¼   tsp. salt
- ⅛   tsp. ground black pepper

1. In a large saucepan cook squash, covered, in enough boiling lightly salted water to cover until tender, about 5 minutes. Drain. Cool vegetables by adding cold water and ice cubes to pan. Drain well.
2. In a serving bowl combine the drained squash, tomatoes, arugula, and herbs. In a screw-top jar combine remaining ingredients. Cover; shake well. Add half to salad; toss to coat. Season to taste with additional salt and pepper. Pass remaining dressing. Makes 8 servings.

EACH SERVING: 82 cal., 7 g total fat (1 g sat. fat), 0 mg chol., 57 mg sodium, 5 g carbo., 2 g fiber, 1 g pro. Daily Values: 19% vit. A, 28% vit. C, 2% calcium, 3% iron.

Grilled Cherry Tomatoes with Garlic

Grilled Pear Tomato Relish

PREP: 10 MINUTES **GRILL:** 5 MINUTES **FAST!**

- 2 cups red and yellow miniature tomatoes, such as pear, currant, grape, or cherry
- 2 tsp. olive oil or cooking oil
- ½ tsp. packed brown sugar
- ⅛ tsp. ground cloves, ginger, or nutmeg

1. In a medium bowl combine all ingredients. Toss gently to mix thoroughly without breaking skins of tomatoes.

2. Heat a grill-top frying pan on the rack of an uncovered grill directly over medium-hot coals or medium-hot gas burner about 5 minutes or until hot. Add tomato mixture to pan; cook and stir for 3 to 5 minutes or until skins begin to pop and tomatoes are softened and heated through. Season to taste with *salt* and *ground black pepper*. Serve over grilled steaks, pork chops, chicken, shrimp, or salmon. Makes 4 servings.

STOVETOP DIRECTIONS: Heat grill pan or medium-size skillet over medium-high heat until hot. Add tomato mixture; cook and stir as directed above.

EACH ¼-CUP SERVING: 39 cal., 2 g total fat (0 g sat. fat), 0 mg chol., 78 mg sodium, 4 carbo., 1 g fiber, 1 g pro. Daily Values: 15% vit. A, 19% vit. C, 1% calcium, 2% iron.

Grilled Pear Tomato Relish

Mosaic Tomato Pie

These side-dish tarts combine a spicy crust with vinaigrette-splashed tomatoes. You won't mind that it takes a bit more time to show off the tomatoes so well.

PREP: 25 MINUTES **BAKE:** 15 MINUTES **COOL:** 15 MINUTES

- 1¼ cups all-purpose flour
- 1 tsp. dried basil, crushed
- ⅛ to ¼ tsp. cayenne pepper
- ¼ tsp. salt
- ⅓ cup shortening
- 4 to 5 Tbsp. cold water
- 3 cups mixed miniature tomatoes, such as currant, grape, pear, and cherry
- ¼ cup finely chopped red onion
- ¼ cup bottled balsamic vinaigrette
- 2 Tbsp. grated Parmesan or other hard grating cheese (optional)

1. Preheat oven to 450°F. In a medium bowl stir together flour, basil, cayenne pepper, and salt. Cut in shortening until pieces are pea size. Sprinkle 1 tablespoon of the water over part of the flour mixture; gently toss with a fork. Push moistened dough to side of bowl. Repeat, using 1 tablespoon water at a time, until flour mixture is moistened; form into a ball. On a lightly floured surface, slightly flatten dough.

2. Roll dough from center to edges into a 12×12-inch square. Cut pastry square into four 6-inch squares. Ease pastry squares into four jumbo muffin cups, pleating sides to fit. Generously prick bottom and sides of pastry with a fork.

3. Bake for 5 to 8 minutes or until just beginning to brown. Meanwhile, in another medium bowl combine tomatoes, red onion, and vinaigrette. Mix to coat tomatoes; spoon tomato mixture into prebaked cups; drizzle any remaining vinaigrette over the tomatoes. If desired, sprinkle with grated cheese. Bake 10 minutes more or until heated through and tomatoes just begin to give up their juices. Cool at least 15 minutes on a wire rack. Makes 4 servings.

EACH SERVING: 365 cal., 23 g total fat (5 g sat. fat), 2 mg chol., 367 mg sodium, 35 g carbo., 3 g fiber, 6 g pro. Daily Values: 24% vit. A, 30% vit. C, 5% calcium, 12% iron.

Home front

GREETINGS FROM THE LINCOLN CAFE

Mt. Vernon, Iowa, offers intrepid travelers a welcome respite from road-tripping. Located about 20 miles north of Iowa City, this tiny town is home to the Lincoln Cafe. Pastry chef Crystal Bounds reinvents homey favorites, such as a PB&J Gelée with Peanut Butter Whip. Chef/owner Matt Steigerwald opened the casual cafe four years ago and since then has been serving up big-city flavors using only local products and a lot of imagination. Lincoln Cafe, 117 1st St. W; Mount Vernon, Iowa; 319/895-4041; www.foodisimportant.com.

TRY THIS

Re-create chef Bounds' dessert at home. Prepare unflavored gelatin dessert mix, substituting grape juice for the water. Add 2 tablespoons lemon juice and 1 teaspoon vanilla extract. Set according to package directions. For the topping, beat together 4 tablespoons peanut butter melted in the microwave oven with 2 cups chilled heavy cream, 4 tablespoons powdered sugar, and 1 teaspoon vanilla extract.

Minty Mixtures

Try a savory alternative to the familiar mint jelly that accompanies spring lamb dishes, without losing the classic flavor combination.

MINT PESTO In a food processor combine 1 cup fresh mint leaves, $1/2$ to 1 teaspoon chopped garlic, 3 tablespoons cooking oil, and a handful of slivered almonds. Top cooked lamb chops.

MINT SOFFRITO In a food processor combine 1 cup fresh mint leaves; 1 medium green sweet pepper, seeded and chopped; 2 green onions, chopped; $1/2$ to 1 teaspoon chopped garlic; 1 tablespoon *each* lime juice and cooking oil; and salt. Use to stuff lamb chops or serve alongside cooked lamb.

MINT AND LIME PEPPER RUB Combine $1/4$ cup chopped fresh mint leaves, 1 tablespoon shredded lime peel, and $1/4$ teaspoon minced garlic. Season with sea salt and ground black pepper. Rub over lamb before roasting.

Mint Soffrito

THE NEW CHOCOLATES

Mexican cooks have been cooking savory dishes with chocolate—the base for mole—for centuries. New on the market are flavored baking bars and chocolate chips and premium cocoa powders. Stir these chocolates into barbecue sauces, chilies, and pork 'n' beans. The chocolates add richness and depth without adding sweetness. Many chocolates have added interesting flavor notes to them: chiles, cayenne pepper, black sesame seeds, cinnamon, ginger, and curry, for example. Exotic Chocolate Chips, 4-oz. package, $8.50, Vosges Chocolate; www.vosgeschocolate.com. Organic cooking chocolate, 5.3-oz. bar, $6.50; Green & Black's; www.chocosphere.com. Unsweetened cocoa, 10 oz., $4.75, Ghirardelli; 800/877-9338 or www.ghirardelli.com.

MAY

LET THE FRESH FLAVOR OF TENDER HERBS TAKE
CENTER STAGE ON YOUR DINNER TABLE THIS
SPRING. FROM ROASTED CHICKEN TO REFRESHING
ICE CREAM, HERBS BRING OUT THE BEST IN EVERY DISH.

Roasted Chicken with Rosemary and
Garlic Herbed Potatoes
page 82

Where Flavor Thrives

Mint Ice Cream
page 82

Stuffed Peppers Mole
page 91

Where Flavor Thrives

FOR MARY RISLEY, THE
ESSENTIAL INGREDIENTS IN ANY
MEAL ARE THE FRESH HERBS
GROWN IN THE BACKYARD OF
HER SAN FRANCISCO HOME.
"THE COOKING EXPERIENCE
SHOULDN'T BE LIMITED TO
THE KITCHEN," SHE SAYS. "IT
BEGINS WITH THE HUNT FOR
FRESH INGREDIENTS."

Mint-Pea Soup

Served warm, this soup has a hint of mint that balances well with the peas. Chill in the refrigerator before serving for a stronger mint flavor.

PREP: 40 MINUTES **COOK:** 20 MINUTES

- 1 medium onion, finely chopped
- 2 Tbsp. butter
- 1 clove garlic, minced
- 5 cups chicken or vegetable stock or three 14-oz. cans chicken or vegetable broth
- 4 cups shelled fresh peas (about 3 lb. in shell) or 4 cups frozen peas
- 2 Tbsp. snipped fresh mint
- 1 tsp. sugar
   Coarse salt and freshly ground black pepper
   Fresh mint leaves (optional)

1. In a large saucepan cook onion in butter over medium heat about 5 minutes or until tender, stirring occasionally. Stir in the garlic; cook 1 minute more. Add stock and peas. Bring to boiling; reduce heat. Simmer, uncovered, for 10 to 15 minutes or until peas are tender. Add the snipped mint and sugar.

2. Blend with an immersion blender* until smooth. Season to taste with salt and pepper. Serve warm or cover and refrigerate until well chilled. Ladle soup into bowls. If desired, garnish with fresh mint leaves. Makes 6 to 8 servings.

*TEST KITCHEN TIP: If no immersion blender is available, cool soup slightly. Transfer the mixture half at a time into a blender. Cover; blend until smooth. Return to saucepan; reheat. Season with salt and pepper. Serve as above.

EACH SERVING: 136 cal., 5 g total fat (2 g sat. fat), 13 mg chol., 925 mg sodium, 17 g carbo., 5 g fiber, 7 g pro. Daily Values: 16% vit. A, 52% vit. C, 3% calcium, 10% iron.

Mint-Pea Soup

There's something about Mary. Say her name and everyone within earshot will

claim to be hungry. That's because Mary Risley, cookbook author, cooking instructor, and founder of San Francisco's Tante Marie's Cooking School in 1979, effervesces about the art of cooking in a way that makes an appetite inevitable.

The key to her art, she says, is freshness. Picked at their prime, ingredients will shine on the plate—and on the palate.

Mary lives on the southern rim of Pacific Heights in a house with a kitchen larger than the typical San Francisco apartment. But it's the garden out back that was the selling point for her. In a city where window boxes are sometimes included in square footage, this 30×100-foot backyard stands out as a culinary promised land. Her garden is densely populated with flowers and herbs that lend aroma to the air and abundant color to the landscape. Rarely does she create a dinner menu for her friends and cooking students that doesn't involve the herbs that she grows just beyond her glass back door.

"Before I cook, I usually see which herbs need picking and develop a dish around them," says Mary, stooping to clip some lemon verbena for a pot of tea. "When you go to the store and you buy herbs out of a plastic container that have been shipped cross-country and refrigerated for days, you will never get the same amount of flavor from those as you will from picking and using your own."

Harvesting herbs in her garden year-round, Mary has found creative uses for nearly all of them. She uses rosemary sprigs as a brush for basting chicken before grilling. When herbs are growing abundantly, she minces some to combine with softened butter, rolls the mixture into a log, wraps it in waxed paper, and freezes for future use on fish or meat. For a sauce for lamb, she chops mint, then mixes it with sugar and white wine vinegar.

Not just for savory dishes, mint remains one of Mary's favorite ice cream flavors. Varieties like chocolate mint make obvious choices for ice cream or sorbet. Mary also enjoys lemon verbena and other herbs in desserts. Marjoram makes a fine sorbet. Young rosemary sprigs are often infused into cream and syrups for dessert, and lavender embellishes shortbread and lends an exciting floral note to fruit compotes and chocolate mousse.

Mary's party favors often include herbs. "One of the simplest, prettiest bouquets I give to people who visit me is a bundle of herbs," she says. "They make the most beautiful bouquets. Often I give a bundle of rosemary, which represents remembrance. It's a way to say I won't forget our time together."

Mint Ice Cream

Mint Ice Cream

Mary loves to add a few grains of salt to the infused cream mixture before freezing. "Salt brings out the sweetness," she says.
PREP: 25 MINUTES **STAND:** 1 HOUR **CHILL:** 2 HOURS
FREEZE: PER MANUFACTURER'S DIRECTIONS

    2 cups whipping cream
    ⅔ cup sugar
    ¾ cup fresh mint or basil leaves (about ¾ oz.)
    1 cup whole milk
       Fresh mint or basil leaves (optional)

1. In a medium saucepan combine cream, sugar, and mint leaves. Cook and stir over medium heat until mixture just begins to boil. Remove from heat; cover; steep for 1 hour. Strain, discarding mint leaves. Add milk to infused cream mixture. Cover and chill for 2 hours or overnight until mixture is completely chilled.

2. Freeze cream mixture in a 1-quart ice cream freezer according to the manufacturer's directions. Ripen ice cream according to manufacturer's directions. Scoop into dessert dishes. If desired, sprinkle with fresh mint. Makes 1 quart.

EACH ½-CUP SERVING: 289 cal., 23 g total fat (14 g sat. fat), 85 mg chol., 36 mg sodium, 19 g carbo., 0 g fiber, 2 g pro. Daily Values: 18% vit. A, 9% vit. C, 8% calcium, 8% iron.

Roasted Chicken with Rosemary and Garlic Herbed Potatoes

Try a rosemary basting brush on a holiday turkey or Cornish hens.
PREP: 30 MINUTES **BRINE:** 6 HOURS
ROAST: 1¼ HOURS **STAND:** 10 MINUTES

    ½ cup kosher salt
    ¼ cup snipped fresh rosemary
    2 3½- to 3¾-lb. whole broiler-fryer chickens
    8 sprigs fresh rosemary
    1 small lemon
    ⅓ cup olive oil
    4 cloves garlic, crushed
    2 lb. red, white, or gold new potatoes
    ¼ tsp. kosher salt or ⅛ tsp. salt
    ¼ tsp. ground black pepper
       Fresh rosemary leaves (optional)
       Lemon peel strips (optional)

1. For brine, in large Dutch oven stir together 1 gallon *water*, the ½ cup salt, and the ¼ cup snipped rosemary until salt is dissolved. Rinse insides of chickens. Submerge chickens in brine. Tie 6 of the rosemary sprigs together with 100%-cotton kitchen string to make a brush. Add rosemary brush to brine mixture. Cover and refrigerate for 6 to 8 hours.

2. Using a vegetable peeler or zester, remove lemon peel, taking care not to remove any white pith. Cut lemon in half; set aside.

3. In a small saucepan combine olive oil, 2 of the garlic cloves, and the lemon peel. Cook, uncovered, over low heat just until warm to the touch; remove from heat and set aside.

4. Preheat oven to 425°F. Remove chickens and rosemary sprigs from brine. Dry chickens with paper towels. Skewer neck skins of chickens to backs. Twist wing tips under backs. In the cavity of each chicken place a lemon half, a sprig of the remaining rosemary, and 1 garlic clove. Tie legs to tails, if present, or to each other. Cut large potatoes into ½-inch slices and halve small potatoes. Place potatoes in a large shallow roasting pan. Sprinkle potatoes with the ¼ teaspoon salt and the pepper. Using the rosemary sprig brush, baste potatoes with some of the oil mixture. Place chickens, breast sides up, on potatoes in pan. Using the rosemary sprig brush, baste the chickens with some of the oil mixture.

5. Roast, uncovered, 30 minutes. Reduce heat to 375°F. Roast for 45 to 60 minutes more or until drumsticks move easily in sockets, chicken is no longer pink (180°F), and potatoes are tender, brushing twice with remaining oil mixture during first 1 hour of roasting. Remove from oven. Cover; let stand 10 minutes before carving.

6. Transfer the chickens to a serving dish; surround with potatoes. If desired, sprinkle chickens and potatoes with fresh rosemary leaves and lemon peel strips. Makes 8 servings.

EACH SERVING OF CHICKEN AND POTATOES: 767 cal., 53 g total fat (13 g sat. fat), 207 mg chol., 947 mg sodium, 20 g carbo., 2 g fiber, 52 g pro. Daily Values: 6% vit. A, 33% vit. C, 5% calcium, 23% iron.

Roasted Chicken with Rosemary and Garlic Herbed Potatoes

Rosemary

Long grown in temperate zones around the world, rosemary is one of the most aromatic herbs. Plant nursery plants or try propagating from cuttings. Rosemary is difficult to grow from seed. The narrow leaves, stems, and blue, pink, or white flowers can be used in cooking. Use rosemary sparingly—its pungent flavor goes a long way. Try with chicken, veal, or lamb. When roasting or grilling meats or poultry, place a few sprigs underneath (or on top). Rosemary can be a star ingredient in focaccia and other breads or in homemade crackers, as well as lentils, potatoes, roasted tomatoes, and summer and winter squash.

Chives

A petite member of the onion family, chives grow as perennials in garden soil, but they demand regular watering and generous mulching because their roots grow close to the surface. Plants appear in spring; to harvest, snip, don't pull. The flavor and texture are best raw. Use scissors to cut chive leaves into tiny sections and generously sprinkle them on potato salads, cheese and butter spreads, and omelets. The pink-and-purple blossoms lend a mild onion taste to salads.

**Lemon-Chive Cheese Dip
with Parmesan Crisps**

Parmesan Crisps

These rich, lemony crackers also pair well with simple seafood salads, light summer soups, and smoked meats.

PREP: 30 MINUTES **BAKE:** 10 MINUTES

4	oz. Parmesan cheese, cut into 1-inch chunks
3/4	cup all-purpose flour
1/4	cup cold butter, cut into 4 pieces
1 1/2	tsp. finely shredded lemon peel
1/4	tsp. freshly ground black pepper
2	Tbsp. cold water
	Kosher salt or sea salt
	Finely shredded lemon peel

1. Put 2 of the chunks of cheese in food processor fitted with chopping blade. Cover; process until cheese is almost ground. Drop in remaining cheese chunks, a few at a time, until all cheese is ground. Remove top; add flour, cold butter, the 1 1/2 teaspoons lemon peel, and the pepper to food processor. With machine running, add water through feed tube; process until mixture just comes together. Shape into a ball.

2. Preheat oven to 400°F. Flatten cheese mixture on a sheet of parchment paper. Top with parchment. Use a rolling pin to roll out a 12-inch square. Remove top sheet of parchment. Invert dough onto baking sheet; remove second parchment. Using fluted pastry wheel, pizza cutter, or sharp knife, cut 2×1 1/2-inch rectangles or 1/2-inch strips. Carefully separate dough using spatula to lift; arrange on baking sheet 1 inch apart. Using fork, prick dough. Sprinkle with salt and additional lemon peel.

3. Bake for 10 to 12 minutes or until golden brown; cool on baking sheet. Makes about 48 rectangles or 24 strips.

EACH RECTANGLE: 50 cal., 3 g total fat (2 g sat. fat), 8 mg chol., 114 mg sodium, 3 g carbo., 0 g fiber, 2 g pro. Daily Values: 2% vit. A, 6% calcium, 1% iron.

Lemon-Chive Cheese Dip

Try this with a citrusy white wine.

PREP: 15 MINUTES **CHILL:** 4 HOURS

4	oz. cream cheese, softened
1/2	cup ricotta cheese
1/2	cup crème fraîche or dairy sour cream
3/4	cup finely snipped fresh chives
1	Tbsp. finely shredded lemon peel
1/4	tsp. kosher salt or sea salt
1/4	tsp. freshly ground black pepper
	Lemon peel and/or fresh chives (optional)
	Crackers and/or vegetable dippers

1. In a medium mixing bowl beat cream cheese with an electric mixer on medium speed until smooth. Beat in ricotta cheese and crème fraîche just until combined. Stir in chives, shredded lemon peel, salt, and pepper. Cover and chill for 4 to 24 hours. If desired, sprinkle with lemon peel and/or fresh chives. Serve with crackers and/or vegetable dippers. Makes 1 1/2 cups dip.

EACH 2-TABLESPOON SERVING: 85 cal., 8 g total fat (2 g sat. fat), 29 mg chol., 80 mg sodium, 1 g carbo., 0 g fiber, 2 g pro. Daily Values: 4% vit. A, 4% vit. C, 5% calcium, 1% iron.

Soaked Cherries with Lavender

Soaked Cherries with Lavender

Mary credits her good friend Vianna LaPlace for this favorite recipe. "I would never have thought of heating the cherries and serving them over crusty bread," she says.

PREP: 15 MINUTES **COOK:** 15 MINUTES

- ½ cup cranberry juice
- ¼ cup packed brown sugar
- 1 tsp. finely snipped fresh lavender buds or ¼ tsp. dried lavender buds, crushed
- 1½ lb. fresh dark and/or light sweet cherries, pitted, or 1¼ lb. (20 oz.) frozen pitted dark sweet cherries
- 4 thick slices country bread
- 2 Tbsp. butter, softened
  Lavender blossoms (optional)
  Almonds or pecans, toasted (optional)

1. In a medium saucepan combine cranberry juice, brown sugar, and lavender. Stir until sugar is dissolved. Add cherries; stir. Bring to boiling, reduce heat. Simmer, uncovered, for 15 minutes.*

2. Lightly grill or toast the bread; spread with butter. Place the bread in 4 dessert bowls. Spoon cherries and juices over the bread. If desired, sprinkle with lavender blossoms and almonds. Serve warm. Makes 4 servings.

*NOTE: For a thicker syrup, remove the cherries with a slotted spoon. Boil gently, uncovered, to the consistency you wish. Return cherries to syrup.

EACH SERVING: 391 cal., 8 g total fat (4 g sat. fat), 15 mg chol., 397 mg sodium, 75 g carbo., 5 g fiber, 7 g pro. Daily Values: 18% vit. A, 9% vit. C, 8% calcium, 8% iron.

Tuna and Marjoram Bean Salad with Anchovy and Caper Vinaigrette

Short on your supply of marjoram? Reach for oregano. Its flavor is more pungent and robust, so you may want to use less.

PREP: 30 MINUTES **STAND:** 1 HOUR
COOK: 2 HOURS **GRILL:** 8 MINUTES

- 1 lb. dried cannellini beans or three 19-oz. cans cannellini beans (white kidney beans), rinsed and drained
- ½ cup fresh marjoram sprigs
- 6 Tbsp. extra virgin olive oil
  Kosher salt and freshly ground black pepper
- 2 to 4 anchovy fillets, drained
- ⅓ cup finely chopped parsley
- 3 Tbsp. drained capers
- 2 cloves garlic, minced
- 1 tsp. Dijon-style mustard
- 6 Tbsp. lemon juice (2 lemons)
- ¼ cup extra virgin olive oil
- 6 4-oz. fresh tuna steaks, about ¾ inch thick*
- 6 ½-inch slices red onion (2 large)
  Fresh marjoram sprigs (optional)

Tuna and Marjoram Bean Salad with Anchovy and Caper Vinaigrette

1. Rinse dried beans, if using. In a Dutch oven combine beans and 8 cups *water*. Bring to boiling; reduce heat. Simmer, covered, for 2 minutes. Remove from heat. Let stand, covered, for 1 hour. (Or place beans in water in Dutch oven. Cover and let soak in a cool place for 6 to 8 hours or overnight.) Drain and rinse beans. Return beans to Dutch oven. Stir in 8 cups fresh *water*; add ½ cup marjoram sprigs and 1 tablespoon of the olive oil. Bring to boiling; reduce heat. Simmer, covered, about 2 hours or until tender. Drain, discarding marjoram sprigs. Cool slightly.

2. Toss cooked beans with 4 tablespoons of the olive oil; season with salt and pepper. Cover; set aside. (If using canned beans, in a saucepan stir together beans, 1½ to 2 tablespoons snipped fresh marjoram, 4 tablespoons olive oil, and salt and pepper to taste. Heat through over medium heat; cover and keep warm.)

3. In a small bowl mash anchovy fillets with a fork. Add parsley, capers, garlic, and mustard; mix thoroughly. Stir in 2 tablespoons of the lemon juice. Add the ¼ cup olive oil, whisking to combine ingredients. Season to taste with salt. Set aside.

4. Brush the tuna and onion slices with remaining 1 tablespoon olive oil; sprinkle lightly with salt and pepper. Grill tuna and onion on rack of uncovered grill directly over medium coals for 4 minutes. Turn and grill 4 to 5 minutes more or until tuna is slightly pink in center and onion is tender. (Or arrange the tuna and onion on unheated rack of broiler pan. Broil 3 to 4 inches from heat for 10 minutes or until tuna is slightly pink in center and onion is tender, turning once.)

5. To serve, spoon beans onto 6 serving plates. Drizzle beans with remaining 4 tablespoons lemon juice. Place a tuna fillet on each plate. Drizzle each serving with anchovy mixture. Serve with red onion slices. If desired, sprinkle with additional marjoram sprigs. Makes 6 servings.

*TEST KITCHEN TIP: Skinless salmon fillets can be used in place of tuna steaks. Salmon will be done when it flakes easily with a fork.

EACH SERVING: 603 cal., 25 g total fat (4 g sat. fat), 52 mg chol., 734 mg sodium, 53 g carbo., 16 g fiber, 44 g pro. Daily Values: 7% vit. A, 45% vit. C, 15% calcium, 26% iron.

Roasted Peppers with Parsley Croutons

Roasted Peppers with Parsley Croutons

These croutons are crisp on the outside, soft on the inside. Toss them over roasted vegetables, salads, or a favorite casserole.

PREP: 30 MINUTES **ROAST:** 20 MINUTES
STAND: 15 MINUTES **COOK:** 10 MINUTES

  6 red, yellow, green, and/or orange sweet peppers
  1 anchovy, minced*
  2 cloves garlic, minced
  ¼ cup extra virgin olive oil
  2 to 3 slices crusty country bread, cut into 1-inch cubes (4 cups)
  2 oz. crumbled goat cheese (chèvre) or feta cheese (optional)
  ½ cup fresh flat-leaf parsley leaves
  ¼ tsp. coarse salt

1. Preheat oven to 425°F. Halve peppers lengthwise; remove stems, seeds, and membranes. Place pepper halves, cut sides down, on a large foil-lined baking sheet. Roast peppers for 20 to 25 minutes or until skins are blistered and dark. (Or broil 4 to 5 inches from heat for 10 to 15 minutes.) Carefully bring foil up around pepper halves to enclose. Let stand about 15 minutes or until cool enough to handle. Using a sharp knife, loosen the edges of the skins from the pepper halves; gently and slowly pull off the skin in strips. Discard skin. Cut peppers in ½-inch strips; transfer to a serving dish.

2. Meanwhile, for croutons, in a large skillet heat anchovy and garlic in hot oil over medium-high heat until garlic just starts to brown. Add bread cubes to skillet. Cook about 8 minutes until lightly browned, stirring occasionally. Sprinkle croutons on peppers. If desired, top with cheese. Sprinkle with parsley and salt. Makes 8 servings.

*NOTE: To substitute bacon for the anchovy, in a large skillet cook 2 slices bacon until crisp. Remove bacon, reserving drippings in skillet. Drain bacon on paper towels. Crumble bacon; set aside. Add 2 tablespoons olive oil to drippings; cook garlic and croutons as above. Assemble as above, sprinkling crumbled bacon on top.

EACH SERVING: 125 cal., 8 g total fat (1 g sat. fat), 0 mg chol., 169 mg sodium, 13 g carbo., 2 g fiber, 2 g pro. Daily Values: 62% vit. A, 291% vit. C, 2% calcium, 6% iron.

Lemon Verbena Tisane

This tisane—an infusion of leaves or flowers—has a light lemon and mint flavor and a sweet scent.

PREP: 5 MINUTES **STAND:** 3 MINUTES

- 12 sprigs fresh lemon verbena or the peel of 1 lemon*
- 4 sprigs fresh mint
- 4 cups boiling water

1. Place fresh herbs and mint in a warm teapot. Add boiling water. Steep for 3 minutes; serve warm. To serve chilled, remove herbs and mint sprigs with a slotted spoon; refrigerate. Makes 6 (6-ounce) servings.

*TEST KITCHEN TIP: Use a vegetable peeler to remove the lemon peel in strips. Scrape any white pith off the lemon peel strips.

EACH SERVING: 1 cal., 0 g total fat, 0 mg chol., 3 mg sodium, 0 mg carbo., 0 mg fiber, 0 mg pro. Daily values: 4% vit. C, 1% calcium, 2% iron.

Lemon Verbena

Known for its strong lemony fragrance, lemon verbena does well in warm climates with moist soil. It can also be container-grown in cold climates and brought indoors during winter months. The deciduous herb needs full sun. Harvest the yellow-green leaves and use them fresh or dried in cooking for a light flavor. Infuse dried leaves in boiling water for a delicate tea or add fresh minced lemon verbena to cooked rice.

Lemon Verbena Tisane

NEW WAYS TO STUFF A PEPPER

BY **STEPHEN EXEL** PHOTOGRAPHS BY **GREG SCHEIDEMANN**

That American suppertime

standard, stuffed sweet peppers, gets updated with a bit of international flair by incorporating seafood, vegetables, and flavorful sauces into the mix. Here are three versions that reflect the diversity of American cooks, with influences from Asia, Mexico, and Italy. Each can be on the table in 30 minutes or less.

Shrimp and Pea Pod Stuffed Peppers get an Asian-style twist with ingredients such as hoisin sauce, sesame seeds, and bok choy. Stuffed Peppers Mole combines precooked ground beef with Spanish-style rice, Mexican cheese blend, and mole sauce; Stuffed Peppers Risotto are filled with precooked chicken, asparagus, tarragon, and rice cooked with whipping cream. Served with a fresh green salad, these cosmopolitan peppers are a complete dinner.

Shrimp and Pea Pod Stuffed Peppers

START TO FINISH: 30 MINUTES **FAST!**

- 4   small or 2 large sweet peppers
- 1   3-oz. pkg. shrimp- or mushroom-flavor ramen noodles
- 8   oz. frozen peeled and deveined cooked shrimp or tub-style firm tofu (bean curd), drained and cubed
- ⅓   cup bottled hoisin or stir-fry sauce
- 1½ cups chopped bok choy
- ¾   cup pea pods, strings and tips removed and halved, or half a 6-oz. pkg. frozen pea pods, thawed and halved
- 4   green onions, thinly sliced
- ¼   tsp. cayenne pepper (optional)
- 2   tsp. sesame seeds, toasted

1. Cut tops off small peppers or halve large peppers lengthwise. Remove membranes and seeds. In a 4-quart Dutch oven immerse peppers in boiling *water* for 3 minutes. Remove; drain peppers, cut sides down, on paper towels.

2. For filling, break noodles. In a saucepan cook noodles and seasoning according to package directions. Add shrimp and cook 30 seconds more. Drain noodle mixture; discard liquid. Return noodle mixture to pot. Add tofu (if using), hoisin sauce, bok choy, pea pods, green onions, and, if desired, cayenne pepper; heat through.

3. Arrange peppers, cut sides up, on a serving platter. Spoon filling into peppers. Spoon any remaining filling around peppers. Sprinkle with toasted sesame seeds. Serve warm or refrigerate and serve cold. Makes 4 servings.

EACH SERVING: 256 cal., 6 g total fat (2 g sat. fat), 111 mg chol., 1,050 mg sodium, 33 g carbo., 4 g fiber, 19 g pro. Daily Values: 80% vit. A, 655% vit. C, 10% calcium, 19% iron.

Shrimp and Pea Pod Stuffed Peppers

GOOD TO KNOW Choose sweet peppers that have a shiny skin and are heavy for their size. Refrigerate them in a plastic bag for up to one week after purchase.

Stuffed Peppers Risotto
START TO FINISH: 30 MINUTES **FAST!**

- ½ cup uncooked Arborio or long grain white rice
- 1¼ cups reduced-sodium chicken broth
- 4 small or 2 large sweet peppers
   Salt and ground black pepper
- 3 oz. Parmesan or Romano cheese
- 1 cup 1-inch pieces asparagus or fresh broccoli florets
- 1 cup cubed cooked chicken
- 2 tsp. snipped fresh tarragon or oregano or ½ tsp. dried tarragon or oregano, crushed
- ¼ cup whipping cream
- ¼ cup pine nuts or chopped walnuts, toasted if desired

1. For filling, in a 2-quart saucepan combine rice and broth; bring to boiling. Reduce heat and simmer, covered, 15 minutes.
2. Meanwhile, cut tops off small peppers, or halve large peppers lengthwise. Remove membranes and seeds. In a 4-quart Dutch oven of boiling water immerse peppers for 3 minutes. Remove; drain, cut sides down, on paper towels. Place in a serving dish, cut sides up. Sprinkle lightly with salt and black pepper; set aside.
3. With a vegetable peeler, shave 1 ounce of the Parmesan in thin strips; set aside. Finely shred or grate the remaining Parmesan; set aside. Stir asparagus, chicken, and herb into rice. Cover and cook 5 minutes more. Stir in whipping cream, shredded or grated cheese, and nuts. Spoon filling into peppers. Top with shaved cheese. Makes 4 servings.
EACH SERVING: 266 cal., 14 g total fat (5 g sat. fat), 54 mg chol., 426 mg sodium, 20 g carbo., 3 g fiber, 16 g pro. Daily Values: 16% vit. A, 88% vit. C, 9% calcium, 15% iron.

Stuffed Peppers Mole

Stuffed Peppers Mole
START TO FINISH: 20 MINUTES **FAST!**

- 4 small or 2 large sweet peppers
- 1 8.8-oz. pouch cooked Spanish-style rice, or long grain and wild rice mix
- 10 to 12 oz. cooked ground beef crumbles or 2 cups cooked ground beef
- ½ cup frozen whole kernel corn
- 3 Tbsp. purchased mole sauce
- 2 Tbsp. water
- ½ cup shredded Mexican cheese blend or shredded cheddar cheese (2 oz.)
   Salt and ground black pepper
- 2 Tbsp. snipped fresh cilantro

1. Cut tops off small peppers or halve large peppers lengthwise. Remove membranes and seeds. In a 4-quart Dutch oven immerse peppers in boiling water for 3 minutes. Remove; drain peppers, cut sides down, on paper towels.
2. For filling, in a saucepan combine rice, beef, corn, mole sauce, and water. Cook, uncovered, over medium heat until heated through, stirring frequently. Remove from heat; stir in cheese. Place peppers, cut sides up, on platter. Sprinkle with salt and black pepper. Spoon filling into peppers. Sprinkle with cilantro. Makes 4 servings.
EACH SERVING: 360 cal., 15 g total fat (7 g sat. fat), 75 mg chol., 732 mg sodium, 29 g carbo., 3 g fiber, 28 g pro. Daily Values: 56% vit. A, 205% vit. C, 11% calcium, 23% iron.

Stuffed Peppers Risotto

A TOUCH OF TARRAGON

BY **STEPHEN EXEL** PHOTOGRAPHS BY **GREG SCHEIDEMANN**

The herb garden's harbinger of spring, tarragon is one of the first perennial herbs to make its appearance as the air and ground warm. It inspires thoughts of light and fresh cooking. The peppery scent and licorice-like flavor pair well with steamed spring vegetables, enliven egg and chicken dishes, and punch up mustard and mayonnaise.

The subtle, elegant flavor of this aromatic herb transforms simple four- and five-ingredient recipes into something complex and sophisticated. Tarragon Ice is a cooling treat for a warm day. Use Fresh Tarragon Yogurt Cheese to top grilled meats or to spread on a toasted bagel. Pour Tarragon Syrup over ice cream or waffles or into tea and sparkling water. Break up a savory Tarragon Custard over spring greens and add a dash of anise-flavor Tarragon Vinegar.

In the garden, tarragon needs well-drained soil and full sun. For culinary use, plant French tarragon from starter plants. (Tarragon seed packets, which are usually the Russian variety, will harvest coarse and tasteless.) Cut back the plant as it grows to prevent it from languishing. This temperate-climate plant needs winter cold to thrive in warm weather. In hot climates, Mexican mint marigold (*Tagetes lucida*) is a close substitute for the flavor.

Tarragon Ice

PREP: 20 MINUTES **COOL:** 30 MINUTES
STAND: 10 MINUTES **FREEZE:** 10 HOURS

    3 cups water
    1 cup sugar
  1/3 cup fresh lemon or lime juice
    1 Tbsp. snipped fresh tarragon

1. In a medium saucepan combine water and sugar. Bring to boiling, stirring to dissolve sugar. Remove from heat; cool 30 minutes. In a 2-quart square baking dish, combine sugar mixture, lemon juice, and tarragon. Cover and freeze about 7 hours or until nearly firm.
2. Break frozen mixture into small chunks. Transfer to a chilled large mixing bowl. Beat with an electric mixer on medium speed until fluffy but not melted. Return mixture to 2-quart square dish; cover and freeze at least 3 hours or until firm.
3. To serve, let stand at room temperature for 10 minutes. Using a large spoon, scrape across surface and spoon into dessert dishes. Makes about 6 cups (twelve 1/2-cup servings).

LOW FAT **EACH 1/2-CUP SERVING:** 64 cal., 0 g total fat, 0 mg chol., 1 mg sodium, 17 g carbo., 0 g fiber, 0 g pro. Daily Values: 5% vit. C.

Tarragon Ice

Tarragon Vinegar

PREP: 15 MINUTES **COOL:** 2 HOURS
STAND: 1 WEEK

- ½ cup tightly packed fresh tarragon
- 2 cups white wine vinegar or cider vinegar

1. Wash tarragon; dry. In stainless-steel saucepan combine tarragon and vinegar; bring to boiling. Remove; cover with cheesecloth; cool about 2 hours. Pour into clean 1-quart jar; submerge tarragon. Cover with nonmetallic lid or plastic wrap; seal with metal lid. Let stand in cool, dark place for 1 to 2 weeks.
2. Line colander with cheesecloth. Strain vinegar. Transfer to clean 1½-pint jar. Cover with nonmetallic lid or plastic wrap; tightly seal with metal lid. Store in cool, dark place up to 6 months. Makes 2 cups.
EACH 1-TABLESPOON SERVING: 5 cal., 0 g total fat, 0 mg chol., 1 mg sodium, 0 g carbo., 0 g fiber, 0 g pro.

Fresh Tarragon Yogurt Cheese

PREP: 15 MINUTES
CHILL: 24 HOURS

- ½ a 32-oz. carton plain yogurt or plain goat's milk yogurt*
- 1 Tbsp. finely snipped fresh tarragon
- ⅛ tsp. salt

1. Line strainer or sieve with cheesecloth. Place over bowl. Spoon in yogurt. Cover with plastic wrap. Refrigerate 24 hours. Remove from refrigerator. Discard drained liquid.
2. Transfer to bowl. Add tarragon and salt. Store, covered, in refrigerator up to 1 week. Makes 16 (1-tablespoon) servings.
*TEST KITCHEN TIP: Use yogurt that contains no gums, gelatin, or fillers, which may prevent whey separating from curd.
EACH SERVING: 18 cal., 1 g total fat (0 g sat. fat), 2 mg chol., 38 mg sodium, 2 g carbo., 2 g pro. Daily Values: 5% calcium.

Tarragon Syrup

PREP: 20 MINUTES **COOL:** 1 HOUR
CHILL: UP TO 2 WEEKS

- 1½ cups water
- 1½ cups sugar
- 3 to 4 sprigs fresh tarragon, slightly crushed

1. In saucepan combine water and sugar. Bring to boiling over medium heat, stirring until sugar dissolves. Add tarragon; boil gently, uncovered, 2 minutes more. Remove from heat; cover and cool in saucepan 1 hour. Strain; discard tarragon. Transfer syrup to covered storage container. Refrigerate up to 2 weeks. Makes 2 cups syrup.
EACH 2-TABLESPOON SERVING: 70 cal., 0 g total fat, 0 mg chol., 0 mg sodium, 18 g carbo., 0 g fiber, 0 g pro.

Tarragon Custard

PREP: 15 MINUTES
STAND: 30 MINUTES
BAKE: 40 MINUTES
COOL: 30 MINUTES
CHILL: 4 HOURS

- 1½ cups whole milk
- 1 Tbsp. coarsely chopped fresh tarragon
  Nonstick cooking spray
- 4 eggs
- ⅛ to ¼ tsp. salt
- ⅛ tsp. ground black pepper

1. In pan combine milk and tarragon. Heat to simmer; remove from heat. Cover; let stand 30 minutes.
2. Meanwhile, lightly coat four 6-ounce custard cups with cooking spray. Place custard cups in square baking dish; set aside. Preheat oven to 325°F.
3. In bowl whisk together eggs, salt, and pepper. Whisk in milk mixture; divide among prepared cups. Place baking dish on oven rack. Pour boiling water in dish to 1 inch depth.
4. Bake for 40 minutes or until knife inserted near centers comes out clean. Cool cups on rack 30 minutes. Cover surface of custards with plastic wrap. Chill 4 hours. Run knife around edges of cups; invert. Makes 4 servings.
EACH SERVING: 129 cal., 8 g total fat (0 g sat. fat), 221 mg chol., 179 mg sodium, 5 g carbo., 9 g pro. Daily Values: 7% vit. A, 13% calcium, 5% iron.

Tarragon Vinegar

Fresh Tarragon Yogurt Cheese

Tarragon Syrup

Tarragon Custard

SPLASH ON FLAVOR

BY **ROBIN KLINE** PHOTOGRAPH BY **JOYCE OUDKERK POOL**

The complex flavors of Asian food

are increasingly popular. If you'd like to prepare these dishes at home but hesitate at the thought of gathering exotic ingredients, here's good news: You can make simple dishes sing with the flavors of ginger, red pepper, sesame, or chiles, using a host of bottled splashes, dressings, and flavored vinegars and oils that are available in specialty foods stores. To update a favorite recipe or enliven deli coleslaw or vegetable salads, add one or two tablespoons of these dressings.

Grilled Pork Noodle Salad, which uses a ginger vinaigrette, a hint of anise, chopped mint, and Thai basil leaves, is an intriguing warm-weather supper of contrasting textures and temperatures. The greens, herbs, and freshly grilled pork top silky rice noodles, and cucumber and lettuce give the salad crunch. For quick serving, cook the noodles and chop the vegetables and herbs ahead of time. Count on quick grilling to finish the dinner.

Grilled Pork Noodle Salad

Grilled Pork Noodle Salad

Try Chinablue Ginger Splash Dressing, available at www.chinablue.com.

PREP: 25 MINUTES **MARINATE:** 1 HOUR
GRILL: 12 MINUTES **STAND:** 25 MINUTES

- 3 boneless pork chops, ½ inch thick, about 12 oz. total
- ½ cup bottled ginger vinaigrette salad dressing or balsamic vinaigrette
- ¾ tsp. anise seeds, crushed
- 1 7-oz. pkg. rice sticks (noodles)
- ⅓ cup salad oil
- 2 cups torn romaine leaves
- 1½ cups peeled, seeded, and thinly sliced cucumber
- ½ cup coarsely chopped mint leaves
- ½ cup coarsely chopped Thai basil leaves or basil leaves
- ½ cup shredded carrot
- ¼ cup chopped roasted peanuts
  Fresh cilantro sprigs
  Lime (optional)

1. Place chops in resealable plastic bag. Add ¼ cup of the ginger vinaigrette and ¼ teaspoon of the anise seeds. Seal bag. Marinate in refrigerator 1 to 4 hours, turning bag occasionally. Drain and discard marinade. Grill chops on rack of uncovered grill over direct medium heat for 12 to 15 minutes or until juices run clear and an instant-read thermometer registers 160°F; turn chops once. Place on cutting board; let stand 5 minutes. Slice diagonally.

2. Cook rice sticks according to package directions. Drain in a colander; rinse with cold water until water runs clear. Let noodles drain 20 minutes; with kitchen shears, snip noodles into 3- to 4-inch lengths. In a bowl toss noodles with oil and remaining anise seeds. Cover and set aside.

3. In a bowl toss lettuce, cucumber, and herbs. If preparing ahead of time (up to 4 hours), cover with damp paper towels and refrigerate.

4. Toss greens with remaining ¼ cup ginger vinaigrette. Divide noodles among 4 plates or shallow soup bowls; top with greens and sliced pork. Top with carrot, peanuts, and cilantro. If desired, squeeze fresh lime on salads. Makes 4 servings.

EACH SERVING: 613 cal., 34 g total fat (6 g sat. fat), 47 mg chol., 692 mg sodium, 54 g carbo., 4 g fiber, 24 g pro. Daily Values: 76% vit. A, 28% vit. C, 7% calcium, 23% iron.

WAKE UP TO THE SIZZLE

BY **RICHARD SWEARINGER** PHOTOGRAPH BY **GREG SCHEIDEMANN**

Country Sausage with Red-Eye Gravy

For an authentic-style sausage, ask the butcher to grind meat through the coarse plate of the meat grinder. As an alternative, cut meat into cubes and finely chop with a chef's knife.

PREP: 25 MINUTES **CHILL:** 8 HOURS **COOK:** 22 MINUTES

1	lb. coarsely ground pork or chopped pork (see above)
½	cup plain croutons, coarsely crushed
¼	cup finely chopped onion
2	cloves garlic, minced
1	tsp. brown sugar
1½	tsp. ground sage
¾	tsp. salt or 1 tsp. kosher salt
½	tsp. dried thyme, crushed
¼	tsp. cayenne pepper
½	cup dried cherries, chopped*
1	Tbsp. cooking oil
2	Tbsp. packed brown sugar
¾	cup strong black coffee or chicken broth
	Prepared biscuits

1. In a medium bowl combine the pork, croutons, onion, garlic, the 1 teaspoon brown sugar, sage, salt, thyme, and cayenne. Mix thoroughly. Gently mix in cherries. Shape mixture into twelve 3-inch patties, using wet hands, if necessary. Arrange on a tray. Cover; chill 8 hours or overnight.

2. In a large skillet fry patties, half at a time, in hot oil over medium heat for 5 minutes on each side or until browned and cooked through (160°F). Remove from heat; keep warm.

3. For the Red-Eye Gravy, stir the 2 tablespoons brown sugar into the drippings in skillet. Stir in the coffee. Bring to boiling. Boil gently, uncovered, for 2 to 3 minutes or until gravy is slightly thickened and a rich reddish brown, scraping the skillet to loosen any crusty bits.

4. Split biscuits. Serve sausage patties on split biscuits with gravy. Makes 12 servings.

*TEST KITCHEN TIP: For an added layer of flavor, soak cherries in ¼ cup bourbon for 15 minutes; drain.

EACH PATTY + 1 TABLESPOON GRAVY: 92 cal., 4 g total fat (1 g sat. fat), 18 mg chol., 171 mg sodium, 9 g carbo., 0 g fiber, 5 g pro. Daily Values: 4% vit. A, 1% vit. C, 1% calcium, 3% iron.

Making sausage patties is a quick,

easy way to create a deliciously memorable breakfast. Served on a biscuit, topped with Red-Eye Gravy made from pan drippings (and an unexpected ingredient: coffee!), the patties exude an aroma that will rouse groggy family members.

This homemade version of sausage is appealing because you can make it as spicy or as mild as you like. The recipe blends classic sausage seasonings of sage, thyme, and garlic—then adds the fruit flavor of dried cherries and a hint of cayenne pepper. Round out breakfast with a bowl of fruit salad, a scrambled egg or two, and your favorite sleepyheads.

Country Sausage with Red-Eye Gravy

CATCH UP ON COCONUT

BY **KEN HAEDRICH** PHOTOGRAPHS BY **GREG SCHEIDEMANN**

A bit of manual labor is needed

to crack open a coconut, and the reward is a rich, fragrant nut meat that adds delicious tropical taste to pancakes, curry dishes, salads, and desserts.

To open a coconut, use a hammer and an ice pick to pierce each of the three soft eyes at one end. Drain the liquid into a container. Lay the coconut on its side and tap with a hammer, rotating to crack open the shell in several pieces. Then use a sturdy blunt knife to pry the white meat from the shell. Although the thin brown skin is edible, it's easily removed with a vegetable peeler. An average coconut yields about 3 cups of grated coconut meat.

Nibble on fresh coconut as a snack. Shred or flake chunks with a food grater or food processor to sprinkle on cereal and salads or fold it into cake batter.

Coconut-Chicken Curry

PREP: 30 MINUTES **STAND:** 30 MINUTES **COOK:** 16 MINUTES

- 1½ lb. skinless, boneless chicken thighs, cut in bite-size pieces
- ½ cup red curry paste
- 1 Tbsp. olive oil
- 1 large onion, coarsely chopped
- 1 recipe Fresh Coconut Milk or one 13.5-oz. can unsweetened or reduced-fat coconut milk
- 1½ cups purchased matchstick carrots or 3 medium carrots, thinly sliced
- 1 tsp. finely shredded lime peel
  Hot cooked rice
  Toasted Coconut Curls
  Snipped fresh cilantro

1. In a bowl combine chicken and curry paste; let stand at room temperature for 30 minutes.

2. Heat a 12-inch skillet over medium heat. Add olive oil, onion, and chicken mixture. Cook over medium heat for 8 to 10 minutes, stirring occasionally, until chicken is tender and no longer pink.

3. Remove chicken from skillet. Carefully add coconut milk to skillet, scraping up crusty bits. Add carrots and lime peel. Bring to boiling; reduce heat and simmer, uncovered, for 5 minutes or until carrots are crisp-tender. Return chicken mixture to skillet. Simmer, uncovered, for 3 to 5 minutes or until liquid thickens slightly. Serve with rice, Toasted Coconut Curls, and snipped cilantro. Makes 4 servings.

FRESH COCONUT MILK: Cut the tip from a young coconut (photo, page 99). Pour out coconut liquid; scoop out coconut meat. In a blender combine coconut liquid and meat; cover and blend until nearly smooth. Add enough chicken or vegetable broth to make 1¼ cups.

TOASTED COCONUT CURLS: Separate coconut meat from the shell in large pieces (see photo, page 99). Slice thinly with a vegetable peeler. Arrange slices on a baking sheet. Bake in a 350°F oven for 2 to 3 minutes or until edges just start to brown. Cool on baking sheet.

EACH SERVING: 561 cal., 28 g total fat (18 g sat. fat), 136 mg chol., 443 mg sodium, 36 g carbo., 2 g fiber, 39 g pro. Daily Values: 100% vit. A, 15% vit. C, 5% calcium, 21% iron.

Coconut-Chicken Curry

Coconut-Mango Salsa

Coconut-Mango Salsa
PREP: 30 MINUTES **CHILL:** 2 HOURS

1 to 2 sweet young coconuts
2 medium ripe mangoes
½ cup chopped radishes (about 7)
¼ cup sliced green onions (2)
1 Tbsp. grated fresh ginger
1 serrano chile pepper (see tip, page 49), seeded and finely chopped
½ tsp. salt
¼ cup Toasted Coconut Curls (page 97)

1. Using a serrated knife cut off the tip end of each coconut (photos, below). Strain ½ cup of the coconut liquid into a food processor or blender. Using a large spoon, scoop out ⅔ cup of the coconut meat; add coconut meat to food processor or blender.
2. Cover; process or blend until coconut mixture is nearly smooth. Transfer to a large serving bowl.
3. Peel, seed, and chop mangoes. Add mangoes, radishes, onions, ginger, pepper, and salt to coconut mixture. Stir to combine. Cover and chill for 2 to 6 hours.
4. Top with Toasted Coconut Curls. Serve with crackers, grilled chicken, ham, or fish. Makes 3 cups (twelve ¼-cup servings).

LOW FAT **EACH ¼-CUP SERVING:** 13 cal., 1 g total fat (1 g sat. fat), 0 mg chol., 27 mg sodium, 2 g carbo., 0 g fiber, 0 g pro. Daily Values: 5% vit. A, 4% vit. C.

INSIDE STORY
You'll find three types of coconuts in major markets.
1. BROWN COCONUT is the most mature and keeps at room temperature up to 6 months. The firm meat is easy to grate or shred.
2. WHITE COCONUT looks like an ivory version of the brown variety, but its meat is sweeter and softer. It can be scooped out with a spoon.
3. SWEET YOUNG COCONUT is the largest and youngest of the trio (coconuts shrink as they mature). A machine shapes it to make it easy to open and use as a drinking vessel for the refreshing liquid inside. The meat—with a puddinglike texture—is yummy in smoothies.

Billowy Coconut Frosting

This recipe makes enough to frost a two-layer cake. It's also luscious on peanut butter cookies or on chocolate cupcakes.

START TO FINISH: 25 MINUTES

- 2 Tbsp. water
- 2 egg whites
- ½ cup granulated sugar
- ½ cup packed brown sugar
- ½ tsp. cream of tartar
- ½ tsp. vanilla
- ½ tsp. coconut extract
- ½ cup sweetened flaked coconut or unsweetened shredded coconut

1. Place water, egg whites, granulated sugar, brown sugar, and cream of tartar in the top of a double boiler or a water bath pan. Place over boiling water (bottom of upper pan should not touch water). Cook, beating with an electric mixer on high speed about 7 minutes or until frosting forms stiff peaks, scraping sides of pan occasionally. Remove from heat; add vanilla and coconut extract. Beat for 2 to 3 minutes more or until frosting is spreading consistency. Fold in ¼ cup of the coconut. Sprinkle remaining coconut on frosted cake or cookies. Makes 3½ cups frosting.

LOW FAT **EACH TABLESPOON FROSTING:** 18 cal., 0 g total fat, 0 mg chol., 3 mg sodium, 4 g carbo., 0 g fiber, 1 g pro.

Billowy Coconut Frosting

SLICE AND SCOOP
Young coconuts without the familiar brown husk can be cut open with a serrated knife. Once open, use the liquid inside to flavor drinks. The soft meat can be eaten with a spoon, like custard, or stirred into frosting.

COCONUT CURLS
Easily shave fresh coconut meat into strips or curls with a vegetable peeler. Toasting the strips in the oven brings out its nutty flavor.

CLAM UP!

BY **STEPHEN EXEL** PHOTOGRAPH BY **JOYCE OUDKERK POOL**

Native Americans invited

early New England settlers to summer clambakes as a gesture of friendship. The tradition of gathering for a simple shellfish supper continues today, and with the country extending from sea to shining sea, the variety of clams—and how they can be prepared—is plentiful (for popular varieties of clams, see chart, opposite).

With their distinctive salty-sweet taste and simple preparation, clams are well suited for casual summer get-togethers. Clam beds are more accessible in the summer, but if you're not the shovel-and-bucket type, buy fresh clams—either in the shell or freshly shucked—from the market. Clams in the shell should be tightly closed; discard any open or cracked shells. The protruding neck of a soft-shell clam should retract when touched. Freshly shucked clams should not smell fishy.

Keep live in-the-shell clams in the refrigerator covered with a wet towel and use them within a day of purchase. They'll keep up to 4 days if you lower the refrigerator temperature to 32°F to 35°F. Before cooking or opening, "purge" the clams by rinsing them several times in ice-cold salted water to rid them of any sand. Hard-shell clams are easier to open if you place them in the freezer for about 10 minutes before shucking. Drain the clams as they're shucked; this liquid is traditionally used in clam chowders. Shucked clams can be refrigerated in tightly covered containers and immersed in their liquor up to one week.

Clams can be prepared in many ways, including steamed, sauteed, baked, cooked, and deep-fried. If you have the grill fired up for a barbecue, Grilled Clams with Three Sauces (recipe, opposite) is an easy dish to start with. Try the three easy stir-together sauces to get out of the cocktail-sauce rut.

Grilled Clams with Three Sauces

Grilled Clams with Three Sauces

PREP: 15 MINUTES **SOAK:** 45 MINUTES **GRILL:** 6 MINUTES

- 36 small hard-shell clams, such as littlenecks (about 5 lb.)
- 1 recipe Stewed Tomato Sauce, Tarragon Butter, or Brandied Cherry Topper

1. Scrub clams under cold running water. In a 6- to 8-quart stockpot stir together 4 quarts *water* and ⅓ cup *salt*. Add clams; let soak for 15 minutes. Drain, discarding water. Rinse clams. Repeat twice.

2. Arrange clams in a single layer on rack of uncovered grill directly over medium-hot coals for 6 to 8 minutes or until opened at least ½ inch, turning once. Remove clams as they open and keep warm while others cook. Discard unopened clams. Serve with topper. Makes 8 to 10 servings.

STEWED TOMATO SAUCE: In saucepan combine ¾ cup bottled chili sauce, 1 pint halved cherry tomatoes, 2 tablespoons lemon juice, and 1 tablespoon adobo sauce. Bring to boiling. Reduce heat; simmer, uncovered, about 30 minutes or until thick. Season to taste with ½ to 1 teaspoon sugar. Makes about 1⅓ cups.

 EACH TABLESPOON (WITH CLAMS): 89 cal., 1 g total fat (0 g sat. fat), 38 mg chol., 104 mg sodium, 4 g carbo., 0 g fiber, 15 g pro. Daily Values: 8% vit. A, 24% vit. C, 5% calcium, 89% iron.

TARRAGON BUTTER: In a mixing bowl beat ½ cup softened unsalted butter with an electric mixer on medium to high speed for 30 seconds. Beat in 1 to 2 cloves minced garlic and 2 to 3 teaspoons snipped fresh tarragon. Chill. To serve, place a tablespoon of butter inside each grilled clam shell; splash with white wine. Makes ½ cup.

EACH TABLESPOON (WITH CLAMS): 196 cal., 13 g total fat (8 g sat. fat), 71 mg chol., 66 mg sodium, 3 g carbo., 0 g fiber, 15 g pro. Daily Values: 16% vit. A, 21% vit. C, 6% calcium, 89% iron.

BRANDIED CHERRY TOPPER: In a saucepan heat ½ cup cherry preserves over low heat until warmed through. Remove from heat. Stir in 1 tablespoon snipped fresh chives, 1 tablespoon brandy, and ¼ teaspoon ground black pepper. Makes ½ cup.

 EACH TABLESPOON (WITH CLAMS): 94 cal., 1 g total fat (0 g sat. fat), 38 mg chol., 65 mg sodium, 5 g carbo., 0 g fiber, 15 g pro. Daily Values: 7% vit. A, 22% vit. C, 5% calcium, 89% iron.

KNOW YOUR CLAMS

	GEODUCK (GOO-EE-DUCK)	QUAHOG (KAY-HOG) FAMILY	RAZOR	STEAMER	BUTTER	PISMO	MANILA
ORIGIN	West Coast	East Coast	West Coast	East Coast	West Coast, especially Puget Sound	West Coast, especially California	West Coast
CHARACTERISTICS	Soft shell; sweet, fleshy taste; serve raw* or sautéed	Hard shell; Surf (1): Largest; best cut up in chowder Cherrystone (2): medium, best baked for hors d'oeuvre Littleneck (3): smallest, delicate, best raw*	Soft shell, large neck, meaty flesh, best steamed but good for baking	Soft shell, steam for best taste, also can be sauteed or deep-fried	Hard shell, small in size, sweet taste, best raw*	Soft shell, large, scarce, flesh is tender and delicious, raw* or steamed	Hard shell (also called Japanese littleneck); most popular; not native to region; raw,* baked or sauteed

*Note: Always purchase seafood from a reputable supplier. Prevent raw and cooked seafood from coming in contact with each other. Do not eat raw seafood if you suffer from liver disease, diabetes, immune disorders, or gastrointestinal disorders.

ADDITIONAL PHOTOGRAPHS COURTESY OF DEPARTMENT OF SEAFOOD AND AQUACULTURE, PACIFIC COAST SHELLFISH GROWERS ASSOCIATION; CALIFORNIA DEPARTMENT OF FISH AND GAME; RICK HARBO, BC SHELLFISH GROWERS ASSOCIATION

JUNE

IT'S THAT TIME OF YEAR AGAIN–THE SEASON TO GROW FRESH AND EAT FRESH. NO TIME FOR THE GROWING PART? CHECK OUT YOUR LOCAL FARMER'S MARKET FOR AN ABUNDANCE OF FRESH SEASONAL FLAVORS.

Chive Butter, Bread Sticks, and Radishes
page 113

Feasting on Summer

Salmon with Sorrel Pesto
page 106

Minted Strawberries with White Wine
page 115

Grilled Colorado Lamb Chops with Lavender
page 109

Feasting
on Summer

Sylvia Tawes and Lyle
Davis head out to the
lettuce patch to snip a
panful of fresh greens.
"We grow food," says Lyle,
"because we love eating."

Green Tea Soda

PREP: 20 MINUTES **CHILL:** SEVERAL HOURS

- 8 bags green tea
- 4 cups boiling water
- 3 Tbsp. honey or sugar
- 4 cups assorted fresh fruit, such as white or regular nectarine wedges, lime slices, blueberries, and/or raspberries
- 1 liter plain or flavored sparkling water, such as raspberry, strawberry, or peach, chilled
- 2 Tbsp. snipped fresh mint or 8 to 10 mint sprigs

1. Add tea bags to boiling water and let stand for 2 to 3 minutes; remove and discard tea bags. Cover and chill brewed tea.

2. Before serving, add honey to chilled tea. Divide tea mixture among eight to ten 12-ounce glasses. Add fruit to each glass and fill with sparkling water. Top with fresh mint. Makes 8 to 10 servings.

EACH SERVING: 55 cal., 0 g fat, 0 mg chol., 25 mg sodium, 14 g carbo., 3 g fiber, 1 g pro. Daily Values: 2% vit. A, 20% vit. C, 1% calcium, 3% iron.

Green Tea Soda

Summer comes slowly to Pastures of Plenty Farm in Longmont, Colorado.

But when Lyle Davis looks out his kitchen window at the adjacent field and sees peonies—3,000 of them—he knows the season is here. The scene never gets old.

Early each summer, he and his wife, Sylvia Tawes, throw a bonfire feast for family and friends at their 1887 farmhouse. For kindling, there's no shortage of old pine boughs and brush cleaned up from the farm's 35 organic acres. Any nip in the air is soon chased away by the blazing fire, the warmth of familiar faces, and hot-off-the-grill foods that burst with the season's bright flavors.

"We know everyone eats with their eyes first. That's why we celebrate food with a vision of abundance and beauty," says Lyle, who grew up on a farm where cooking—good, unfussy cooking inspired by his mother's garden—shaped most of his family traditions. "I derive a lot of my sense of self through those family rituals, so I wanted to share them and pass them on," he says.

You could call the early summer bonfire a feast of firsts. It coincides with the farm's first crops and Lyle's first trips of the year to sell them at the farmers' markets in nearby Boulder, Denver, and the mountain town of Evergreen. Eleven-year-old Clinton often helps his dad on market days. The feast marks the beginning of a busy wedding season for another of Lyle's businesses, Big Bang Catering. And the first of dozens of Davis family meals shared outdoors in the early summer sunshine, just steps from the fields that provide much of the bounty on the table.

"Most of the menu is a harbinger of warm days to come," Sylvia says of the annual feast. Vibrant green is the unifying motif—from pencil-thin spears of roasted asparagus to sorrel pesto for wild salmon to a simple dessert of lime zinger cookies, the crunchy sidekick to strawberries tossed with fresh mint and a crisp white wine. "After the brown of the Colorado winter, we just long for green," explains Sylvia.

For the charming takeaway gifts, bees do most of the work. Small jars of local honey, which Lyle buys in bulk at the farmer's market, have handwritten notes attached reading, "To a sweet future!" In months to come, the golden contents are a reminder of simple pleasures to be had from sunshine, good food cooked and savored with friends, and the glimpse of peonies out the kitchen window.

Quinoa Salad with Roasted Green Chiles

Quinoa (keen-wah) is a nutty-flavor grain that grows easily in Colorado's high altitudes. Couscous substitutes well in this fresh-tasting salad when quinoa is not available.

PREP: 45 MINUTES **ROAST:** 20 MINUTES
STAND: 45 MINUTES **COOK:** 25 MINUTES

1¼ lb. fresh Anaheim chile peppers, poblano chile peppers, banana chile peppers (see note, page 49), and/or red sweet peppers
2 cups quinoa or 4 cups cooked couscous
2 cups water
1 cup chopped green onions
2 Tbsp. butter
⅓ cup extra virgin olive oil
⅓ cup lime juice
4 cloves garlic, minced
½ tsp. sea salt or salt
¼ tsp. freshly ground black pepper
2 cups fresh cilantro, lightly chopped
⅔ cup pine nuts or slivered almonds, toasted
Bibb or Boston Lettuce
Whole roasted peppers*

1. Preheat oven to 425°F. Halve chile peppers lengthwise. Remove stems, seeds, and membranes. Place pepper halves, cut sides down, on a foil-lined baking sheet. Roast for 20 to 25 minutes or until skins are blistered and dark. Carefully fold foil up and around pepper halves to enclose; let stand about 15 minutes. Use a sharp knife to loosen the edges of the skins; gently and slowly pull off the skin in strips. Cut peppers in bite-size strips. Set aside.

2. In a fine sieve thoroughly rinse the quinoa in cold water. In a medium saucepan combine quinoa and the 2 cups water. Bring to boiling; reduce heat. Simmer, covered, for 25 minutes. Remove from heat. Uncover; let stand about 30 minutes.

3. Meanwhile, in a medium skillet cook green onions in the 2 tablespoons hot butter until tender. Remove from heat. Cool.

4. For vinaigrette, in a small screw-top jar combine olive oil, lime juice, garlic, sea salt, and black pepper. Cover; shake well to combine.

5. In a bowl toss cooked quinoa, roasted pepper strips, cooked green onions, vinaigrette, cilantro, and pine nuts. Stir until combined. Line a platter with lettuce. Top with salad and roasted peppers. Top with additional whole roasted peppers. Serve at room temperature. Makes 8 to 10 servings.

*TEST KITCHEN TIP: While roasting peppers, add additional whole small peppers to use as garnish. Roast but do not peel the small peppers.

EACH SERVING: 366 cal., 21 g fat (4 g sat. fat), 8 mg chol., 147 mg sodium, 39 g carbo., 4 g fiber, 11 g pro. Daily Values: 40% vit. A, 230% vit. C, 7% calcium, 36% iron.

Salmon with Sorrel Pesto

PREP: 15 MINUTES **ROAST:** 12 MINUTES

½ cup olive oil
2 cups lightly packed fresh sorrel or basil leaves
½ cup pine nuts, toasted
4 cloves garlic
Sea salt or salt
Ground black pepper
Olive oil
8 4- to 6-oz. wild-caught or farm-raised skinless salmon fillets, about 1 inch thick

1. Preheat oven to 450°F. For Sorrel Pesto, in a food processor or blender combine ¼ cup of the olive oil, sorrel, pine nuts, and garlic. Cover; process while drizzling up to ¼ cup remaining olive oil, scraping down sides of processor as necessary. Season to taste with salt and pepper. Set aside.

2. Brush a roasting pan with olive oil. Place fish fillets in prepared pan. Lightly brush fish with olive oil; sprinkle with salt and pepper. Roast, uncovered, for 12 minutes or until fish flakes easily when tested with a fork. Serve with Sorrel Pesto. Makes 8 servings.

EACH FILLET + 2 TABLESPOONS PESTO: 351 cal., 27 g fat (4 g sat. fat), 62 mg chol., 102 mg sodium, 3 g carbo., 0 g fiber, 26 g pro. Daily Values: 1% vit. A, 1% vit. C, 2% calcium, 11% iron.

Quinoa Salad with Roasted Green Chiles
Salmon with Sorrel Pesto

Roasted Lemony Asparagus
Grilled Colorado Lamb Chops with Lavender

Roasted Lemony Asparagus

In Colorado, wild asparagus can still be found along creeks and irrigation ditches. Take your own route to a local farmer's market to find a supply of fresh asparagus.

PREP: 15 MINUTES **ROAST:** 10 MINUTES

2	lb. asparagus spears
¼	cup extra virgin olive oil
¼	tsp. sea salt or salt
	Freshly ground black pepper
2	Tbsp. chopped preserved lemon*

1. Preheat oven to 400°F. Snap off woody bases from asparagus; discard. If stems are tough, remove outer layers with a vegetable peeler. Arrange asparagus in a single layer in a 15×10×1-inch baking pan. Drizzle with olive oil and sprinkle with sea salt. Roast, uncovered, for 10 to 15 minutes or until crisp-tender. Season with freshly ground black pepper. Sprinkle with chopped preserved lemons. Makes 8 to 10 servings.

GRILL METHOD: Prepare asparagus spears as above. Place in a 13×9-inch disposable foil pan. Drizzle with olive oil and sprinkle with sea salt. Place pan directly over medium coals; grill for 10 to 15 minutes or until asparagus is crisp-tender, occasionally turning asparagus with tongs. Serve as above.

*TEST KITCHEN TIP: If preserved lemon is not available, in a small bowl combine 2 tablespoons finely shredded lemon peel and ½ teaspoon salt; sprinkle on roasted asparagus.

EACH SERVING: 76 cal., 7 g fat (1 g sat. fat), 0 mg chol., 781 mg sodium, 4 g carbo., 2 g fiber, 2 g pro. Daily Values: 8% vit. A, 22% vit. C, 2% calcium, 7% iron.

Grilled Colorado Lamb Chops with Lavender

The four bulbs of garlic can be separated into cloves and peeled up to 24 hours ahead. Store the peeled cloves in a food-safe container in the refrigerator.

PREP: 45 MINUTES **GRILL:** 12 MINUTES

16	to 20 lamb rib or loin chops, cut 1 inch thick (4 to 5 lb.)
1	Tbsp. dried lavender or finely shredded lemon peel
1	Tbsp. dried Italian seasoning, crushed
1½	tsp. freshly ground black pepper
1	tsp. sea salt or salt
4	bulbs garlic, separated into cloves and peeled
2	Tbsp. extra virgin olive oil
2	lemons, halved (optional)
	Fresh lavender (optional)

1. Trim fat from chops. In a small bowl combine dried lavender, Italian seasoning, pepper, and sea salt. Rub onto lamb chops. Cover and refrigerate up to 4 hours.

2. In a medium skillet cook garlic cloves in hot oil over medium heat for 15 to 20 minutes or until golden and soft, stirring occasionally and turning down heat if oil splatters. Remove from heat; cover and keep warm.

3. Meanwhile, for a charcoal grill, place chops on the rack of an uncovered grill directly over medium coals and grill until desired doneness, turning once halfway through grilling. Allow 12 to 14 minutes for medium-rare doneness (145°F) and 15 to 17 minutes for medium doneness (160°F). (For a gas grill, preheat grill. Reduce heat to medium. Place chops on grill rack over heat. Cover; grill as above.) Transfer to serving plates. Spoon garlic cloves on grilled chops. If desired, squeeze fresh lemon juice on chops and top with fresh lavender. Makes 8 to 10 servings.

 EACH SERVING: 215 cal., 12 g fat (3 g sat. fat), 64 mg chol., 263 mg sodium, 6 g carbo., 2 g fiber, 21 g pro. Daily Values: 1% vit. A, 8% vit. C, 6% calcium, 13% iron.

Pizza Bar for a Crowd

This works as well for a dinner party as it does for a soccer team party. To create a kid-centric event both fun and educational, place ingredients—for each guest, provide ³/₄ cup shredded cheese, ¹/₃ to ¹/₂ cup sauce, and 1 cup of toppers—in separate bowls for easy assembly.

PREP: 10 MINUTES PER PIZZA **BAKE:** 15 MINUTES

    Parchment paper
    All-purpose flour
1 recipe Pizza Dough* (right)
Sauces: pizza sauce, barbecue sauce, olive oil
Meats: precooked ground beef or Italian sausage, sliced pepperoni, chopped or shredded cooked chicken, sliced or chopped cooked ham, precooked chorizo sausage
Vegetables: sliced fresh mushrooms; fresh tomatoes; sweet peppers; green, black, and/or kalamata olives; chopped onion
Cheeses: shredded mozzarella or sliced fresh mozzarella cheese; shredded or grated Parmesan cheese; crumbled feta cheese
Herbs: whole or torn fresh basil leaves or dried basil, crushed; snipped fresh or dried rosemary or thyme
Garlic: minced or coarsely chopped

1. Preheat oven to 425°F. From parchment paper cut 8-inch squares. Lightly sprinkle parchment with flour.
2. Place divided dough on parchment pieces. Roll dough pieces in 4- to 6-inch circles. Top pizza dough with choice of sauces, meats, vegetables, cheeses, herbs, and garlic.
3. Keeping pizzas on parchment, transfer to baking sheets. Bake for 15 to 20 minutes or until crust is lightly browned and cheese is melted. Makes 8 servings.

*TEST KITCHEN TIP: A 1-pound loaf of bread dough or a 13.8-ounce package of refrigerated pizza dough may be substituted for homemade pizza dough. Each will yield 4 to 6 individual dough rounds depending on how thinly the dough is rolled.

Pizza Dough
PREP: 30 MINUTES

2³/₄ to 3¹/₄ cups all-purpose flour
1 pkg. active dry yeast
¹/₂ tsp. salt
1 cup warm water (120°F to 130°F)
2 Tbsp. cooking oil or olive oil

1. In a large mixing bowl combine 1¹/₄ cups of the flour, the yeast, and salt; add warm water and oil. Beat with an electric mixer on low speed for 30 seconds, scraping bowl constantly. Beat on high speed for 3 minutes. Using a wooden spoon, stir in as much of the remaining flour as you can.
2. Turn dough out onto a lightly floured surface. Knead in enough remaining flour to make a moderately stiff dough that is smooth and elastic (6 to 8 minutes total) . Divide dough into 8 pieces. Cover; let rest for 10 minutes. Makes 8 pizza pieces.

EACH DOUGH PIECE: 176 cal., 4 g fat (1 g sat. fat), 0 mg chol., 147 mg sodium, 30 g carbo., 1 g fiber, 4 g pro. Daily Values: 1% calcium, 11% iron.

WHEN THE KIDS CALL FOR PIZZA, GIVE THEM WHAT THEY WANT! THIS INTERACTIVE PROJECT IS FUN, FRESH, AND RESULTS IN A PERSONALIZED PIZZA EACH CHILD WILL LOVE.

Pizza Bar for a Crowd

Chive Butter, Bread Sticks, and Radishes

Chive Butter, Bread Sticks, and Radishes

Salt will cling to the radishes when they remain wet after rinsing.

START TO FINISH: 15 MINUTES **FAST!**

⅓ cup butter, softened
2 Tbsp. snipped chives (with blossoms, if desired)
1 12-oz. baguette
1 bunch (12 oz.) radishes with tops, trimmed and root tips removed
¼ cup sea salt or kosher salt

1. In a bowl combine butter and chives. Cut baguette in half crosswise, then cut halves lengthwise to make 8 to 10 bread sticks.

2. Spread butter mixture on cut sides of bread sticks. Serve bread with radishes and salt for dipping. Makes 8 to 10 servings.

EACH SERVING: 233 cal., 10 g fat (5 g sat. fat), 21 mg chol., 961 mg sodium, 31 g carbo., 2 g fiber, 5 g pro. Daily Values: 6% vit. A, 10% vit. C, 6% calcium, 9% iron.

Artichokes with Tarragon Drizzle

Sylvia Tawes' family hails from California's Monterey Peninsula, where artichokes are more popular than potatoes at dinner. Sylvia serves them as often as possible.

PREP: 25 MINUTES **COOK:** 20 MINUTES **GRILL:** 12 MINUTES

4 to 5 large whole artichokes or 12 to 15 baby artichokes
1 recipe Tarragon Drizzle
Extra virgin olive oil
2 lemons, each cut in 8 to 10 wedges

1. Wash large artichokes; trim stems, if desired, and remove loose outer leaves. Snip off the sharp leaf tips. If using baby artichokes, remove outer leaves to reach pale green or yellow leaves on bottom half. Cut darker green portion of leaves off top half of artichoke; discard. Cut off stem and trim any remaining green from base of baby artichokes.

2. In a Dutch oven bring a large amount of lightly salted water to boiling; add artichokes. Return to boiling; reduce heat. Simmer, covered, for 20 to 30 minutes for large artichokes or 10 minutes for baby artichokes or until a leaf pulls out easily.

3. Place artichokes in a large bowl of ice water to cool completely. Drain artichokes upside down on paper towels. Cut artichokes in half from top through stem; use a spoon to scoop out the fibrous cores, leaving the hearts and leaves intact.

4. Prepare Tarragon Drizzle. Brush artichoke halves with olive oil. For a charcoal grill, place artichokes, cut sides down, on the rack of an uncovered grill directly over medium coals. Grill for 7 minutes; turn artichokes and grill for 5 to 7 minutes. (For a gas grill, preheat grill. Reduce heat to medium. Place artichokes on grill rack over heat. Cover and grill as above.)

5. On a serving platter place grilled artichokes, cut sides up. Shake Tarragon Drizzle; pour some over artichokes; pass remaining with platter. Serve with lemon wedges. Makes 8 to 10 servings.

TARRAGON DRIZZLE: In a screw-top jar combine ⅔ cup extra virgin olive oil, ⅓ cup white wine vinegar, ⅓ cup thinly sliced green onion, 2 tablespoons Dijon-style mustard, and 2 tablespoons snipped fresh tarragon or 2 teaspoons dried tarragon, crushed. Cover and shake well. Season to taste with sea salt and ground black pepper.

EACH SERVING: 131 cal., 11 g fat (1 g sat. fat), 0 mg chol., 153 mg sodium, 8 g carbo., 4 g fiber, 3 g pro. Daily Values: 1% vit. A, 18% vit. C, 3% calcium, 5% iron.

Artichokes with Tarragon Drizzle

Petite Fruit Tarts

Petite Fruit Tarts

For juicier fruits, such as berries, fold up pastry around the edges (photo, bottom).

PREP: 1 HOUR **CHILL:** 1 HOUR **BAKE:** 20 MINUTES

2	cups all-purpose flour
1/3	cup sugar
3/4	cup cold butter
2	egg yolks, beaten
1/4	cup dairy sour cream
3	Tbsp. ice water
2/3	cup sugar
1/4	cup all-purpose flour
6	to 8 cups fresh fruit, such as sliced nectarines, coarsely chopped apples, halved strawberries, blueberries, blackberries, raspberries, and/or sliced apricots
1/4	to 1/3 cup sugar
2	Tbsp. snipped fresh lavender or lemon thyme (optional)

1. In a medium bowl stir together the 2 cups flour and the 1/3 cup sugar. Using a pastry blender, cut butter into flour mixture until pieces are pea size. In a small bowl stir together egg yolks, sour cream, and ice water. Gradually stir egg yolk mixture into flour mixture. Using your fingers, gently knead the dough just until a ball forms. Cover dough with plastic wrap; chill for 1 hour or until dough is easy to handle.

2. Divide dough into 8 portions. Place on lightly floured pieces of parchment paper. Roll dough into 6- to 7-inch free-form squares or circles. Transfer, on parchment, to baking sheets.

3. Preheat oven to 375°F. In a small bowl combine 2/3 cup sugar and 1/4 cup flour. Sprinkle a scant 2 tablespoons of the sugar mixture on each pastry shape to within 1/2 inch of the edges. In a large bowl combine fruit and the 1/4 to 1/3 cup sugar; toss gently.

4. Place fruit on the pastry, using 3/4 to 1 cup fruit for each tart. For juicier fruits, fold up pastry edges slightly to form a lip. Bake tarts for 20 to 25 minutes or until fruit is tender and pastry edges are golden brown. If desired, sprinkle pastry with lavender or lemon thyme. Makes 8 servings.

EACH SERVING: 467 cal., 21 g fat (10 g sat. fat), 102 mg chol., 136 mg sodium, 66 g carbo., 3 g fiber, 5 g pro. Daily Values: 20% vit. A, 9% vit. C, 3% calcium, 11% iron.

A bounty of summer fruits and a scatter of lemon thyme and lavender grace individual tarts that guests build and bake themselves.

Zingy Lime Flower Cookies

The flavors of these cookies are a cool accompaniment to Latin-inspired meals, afternoon tea, or summer feasts.

PREP: 1¼ HOURS CHILL: 2 HOURS BAKE: 8 MINUTES PER BATCH

- 1 lime
- ½ cup butter, softened
- ½ cup granulated sugar
- ½ tsp. baking powder
- ⅛ tsp. salt
- 1 egg
- 1 Tbsp. lime juice
- 1½ tsp. vanilla
- 1½ cups all-purpose flour
- 1½ cups powdered sugar
- 1 to 2 Tbsp. lime juice
  Finely shredded lime peel (optional)

1. With a zester, remove lime peel from lime; set aside. In a large mixing bowl beat butter with an electric mixer on medium to high speed for 30 seconds. Add granulated sugar, baking powder, and salt. Beat until combined, scraping sides of bowl occasionally. Beat in egg, the 1 tablespoon lime juice, and vanilla until combined. Beat in as much of the flour as you can with the mixer. Stir in any remaining flour and 1 teaspoon of the lime peel. Divide dough in half. Cover and chill at least 2 hours or up to 3 days.

2. Preheat oven to 350°F. On a well-floured surface, roll half the dough at a time to ⅛-inch thickness. Using a 2- or 3-inch flower-shape cookie cutter, cut dough in shapes. Place cookies 1 inch apart on an ungreased cookie sheet.

3. Bake for 8 to 10 minutes for the 2-inch cookies or 10 to 12 minutes for the 3-inch cookies or until edges just start to brown. Transfer to a wire rack to cool.

4. For icing, in a bowl stir together the powdered sugar and the 1 to 2 tablespoons lime juice until well combined and of drizzling consistency. Drizzle or spread icing on cooled cookies. If desired, sprinkle with additional lime peel. Makes about 60 two-inch cookies or 30 three-inch cookies.

 EACH 2-INCH COOKIE: 43 cal., 2 g fat (1 g sat. fat), 8 mg chol., 20 mg sodium, 6 g carbo., 0 g fiber, 0 g pro. Daily Value: 1% vit. A, 1% iron.

Minted Strawberries with White Wine

For a nonalcoholic version, use white grape juice instead of wine and reduce the sugar to 2 tablespoons.

PREP: 20 MINUTES STAND: 1 HOUR

- 6 cups strawberries
- 1 cup sugar
- 2 bunches fresh mint (1½ oz.)
- 2 to 3 cups dry white wine such as Sauvignon Blanc
  Fresh mint sprigs

1. Halve large berries; leave hulls on a few berries. Place berries in a large bowl; sprinkle with sugar and cover bowl with plastic wrap. Let stand at room temperature at least 1 hour, stirring once or twice.

2. Remove mint leaves from one bunch of mint. Stack 6 to 8 leaves together; roll the stacked leaves. Slice across the roll to create narrow strips. Repeat with remaining leaves. Add the shredded mint to strawberries just before serving.

3. To serve, evenly divide the minted berries and juices among 8 glasses; pour wine over berries until just covered. Garnish with mint sprigs. Makes 8 servings.

EACH SERVING: 170 cal., 0 g fat, 5 mg sodium, 33 g carbo., 2 g fiber, 1 g pro. Daily Values: 117% vit. C, 3% calcium, 14% iron.

Minted Strawberries with White Wine
Zingy Lime Flower Cookies

TREAT DAD TO BREAKFAST

BY **BRIDGET NELSON** PHOTOGRAPHS BY **GREG SCHEIDEMANN**

Hit a home run this Father's Day

and surprise Dad with breakfast in bed. The lineup: flavorful dishes that are hearty and from the heart. They're also quick to prepare, so you can get them ready and delivered before Dad wakes up. Enlist the whole team to help—kids of all ages can lend a hand in the kitchen with this easy meal.

Basil Scrambled Eggs with Corn Bread Toast is a twist on basic breakfast fare. For extra flavor and texture add a little shredded cheese or diced green chile peppers to the corn bread batter before baking. Top the toast with scrambled eggs and hash browns and sprinkle on fresh basil to dress up the meal. Serve with make-ahead ketchup that has finely shredded basil stirred in.

For a morning dessert, put a spin on banana splits with Banana Breakfast Sundaes. Slice and halve bananas, with kids spooning on vanilla yogurt, drizzling with melted chocolate, and sprinkling on some blueberries and granola.

Now the best part. Tray in hands, tiptoe to the bedroom to surprise Dad. Deliver the tray along with homemade cards and the Sunday paper. Add a few small gifts, such as a new book, tickets to a baseball game, or a handmade coupon book from the kids with such offers as, I'll help mow the lawn or I'll clear the table.

Dad will appreciate this savory breakfast of Basil Scrambled Eggs with Corn Bread Toast even more when it's accompanied by homemade cards, a dish towel to use as a napkin, and a fresh flower or two.

Basil Scrambled Eggs with Corn Bread Toast

Basil Scrambled Eggs with Corn Bread Toast

Get kids involved and ask them to help prepare the eggs and toast. They can stir the cheese into the corn bread batter or add the finely shredded basil to the ketchup.

PREP: 25 MINUTES **BAKE:** 20 MINUTES **COOL:** 15 MINUTES

- 1 8-oz. pkg. corn bread mix
- 1 cup shredded cheddar cheese
- ½ a 32-oz. pkg. frozen hash brown potatoes (about 3½ cups)
- 6 eggs
- ⅓ cup milk, half-and-half, or light cream
- ¼ tsp. salt
- Dash ground black pepper
- 1 Tbsp. butter or margarine
- ½ cup snipped fresh basil*

1. Preheat oven to 400°F. Prepare corn bread mix according to package directions, stirring ½ cup of the cheese into the batter. Spread batter in a greased 8×4-inch loaf pan. Bake 20 minutes or until corn bread is lightly browned and a wooden toothpick inserted near center comes out clean. Cool corn bread in pan on a wire rack for 10 minutes. Remove corn bread from pan; cool completely.

2. In a large skillet, prepare hash brown potatoes according to package directions. Sprinkle potatoes with remaining ½ cup cheese during last 2 minutes of cooking. Set aside; keep warm.

3. Preheat oven to 300°F. Slice corn bread loaf into eight 1-inch-thick slices. Lay slices on a baking sheet. Place in oven to warm. Meanwhile, in a medium bowl beat together eggs, milk, salt, and pepper with a wire whisk just until combined. In a large skillet melt butter over medium heat and pour in egg mixture. Cook over medium heat, without stirring, until eggs begin to set on the bottom and around the edge.

4. With a spatula, lift and fold the partially cooked egg mixture to let the uncooked portion flow underneath. Cook over medium heat for 2 to 3 minutes or until egg mixture is cooked through but still glossy and moist. Remove from heat immediately.

5. To serve, place 2 slices of corn bread on each of four plates. Divide scrambled eggs and hash browns among the plates. Sprinkle eggs and hash browns with fresh basil. Makes 4 servings.

*TEST KITCHEN TIP: Finely shred additional basil to stir into ketchup. Serve alongside eggs, potatoes, and corn bread.

NOTE: For variation, omit cheese stirred into bread batter; stir in one 4-ounce can diced green chile peppers, drained.

EACH SERVING: 635 cal., 31 g fat (11 g sat. fat), 396 mg chol., 960 mg sodium, 66 g carbo., 2 g fiber, 26 g pro. Daily Values: 21% vit. A, 17% vit. C, 38% calcium, 23% iron.

Banana Breakfast Sundaes

Banana Breakfast Sundaes

If blueberries aren't one of Dad's favorite fruits, substitute a handful of another fruit for an extra bit of flavor.

START TO FINISH: 15 MINUTES

- 2 oz. bittersweet chocolate, coarsely chopped
- 2 ripe medium bananas, peeled, halved, and split lengthwise
- 2 6-oz. cartons vanilla low-fat yogurt or 2 cups vanilla frozen yogurt
- ¼ cup low-fat granola
- Blueberries

1. In a small saucepan heat chocolate just until melted. Or place chocolate in a microwave-safe bowl and heat on 70% power (medium-high) for 1½ to 2 minutes, stirring every 30 seconds.

2. In separate bowls place two banana quarters. Top bananas with yogurt, drizzle with melted chocolate, sprinkle with granola, and top with blueberries. Makes 4 sundaes.

EACH SUNDAE: 218 cal., 7 g fat (4 g sat. fat), 4 mg chol., 73 mg sodium, 38 g carbo., 3 g fiber, 6 g pro. Daily Values: 3% vit. A, 10% vit. C, 16% calcium, 5% iron.

NASTURTIUM'S PEPPERY PUNCH

BY **STEPHEN EXEL** PHOTOGRAPHS BY **GREG SCHEIDEMANN**

Individual petals add a decorative touch to butter pats. Perch fully opened bright blossoms on top of cheeses, such as goat, Brie, or Camembert.

Bright, multicolor flowers

Bright, multicolor flowers and lily pad-shape leaves identify the edible ornamental plant nasturtium. A member of the cress family (it is also called "Indian cress"), it perks up fresh summer dishes with its pungent, peppery flavor.

Toss young nasturtium leaves into a fresh green salad. Shredded or chopped, the leaves can be stirred into chilled soups, cooked in quiches or omelets, or blended with soft cheese for sandwich spreads. They combine well with basil, dill, parsley, and sorrel. The delicate flowers are both decorative and tasty. For a spicy note, they can be scattered on soups, pressed into cheeses and butter, sprinkled across sandwiches (a superb complement to red meats), and floated atop fruit-based drinks. Add the flowers to a salad after it has been tossed with dressing; otherwise the buds will absorb the oil and wilt.

Nasturtiums give punch to a container or herb garden as well. The plant blooms in mixtures of brilliant orange, yellow, and red amid trailing heart-shape leaves. It prefers not to be fussed with and requires only minimal attention; a half day or more of direct sun will keep it happy. Nasturtiums do best with warm days and cool nights and fertilizer that is high in phosphate (with 30 as a middle number, for example). Well-drained average soil is essential; otherwise the plants will produce abundant leaves and very few flowers.

Avoid consuming flowers that have been treated with pesticides. Purchase flowers labeled "edible" only from reliable food markets.

In salads, nasturtiums add beauty and flavor. Toss in the flowers at the last minute to keep them fresh. Choose milder greens, such as lamb's lettuce and butter (or Bibb), or simple leaf lettuces, such as oak or red leaf, to balance the pungent flowers.

A scatter of nasturtium buds livens up all sorts of sandwiches, from elegant fare such as beef tenderloin to something as simple as an open-face grilled cheese (add the flowers after the sandwich has been cooked). Try nasturtiums with a cold chicken or pork sandwich and a dab of mayonnaise or mild mustard.

Home front

Brewing Good

When buying coffee you may have noticed labels that read "Fair Trade Certified." The designation on items ranging from chocolate to bananas to tea guarantees that workers from developing countries receive a living wage for the items they produce. "We want to give back to our farmers and their families. If that means we pay a little bit more for far superior coffee, then so be it," says Mark Ottinger, CEO of Ugly Mug Coffee in Memphis, which sells 100% Fair Trade organic coffee. The Fair Trade Labeling Organization, or FLO, provides international standards for nonprofit organizations to become Fair Trade certified. Look for the logo on the packaging.
—Mikhael Romain

The Fair Trade Certified label

CLEAN MACHINE

For the perfect cup of joe, experts at Gevalia Kaffe fine coffees recommend cleaning your coffeemaker once a month. Mix 2 tablespoons white vinegar with 12 cups of cold water; run through the coffeemaker. Repeat using fresh water only.

Just Dip

Brothers Jack and Sabi Kampeas opened their cafe, Kitchen Commune, in New York City's Soho neighborhood in mid-January. Cafe offerings include bumped-up lunch fare such as a panini stuffed with barbecue duck confit with herbed goat cheese and roasted bell peppers. The real menu star is mayonnaise. Jack and Sabi flavor their homemade mayo with savory ingredients and serve alongside twice-fried french fries. Try their idea at home with purchased mayonnaise and serve with chips or veggies, as a dipper for chicken, or spread on a roast beef sandwich. Kitchen Commune, 448 Broadway (Grand St.), NY; 212/680-0140. www.kitchencommune.com

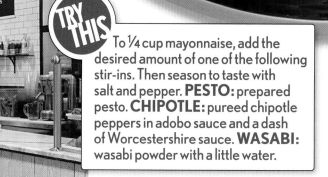

TRY THIS To ¼ cup mayonnaise, add the desired amount of one of the following stir-ins. Then season to taste with salt and pepper. **PESTO:** prepared pesto. **CHIPOTLE:** pureed chipotle peppers in adobo sauce and a dash of Worcestershire sauce. **WASABI:** wasabi powder with a little water.

JULY

A TRADITIONAL BARBECUE WITH FRIENDS AND FAMILY IS THE PERFECT WAY TO CELEBRATE INDEPENDENCE DAY. WHETHER YOU'RE FEEDING FOUR OR FORTY, THIS MENU HAS YOU COVERED.

Red, White, and Blueberry Shortcake
page 134

Smoke, Sauce, and Friends

Plus

Best of Season—

Your Best Summer Weekend—

Star Sugar Cookies
page 133

Beef Brisket
page 128

Cherry Chocolate Chip Cookies
page 135

Smoke, Sauce, and Friends

One man's recipe for the
perfect Fourth of July BBQ party

Brisket Barbecue Sauce

PREP: 20 MINUTES   **COOK:** 30 MINUTES   **COOL:** 38 MINUTES

- 1   large onion, coarsely chopped (1 cup)
- 1   Tbsp. cooking oil
- 1   14½-oz. can whole tomatoes with juice, cut up
- 1   10¾-oz. can tomato puree
- ⅔   cup white vinegar
- ¼   cup orange juice
- 2   Tbsp. Dijon-style mustard
- 1   Tbsp. granulated sugar
- 1   Tbsp. packed brown sugar
- 1   Tbsp. molasses
- 2   tsp. salt
- 1   tsp. liquid smoke
- ½   tsp. paprika
- ½   tsp. freshly ground black pepper

1. In a large saucepan cook onion in hot oil over medium heat about 8 minutes or until golden brown, stirring frequently.

2. Stir in remaining ingredients. Bring to boiling; reduce heat. Simmer, uncovered, for 30 to 40 minutes or until sauce is thickened, stirring occasionally. Remove from heat; cool sauce for 30 minutes.

3. Transfer sauce, half at a time, to a blender or food processor. Cover and blend or process sauce until smooth. Store, tightly covered, in the refrigerator up to 1 month. Makes 3½ cups sauce.

SERVINGS FOR 25 OR 50: For 25 servings, double all ingredients. For 50 servings, quadruple the ingredients. For either amount, cook onions as directed in a 6-quart Dutch oven. Stir in remaining ingredients and simmer, uncovered, for 30 or 40 minutes or until sauce is thickened. Set aside to cool. Process about 2 cups at a time. Serve at once or cover and chill up to 3 days. Reheat before serving or let stand at room temperature for 1 to 2 hours before serving. Fifty servings equals about 15 cups; serve the sauce in small bowls and refill as needed.

EACH ¼-CUP SERVING: 48 cal., 1 g total fat, 0 mg chol., 499 mg sodium, 9 g carbo., 1 g fiber, 1 g pro. Daily Values: 2% vit. A, 17% vit. C, 2% calcium, 4% iron.

BY JUDITH GAINES   PHOTOGRAPHS BY JAMES CARRIER   FOOD STYLING BY CHARLES WORTHINGTON

If you hear "barbecue" you imagine the tangy, smoky flavors of Memphis, Kansas City, Texas,

and... New Hampshire? Unlikely as it seems, steps from the town green of Amherst, on an old stagecoach route, sits an outpost of barbecue zeal. It's the 151-year-old home of Jeff and Beth Davis, whose annual Fourth of July celebration of the magical mix of smoke, meat, and sauce has become a local legend in their setting of dignified Colonial homes.

The family pulls it off with some help from their friends, a remarkable feat given the size of the gathering—nearly 250 attended last year!

All the recipes are basic traditional classics, nothing fussy or labor intensive. To get everything done on time, they keep to a strict schedule. With limited time and cooking space on the Fourth, anything that can be done ahead of time is a bonus. Early on the morning of July 2, Jeff applies a spicy coating (recipe, page 132) to the pork butts and vigorously rubs it in. He uses a mixture of charcoal lumps and chunks of hardwood in his barrel smoker and lets the pork smoke all day at 200°F to 250°F. The next day he repeats the process with the briskets.

Frozen cookies, made about a month earlier, are thawed the day before the party. The Davises have found that the corn bread tastes better when it has a day to sit and dry out a bit. They slice the pork in a 14-cup Cuisinart food processor two days before, then reheat it in the vinegar sauce in batches on the Fourth. The briskets, which don't reheat as well, are resmoked whole for a few hours on the Fourth, then cut in thin slices.

To prevent soggy slaw, the cabbage is shredded the morning of the Fourth but not mixed with the dressing until just before the party. Beans are cooked overnight on very low heat.

On Independence Day morning, with everything carefully controlled, there's time to attend the town parade. Shortly after noon, invitees head to the Davis home. Under a large white tent in the backyard, they help themselves to brisket and pulled pork, with extra sauces on the side, and to corn bread, baked beans, and coleslaw. The atmosphere is casual and relaxed.

This party is about more than the food, however. For the Davis family, it's a way to come together each year for an event that has become a shared source of pride. For them, as for the guests, "it's also a nice way to reconnect with people we may not see much socially at any other time of year," says Beth.

Bill Durling, one of the Davises' friends, voices a frequently heard view. "We wouldn't miss this. It's legendary," he says. "And every year the crowd gets bigger."

Pulled Pork Shoulder

This recipe and its peppery, vinegary sauce take their cues from the barbecues of North and South Carolina.

PREP: 15 MINUTES **SMOKE:** 4 HOURS **STAND:** 15 MINUTES

6 to 8 hickory wood chunks or 3 cups hickory wood chips
⅓ cup Davis Dry Rub (recipe, page 132)
1 5- to 5½-lb. boneless pork shoulder roast (sold in some regions as Boston butt)
1 recipe Vinegar Barbecue Sauce (recipe, page 132)
12 to 18 soft white hamburger buns
Bottled hot pepper sauce (optional)
Kohlrabi Coleslaw (recipe, right)

1. SMOKER INSTRUCTIONS: At least 1 hour before smoke-cooking, soak wood chunks or chips in enough water to cover. Drain before using.

2. Sprinkle Davis Dry Rub evenly over roast; rub in with your fingers. In a smoker arrange preheated coals, drained wood chunks, and water pan according to manufacturer's directions. Pour water into pan. Place roast on the grill rack over water pan. Cover; smoke for 4 to 5 hours or until roast is very tender. Add additional coals and water as needed to maintain temperature and moisture. (Do not add more wood after the first 2 hours of smoking. Too much smoke makes roast bitter.)

3. Remove roast from smoker. Cover roast with foil; let stand for 15 minutes. Using two forks, gently pull the roast into long thin strands. Mix about 1½ cups Vinegar Barbecue Sauce with the pork to moisten the pork.

4. To serve, pile pork onto buns. If desired, sprinkle with hot pepper sauce. Serve with remaining Vinegar Barbecue Sauce and Kohlrabi Coleslaw. Makes 12 (4¼-ounce) to 18 servings.

SERVINGS FOR 25 : Prepare two 5- to 5½-pound boneless pork shoulder roasts. Smoke two roasts at a time on a smoker or grill. Prepare Vinegar Barbecue Sauce for 25. Pull pork as in Step 3. To serve, combine each pulled roast with 1½ cups sauce in a 4-quart Dutch oven. Replenish pork as needed; do not allow pork to sit out for more than 2 hours.

SERVINGS FOR 50 : Prepare four 5- to 5½-pound boneless pork shoulder roasts. Smoke two roasts at a time on a smoker or grill. Prepare Vinegar Barbecue Sauce for 50. Pull pork as in Step 3. To serve, combine each pulled roast with 1½ cups sauce in a 4-quart Dutch oven. Replenish pork as needed; do not allow pork to sit out more than two hours.

GAS GRILL INSTRUCTIONS: Start with a full tank of propane. Adjust heat for indirect cooking over medium-low heat. Add soaked wood chunks according to manufacturer's directions. Or wrap in foil and add to grill. Place pork shoulder on a rack in a roasting pan; set pan on grill rack over the unlit burner. Add ½ inch of water to pan. Cover and smoke 4 hours or until very tender, adding water to pan if necessary. Do not add more wood after the first 2 hours of smoking. Serve as directed above.

CHARCOAL GRILL INSTRUCTIONS: Prepare grill for indirect grilling. Arrange medium-hot coals around a foil drip pan. Fill drip pan with 1 inch of hot water. Test for medium heat above the drip pan. Add presoaked chunks or chips to coals. Place roast on grill rack and cover. Smoke as directed in gas grill instructions, making sure to check food, temperature, and water once every hour. Do not add more wood after the first 2 hours of smoking. Serve as directed in Step 4.

MAKE-AHEAD DIRECTIONS: Prepare through Step 3. Cover; refrigerate up to 3 days. Reheat in a large pot over medium heat, stirring occasionally.

EACH SERVING: 439 cal., 15 g total fat, (5 g sat fat) , 125 mg chol., 1,012 mg sodium, 34 g carbo., 2 g fiber, 42 g pro. Daily Values: 11% vit. A, 3% vit. C, 10% calcium, 26% iron.

Kohlrabi Coleslaw

PREP: 30 MINUTES

¾ cup mayonnaise
¼ cup white vinegar
2 Tbsp. sugar
2 tsp. celery seeds (optional)
½ tsp. salt
¼ tsp. ground black pepper
1 lb. green cabbage, chopped or finely shredded (9 cups)
2 medium carrots, finely shredded* (1 cup)
1 cup shredded kohlrabi, jicama, or radishes*
1 cup snipped flat-leaf parsley

1. For dressing, in a medium bowl combine mayonnaise, vinegar, sugar, celery seeds (if desired), salt, and pepper. Set aside.

2. In a 4-quart bowl combine the cabbage, carrots, kohlrabi, and parsley. Stir in the dressing; mix well. Cover and refrigerate until serving time or up to 24 hours. Serve with a slotted spoon. Makes 12 servings.

SERVINGS FOR 25: Double the recipe above.

SERVINGS FOR 50: Prepare the 25-serving recipe twice.

***TEST KITCHEN TIP:** Use the shredding blade of a food processor to shred the cabbage, carrots, and kohlrabi. Instead of the cabbage and carrots, you can also substitute one 16-ounce package of shredded cabbage with carrot (coleslaw mix).

EACH SERVING: 124 cal., 11 g total fat (2 g sat fat), 5 mg chol., 209 mg sodium, 7 g carbo., 2 g fiber, 1 g pro. Daily Values: 33% vit. A, 50% vit. C, 4% calcium, 4% iron.

Kohlrabi Coleslaw, Pulled Pork Shoulder, and Beef Brisket
page 128

Pan-Baked Beans
page 130

Beef Brisket

To keep underside of brisket from getting charred during cooking, smoke it on foil.

PREP: 1 HOUR **SMOKE:** 5 HOURS **STAND:** 15 MINUTES

  6 to 8 hardwood chunks, such as mesquite or hickory
  ½ cup Davis Dry Rub (recipe, page 132)
  1 5-lb. fresh beef brisket
  1 recipe Brisket Barbecue Sauce (recipe, page 125)

1. SMOKER INSTRUCTIONS: At least 1 hour before grilling, soak wood chunks in enough water to cover. Drain before using.

2. Sprinkle Davis Dry Rub evenly over brisket; rub in with your fingers. Cut a sheet of foil slightly larger than the brisket. Poke several holes in the foil. Place brisket on foil.

3. In a smoker arrange preheated coals, about half the drained wood chunks, and a water pan according to the manufacturer's directions. Pour hot water into pan. Place brisket and foil on the grill rack over water pan. Cover; smoke for 5 to 6 hours or until brisket is tender. Test tenderness by inserting fork into center of brisket and twisting. When fork twists easily, brisket is ready. Add additional coals, wood chunks, and water as needed. (Do not add wood after the first 2 hours of smoking. Too much smoke makes meat bitter.)

4. Remove brisket from smoker. Cover and let stand 15 minutes. Meanwhile, heat Brisket Barbecue Sauce in a saucepan over low heat. To serve brisket, trim away crusty outer layer; serve separately. Thinly slice brisket across the grain (photo, below). Serve with Brisket Barbecue Sauce on the side. Makes 12 (4¼-ounce) servings.

CHARCOAL GRILL INSTRUCTIONS: At least 1 hour before grilling, soak 6 to 8 wood chunks in enough water to cover. Prepare grill for indirect grilling; arrange lit coals around a drip pan. Fill drip pan with hot water. Add half the wood chunks to coals. Place brisket and foil on grill rack over the drip pan. Cover and grill for 2½ hours. Turn brisket and continue grilling for 1½ to 2 hours or until brisket is tender. Add additional coals and wood as needed to maintain temperature and smoke. (Do not add additional wood after the first 2 hours of grilling. Too much smoke gives food a bitter flavor.) Test by inserting fork into center of brisket and twisting. When fork twists easily, brisket is ready. Serve as directed in Step 4.

GAS GRILL INSTRUCTIONS: Be sure to begin with a full tank of propane. Adjust heat for indirect cooking over medium-low heat. Add soaked wood chunks according to manufacturer's directions. Or wrap in foil and add to grill.* Place a small can or pan of hot water on the side of the grill rack over a lit burner. Place brisket, fat side up, on a rack in a roasting pan; set pan on grill rack over the unlit burner. Cover and grill for 2½ hours or until brisket is very dark brown. Wrap brisket in foil; return to grill directly on grill rack. Cook 1½ to 2 hours more or until tender. Serve as directed in Step 4.

SERVINGS FOR 25: Double the recipe for both Davis Dry Rub and Brisket Barbecue Sauce and use two 5- to 5½-pound fresh beef briskets. Prepare each brisket as directed at left. Wrap each in heavy foil after slicing; refrigerate up to 2 days.

SERVINGS FOR 50: Quadruple the recipe for both Davis Dry Rub and Brisket Barbecue Sauce and use four 5- to 5½-pound fresh beef briskets. Prepare briskets as directed at left, smoking two at a time. Wrap each in heavy foil after slicing; refrigerate up to 2 days.

*TEST KITCHEN TIP: To make a foil packet for smoking on a gas grill, place half the soaked wood chunks in the center of a 12×18-inch sheet of heavy foil. Bring up two opposite edges of foil and make a pouch with an opening in the top of packet for smoke to escape. Repeat with remaining wood and a second sheet of foil. Place packets directly over heat on lava rocks, ceramic briquettes, or grates above the burner.

NOTE: To reheat on a charcoal grill, arrange medium-hot coals around the edge of the grill. Test for medium heat in the center of the grill. Place chilled brisket packets in the center of the grill rack, not over the heat. Cover and grill for 30 minutes or until heated through. For a gas grill, preheat grill. Reduce heat to medium. Adjust for indirect cooking. Grill as above. Packets also can be reheated in a 350°F oven for about 30 minutes.

EACH SERVING: 423 cal., 18 g total fat (6 g sat fat), 145 mg chol., 1,249 mg sodium, 13 g carbo., 2 g fiber, 51 g pro. Daily Values: 17% vit. A, 18% vit. C, 5% calcium, 33% iron.

FOR TENDER BRISKET

To ensure that guests get tender brisket, it's important to slice across the grain. Look closely before cooking; notice that meat fibers run in one direction. Carve roasted meat across the grain, cutting the fibers into short sections.

Pulled Pork Shoulder
page 126

Beef Brisket

BEEF
BRISKET

Pan-Baked Beans

For 50 servings, we recommend preparing two smaller batches; there's less danger of burning beans at the bottom of the pot.

PREP: 40 MINUTES **COOK:** 1¾ HOURS **STAND:** 1 HOUR

- 1 lb. dried navy beans
- 1 lb. sliced bacon, cut up
- 2 large onions, chopped (2 cups)
- 1 cup ketchup
- 1 cup molasses
- 3 Tbsp. prepared yellow mustard
- 2 tsp. dried oregano, crushed (optional)
- ½ tsp. salt
- ½ tsp. ground black pepper

1. Rinse and drain beans. In a 4- to 6-quart Dutch oven combine beans and 8 cups *water*. Bring to boiling; reduce heat. Simmer for 2 minutes. Remove from heat. Cover and let stand for 1 hour. (Or place beans and water in Dutch oven. Cover and let soak in a cool place for 6 to 8 hours or overnight.) Drain and rinse beans.

2. In the Dutch oven cook bacon and onions until bacon is crisp. Drain off fat. Add the beans and 6 cups fresh *water* to Dutch oven. Bring to boiling; reduce heat. Simmer, covered, for 1¼ to 1½ hours or until beans are tender, stirring occasionally.

3. Stir in the ketchup, molasses, mustard, oregano, salt, and pepper. Bring to boiling; reduce heat. Simmer, uncovered, for 30 to 45 minutes more or until desired consistency, stirring occasionally. Makes ten to twelve ⅔-cup servings.

SERVINGS FOR 25: Prepare as above, doubling amounts of all ingredients. Soak beans in 12 cups water in an 8- to 10-quart pot. Cook half the onions and bacon at a time. Cook the beans as above, except stir in 10 cups of water in Step 2. Cook, uncovered, in Step 3 for 1 to 1¼ hours, stirring beans frequently.

SERVINGS FOR 50: Prepare the 25-serving recipe twice (do not double the recipe; beans may burn at the bottom of pot).

TEST KITCHEN TIP: To reheat, cook over medium-low heat, stirring occasionally, until bubbling, about 30 minutes.

EACH SERVING: 429 cal., 11 g total fat (4 g sat. fat.), 21 mg chol., 788 mg sodium, 62 g carbo., 12 g fiber, 16 g pro. Daily Values: 5% vit. A, 11% vit. C, 14% calcium, 22% iron.

CORN BREAD is a classic that the Davises have changed a little from its Southern roots; they add a dash of sugar to give it Northern appeal. The day is low-key, with no organized activities beyond food and mingling; but there is careful thought given to feeding all ages at the event, including a peanut butter sandwich buffet that keeps the kids happy.

Davis Family Corn Bread

Make this recipe to serve 24 or serve 12 and have leftovers. Toasted corn bread with honey and butter is a sensational breakfast.

PREP: 10 MINUTES **BAKE:** 35 MINUTES

- 2½ cups all-purpose flour
- 2 cups yellow cornmeal
- ½ cup sugar
- 4 tsp. baking powder
- 1 tsp. salt
- 3 eggs
- 2¼ cups whole milk
- ½ cup butter, melted

1. Preheat oven to 350°F. Grease a 13×9×2-inch disposable foil pan or coat with nonstick cooking spray; set aside.

2. In an extra-large mixing bowl stir together the flour, cornmeal, sugar, baking powder, and salt. In a medium bowl mix together eggs, milk, and melted butter. Add to the dry ingredients and stir until just mixed. (Do not overmix batter.)

3. Pour into pan. Bake 35 to 40 minutes or until a wooden skewer inserted in center comes out clean. Using a sharp knife and sawing motion, cut corn bread into 24 (approximately 2-inch) squares. Makes 24 servings.

SERVINGS FOR 50: Make the 24-serving recipe three times.

TEST KITCHEN TIP: The corn bread is better when made 1 day ahead. Cover tightly with foil. Store at room temperature. Or bake up to 2 months ahead; wrap, label, and freeze.

EACH SERVING: 190 cal., 7 g total fat (4 g sat.fat), 47 mg chol., 219 mg sodium, 28 g carbo., 1 g fiber, 5 g pro. Daily Values: 5% vit. A, 6% calcium, 5% iron.

Davis Family Corn Bread

Davis Dry Rub

This rub also works wonders for fish, chicken, pork—even vegetables on the grill. It easily doubles and it stores, tightly covered, up to six months.

START TO FINISH: 10 MINUTES FAST!

- ½ cup paprika
- ⅓ cup ground black pepper
- ¼ cup salt
- ¼ cup chili powder
- ¼ cup ground cumin
- ¼ cup packed brown sugar
- 3 Tbsp. granulated sugar
- 2 Tbsp. cayenne pepper

1. In a small bowl stir together the paprika, black pepper, salt, chili powder, cumin, brown sugar, granulated sugar, and cayenne pepper. Transfer to a small airtight container or bag. Store at room temperature up to 6 months. Makes about 2 cups rub.

EACH TABLESPOON: 29 cal., 1 g total fat (0 g sat fat), 0 mg chol., 887 mg sodium, 6 g carbo., 2 g fiber, 1 g pro. Daily Values: 23% vit. A, 2% vit. C, 2% calcium, 6% iron.

Vinegar Barbecue Sauce

For a milder heat level, use the lesser amount of crushed red pepper.

PREP: 10 MINUTES **STAND:** 6 HOURS

- 3 cups cider vinegar
- 6 Tbsp. sugar
- 1 Tbsp. dry mustard
- 2 to 4 tsp. crushed red pepper
- 2 tsp. bottled hot pepper sauce
- 1½ tsp. salt
- 1½ tsp. ground black pepper

Brisket Barbecue Sauce
page 125
Vinegar Barbecue Sauce

1. In a clean 1-quart jar mix together vinegar, sugar, mustard, crushed red pepper, hot pepper sauce, salt, and black pepper. Cover and shake well. Let stand at room temperature for 6 hours to meld flavors. Use to prepare Pulled Pork Shoulder or refrigerate, tightly covered, up to 7 days. Makes about 3¼ cups.

SERVINGS FOR 25: In a 2- or 3-quart bowl whisk together 6 cups cider vinegar, ¾ cup sugar, 2 tablespoons dry mustard, 1 to 3 tablespoons crushed red pepper, 2 tablespoons bottled hot pepper sauce, 1 tablespoon salt, and 1 tablespoon ground black pepper. Cover and let stand at room temperature 6 hours to meld flavors. Use to prepare Pulled Pork Shoulder or refrigerate, tightly covered, up to 7 days. Makes about 7 cups.

SERVINGS FOR 50: In a 3- to 4-quart bowl whisk together 12 cups cider vinegar, 1½ cups sugar, ¼ cup dry mustard, 3 to 5 tablespoons crushed red pepper, 3 tablespoons bottled hot pepper sauce, 2 tablespoons salt, and 2 tablespoons ground black pepper. Cover and let stand at room temperature 6 hours to meld flavors. Use to prepare Pulled Pork Shoulder or refrigerate, tightly covered, up to 7 days. Makes about 13 cups.

EACH TABLESPOON: 8 cal., 0 g total fat, 0 mg chol., 68 mg sodium, 2 g carbo., 0 g fiber, 0 g pro. Daily Values: 1% iron.

Peanut Butter Cookies

PREP: 40 MINUTES **CHILL:** 1 HOUR **BAKE:** 8 MINUTES PER BATCH

- ½ cup peanut butter
- ½ cup butter, softened
- ½ cup granulated sugar
- ½ cup packed brown sugar
- ½ tsp. baking soda
- ¼ tsp. salt
- 1 egg
- ½ tsp. vanilla
- 1¼ cups all-purpose flour
- Granulated sugar

1. In a large mixing bowl beat peanut butter and butter with electric mixer on medium to high speed for 30 seconds. Add granulated sugar, brown sugar, baking soda, and salt. Beat until combined, scraping sides of bowl occasionally. Beat in egg and vanilla until combined. Beat in as much of the flour as you can with the mixer. Stir in any remaining flour. Cover and refrigerate dough about 1 hour or until easy to handle.

Peanut Butter Cookies and
Star Sugar Cookies

2. Preheat oven to 375°F. Shape dough in 1-inch balls. Place balls 2 inches apart on an ungreased cookie sheet. Flatten the cookies by making crisscross marks with fork tines, dipping fork in sugar between flattening each cookie. Bake about 8 minutes or until edges are lightly browned. Transfer to wire racks. Cool completely. Makes 3 dozen cookies.

PEANUT BUTTER-TOFFEE COOKIES: Stir 1 cup toffee pieces, chocolate-covered toffee pieces, or coarsely chopped chocolate-covered English toffee bar into the dough with the flour.

TEST KITCHEN TIP: Double this recipe to make 6 dozen cookies.

EACH PEANUT BUTTER COOKIE: 82 cal., 4 g total fat (2 g sat. fat), 13 mg chol., 71 mg sodium, 9 g carbo., 0 g fiber, 2 g pro. Daily Values: 1% calcium, 2% iron.

Star Sugar Cookies

PREP: 45 MINUTES **CHILL:** 1 HOUR **BAKE:** 5 MINUTES PER BATCH

- 1 cup butter, softened
- 1 cup sugar
- 1½ tsp. baking powder
- ½ tsp. salt
- ¼ tsp. ground nutmeg
- 1 egg
- 2 Tbsp. milk
- 1 tsp. vanilla
- 3 cups all-purpose flour
- Granulated sugar, red- and blue-color sugar, or sprinkles

1. In large mixing bowl beat butter with electric mixer on medium to high speed for 30 seconds. Add sugar, baking powder, salt, and nutmeg. Beat until combined, scraping sides of bowl occasionally. Beat in egg, milk, and vanilla until combined. Beat in as much flour as you can with the mixer. Stir in any remaining flour. Divide dough in halves. Wrap; refrigerate dough for 1 hour or until easy to handle.

2. Preheat oven to 375°F. On a lightly floured surface, roll half the dough to ⅛-inch thickness.* Refrigerate remaining dough until ready to roll. With a 3-inch star-shape cookie cutter, cut dough. Place 1 inch apart on ungreased cookie sheets. Sprinkle with sugar.

3. Bake for 5 to 6 minutes or until edges are light brown. Transfer cookies to wire racks to cool. Makes about 9 dozen cookies.

*****TEST KITCHEN TIP:** For thicker, cakier cookies, roll dough to ¼-inch thickness. Bake for 8 to 9 minutes. Makes about 4½ dozen cookies.

 EACH THIN COOKIE: 35 cal., 2 g total fat (1 g sat. fat), 7 mg chol., 73 mg sodium, 4 g carbo., 0 g fiber, 0 g pro. Daily Values: 1% vit. A, 2% calcium, 1% iron.

Red, White, and Blueberry Shortcake

PREP: 15 MINUTES **BAKE:** 18 MINUTES **STAND:** 10 MINUTES

½ cup dried blueberries and/or cranberries (optional)
2 cups all-purpose flour
⅔ cup sugar
2 tsp. baking powder
½ tsp. salt
½ cup cold butter, cut into 8 to 12 pieces
¾ cup milk
2 eggs, lightly beaten
3 cups fresh strawberries, stemmed and quartered
1½ cups fresh blueberries
2 Tbsp. sugar
1 7-oz. can pressurized whipped dessert topping

1. Preheat oven to 375°F. If desired, place the dried berries in a small bowl; cover with boiling water. Let stand for 10 minutes; drain well. Meanwhile, grease and flour a 15×10×1-inch baking pan; set aside.
2. In a large bowl combine flour, the ⅔ cup sugar, baking powder, and salt. Using a pastry blender or two knives, cut in butter until mixture resembles coarse crumbs. Add milk and eggs, stirring just until dry ingredients are moistened. Stir in drained dried fruit, if using. Spoon batter into pan, spreading evenly with a thin metal spatula. Bake for 18 to 20 minutes or until evenly golden. Cool on a wire rack.*
3. In a medium bowl combine strawberries and blueberries. Sprinkle with 2 tablespoons sugar. Toss gently. Cover; let stand 10 minutes or up to 1 hour.
4. Using a 3-inch star-shape cutter, cut shapes from cake. To serve, place a single shortcake star in a small shallow bowl or on a serving plate; spoon berry mixture over the shortcake and top the berries with about 1 to 2 tablespoons of whipped topping. Makes 16 to 18 servings.

SERVINGS FOR 25: Prepare two shortcake recipes. Use 5 cups fresh strawberries, 3 cups fresh blueberries, and 3 tablespoons sugar. Three cans of pressurized whipped dessert topping are sufficient.
SERVINGS FOR 50: Prepare three shortcakes. Use 9 cups fresh strawberries, 4½ cups fresh blueberries, and ⅓ cup sugar. Four or five cans of pressurized whipped dessert topping are sufficient.
*TEST KITCHEN TIP: Shortcakes can be made ahead and frozen whole for up to 1 month. Thaw before cutting into stars.
EACH SERVING (1 SHORTCAKE + ¼ CUP BERRIES): 208 cal., 9 g total fat (5 g sat. fat), 53 mg chol., 158 mg sodium, 27 g carbo., 2 g fiber, 3 g pro. Daily Values: 5% vit. A, 29% vit. C, 4% calcium, 5% iron.

Molasses Ginger Cookies

PREP: 30 MINUTES **CHILL:** 3 HOURS **BAKE:** 9 MINUTES PER BATCH

2¼ cups all-purpose flour
1½ tsp. baking soda
½ tsp. ground cinnamon
¼ tsp. ground ginger
¼ tsp. ground nutmeg
¼ tsp. ground cloves
½ cup butter, softened
¾ cup granulated sugar
½ cup dark molasses
1 egg
½ cup coarse raw sugar or granulated sugar

1. In a medium bowl stir together flour, baking soda, cinnamon, ginger, nutmeg, and cloves. In a large mixing bowl beat butter with an electric mixer on low speed for 30 seconds. Add the ¾ cup granulated sugar. Beat until combined, scraping sides of bowl occasionally. Beat in molasses and egg until combined. Beat in as much of the flour mixture as you can with the mixer. Stir in any remaining flour mixture. Cover and refrigerate 3 hours or until easy to handle.
2. Preheat oven to 350°F. Shape dough into 1-inch balls. Roll balls in the ½ cup raw sugar. Place balls on parchment-lined cookie sheet or on ungreased cookie sheet.
3. Bake for 9 to 11 minutes or until edges are firm and tops are puffed; do not overbake. Cool on cookie sheet for 1 minute. Transfer cookies to wire racks. Cool.* Makes about 4 dozen cookies.
*TEST KITCHEN TIP: To store, arrange in layers separated by waxed paper in an airtight container; cover. Store at room temperature for up to 3 days or freeze for up to 3 months.
EACH COOKIE: 68 cal., 2 g total fat (1 g sat. fat), 9 mg chol., 130 mg sodium, 12 g carbo., 0 g fiber, 1 g pro. Daily Values: 1% vit. A, 3% calcium, 3% iron.

Red, White, and Blueberry Shortcake

Cherry Chocolate Chip Cookies

Butterscotch Cookies
PREP: 30 MINUTES **BAKE:** 9 MINUTES PER BATCH

  1   **cup butter, softened**
 ⅔   **cup granulated sugar**
 ⅔   **cup packed brown sugar**
  1   **tsp. baking soda**
 ½   **tsp. salt**
  2   **eggs**
  1   **tsp. vanilla**
2½   **cups all-purpose flour**
  1   **11-oz. pkg. butterscotch pieces**

1. Preheat oven to 375°F. In a large mixing bowl beat butter with an electric mixer on medium to high speed for 30 seconds. Add granulated sugar, brown sugar, baking soda, and salt. Beat until combined, scraping sides of bowl occasionally. Beat in eggs and vanilla until combined. Beat in as much of the flour as you can with the mixer; stir in any remaining flour and the butterscotch pieces.

2. Drop dough by rounded teaspoonfuls about 2 inches apart onto ungreased cookie sheets. Bake for 9 to 10 minutes. Rotate cookie sheets halfway through bake cycle. Remove from cookie sheets immediately and cool on wire racks. Makes 4 dozen cookies.

EACH COOKIE: 119 cal., 6 g total fat (4 g sat. fat), 19 mg chol., 89 mg sodium, 15 g carbo., 0 g fiber, 1 g pro. Daily Values: 3% vit. A, 1% calcium, 2% iron.

Cherry Chocolate Chip Cookies
PREP: 25 MINUTES **BAKE:** 9 MINUTES PER BATCH

  1   **cup butter, softened**
  1   **cup granulated sugar**
  1   **cup packed brown sugar**
  1   **tsp. baking soda**
  1   **tsp. salt**
  2   **eggs**
1½   **tsp. vanilla**
  3   **cups all-purpose flour**
  1   **12-oz. pkg. semisweet chocolate pieces**
  1   **cup snipped dried cherries**

1. Preheat oven to 375°F. In a large mixing bowl beat butter with an electric mixer on medium to high speed for 30 seconds. Add sugars, baking soda, and salt. Beat until combined, scraping sides of bowl occasionally. Beat in eggs and vanilla until combined. Beat in as much of the flour as you can with the mixer. Stir in any remaining flour. Stir in chocolate pieces and cherries.

2. Drop dough by tablespoons 2 inches apart onto ungreased cookie sheets. Bake 9 minutes. Transfer cookies to racks. Cool completely. Makes 4 dozen cookies.

EACH COOKIE: 136 cal., 6 g total fat (4 g sat. fat), 19 mg chol., 206 mg sodium, 20 g carbo., 1 g fiber, 2 g pro. Daily Values: 3% vit. A, 4% calcium, 6% iron.

Enhance simple syrups with herbs, citrus peel, and vanilla beans. Store them in the fridge and bring them out to make a splashy debut on a big bowl of freshly sliced fruits or in a favorite drink.

SIMPLE SYRUPS JAZZ UP FLAVOR

BY **JEANNE AMBROSE** PHOTOGRAPHS BY **GREG SCHEIDEMANN**

People who live in the South—where sweet

tea reigns supreme—are aware of the magic that results when simple syrups are stirred into favorite beverages. Sweetness enhances the natural flavor of tea while dissolving its bitter edge. Infused with bold flavors, simple syrups become dazzling drizzlers to stir into drinks, pour over cakes, or spoon on waffles and pancakes.

Making simple syrups is as easy as dissolving sugar in water over heat. Spruce up the syrup by dropping in a few sprigs of rosemary, crushed mint, fresh lemon and ginger, or a split vanilla bean. Let the flavors blend as the syrup cools.

Herbs infused into syrup offer a bold, fresh taste to iced tea and lemonade. Drizzled over pound cake, the lemon-ginger syrup adds a tart-sweet taste. The vanilla version is divinely subtle when splashed over a fruit salad.

Flavored Simple Syrups
PREP: 15 MINUTES **COOL:** 1 HOUR **CHILL:** UP TO 2 WEEKS

1½ cups water
1½ cups sugar
Fresh Herb, Lemon-Ginger, or Vanilla Infusion

Take on a mix-and-match attitude to come up with many creative infusion combinations. Fruits (oranges, berries, or kiwifruit) pair well with all three infusions. A splash over sorbets promises a refreshing dessert. Any of these flavored syrups will shake up ice water.

1. In a saucepan combine water and sugar. Bring to boiling over medium heat, stirring until sugar is dissolved. Add one of the infusions; boil gently, uncovered, for 2 minutes more. Remove from heat; cover and cool in saucepan for 1 hour. Remove and discard infusion ingredients. Transfer syrup to a covered storage container. Refrigerate up to 2 weeks. Makes 2 cups syrup.
EACH TABLESPOON: 35 cal., 0 g total fat, 0 mg chol., 0 mg sodium, 9 g carbo., 0 g fiber, 0 g pro.

VANILLA INFUSION: Add one fresh vanilla bean, halved lengthwise, to the hot sugar-water mixture. If desired, after cooling, remove the vanilla bean and use the tip of a small sharp knife to scrape the seeds from the bean halves into the syrup (flecks of dark seeds will color the crystal-clear syrup). Drizzle syrup over slices of cantaloupe, strawberries, or other cut-up fresh fruit.

FRESH HERB INFUSION: Add three 3- to 4-inch sprigs fresh rosemary; ¾ cup mint leaves, slightly crushed; or ¾ cup basil leaves, slightly crushed, to the hot sugar-water mixture. Proceed as directed above. Pass syrup with iced tea to sweeten. Or to use in lemonade, combine equal parts water, fresh lemon juice, and infused syrup. Sweeten as desired with additional syrup.

LEMON-GINGER INFUSION: Add three 1×3-inch strips of lemon peel and a 1-inch piece of ginger, thinly sliced, to the hot sugar-water mixture. Proceed as directed in Step 1. Drizzle syrup over pound cake or strawberry shortcake.

Vanilla

Fresh Herb

Lemon-Ginger

YOUR Best Summer Weekend

Hot Diggedy

For a new twist on an old dog, use these Major League-city franks as role models.

DENVER The Denver Dog comes hot off the roller grill at Coors Field and is topped with green chili sauce, shredded cheese, and jalapeños.

ATLANTA Always a hit at Turner Field, the Georgia Dog takes on a regional accent with coleslaw and Vidalia onion relish.

BOSTON The classic Fenway Park Frank is smothered in mustard and relish.

BY **LISA FREDERICK**
PHOTOGRAPHS BY **ANDY LYONS**

Preserving Friendship

BY **STEPHEN EXEL**

When five friends meet over several weekends each summer to can the season's produce, the gatherings yield much more than dozens of pies and jars of tomato sauce. Dee Kiehne, Karen Koch, Carrie Crawford, Sara Schneider, all from Des Moines, Iowa, and Sherry Sandahl, from Savage, Minnesota, have been canning together for 10 years, and the activity has forged enduring friendships.

"Getting together keeps us aware of what each other is going through. We support each other through our tragedies and our triumphs," Sherry says.

The canning weekends are so special that the women have been journaling the event since 2000. In addition to practical information, such as recipes, they record the flow of their lives: graduations, job changes, gossip. The journal stays out all weekend; everyone takes turns writing as the mood strikes. Saturday and Sunday are mostly dedicated to canning (one weekend may yield 75 pints of pickled green beans), and everyone pitches in Saturday night to cook a festive dinner.

"The produce we put up seems secondary to the relationships and fun we're having until you open a jar months later," Dee says. "That brings back a flood of memories and the tastes of summer."

AUGUST

SAVOR SUMMER'S
HARVEST WITH A FEAST
OF FRESH-FROM-THE-
FIELD FAVORITES.

**Roasted Late-Summer Apples
with Ginger Ale Ice**
page 150

A Harvest of Inspiration

Sweet Corn Soup
page 148

Pork Roast, Eggplant, and White Beans
page 149

Summer Vegetables and Herb Dressing
page 152

A Harvest
of Inspiration

Six renowned chefs gather on an
Iowa farm; the result is recipes
that are simple and delicious.

BY **RICHARD SWEARINGER** PHOTOGRAPHS BY **JEFF KAUCK** FOOD STYLING BY **JOSEPHINE ORBA** FOOD PROP STYLING BY **ANDREA KUHN** PRODUCED BY **JESSICA THOMAS**

Peach Crisp

Colorado, Tricia Cyman's home state, is renowned for its peaches. This recipe brings out the best in any peach.

PREP: 20 MINUTES **BAKE:** 40 MINUTES

- 1/4 cup granulated sugar
- 2 Tbsp. all-purpose flour
- 1 tsp. ground cinnamon
- 7 cups 1/2-inch fresh or frozen peach slices (8 peaches, about 3 1/2 lb.) or 1/2-inch slices cooking apples, such as Granny Smith
- 2 Tbsp. honey
- 2/3 cup coarsely crushed graham crackers (5 squares)
- 2/3 cup packed brown sugar
- 1/3 cup all-purpose flour
- 2 Tbsp. rolled oats
- 1/4 tsp. ground cinnamon
- 1/3 cup butter
- 1 recipe Smokehouse Ice Cream (optional) (recipe, page 144)

1. Preheat oven to 375°F. For filling, in a bowl stir together granulated sugar, the 2 tablespoons flour, and the 1 teaspoon cinnamon. Add peaches; toss to coat. Spread in 2-quart rectangular baking dish. Drizzle honey over peaches; set aside.

2. For topping, in a bowl stir together crushed graham crackers, brown sugar, the 1/3 cup flour, the rolled oats, and the 1/4 teaspoon cinnamon. Using a pastry blender, cut in butter until mixture resembles coarse crumbs. Sprinkle topping evenly over the peach mixture.

3. Bake, uncovered, for 40 to 45 minutes or until topping is golden brown. Serve warm; if desired, top with Smokehouse Ice Cream. Makes 8 servings.

EACH SERVING: 306 cal., 8 g fat (5 g sat. fat), 20 mg chol., 101 mg sodium, 58 g carbo., 4 g fiber, 2 g pro. Daily Values: 21% vit. A, 17% vit. C, 3% calcium, 7% iron.

Peach Crisp

The flavor of a peach tugged directly from the tree makes chef Tricia Cyman's hazel eyes light up.

"Perfect! You have to try this," she says, beckoning to five other chefs visiting this farmhouse nestled in central Iowa.

Each takes a bite and passes it along, ideas for fresh peaches—stir-frying, roasting, grilling—darting around. Before reaching a consensus on cobbler versus crisp, talk skips to the potatoes growing a few hundred yards away and how wonderful they would be cooked and tossed with just a little olive oil and salt. Chefs are usually known for complicated recipes, but visiting a farm where freshness prevails turns thoughts to simple recipes and quick preparations.

"These are not fancy ingredients," says Jeff Jackson, chef of the Lodge at Torrey Pines in California. "They require respect and restraint. They're very happy on their own."

Invited to Iowa by hog farmer Paul Willis and cattle rancher Bill Niman to see firsthand how some of the best-tasting meat and produce in the country is grown, this group of chefs enjoys a day that turns from lecture to love-in. Chefs and farmers stroll through pastures filled with sows and piglets.

Jackson and Cyman, visiting Iowa along with chefs Paul Canales of California, Christopher Beischer of New York, Andrea Reusing of North Carolina, and Bruce Sherman of Illinois, purchase meat for their restaurants from Niman Ranch, Inc. This beef-, pork-, and lamb-producing company recognizes that animals raised on all-natural feed without antibiotics or hormones have a distinct—and they say better—flavor over conventionally raised meat.

The group begins the tour with a stop at the third-generation vegetable farm owned by Larry Cleverley, who is friend and business partner of Niman and Willis and grows vegetables without pesticides or other chemicals.

The main event is up the road, however, at the 800-acre hog and grain farm of Paul Willis. Willis and Niman are united by a common goal: pork chops with bold, meaty flavors and beef roasts that are tender and savory. The producers rely on a combination of age-old techniques and modern science. While feed has no chemical additives and animals receive lots of hands-on attention, there are computers everywhere and plenty of modern labor-saving farm machinery.

Inspired by their visits to the farms, these chefs created tantalizing recipes with short ingredient lists and simple techniques—the focus on letting the natural flavors of basic ingredients shine through.

Smokehouse Ice Cream

This yummy dessert from chef Jeff Jackson, of the Lodge at Torrey Pines near San Diego, has a rich, faintly smoky flavor.

PREP: 15 MINUTES **CHILL:** 4 HOURS **FREEZE:** 4 HOURS

- 2 slices wood-smoked bacon
- 1 cup whole milk
- 1/3 cup sugar
- 3 egg yolks, lightly beaten
- 1 cup whipping cream
- 1/2 tsp. vanilla
- 1 recipe Peach Crisp (optional) (recipe, page 145)

1. In a skillet cook bacon over medium heat until crisp and browned. Remove bacon from skillet; drain well on paper towels. Separate meat of bacon from fat; finely chop meat. Discard fat.
2. For custard, in a 2-quart saucepan combine milk, sugar, egg yolks, and chopped bacon. Cook and stir over medium heat until mixture just coats the back of a clean metal spoon.* To cool, place custard in a large bowl of ice water for 1 to 2 minutes, stirring constantly.
3. Pour custard in a bowl; cover with plastic wrap. Refrigerate 4 to 24 hours. Strain out bacon; discard. Stir whipping cream and vanilla into chilled custard.
4. Freeze cream mixture in 1 1/2- to 2-quart ice cream freezer according to manufacturer's directions. Transfer to freezer container; seal and freeze 4 hours. If desired, serve with Peach Crisp. Makes 2 1/2 cups; 10 (1/4-cup) servings.

*TEST KITCHEN TIP: Coating on the spoon should be fairly thick. When you draw a finger through the coating, the edges along the path should hold their shape.

EACH 1/4-CUP SERVING ICE CREAM: 150 cal., 12 g fat (8 g sat. fat), 100 mg chol., 50 mg sodium, 9 g carbo., 0 g fiber, 3 g pro. Daily Values: 9% vit. A, 5% calcium, 1% iron.

Steak with Squash and Arugula

Chef Paul Canales nods to his Italian roots in using a thin ribeye. Thin steaks are preferred in Italy, he says.

PREP: 30 MINUTES **GRILL:** 8 MINUTES

- 1/4 cup white wine or white balsamic vinegar
- 2 cloves garlic, minced
- 1/2 tsp. kosher or sea salt or 1/4 tsp. salt
- 1/4 cup extra virgin olive oil
- 1 medium yellow summer squash or zucchini, thinly sliced
- 1 cup baby pattypan squash, halved
- 1 cup yellow or red pear tomatoes or cherry tomatoes, halved
- 1/4 cup finely chopped yellow sweet pepper
- 4 boneless beef ribeye steaks, cut 3/4 to 1 inch thick (2 1/2 to 3 lb. total)
  Sea salt, kosher salt, or salt
  Freshly ground black pepper
- 5 cups loosely packed arugula* or baby spinach
- 2 Tbsp. snipped fresh flat-leaf parsley

1. In a bowl combine vinegar, garlic, and the 1/2 teaspoon salt. Cover; let stand at room temperature 20 minutes. Whisk in olive oil. Add yellow and baby pattypan squashes, tomatoes, and sweet pepper. Toss gently. Set aside. Season steaks with additional salt and black pepper.
2. FOR A CHARCOAL GRILL: Grill steaks on the rack of an uncovered grill directly over medium coals to desired doneness, turning once halfway through. Allow 8 to 12 minutes for medium rare (145°F), 10 to 15 minutes for medium (160°F).
FOR A GAS GRILL: Preheat grill. Reduce heat to medium. Place steak on grill rack over heat. Cover and grill as above.
3. Add arugula and parsley to tomato mixture; toss gently to combine; serve with grilled steaks. Makes 4 servings.

*TEST KITCHEN TIP: Arugula, a salad green, adds a peppery note to this dish.

EACH SERVING WITH VEGETABLES: 602 cal., 36 g fat (10 g sat. fat), 165 mg chol., 470 mg sodium, 6 g carbo., 2 g fiber, 59 g pro. Daily values: 17% vit A, 18% vit. C, 9% calcium, 39% iron.

Steak with Squash and Arugula

Pork Chops with
Gorgonzola and Pears

SENSATIONALLY FRESH
INGREDIENTS CALL FOR
SIMPLE PREPARATION
TECHNIQUES.

Pork Chops with Gorgonzola and Pears

Paul Canales uses an entire Niman Ranch hog each week at Oliveto, his Italian-country restaurant in Oakland, California. He recommends using a mild Gorgonzola.

PREP: 10 MINUTES **COOK:** 20 MINUTES

- 4 pork rib chops,* cut ³/₄ to 1 inch thick
  Sea salt, kosher salt, or salt
- 2 Tbsp. olive oil
- 2 medium ripe pears, peeled, cored, and cut into 8 wedges each
- 2 Tbsp. butter
- ¼ cup dry white wine or apple juice
- ¼ cup whipping cream
- 8 oz. creamy Gorgonzola or blue cheese, cut up
  Freshly ground black pepper
  Additional Gorgonzola cheese, cut in chunks (optional)

1. Sprinkle pork chops with salt. In a 12-inch skillet cook pork chops in hot oil over medium heat for 5 minutes. Turn chops and cook 5 minutes more or until browned and juices run clear (160°F). Transfer chops to a serving platter. Drain fat from skillet.

2. In same skillet cook pear wedges in butter over medium-high heat for 5 minutes or until browned, turning once. Add pears to platter.

3. For sauce, add wine and cream to skillet. Bring to boiling; reduce heat. Boil gently, uncovered, 1 to 2 minutes or until slightly thickened. Add the 8 ounces Gorgonzola; whisk until cheese is almost melted. Remove from heat. Serve with pork and pears. Sprinkle with pepper; if desired, serve with additional cheese. Makes 4 servings.

*TEST KITCHEN TIP: Rib chops are notable for flavor and juiciness.

EACH SERVING: 618 cal., 46 g fat (24 g sat fat), 147 mg chol., 1,105 mg sodium, 14 g carbo., 4 g fiber, 34 g pro. Daily Values: 21% vit. A, 6% vit. C, 35% calcium, 4% iron.

Chefs Jeff Jackson, far left, and Paul Canales, right, survey a pasture where Paul Willis raises hogs. On Niman Ranch farms, the animals live outdoors, a return to the roots of hog farming and a departure from the practices of most large-scale hog operations where animals are raised in climate-controlled buildings.

Sweet Corn Soup

Sweet Corn Soup

From Chicago's North Pond restaurant, chef Bruce Sherman marries Paris, Southeast Asia, and London influences for this spin on a Midwest classic.

PREP: 30 MINUTES **COOL:** 10 MINUTES

12	fresh ears of corn
1	Tbsp. cooking oil
1	small apple, peeled and chopped (about $^2/_3$ cup)
1	small carrot, chopped (about $^1/_3$ cup)
1	small onion, chopped (about $^1/_3$ cup)
1	clove garlic, minced
2	14-oz. cans reduced-sodium chicken broth
	Salt and ground black pepper
2	limes
2	to 3 Tbsp. snipped fresh thyme or parsley
2	Tbsp. butter, cut in 6 to 8 pieces and softened (optional)
	Bottled hot pepper sauce (optional)

1. Remove husks from corn. Scrub corn with a stiff brush to remove silk; rinse. Cut kernels from cobs* (you should have about 6 cups). In a 4-quart Dutch oven bring 2 quarts lightly salted *water* to boiling. Add corn; return to boiling. Cook, uncovered, for 1½ minutes, stirring occasionally. Drain well; set aside.

2. In a large saucepan heat oil over medium heat. Add apple, carrot, onion, and garlic; cook and stir for 3 to 4 minutes or until vegetables are tender but not brown. Add chicken broth. Bring to boiling; reduce heat. Cover and cook 2 minutes more.

3. Cool vegetable mixture slightly, about 10 minutes. Add half the cooked corn (about 2 ½ cups). Place vegetable mixture, one-third at a time, in blender or food processor. Cover and blend or process until nearly smooth; return to large saucepan. Add remaining corn; heat through. Season to taste with salt and pepper.

4. Peel and section limes; finely chop sections. Combine lime sections and thyme. To serve, ladle soup into bowls. If desired, top with a pat of butter. Sprinkle with lime-herb mixture. If desired, pass hot pepper sauce. Makes 6 to 8 servings.

*TEST KITCHEN TIP: Cut corn from cob by steadying one end on cutting board and slicing downward with a sharp knife.

EACH SERVING: 204 cal., 4 g fat (1 g sat. fat), 0 mg chol., 444 mg sodium, 41 g carbo., 6 g fiber, 8 g pro. Daily Values: 25% vit. A, 36% vit. C, 2% calcium, 7% iron.

Pork Roast, Eggplant, and White Beans

Chef Jeff Jackson's recipe can also be made with a 2- to 3-pound single loin roast. Reduce roasting time to 1 1/4 to 1 3/4 hours.

CHILL: OVERNIGHT **PREP:** 40 MINUTES
ROAST: 1 3/4 HOURS **STAND:** 15 MINUTES

- 1 4- to 6-lb. pork center rib roast (8 ribs)
- 2 Tbsp. snipped fresh rosemary or 2 tsp. dried rosemary, crushed
- 1 Tbsp. extra virgin olive oil or olive oil
- 3 cloves garlic, minced
- 1/2 cup extra virgin olive oil or olive oil
- 2 white eggplants, halved lengthwise (8 to 10 oz. each), or 2 small eggplants
- 8 oz. baby yellow pattypan squash, halved, or yellow summer squash, cubed
- 1 15-oz. can cannellini beans (white kidney beans), rinsed and drained
- 1 cup chicken broth or dry white wine
- 2 Tbsp. snipped fresh sage or 2 tsp. dried leaf sage, crushed
- 1/2 tsp. finely shredded lemon peel
  Salt and ground black pepper

1. In a shallow pan rub roast with rosemary, the 1 tablespoon olive oil, and the garlic. Cover; refrigerate overnight.

2. Preheat oven to 325°F. Place meat, backbone side down, in a shallow roasting pan. Insert meat thermometer. Roast pork for 1 3/4 to 2 1/2 hours or until thermometer registers 155°F. Remove roast from oven; cover with foil; let stand 15 minutes before carving.* (Meat temperature will rise 5°F while standing.)

3. In a 12-inch skillet heat the 1/2 cup olive oil over medium-high heat. Add eggplant to skillet, cut sides down; cook about 10 minutes or until eggplant flesh is darkened and tender, adding pattypan squash to skillet the last 5 minutes of cooking. Stir in beans, broth, sage, and lemon peel. Cook, covered, 5 minutes more or until squash is tender. Season to taste with salt and pepper. Serve pork with eggplant mixture. Makes 8 servings.

*TEST KITCHEN TIP: Letting the roast stand before carving allows juices to reabsorb.

EACH SERVING: 374 cal., 23 g fat (5 g sat. fat), 71 mg chol., 324 mg sodium, 12 g carbo., 4 g fiber, 33 g pro. Daily Values: 2% vit. A, 10% vit. C, 6% calcium, 11% iron.

Slow-Roasted Beef Tenderloin

Tricia Cyman creates specialties such as Lavender Rack of Lamb for her restaurant at Devil's Thumb Ranch in Colorado. Roasting beef over a bed of herbs infuses the meat with fragrance.

PREP: 20 MINUTES **ROAST:** 50 MINUTES **STAND:** 10 MINUTES

- 1 2 1/2- to 3-lb. beef tenderloin
- 2 Tbsp. cooking oil
- 1 to 2 cloves garlic, minced
- 1 tsp. cracked black pepper
- 1/2 tsp. sea salt or kosher salt, or 1/4 tsp. salt
- 4 sprigs fresh rosemary
- 4 sprigs fresh oregano
- 4 sprigs fresh thyme
- 1 recipe Mushroom Tumble or Horseradish Cream
  Fresh thyme sprigs

1. Preheat oven to 250°F. Drizzle tenderloin with cooking oil. Rub minced garlic evenly over the surface of the meat. Sprinkle with pepper and salt.

2. Place rosemary, oregano, and thyme sprigs in the bottom of a 13×9×2-inch baking pan. Add a roasting rack. Place meat on rack.

3. Roast meat, uncovered, 20 minutes.* Increase oven temperature to 425°F. Roast until an instant-read thermometer inserted in thickest part of meat registers 135°F (about 30 to 40 minutes). Remove from oven. Cover loosely with foil. Let stand 10 minutes.

4. Serve beef with Mushroom Tumble or Horseradish Cream; sprinkle with fresh thyme sprigs. Makes 8 to 10 servings.

MUSHROOM TUMBLE: In an extra-large bowl toss together 6 cups assorted mushrooms (halve any large mushrooms and remove stems, if necessary), such as chanterelle, portobello, shiitake, and oyster, with 3 tablespoons olive oil, 2 tablespoons lemon juice, and 1 teaspoon reduced-sodium soy sauce. Cook, uncovered, in a large skillet over medium heat until tender, about 10 minutes. Sprinkle with coarse sea salt and cracked black pepper.

HORSERADISH CREAM: In a small bowl stir together one 7- to 8-ounce carton crème fraîche or dairy sour cream and 2 tablespoons prepared horseradish. Stir in 1/8 teaspoon each salt and ground black pepper. Serve immediately or cover and refrigerate up to 3 days. Remove from refrigerator; allow to stand 30 minutes before serving. Makes 1 cup.

*TEST KITCHEN TIP: Slow roasting in the early stages ensures that the meat is tender.

EACH SERVING WITH 1/4 CUP MUSHROOMS: 316 cal, 20 g fat (5 g sat fat), 87 mg chol, 238 mg sodium, 3 g carbo, 1 g fiber, 32 g pro. Daily Values: 3% vit. C, 1% calcium, 24% iron.

"It strikes me as worthwhile life's work to create food that's safe and nutritious."

Bill Niman and his wife, Nicolette Hahn Niman, pay attention to detail. "I try to see every animal every day," says Nicolette. "I walk through them or ride through on horseback to look for injuries or illness and just to make sure they are all there." Bill, a teacher before founding Niman Ranch on 11 acres north of San Francisco in 1970, now has more than 500 independent family farmers raising livestock for him. He's also an author; *The Niman Ranch Cookbook* is part recipe collection, part chronicle of his transformation from Minneapolis grocer's son to a leader in agriculture.

Along with the Nimans, thousands of farmers and ranchers are raising livestock on a small scale. Look for their products at farmers' markets.

Roasted Late-Summer Apples

Chef Jeff Jackson believes less cooking equals more flavor. He has a talent for combining ingredients in unexpected ways, such as baked apples served with a scoop of Ginger Ale Ice melting over the top.

PREP: 30 MINUTES **BAKE:** 20 MINUTES **COOL:** 30 MINUTES

   1   cup apple juice
 1/3   cup golden raisins
 1/3   cup chopped pecans
   3   Tbsp. butter, softened
   3   Tbsp. packed brown sugar
 1/2   tsp. ground cinnamon
   6   small apples, such as Jonathan (about 1 1/2 lb.), or 6 medium apples, such as Granny Smith or Braeburn* (about 2 lb.)
   1   recipe Ginger Ale Ice (optional) (recipe, right)

1. In a small saucepan bring 1/2 cup of the apple juice and the raisins to boiling. Remove from heat; let stand for 20 minutes. Drain, reserving liquid.
2. Preheat oven to 425°F. In a small bowl combine drained golden raisins, pecans, butter, brown sugar, and ground cinnamon.
3. Core apples. If desired, score apples with a sharp knife around the circumference of each. Spoon nut mixture into cavity of apples. Place stuffed apples in a 2-quart rectangular baking dish. Pour the reserved liquid and the remaining apple juice around apples.
4. Bake, covered, for 10 minutes (15 minutes for medium apples). Uncover and bake for 10 minutes more (20 minutes more for medium apples) or until apples are just tender enough to be easily pierced with a sharp knife, spooning juices over filling once or twice. Cool about 30 minutes before serving. If desired, serve with Ginger Ale Ice. Makes 6 servings.

*TEST KITCHEN TIP: Small apples are sold in prepackaged plastic bags in the produce department of supermarkets. If using medium apples, increase amounts to 1/2 cup raisins, 1/2 cup chopped pecans, 1/4 cup butter, 1/4 cup packed brown sugar, and 3/4 teaspoon ground cinnamon

EACH SERVING: 219 cal., 10 g fat (4 g sat. fat), 15 mg chol., 47 mg sodium, 34 g carbo., 4 g fiber, 1 g pro. Daily Values: 5% vit. A, 8% vit. C, 3% calcium, 4% iron.

Ginger Ale Ice KID FRIENDLY

PREP: 5 MINUTES **FREEZE:** 6 HOURS

   1   cup water
 1/2   cup sugar
   1   12-oz. bottle or can ginger ale

1. In a medium saucepan combine water and sugar. Cook and stir over medium heat until sugar is dissolved. Remove from heat. Stir in ginger ale.
2. Pour ginger ale mixture into a 2-quart baking dish. Cover and freeze about 6 hours or until completely frozen, stirring after 2 hours.*
3. Just before serving, break up mixture with a fork until fluffy. If desired, serve with Roasted Late-Summer Apples (left). Makes 6 (2/3-cup) servings.

*TEST KITCHEN TIP: Freeze Ginger Ale Ice up to 2 weeks. To serve, let stand at room temperature about 20 minutes.

LOW FAT **EACH SERVING:** 83 cal., 0 g fat, 0 mg chol., 5 mg sodium, 21 g carbo., 0 g fiber, 0 g pro. Daily Values: 1% iron.

Clockwise from above left: Rows of arugula at Cleverley Farms. Chef Bruce Sherman of Chicago examining red potatoes; the peaches outside Larry Cleverley's back door. Bill Niman explains the mixture of grain and other plants he uses for cattle feed to chef Andrea Reusing. At Paul Willis' farm, chefs get a first-hand look at livestock raised for Niman Ranch. Unprocessed grains, such as corn, are fed to hogs on the ranch. Larry Cleverley begins the process of washing lettuce in his farmyard. Tricia Cyman with a basket of the peaches that inspired Peach Crisp (recipe, page 143).

Summer Vegetables and Herb Dressing

Simple is delicious, a lesson taught by chef Chris Beischer, who works at Jo Jo and The Mercer Kitchen in New York.

START TO FINISH: 40 MINUTES

- ½ cup seasoned rice vinegar or white wine vinegar
- ½ cup extra virgin olive oil
- 3 Tbsp. finely chopped fresh flat-leaf parsley, basil, and/or chives
- ½ tsp. sea salt, kosher salt, or salt
- ½ tsp. ground black pepper
- 4 cups fresh vegetables, such as scrubbed baby beets, halved or quartered; trimmed baby carrots with tops; trimmed fresh wax or green beans; and/or trimmed snap pea pods
- 3 cups radishes, halved; sweet peppers, cut into strips; green onions, trimmed and cut into 4-inch lengths; cucumber pieces; avocado slices; and/or small yellow or red tomatoes
- 4 cups mesclun
  Fresh flat-leaf parsley or basil leaves and/or chives

1. For Herb Dressing, in screw-top jar combine vinegar, olive oil, finely chopped herbs, salt, and black pepper. Cover and shake well; set aside.

2. In a 12-inch skillet bring 1 inch lightly salted *water* to boiling. Add beets, carrots, and/or green beans. Return to boiling, reduce heat, and cook 3 to 4 minutes or until vegetables are crisp-tender. Add pea pods, if using, the last 1 minute of cooking. To cool, use a slotted spoon to transfer vegetables to a large bowl filled with ice water.

3. Drain vegetables. On a large platter arrange mesclun and vegetables. Sprinkle with additional herbs; pass dressing. Makes 8 servings.

EACH SERVING: 163 cal., 14 g fat (2 g sat. fat), 0 mg chol., 333 mg sodium, 10 g carbo., 3 g fiber, 2 g pro. Daily Values: 47% vit. A, 45% vit. C, 5% calcium, 6% iron.

Amid rows of lettuce at Cleverly Farms, Larry Cleverley and chefs Jeff Jackson, Andrea Reusing, and Paul Canales discuss the menu for a dinner Niman Ranch holds each year for its pork producers. Niman buys meat from more than 500 farmers across the country.

Summer Vegetables
and Herb Dressing

A PLATTER OF FRESH
HOMEGROWN VEGETABLES
IS A DIVINE APPETIZER—
NUTRITIOUS, DELICIOUS,
AND BEAUTIFUL!

Summer's Gold

BY **DOUG HALL** AND **STEPHEN EXEL** PHOTOGRAPHS BY PETE KRUMHARDT FOOD STYLING BY **DIANNA NOLIN** PROP STYLING BY LORI TURSI GROTE AND SUE MITCHELL

W hen second-grade students study the magic of seeds, pressing the dry grains into soil-filled paper cups, often it's marigolds they plant. Teachers know that this eager-to-please flower will quickly be up and growing. At home, budding gardeners receive an early boost of confidence when their parents choose trouble-free marigolds for them to grow. Once seedlings begin to bloom, the flowers continue nonstop, yielding a summer of cheerful bouquets and garlands.

Marigold colors pack all the heat of the summer sun: gold, saffron, lemon, mahogany, and orange. There are even pale butter-color varieties, although they lack the lusty vigor of their flashier siblings. When strung into leis, crowns, or floral boas, petal-packed marigolds are substantial enough to resist wilting for hours—long enough for a day of playing dress-up.

Marigolds grow in several familiar forms. The French type is low and compact with prolific blossoms about an inch across. Because of their uniformly short stature, French marigolds are often used to edge flower beds. As blooms fade, they disappear in the fresh growth of foliage and new flowers, eliminating the need for deadheading.

African marigolds are known for their large ruffled carnationlike flowers. Some grow 24 inches or taller; these are the ones to choose when you want flowers for cutting.

Although most marigolds are sharply pungent, a third type, the Signets, is good enough to eat. Signet varieties, such as 'Lemon Gem' and 'Tangerine Gem', are dense with fine, ferny leaves and spangled with five-petal blooms. Snipped petals add confetti colors to recipes. Along with the leaves, they provide a spicy herbal flavor, a tang of citrus, and a hint of tarragon.

Use the bit of licorice flavor to inspire a Signet marigold tea party menu as a reward for small gardeners. The petals and leaves flavor cream-cheese-filled Petal Tea Sandwiches and a five-ingredient Marigold Vinaigrette drizzled over crisp lettuce. For dessert, stir snipped marigold leaves and petals into a white cake mix to give a lively citrus flavor to Flower Power Mini Cupcakes.

In gardens, marigolds are at their dazzling best when their companions are bold enough to stand up to the brilliant colors. For a jazzy summer bed, combine marigolds with dramatic foliage plants, such as cannas, ornamental grasses, and sun-tolerant coleus, and with other hot-hue flowers. Marigolds of all types thrive in containers. Because they are annuals, they live for just one growing season, succumbing to the first frost of fall. Love them while they last!

GARDEN PARTY WITH MARIGOLD GOODIES **Serve** summer snacks at a marigold-bedecked table (right) placed at the edge of the garden. The menu features petals and foliage of Signet marigolds, as in the orange-flavored Marigold Sipper.

Marigold Sipper
PREP: 15 MINUTES **COOK:** 10 MINUTES **CHILL:** OVERNIGHT

- 1 cup water
- 1 cup sugar
- 2 medium oranges, cut in 1/2-inch slices
- 30 to 40 sprigs Signet marigolds, 4 to 5 inches long
  Carbonated water, chilled
  Ice cubes
  Signet marigold sprigs

1. In a large saucepan combine water and sugar. Add orange slices. Bring to boiling, stirring occasionally. Reduce heat and simmer, covered, for 5 minutes. Remove from heat; stir in marigold sprigs. Cover; steep for 3 minutes. Strain syrup with a fine-mesh sieve; discard sprigs. Cool syrup completely. Cover and refrigerate.

2. For each serving, pour about 1/4 cup syrup and 1/2 cup carbonated water into a glass filled with ice cubes. (For a less sweet beverage, add additional carbonated water to taste.) Float additional marigold sprigs in each glass. Makes 6 servings (1 2/3 cups syrup).

LOW FAT **EACH SERVING:** 173 cal., 0 g fat (0 g sat. fat), 0 mg chol., 34 mg sodium, 45 g carbo., 1 g fiber, 0 g pro. Daily Values: 2% vit. A, 46% vit. C, 3% calcium.

Marigold Sipper

**Flower Power
Mini Cupcakes**

Flower Power Mini Cupcakes

For milder flavor, use the smaller measure of snipped leaves.
PREP: 35 MINUTES **BAKE:** 10 MINUTES

 1 pkg. 1-layer white cake mix
 1/3 cup Signet marigold petals
 1/3 to 1/2 cup snipped Signet marigold leaves
 1 recipe Butter Cream Frosting
   Signet marigold leaves and blossoms

1. Preheat oven to 350°F. Line 1 3/4-inch muffin cup pan with paper bake cups; set aside.
2. Prepare cake mix according to package directions. Stir in Signet marigold petals and leaves. Fill each cup two-thirds full with batter (scant tablespoon per cup). Bake 10 to 12 minutes or until a wooden toothpick inserted in centers comes out clean.
3. Remove cupcakes to wire rack. Cool completely. Frost with Butter Cream Frosting. Top with additional Signet marigold leaves and blossoms. Makes about 32 cupcakes.
BUTTER CREAM FROSTING: In medium mixing bowl beat 1/3 cup softened butter until smooth. Gradually add 1 cup powdered sugar, beating well. Slowly beat in 2 tablespoons milk and 1 teaspoon vanilla. Gradually beat in 2 cups powdered sugar, adding additional milk as necessary to reach spreading consistency. If desired, tint with yellow food coloring. Makes 1 1/3 cups frosting.
EACH FROSTED CUPCAKE: 86 cal., 3 g fat (1 g sat. fat.), 5 mg chol., 48 mg sodium, 16 g carbo., 0 g fiber, 0 g pro. Daily Values: 1% vit. A, 1% iron.

Signet Marigold Biscuits
PREP: 30 MINUTES **BAKE:** 11 MINUTES

 3 cups all-purpose flour
 1 Tbsp. baking powder
 1 Tbsp. sugar
 1 tsp. salt
 3/4 tsp. cream of tartar
 3/4 cup butter
 1 1/4 cups buttermilk
 1 egg white
 1 Tbsp. water
   Signet marigold flowers and leaves

1. Preheat oven to 450° F. In a large bowl stir together flour, baking powder, sugar, salt, and cream of tartar. Using a pastry blender, cut in butter until mixture resembles coarse crumbs. Make a well in center of flour mixture. Add buttermilk all at once. Using a fork, stir just until moistened.
2. Turn dough out onto lightly floured surface. Knead by folding and gently pressing dough 4 to 6 strokes, just until dough holds together. Pat or lightly roll to 1/2 inch thick. Cut dough with floured 1 1/2-inch round, oval, or flower cookie cutter, rerolling scraps as needed. Place biscuits 1 inch apart on ungreased baking sheet; bake for 8 minutes.
3. Meanwhile, in a small bowl combine egg white and water. Brush biscuits with egg white mixture. Arrange Signet marigold flowers and leaves on biscuit tops. Brush again with egg white mixture. Return to oven; bake for 3 minutes more or until golden.
4. Remove biscuits from sheet; cool on wire rack. Makes 38 biscuits.
EACH BISCUIT: 72 cal., 4 g fat (2 g sat fat), 11 mg chol., 118 mg sodium, 8 g carbo., 0 g fiber, 1 g pro. Daily Values: 2% vit. A, 2% calcium, 2% iron.

YOU CAN DO IT
When cooking with marigolds, select blossoms and young leaves with no sign of wilting or browning. Immerse blossoms in cool water to rid them of any insects. Dry by patting with paper towels. Store unused Signet marigolds in a folded paper towel placed in a food-safe bag in refrigerator. Use marigold petals and foliage in salads, breads, and egg and vegetable dishes. Whole blossoms can serve as garnish. Never consume flowers that have been treated with pesticides.

Petal Tea Sandwiches

Signet marigolds are one of the best-tasting varieties of the flower. For more information, see tip box, page 156.

PREP: 20 MINUTES **STAND:** 30 MINUTES **CHILL:** 3 HOURS

- 1 8-oz. pkg. cream cheese
- 2 Tbsp. Signet marigold leaves
- 1 Tbsp. Signet marigold petals
- 2 Tbsp. snipped fresh chives
- 1 recipe Signet Marigold Biscuits (left) or thinly sliced firm-textured white, wheat, or rye bread, toasted
   Signet marigold flowers (optional)
   Cucumber and radish slices (optional)
   Watercress (optional)

1. Let cream cheese stand at room temperature for 30 minutes. In a bowl combine Signet marigold leaves and petals; use kitchen scissors to coarsely snip. Stir in chives. Spread chive mixture on plastic wrap or waxed paper. Shape cream cheese into a log about 2 inches in diameter.* Roll cheese log over chive mixture to evenly coat, pressing slightly so mixture adheres. Wrap log in plastic wrap. Refrigerate 3 to 24 hours (or freeze up to 1 hour).

2. To serve, split biscuits or cut bread in shapes using 2-inch cookie cutters. Slice cheese log in thin rounds; place rounds between biscuit halves. If desired, top with whole Signet marigold flowers, cucumber and/or radish slices, and watercress. Makes 38 sandwiches.

*****TEST KITCHEN TIP:** For fewer sandwiches, halve filling; use for 16 to 18 biscuits. Wrap and freeze remaining biscuits up to 3 months.

EACH SANDWICH: 93 cal., 6 g fat (3 g. sat fat, 17 mg chol., 135 mg sodium, 8 g carbo., 0 g fiber, 2 g pro. Daily Values: 4% vit. A, 2% calcium, 3% iron.

Marigold Vinaigrette

PREP: 20 MINUTES

- ⅓ cup olive oil or salad oil
- ⅓ cup rice vinegar
- 2 Tbsp. Signet marigold petals
- 2 Tbsp. snipped Signet marigold leaves
- 1 tsp. sugar
   Iceberg lettuce wedges or mesclun
   Signet marigold leaves and blossoms (optional)

1. In a screw-top jar combine oil, vinegar, Signet marigold petals, marigold leaves, and sugar. Cover and shake well.

2. Drizzle vinaigrette on lettuce wedges. If desired, top salads with additional Signet blossoms and leaves. Makes about 1 cup dressing.

EACH TABLESPOON DRESSING: 43 cal., 4 g fat (1 g sat. fat), 0 mg chol., 0 mg sodium, 0 g carbo., 0 g fiber, 0 g pro.

Petal Tea Sandwiches and Marigold Vinaigrette

PRESERVING HERBS

BY **RICHARD SWEARINGER** PHOTOGRAPHS BY **COLLEEN DUFFLEY**

When summer fills your garden with more herbs than you can use, freeze or dry them to keep the fresh flavor.

What to Keep

The best herbs for preserving are ones that have robust flavor, such as oregano, mint, tarragon, marjoram, sage, basil, thyme, and rosemary.

How to Harvest

To keep plants producing as long as possible, treat them gently at harvest time. Experts at the Better Homes and Gardens® Test Garden recommend cutting before the heat of the day to reduce stress on the plant. Look for stalks that haven't bloomed and snip just above a leaf. Snipping the youngest portion of the plant encourages it to grow more densely (the more you cut, the more new growth is encouraged). If you want blossoms, either for garnishing or cooking, be aware that once a plant flowers, growth slows and the plant's life is shortened.

For drying, limit bundles to five to seven stems. Let the plants flower if you want the beauty of dried blossoms; the trade-off is a shorter life span for the plants.

How to Preserve

To dry and preserve herbs, tie together and hang bunches upside down in a cool, preferably dark, place—a guest room closet, a shady spot in the yard sheltered from rain, or basement—until the leaves crumble easily. Keep bunches small; if bunches are too big, they'll develop mold. You can also dry individual leaves of some large-leaf plants, such as sage, between paper towels.

To freeze herbs, chop them in a food processor, adding enough oil to form a paste, then freeze in ice cube trays. (To prevent basil from turning black while frozen, dip in boiling water for 20 seconds, then into ice water.) Once frozen, remove cubes from trays and wrap individually in plastic; store in the freezer. If plastic doesn't stick well to cubes, overwrap them in foil.

How to Use

In general, 1 teaspoon of crushed dried herbs is equal to 1 tablespoon of chopped fresh herbs. An exception is basil; about 2 teaspoons of dried equals 1 tablespoon of fresh herbs.

Ice cube trays (above) are an ideal way to freeze herbs. Each cube equals about 1 tablespoon, the amount called for in many recipes that serve four. Dry large-leaf herbs (left) between sheets of paper towels.

SUMMER PARTY NIBBLES

BY **STEPHEN EXEL** PHOTOGRAPHS BY **GREG SCHEIDEMANN [N] HAUS FOTO**

A perfect mix of summer food and fun, these small bites are kitchen and company friendly. With just a few ingredients and a few minutes, you'll have sophisticated fare to share with guests on the deck or patio.

To ensure that on-deck snacking is safe as well as tasty, serve food immediately after preparation or removing from the refrigerator. If there are any leftovers (doubtful!), put them in the refrigerator within 2 hours of serving—just 1 hour if it's 90°F or hotter outdoors.

Brie Queso Fundido
On a microwave-safe serving plate microwave an 8-ounce round of Brie for 2 minutes on medium power (50%) or until Brie is soft. Spoon ¼ cup bottled green salsa over Brie. Serve with radish slices, corn bread twists, or tortilla chips.

Spicy Potatoes and Corn

Halve 1 pound of new potatoes; toss with 2 tablespoons olive oil. Place in a 15×10×1-inch baking pan. Brush 2 ears of corn with 1 tablespoon olive oil; add to pan. Lightly sprinkle potatoes and corn with salt and ground chipotle pepper or chili powder. Roast in a 425°F oven for 25 to 30 minutes or until potatoes are tender. Cool just until corn can be handled; cut corn off cob. Place potatoes, cut sides down, on a serving plate; top with corn and sprinkle with ¼ cup chopped prosciutto.

Roasted Asparagus with Tomato Jam

Toss 1½ pounds trimmed asparagus with olive oil, salt , and black pepper. Roast, uncovered, at 425°F for 12 to 15 minutes or until crisp-tender. In a large skillet cook 2 cups chopped tomato and ½ cup chopped red sweet pepper in 1 tablespoon olive oil about 10 minutes or until tender. Season to taste with salt, black pepper, and prepared horseradish. Cool. If desired, puree mixture for a smoother jam.

Herbed Crab Salad

Stir 3 tablespoons chopped, toasted almonds and 1 to 2 tablespoons chopped parsley, flat-leaf parsley, basil, or cilantro into 1 cup purchased crab salad. Serve on pumpernickel party bread.

Marinated Olives

In a bowl combine 2 cups green and/or kalamata olives, ¼ cup olive oil, 1 tablespoon lemon juice, 1 teaspoon shredded lemon peel, 3 garlic cloves, 1 teaspoon *each* dried oregano, dried rosemary, and dried thyme, crushed. Cover and chill overnight. Drain olives; discard marinade. Serve immediately.

Lemon-Watermelon Bites

Top 6 cups seedless watermelon chunks with 2 ounces goat cheese (chèvre). Drizzle about 1 tablespoon lemon-flavor olive oil or olive oil over all. Season to taste with salt and pepper.

Home front

Smoke Signals

Give grilled foods extra-smoky flavor with cedar papers.
Soak the papers in water, wrap around food, grill, then toss after the meal. Try the papers with seafood, vegetables, pears, peaches, tofu, and soft cheeses. (Imagine a cedar-grilled wedge of melty Camembert on crusty bread!) For a striking presentation, tie an herb sprig or green onion around the roll before grilling. $36 for a pack of 50 six-inch papers; Korin Japanese Trading Company; korin.com.

Wonder Soap
Love to cook but hate stinky hands from garlic, onion, and cheese? Famed L.A. chef Yossi Faigenblat created a line of highly effective odor-neutralizing products, including this hand soap. $24; chefyossi.com.

CHEESE, U.S.A. STYLE
The ultimate adventure for cheese lovers awaits in the Chicago store of Greg O'Neill and Ken Miller. Pastoral Artisan Cheese, Bread & Wine offers a tasty tour of culinary offerings from small producers across the country. Sample these! 773/472-4781; pastoralartisan.com.

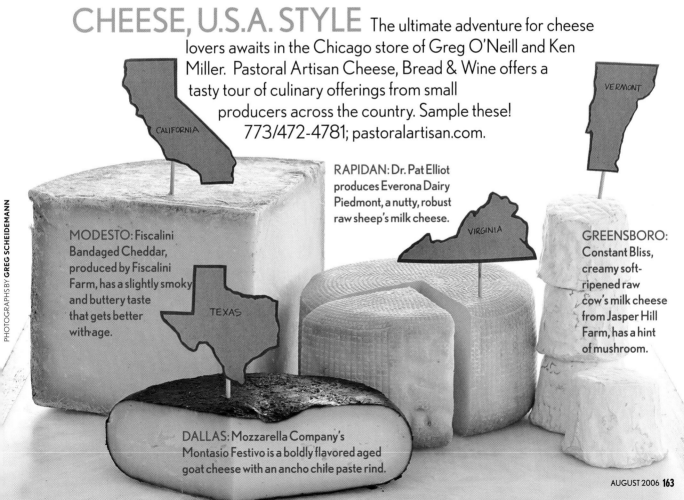

RAPIDAN: Dr. Pat Elliot produces Everona Dairy Piedmont, a nutty, robust raw sheep's milk cheese.

MODESTO: Fiscalini Bandaged Cheddar, produced by Fiscalini Farm, has a slightly smoky and buttery taste that gets better with age.

GREENSBORO: Constant Bliss, creamy soft-ripened raw cow's milk cheese from Jasper Hill Farm, has a hint of mushroom.

DALLAS: Mozzarella Company's Montasio Festivo is a boldly flavored aged goat cheese with an ancho chile paste rind.

SEPTEMBER

Hazelnut–Brown Butter Trout
page 167
Green Beans with Tomato and Basil
page 172

On-the-Go Weekend Recipes

**Blue Cheese
Steak Sandwiches**
page 172

**Mixed Berry-Corn
Mini Loaves**
page 176

**Pretzel Snack Mix
Bite-Size Oatmeal Cookies
Melon Salad with Lime Syrup**
page 179

WHETHER YOU'RE HEADING TO A CABIN FOR A LONG WEEKEND OR JUST STAYING HOME WITH THE PHONE UNPLUGGED, THESE 16 RECIPES ARE SO FAST AND EASY THAT COOKING BECOMES PART OF THE GETAWAY FUN.

on-the-go weekend RECIPES

BY **RICHARD SWEARINGER** AND **MARGE PERRY**   PHOTOGRAPHS BY **TINA RUPP**

Sizzle fresh trout in a hot pan with hazelnuts, balsamic vinegar, and lemon juice. The bed of green onion tops is much more than pretty presentation. Heat from the fish wilts the onions to release subtle flavor. Alongside, slender green beans are flash-cooked with the white of green onions, a little garlic, and a healthy fistful of basil.

Hazelnut-Brown Butter Trout

Other fish to try with this recipe are salmon, halibut, and catfish.
PREP: 30 MINUTES **COOK:** 20 MINUTES

- 4   10- to 12-oz. pan-dressed trout
- 3/4   to 1 tsp. ground cumin
- 3/4   tsp. salt
- 1/4   tsp. ground black pepper
- 1   Tbsp. olive oil
- 1   bunch green onions, cut into thin strips
- 4   Tbsp. butter
- 1/4   cup hazelnuts (filberts), coarsely chopped
- 2   Tbsp. lemon juice
- 2   Tbsp. balsamic vinegar

1. Spread each trout open; sprinkle meaty sides with cumin, salt, and 1/8 teaspoon of the pepper. Heat oil in large nonstick skillet over medium-high heat. Add two trout, skin sides up; cook for 2 minutes. Turn skin sides down; cook 2 to 3 minutes more or until fish flakes easily when tested with fork. Line 4 plates with green onion strips. Transfer fish to plates, skin sides down. Cover; keep warm. Add additional oil, as needed, to fry remaining fish. Cook as above. Transfer to plates. Cover; keep warm.

2. Reduce heat to medium. Add butter and hazelnuts to skillet; cook, stirring often, 1 1/2 to 2 minutes until butter and nuts begin to brown. Stir in lemon juice and vinegar; cook for 30 seconds until slightly thickened (aroma will be strong). Add remaining 1/8 teaspoon pepper. Pour nut mixture over trout; serve immediately. Makes 4 servings.

TEST KITCHEN TIP: To substitute pork chops in this recipe, use four 3/4-inch-thick boneless or bone-in pork chops. Reduce salt to 1/2 teaspoon. Cook over medium-high heat 8 to 10 minutes until browned and slightly pink in center (or desired doneness) turning once.

EACH SERVING: 599 cal., 35 g fat (13 g sat. fat), 197 mg chol., 624 mg sodium, 7 g carbo., 2 g fiber, 61 g pro. Daily Values: 28% vit. C, 23% calcium, 10% iron.

M ENU FOR A LONG WEEKEND

After a little prep time, these recipes will feed your family from Friday evening through Sunday evening. Here's how to make it happen.

Thursday evening: Set aside a couple of hours to prepare the Pretzel Snack Mix, Apple-Spice Hummus Dip, Summer Vegetable Pasta Salad, Bite-Size Oatmeal Cookies, and the mixes for Ready-to-Go Prosciutto Biscuits and the Mixed Berry-Corn Mini Loaves. Knead together the dough for the Peanut Butter Surprise S'mores and Cookie-Fruit Crisp and season the Spice-Rubbed Flank Steak.

Friday dinner: No-Fuss Snack Mix Chicken, Summer Vegetable Pasta Salad, Mixed Berry-Corn Loaves, Peanut Butter Surprise S'mores.

Saturday lunch: Zesty Lemon-Chicken Salad Sandwiches, Apple-Spice Hummus Dip.

Saturday dinner: Spice-Rubbed Flank Steak, Grilled Nectarine Relish, Ready-to-Go Prosciutto Biscuits, Cookie-Fruit Crisp.

Sunday lunch: Blue Cheese Steak Sandwiches.

Sunday dinner: Hazelnut-Brown Butter Trout, Green Beans with Tomato and Basil.

No-Fuss Snack Mix Chicken

Summer Vegetable Pasta Salad
page 173

The savory crunch of this meal comes from a coating of crushed pretzels and nuts. Cook extra chicken to make Zesty Lemon-Chicken Salad Sandwiches for lunch the next day.

No-Fuss Snack Mix Chicken

Diners will never guess that the snack mix you've been eating all weekend is also the coating for this chicken. Baking transforms the flavors deliciously.

START TO FINISH: 1 HOUR 10 MINUTES

- 1 cup butter, melted
- 4 cups Pretzel Snack Mix (recipe, page 179) or purchased snack mix, crushed*
- 5 to 5½ lb. meaty chicken pieces** or 6 skinless, boneless chicken breast halves (about 2½ lb.)

1. Preheat oven to 375°F. Line a 15×10×1-inch baking pan with aluminum foi; set aside. Place melted butter in shallow dish or pie plate. In another shallow dish or on waxed paper place crushed snack mix. Remove skin from meaty chicken pieces. Dip chicken in butter to coat; dip in snack mix to coat evenly. Place chicken in prepared pan.

2. Bake until chicken is no longer pink (170°F for breasts; 180°F for thighs and drumsticks). Allow 50 to 60 minutes for meaty chicken pieces or 30 minutes for skinless, boneless breast halves.

3. In a resealable storage bag or storage container with tight-fitting lid reserve 2 breast halves or 4 legs or thighs for Zesty Lemon-Chicken Salad Sandwiches; refrigerate up to 2 days. Makes 4 servings plus enough for Zesty Lemon-Chicken Salad Sandwiches (recipe, page 171).

*TEST KITCHEN TIP: To crush snack mix, place in resealable plastic bag. Remove excess air and close bag. Roll a rolling pin over snack mix in bag. (Or place snack mix in food processor bowl; cover and process until crushed.)

**TEST KITCHEN TIP: When purchasing meaty chicken pieces, figure 1 breast half or 2 legs or thighs per serving. A serving of chicken is about 4 ounces of boneless.

EACH SERVING: 863 cal., 61 g fat (28 g sat. fat), 249 mg chol., 715 mg sodium, 23 g carbo., 3 g fiber, 58 g pro. Daily Values: 1% vit. C, 7% calcium, 17% iron.

Grilled Nectarine Relish and Ready-To-Go Prosciutto Biscuits
Page 174

Spice-Rubbed Flank Steak

Before you even leave home, this steak is absorbing the rich flavors of cumin, garlic, and chili powder. Later, while it's on the grill, make a topping of nectarines and onions. For hot biscuits, just add milk to the make-ahead biscuit mix, cut out, and bake. The next day, slice leftover steak for Blue Cheese Steak Sandwiches.

Turn a standby into a standout. Make sandwiches from No-Fuss Snack Mix Chicken leftovers, adding these delicious differences: shreds of lemon zest and a generous stir-in of chopped red onion.

Spice-Rubbed Flank Steak

To have meat already cooked for Blue Cheese Steak Sandwiches (recipe, page 172), prepare and grill two steaks. Otherwise, one steak serves four with a little left over.

PREP: 20 MINUTES **CHILL:** UP TO 3 DAYS
GRILL: 17 MINUTES **STAND:** 10 MINUTES

- 1 Tbsp. packed brown sugar
- 2 tsp. ground cumin
- 2 tsp. garlic powder
- 2 tsp. chili powder
- 1 tsp. onion powder
- ½ tsp. salt
- ¼ tsp. ground black pepper
- 1 or 2 (1¾-lb.) flank steaks, trimmed of visible fat
  Grilled Nectarine Relish (recipe, page 174)

1. In a small bowl combine brown sugar, cumin, garlic powder, chili powder, onion powder, salt, and pepper. Rub mixture on both sides of flank steak. Wrap in plastic wrap; chill up to 3 days.

2. For a charcoal grill, place flank steak on grill rack directly over medium coals. Grill 17 to 21 minutes or until an instant-read thermometer inserted in center of meat registers 160°F (medium), turning once halfway through grilling. (For a gas grill, preheat grill. Reduce heat to medium. Place flank steak on grill rack over heat. Cover and grill as above.)

3. Transfer steak to a cutting board and let stand, loosely covered with aluminum foil, for 10 minutes. Thinly slice diagonally across the grain (cover and refrigerate half the steak for Blue Cheese Steak Sandwiches, page 172). Serve sliced steak with Grilled Nectarine Relish. Makes 4 servings plus leftovers for sandwiches.

TEST KITCHEN TIP: To broil, place meat on unheated rack of broiler pan. Broil 4 to 6 inches from heat for 15 to 20 minutes or until an instant-read thermometer inserted in the center registers 160°F (medium), turning once.

EACH SERVING: 729 cal., 31 g fat (9 g sat. fat), 49 mg chol., 1,162 mg sodium, 77 g carbo., 5 g fiber, 35 g pro. Daily Values: 7% vit. A, 87% vit. C, 19% calcium, 33% iron.

Zesty Lemon-Chicken Salad Sandwiches

To get a head start on this recipe, prepare the mayonnaise mixture at home, cover tightly, and keep refrigerated.

START TO FINISH: 25 MINUTES

- ⅓ cup mayonnaise
- 3 Tbsp. finely chopped red onion
- 3 Tbsp. finely chopped celery
- 1 tsp. finely shredded lemon peel
- 2 tsp. fresh lemon juice
- 2 cups chopped , cooked chicken (reserved from No-Fuss Snack Mix Chicken, bones removed if present)
  Romaine lettuce leaves, arugula, or lettuce
- 8 slices wheat bread, toasted if desired
- 8 thin tomato slices (about 1 medium tomato)

1. In a medium bowl stir together mayonnaise, onion, celery, lemon peel, and lemon juice. Add chopped chicken, stir to coat; set aside.

2 Arrange lettuce leaves on 4 bread slices; top with tomato slices. Spoon chicken mixture on tomato slices; top with remaining bread slices. Serve immediately or wrap with plastic wrap and refrigerate up to 6 hours. Makes 4 sandwiches.

TEST KITCHEN TIP: Serve this sandwich on multigrain bread slices or hearty rolls.

EACH SANDWICH: 580 cal., 30 g fat (8 g sat. fat), 83 mg chol., 831 mg sodium, 49 g carbo., 7 g fiber, 30 g pro. Daily Values: 11% vit. C, 7% calcium, 19% iron.

Zesty Lemon-Chicken Salad Sandwich

**Blue Cheese
Steak Sandwiches**

Wrapped and ready for an afternoon of adventure, this sandwich combines slices of Spice-Rubbed Flank Steak with dressing made from blue cheese, mayo, and a splash of Worcestershire sauce.

Blue Cheese Steak Sandwiches

Together with the peppery punch of arugula, the classic combination of blue cheese and beef transforms last night's Spice-Rubbed Flank Steak (recipe, page 171).

START TO FINISH: 15 MINUTES

- ⅓ cup crumbled blue cheese
- ⅓ cup mayonnaise
- 1 tsp. Worcestershire sauce
- 1 tsp. white wine vinegar
- 8 slices sourdough bread or 4 sandwich rolls, toasted
  Spice-Rubbed Flank Steak slices (recipe, page 171)
- ½ cup fresh arugula
- ½ cup bottled roasted red sweet pepper

1. In a small bowl combine blue cheese, mayonnaise, Worcestershire sauce, and vinegar. Spread one side of toasted bread slices with blue cheese mixture. On half the slices, divide sliced steak, arugula, and sweet pepper; top with toast slices. If desired, secure with wooden picks. Makes 4 sandwiches.

TEST KITCHEN TIP: About half the tasters who tried this recipe enjoyed it on toast; the other half preferred it on plain bread.

EACH SANDWICH: 254 cal., 9 g fat (3 g sat. fat), 34 mg chol., 499 mg sodium, 21 g carbo., 2 g fiber, 23 g pro. Daily Values: 13% vit. C, 5% calcium, 11% iron.

Green Beans with Tomato and Basil

At the end of the weekend, when a few choice odds and ends remain in the vegetable bin, showcase them in this recipe, substituting any vegetables on hand for the green beans and onion.

START TO FINISH: 25 MINUTES

- 1 Tbsp. olive oil
- 1 medium onion, chopped
- 1 bunch green onions, white part only
- 2 cloves garlic, minced
- 4 cups trimmed fresh green beans (about 10 oz.) or frozen whole green beans, thawed
- ¼ cup water
- ¼ cup chopped fresh basil or flat-leaf parsley
- ¼ tsp. salt
- ⅛ tsp. ground black pepper
- 2 small tomatoes, cut into wedges

1. In a large skillet heat oil over medium-high heat. Add onion, white part of green onions, and garlic; cook and stir for 3 minutes. Add green beans; cook for 2 minutes more, tossing with tongs frequently. Add water; bring to boiling; reduce heat. Simmer, covered, for 7 to 9 minutes or until beans are crisp-tender. Stir in basil, salt, and pepper. Serve with tomato wedges. Makes 4 servings.

TEST KITCHEN TIP: To give this recipe Southern flair, add ½ cup chopped ham at the same time as the onions and garlic.

EACH SERVING: 84 cal., 4 g fat (1 g sat. fat), 0 mg chol., 155 mg sodium, 12 g carbo., 5 g fiber, 3 g pro. Daily Values: 36% vit. C, 6% calcium, 8% iron.

Peace of mind takes just 30 minutes. Tuck a bowl of this salad in the fridge or ice chest and you'll be ready with a delicious side dish.

Summer Vegetable Pasta Salad

Summer Vegetable Pasta Salad

To serve this recipe at more than one meal, double the ingredient amounts—saving prep time for another meal.

PREP: 30 MINUTES **CHILL:** 4 HOURS (OPTIONAL)

- 8 oz. dried campanelle, penne, or mostaccioli pasta (2⅓ cups)
- 5 Tbsp. extra virgin olive oil
- 6 to 8 cloves garlic, thinly sliced
- 1 medium zucchini (8 oz.) trimmed and cut into matchstick-size strips (2 cups)
- 8 oz. sugar snap peas, strings removed
- 2 cups cherry or grape tomatoes, halved
- 1 shallot, finely chopped (3 Tbsp.)
- 1 Tbsp. sherry vinegar or white wine vinegar
- 1 Tbsp. Dijon-style mustard
- ½ tsp. salt
- ¼ tsp. ground black pepper
- 3 Tbsp. chopped fresh parsley
   Finely shredded Asiago cheese (optional)

1. Bring a large pot of lightly salted water to boiling; add pasta and cook according to package directions. Drain and rinse pasta under cold water; drain again. Transfer pasta to a large bowl.

2. Heat 1 tablespoon of the oil in a large nonstick skillet over medium-high heat. Add the garlic; cook 30 seconds until fragrant. Add zucchini; cook and stir for 1 minute. Add snap peas; cook 30 seconds. Stir in tomatoes; cook 30 seconds or until beginning to soften. Add vegetable mixture to pasta in bowl; toss well.

3. For shallot-mustard dressing, in a small bowl combine shallot, vinegar, mustard, salt, and pepper. Slowly whisk in remaining oil; stir in parsley. Pour dressing over pasta mixture; toss well. Serve immediately or cover and refrigerate for 4 hours or up to 3 days to allow flavors to meld. If desired, before serving, sprinkle each serving with Asiago cheese. Makes 4 to 6 servings.

TEST KITCHEN TIP: To cut preparation time, use ⅓ cup bottled vinaigrette salad dressing in place of shallot-mustard dressing.

EACH SERVING: 434 cal., 18 g fat (2 g sat. fat), 0 mg chol., 404 mg sodium, 57 g carbo., 5 g fiber, 12 g pro. Daily Values: 59% vit. C, 7% calcium, 19% iron.

GLOSSARY

Here are some terms you'll see in the recipes:

Cumin (KUH-min) This spice adds a unique, slightly nutty, earthy flavor and aroma to food. You might be familiar with it as one of the flavors in chili powder or from pickles and sausages.

Flank steak A wide, relatively thin steak that takes well to rubs and marinades. It's at its best when sliced across the grain in thin portions.

Prosciutto A dry, salt-cured ham from Italy. Unlike domestic hams, it is not smoked.

Pan-dressed A "pan-dressed trout" is one that is cleaned and split down the backbone so it cooks evenly. Trout can also be cooked whole, but it will take a minute or two longer.

Ready-to-Go Prosciutto Biscuits

Assemble dry ingredients, cold butter, prosciutto, and cheese in a resealable plastic bag before you leave home (see tip, below).
PREP: 20 MINUTES **BAKE:** 12 MINUTES

- 1⅓ cups all-purpose flour
- 1 tsp. baking powder
- 1 tsp. fennel seeds, crushed
- ½ tsp. sugar
- ¼ tsp. salt
- ¼ tsp. baking soda
- 6 Tbsp. cold butter, cut up
- 2 oz. sharp provolone or cheddar cheese, shredded (½ cup)
- 1 oz. thinly sliced prosciutto or cooked ham, finely chopped (about ⅓ cup)
- ½ cup milk

1. Preheat oven to 425°F. In a medium bowl stir together flour, baking powder, fennel seeds, sugar, salt, and baking soda. Using a pastry blender, cut in butter until flour mixture resembles coarse crumbs. Stir in cheese and prosciutto.

2. Make a well in center of flour mixture; add milk all at once. Using a fork, stir just until moistened. Turn dough out onto a lightly floured surface. Knead dough by folding and gently pressing 4 to 6 strokes or just until dough holds together. Lightly roll dough to 9×5-inch rectangle. Using a long knife or pizza cutter, cut dough lengthwise in half, then crosswise in fourths, making 8 rectangles.

3. Arrange dough pieces on ungreased baking sheet. Bake 12 to 14 minutes or until biscuits are golden brown; remove from baking sheet and serve warm. Makes 8 biscuits.

BASIC BISCUITS: Prepare as above, except omit fennel, cheese, and prosciutto; increase salt to ½ teaspoon.

TEST KITCHEN TIP: To make ahead, prepare as above through Step 1. Place flour mixture in airtight storage container. Cover and refrigerate up to 3 days. To use, let stand at room temperature for 10 minutes. Continue as directed in Step 2. Bake time may increase by 1 to 2 minutes.

EACH BISCUIT: 187 cal., 11 g fat (7 g sat. fat), 31 mg chol., 368 mg sodium, 16 g carbo., 1 g fiber, 5 g pro. Daily Values: 9% calcium, 6% iron.

Grilled Nectarine Relish

To prevent fruit from sticking to grill racks, first lightly grease or coat the cold grill rack with nonstick cooking spray before heating.
PREP: 15 MINUTES **GRILL:** 16 MINUTES

- 1 peach, halved and pitted
- 1 nectarine, halved and pitted
- 1 plum, halved and pitted
- 2 Tbsp. sugar
- 1 Tbsp. cooking oil
- 1 medium sweet onion, cut into ¼-inch slices
- 1 Tbsp. cider vinegar or white wine vinegar
- ½ tsp. salt
- ⅛ tsp. ground black pepper

1. In a medium bowl toss peach, nectarine, and plum halves with 1 tablespoon of the sugar and 2 teaspoons of the oil. Brush onion slices with remaining oil.

2. For a charcoal grill, place fruit and onion slices on rack of uncovered grill directly over medium heat. Grill fruit for 14 to 16 minutes and onion slices for 16 to 18 minutes or until well marked and slightly tender, turning once.

3. Cut fruit in narrow wedges; halve onion slices. In a medium bowl stir together cooked fruit and onion, the remaining 1 tablespoon sugar, the vinegar, salt, and pepper. Serve with Spice-Rubbed Flank Steak or ham. Makes 4 servings.

TEST KITCHEN TIP: In place of a grill, place prepared fruit and onion on unheated rack of broiler pan. Broil 4 to 6 inches from heat. Allow 4 minutes for fruit to heat through; allow 16 to 18 minutes for onion slices or until browned and slightly tender, turning once.

EACH SERVING: 103 cal., 4 g fat (1 g sat. fat), 0 mg chol., 292 mg sodium, 18 g carbo., 2 g fiber, 1 g pro. Daily Values: 12% vit. C, 1% calcium, 2% iron.

Apple-Spice Hummus Dip

Apple-Spice Hummus Dip

This chickpea dip is based on a Mediterranean favorite—hummus, which is usually quite garlicky and rich. We've kept the same protein-rich blend of chickpeas and nuts, lightened the flavor by omitting garlic, and added intriguing flavor with apples and spices.

START TO FINISH: 20 MINUTES

- 2 15-oz. cans garbanzo beans, rinsed and drained
- 1 sweet apple (such as Golden Delicious), peeled and chopped
- ⅓ cup lemon juice
- ¼ cup creamy peanut butter or tahini
- 2 to 3 Tbsp. water
- ½ tsp. salt
- ½ tsp. apple pie spice
- ¼ tsp. cayenne pepper (optional)

Cayenne pepper (optional)

Apple slices, carrot slices, and/or whole wheat crackers

1. In a food processor or blender place half of the following ingredients: garbanzo beans, chopped apple, lemon juice, peanut butter, water, salt, apple pie spice, and, if desired, cayenne pepper. Cover and process or blend until smooth; transfer to bowl. Repeat with the remaining half of above ingredients; combine with the previously blended batch. Cover; refrigerate up to 3 days. If desired, before serving, sprinkle with cayenne pepper.

2. Serve dip with apple slices, carrot slices, and/or whole wheat crackers. Makes 3 cups (24 two-tablespoon servings).

EACH 2-TABLESPOON SERVING: 62 cal., 2 g fat (0 g sat. fat), 0 mg chol., 167 mg sodium, 10 g carbo., 2 g fiber, 2 g pro. Daily Values: 5% vit. C, 1% calcium, 3% iron.

When it's time to recharge, serve this peanutty—and not too sweet—dip that packs enough protein to fuel activities for the rest of the day.

Cookie-Fruit Crisp

No bowl? Combine fruit, flour, brown sugar, and lemon juice in the baking pan.

PREP: 40 MINUTES **BAKE:** 55 MINUTES **COOL:** 45 MINUTES

- 8 cups fresh fruit, such as thinly sliced, pitted nectarines, peaches, and/or plums, or blueberries
- 3 Tbsp. all-purpose flour
- 2 Tbsp. packed brown sugar
- 1 Tbsp. fresh lemon juice
- 1 tsp. ground cinnamon
- ½ an 18-oz. pkg. refrigerated sugar cookie dough
- ½ cup graham cracker crumbs
- ⅓ cup chopped hazelnuts (filberts)* or pecans, toasted if desired
- 1 recipe Powdered Sugar Icing or honey

1. Preheat oven to 350°F. In a large bowl combine fruit, flour, brown sugar, lemon juice, and cinnamon. Toss to coat; transfer to a 10-inch oven-safe skillet or 7⅞×7⅞×1⅞-inch foil pan. Set aside.
2. In a medium bowl combine dough and graham cracker crumbs; knead until well combined. Divide dough in 9 portions. With hands, on a lightly floured surface flatten each portion to 2½-inch round. Arrange rounds on fruit mixture; sprinkle with nuts.
3. If using foil pan, place on baking sheet. Bake for 55 to 60 minutes or until filling is bubbly around edges and top is golden brown. Cool on wire rack for 45 minutes. Before serving, drizzle with Powdered Sugar Icing; serve warm. Makes 6 to 9 servings.

POWDERED SUGAR ICING: In a small bowl combine ½ cup powdered sugar, ¼ teaspoon vanilla, and 1 teaspoon milk. Stir in additional milk, ½ teaspoon at a time, until icing is drizzling consistency.

*TEST KITCHEN TIP: To toast hazelnuts, spread nuts in a single layer in a shallow baking pan. Bake at 350°F for 10 to 15 minutes or until light golden brown, watching carefully and stirring once or twice so nuts do not burn. Place nuts on a clean kitchen towel, fold towel over nuts, and rub vigorously to remove loose skins.

EACH SERVING: 411 cal., 14 g fat (3 g sat. fat), 12 mg chol., 220 mg sodium, 69 g carbo., 5 g fiber, 5 g pro. Daily Values: 19% vit. C, 6% calcium, 11% iron.

Mixed Berry-Corn Mini Loaves KID FRIENDLY

Prepare these for dinner, then toast leftovers to serve for breakfast.

PREP: 25 MINUTES **BAKE:** 18 MINUTES **COOL:** 5 MINUTES

- Nonstick cooking spray
- 1 cup yellow cornmeal
- 1 cup all-purpose flour
- ⅔ cup sugar
- 2 tsp. baking powder
- ¼ tsp. salt
- ⅔ cup milk
- ⅓ cup corn, canola, or vegetable oil
- 2 large eggs, lightly beaten
- 2 tsp. finely shredded orange peel
- ¾ cup raspberries
- ¾ cup blueberries
- Citrus Butter (recipe above)

1. Preheat oven to 400°F. Coat five 5¾×3×2-inch disposable foil loaf pans or disposable foil muffin cups (layer two liners) with cooking spray.
2. In a large bowl combine cornmeal, flour, sugar, baking powder, and salt. Add milk, oil, eggs, and orange peel. Stir to combine. Gently stir in raspberries and blueberries. Evenly divide batter among loaf pans or muffin cups.
3. Bake until tops are lightly golden and a toothpick inserted in center comes out clean. Allow 18 to 20 minutes for loaves; 12 to 15 minutes for muffins. Cool in pans for 5 minutes. Remove from pans; cool on wire rack before serving. Serve with Citrus Butter. Makes 5 loaves (5 servings each) or 12 to 14 muffins.

TEST KITCHEN TIP: To make biscotti from loaves, use a serrated knife to cut loaves lengthwise in ½-inch slices. Place slices, cut sides down, on ungreased baking sheets. Bake at 325°F for 10 minutes. Turn slices over; bake 10 to 15 minutes more or until dry and crisp. Transfer to wire rack to cool.

MAKE-AHEAD DIRECTIONS: To assemble ingredients ahead, combine dry ingredients in a large resealable plastic bag. Combine wet ingredients in a screw-top jar and store in cooler. To bake, pour the wet ingredients into dry; seal bag and knead to mix. Open bag and add berries; knead gently (berries will be mashed). Cut a 1-inch hole in bottom corner of bag; pipe batter into prepared cups.

EACH SERVING: 197 cal., 7 g fat (1 g sat. fat), 36 mg chol., 106 mg sodium, 29 g carbo., 2 g fiber, 4 g pro. Daily Values: 5% vit. C, 4% calcium, 5% iron.

FOR CAMPFIRE CREATIONS OFFER EVERYONE A CHOICE OF CHOCOLATE—WHITE, MILK, OR SEMISWEET—AS WELL AS PEANUT BUTTER AND REFRESHING CHUNKS OF FRUIT.

Peanut Butter Surprise S'mores

To make both this recipe and the Cookie-Fruit Crisp, prepare both recipes' cookie dough-graham cracker crumb mixture at one time.

START TO FINISH: 35 MINUTES

- ½ 18-oz. pkg. refrigerated sugar cookie dough
- ½ cup graham cracker crumbs
- ¼ cup peanut butter
- 4 thin slices peach or plum
- 2 or 3 (1.5-oz.) bars dark, milk, or white chocolate
- 1 10 to 12-oz. pkg. marshmallows

1. Preheat oven to 350°F. In a medium bowl break up cookie dough and gently knead in graham cracker crumbs until evenly combined. Divide dough in 8 balls; place 2 inches apart on large ungreased baking sheet. Pat balls with fingers to ¼-inch thickness. Bake for 10 to 12 minutes or until cookies are lightly browned. Cool completely on a wire rack about 10 minutes.

2. On half the cookies spread flat side with 1 tablespoon peanut butter. Place fruit on peanut butter; top with a piece of chocolate.

3. Place marshmallows on one end of a long skewer; hold over campfire flame for 30 to 60 seconds, turning frequently until toasted. Place 2 to 3 toasted marshmallows on each chocolate; top each with a second cookie. Makes 4 servings.

EACH SERVING: 581 cal., 30 g fat (10 g sat. fat), 20 mg chol., 412 mg sodium, 76 g carbo., 3 g fiber, 9 g pro. Daily Values: 1% vit. C, 7% calcium, 16% iron.

S'MORES INDOORS

S'mores are easy to prepare even without a campfire. Preheat an oven to 350°F. Arrange half the cookies on a baking sheet; spread each with peanut butter, then top with chocolate squares and a marshmallow. Bake for 5 minutes or until marshmallow puffs and chocolate is melted. Remove from oven, top with second cookie, and serve.

SHOPPING LIST

Below is a shopping guide to everything you'll need for three days of meals.

Produce
5 lb. fresh fruit: nectarines, peaches, and/or plums
Berries: 1 pint fresh raspberries, 1 pint blueberries
Melons: 1 small watermelon, 1 medium honeydew, 1 medium cantaloupe
6 lemons
4 apples
1 orange
2 limes
1 head romaine lettuce
1 small bunch celery
1 medium zucchini
1 lb. fresh or frozen green beans
Carrots
8 oz. sugar snap peas
Tomatoes: 4 medium tomatoes and 1 pint cherry or grape tomatoes
3 medium onions
2 bunches green onions
2 shallots
2 bulbs garlic
1 bunch fresh arugula
Herbs: 2 bunches fresh basil, 1 bunch fresh parsley

Dairy
2 lb. butter
2 oz. sharp provolone or cheddar cheese
2 oz. crumbled blue cheese
2 percent milk (for baking)
3 large eggs
Shredded Asiago cheese

Bread
Sandwich bread or rolls
Baked cheddar cheese crackers
Bite-size square pretzel snaps

Meat, Poultry & Fish
5 to 5½ lb. chicken pieces
4 (10- to 12-oz.) trout
1 or 2 (1¾- to 2-lb.) flank steaks
1 oz. prosciutto or thinly sliced ham

Pantry Items
Cornmeal
Rolled oats
Flour
Granulated sugar
Brown sugar
Baking soda
Baking powder
Mayonnaise
Vanilla
Olive oil
Nonstick cooking spray
Corn, canola, or vegetable oil
Balsamic vinegar
Sherry, cider, or white wine vinegar
Dijon-style mustard
Worcestershire sauce
12-oz. jar roasted red sweet peppers
1 box graham crackers
12-oz. bag marshmallows
12-oz. can peanuts
12-oz. pkg. miniature semisweet chocolate pieces
18-oz. pkg. refrigerated sugar cookie dough
2 (1.5-oz.) bars dark chocolate, milk chocolate, or white chocolate
2 (15-oz.) cans garbanzo beans
Dried campanelle pasta
8 oz. hazelnuts (filberts)
Chopped dried fruit
Creamy peanut butter
Pecans

Spices
Apple pie spice
Cinnamon
Chili powder
Cayenne pepper
Cumin
Fennel seeds
Garlic powder
Italian seasoning
Onion powder

Pretzel Snack Mix

Bite-Size Oatmeal Cookies

Melon Salad with Lime Syrup

THE SNACKS

A successful outing requires treats always ready for nibbling.

Pretzel Snack Mix Herbs make this blend of pretzels, nuts, and miniature crackers stand out from typical trail mixes. With no candy involved, it makes a delicious coating for No-Fuss Snack Mix Chicken (recipe, page 169).

Bite-Size Oatmeal Cookies To our best oatmeal cookie recipe, we added tiny chocolate chips and dried fruit. Unlike some cookie recipes that have to be made just so, this one is easy to modify. Supersize them, add only raisins, or include a variety of candy and nuts.

Melon Salad with Lime Syrup We chose melons for this recipe because they hold up well in the fridge for a few days.

Pretzel Snack Mix

Reserve 4 cups of this yummy snack mix to make the No-Fuss Snack Mix Chicken recipe (page 169).
PREP: 10 MINUTES **BAKE:** 45 MINUTES

- 6 cups baked cheddar cheese crackers
- 1 9-oz. pkg. bite-size square pretzel snaps (5 cups)
- 1 12-oz. can peanuts
- ½ cup butter, melted
- 2 Tbsp. dried Italian seasoning, crushed
- 1 clove garlic, finely minced
- ¼ tsp. freshly ground black pepper

1. Preheat oven to 300°F. In roasting pan combine crackers, pretzels, and peanuts. In small bowl stir together melted butter, Italian seasoning, garlic, and pepper; drizzle over cracker mixture; stir to evenly coat.
2. Bake, uncovered, for 45 minutes, stirring every 15 minutes. Spread snack mix on large sheet of foil to cool. Store in airtight container. Makes 20 (½-cup) servings (plus 4 cups for No-Fuss Snack Mix Chicken).
EACH ½-CUP SERVING: 204 cal., 13 g fat (4 g sat. fat), 11 mg chol., 269 mg sodium, 17 g carbo., 2 g fiber, 6 g pro. Daily Values: 1% vit. C, 3% calcium, 4% iron.

Bite-Size Oatmeal Cookies

Also use these cookies, which store well at room temperature up to 3 days, in place of the sugar cookies used for the Peanut Butter Surprise S'mores recipe (page 177).
PREP: 20 MINUTES **BAKE:** 6 MINUTES PER BATCH

- ½ cup butter, softened
- ⅓ cup packed brown sugar
- ¼ cup granulated sugar
- ¾ tsp. baking powder
- ½ tsp. baking soda
- ½ tsp. ground cinnamon
- ¼ tsp. salt
- ⅛ tsp. ground allspice
- 1 egg
- 1 tsp. vanilla
- ¾ cup all-purpose flour
- 1 cup quick-cooking rolled oats
- ½ cup miniature semisweet chocolate pieces
- ⅓ cup chopped dried fruit such as cranberries, tart cherries, or blueberries

1. Preheat oven to 375°F. In a mixing bowl beat butter with electric mixer on medium speed 30 seconds. Beat in sugars, baking powder, baking soda, cinnamon, salt, and allspice. Beat in egg and vanilla until combined. Beat in flour and oats. Stir in chocolate pieces and dried fruit.
2. Drop cookies by small spoonfuls about 2 inches apart onto ungreased cookie sheet. Bake 6 to 8 minutes or until cookies are golden. Transfer to rack; cool. Makes 48 cookies.
EACH COOKIE: 59 cal., 3 g fat (2 g sat. fat), 9 mg chol., 72 mg sodium, 8 g carbo., 1 g fiber, 1 g pro. Daily Values: 2% calcium, 2% iron.

Melon Salad with Lime Syrup

PREP: 20 MINUTES **COOK:** 3 MINUTES **COOL:** 10 MINUTES

- ¼ cup sugar
- ¼ cup water
- 2 tsp. finely shredded lime peel
- 3 Tbsp. fresh lime juice
- ⅛ to ¼ tsp. cayenne pepper (optional)
- 4 cups cubed watermelon (about half a small melon)
- 4 cups seeded and cubed honeydew (about half a medium melon)
- 4 cups seeded and cubed cantaloupe (1 small melon)

1. For Lime Syrup, in a small saucepan combine sugar and water; cook over medium-high heat. Bring to boiling; cook 3 minutes until syrupy. Remove from heat; transfer to a small bowl. Cool 10 minutes. Stir in lime peel, lime juice, and cayenne pepper. Cover; refrigerate.
2. To serve, combine melons and Lime Syrup in bowl. Makes 12 (1-cup) servings.
TEST KITCHEN TIP: Cayenne pepper makes the salad spicier as it sits. For milder heat, add a dash of cayenne pepper before serving.
EACH SERVING: 87 cal., 0 g fat, 0 mg chol., 22 mg sodium, 22 g carbo., 1 g fiber, 1 g pro. Daily Values: 69% vit. C, 2% calcium, 2% iron.

HOW TO PACK IT ALL

Getting away for the weekend is as easy as you make it.

Keep it simple You won't need much cooking equipment. Just pack essentials for the recipes you choose. Consider packing a baking sheet, barbecue tongs, a large all-purpose bowl, your favorite knife, and a 10-inch skillet.

Keep it organized Make use of plastic storage boxes or extra-large (2×1.7-foot) resealable plastic bags to divide and group food by the day it will be used.

Keep it cool Pack enough ice to keep all the perishables cold en route to your destination—a 10-pound bag of ice should be sufficient. You can also use plastic milk jugs filled nearly full with water and frozen for several hours or refrigerant gel packs in your cooler.

EASY TOMATO SAUCE

BY **MAGGIE MEYER** PHOTOGRAPHS BY **COLLEEN DUFFLEY**

Ancho Chile Tomato Sauce

Chile powder adds smoky depth and a kick of spice to this sauce.

PREP: 15 MINUTES **COOK:** 15 MINUTES

- 2¼ lb. tomatoes (5 or 6)
- 2 Tbsp. olive oil
- ½ cup finely chopped onion
- 2 cloves garlic, minced
- 1 Tbsp. ancho chile powder
- ¼ cup snipped fresh basil or cilantro
- ¾ tsp. salt

1. Core and halve tomatoes; squeeze out and discard seeds. Cut tomatoes in chunks. One-third at a time, place tomato chunks in food processor or blender. Process with several on/off turns; tomatoes should remain chunky. Transfer to medium bowl. You should have about 3¼ cups tomatoes. Set aside.

2. In a medium saucepan, heat oil over medium heat. Add onion; cook and stir until tender but not brown (3 minutes). Stir in garlic and chile powder; cook and stir for 1 minute. Stir in tomatoes. Bring to boiling; reduce heat. Simmer gently, uncovered, about 15 minutes or until sauce is thickened. Stir in basil and salt; heat through. Makes 3 cups.

TEST KITCHEN TIP: Double the recipe and make several batches of sauce to store. Cover and refrigerate up to 1 week, or freeze up to 3 months.

EACH ¼-CUP SERVING: 40 cal., 3 g fat (0 g sat. fat), 0 mg chol., 150 mg sodium, 4 g carbo., 1 g fiber, 1 g protein. Daily Values: 17% vit. A, 16% vit. C, 1% calcium, 2% iron.

When blessed with surplus tomatoes, make extra sauce to share! Dress a container with a label and ribbon for a gift from the kitchen. Be sure to include storage directions.

CAPTURE THE ESSENCE OF FRESH TOMATO IN THIS THICK, DELICIOUS SAUCE. SERVE IT OVER PASTA FOR A QUICK MEAL OR USE IN A FAVORITE MEAT LOAF, LASAGNA, OR PIZZA RECIPE.

DESSERT FIGS

These four luscious, simple desserts use fresh or dried figs. That means divine sweets year-round for family or guests.

BY **STEPHEN EXEL** PHOTOGRAPHS BY **COLLEEN DUFFLEY**

FIGTASTIC SHORTCAKE
Top purchased shortcake with quartered fresh figs (left). Drizzle with orange juice; top with a spoonful of mascarpone cheese and orange peel.

CHOCOLATE FIGS
Dip figs, fresh or dried, in chocolate melted with a dab of shortening (above). Chill 15 minutes before serving.

FIG CAKE
Add chopped dried figs and pistachios to a sour cream coffee cake recipe (above).

FIG SAUCE
Snip dried figs; soak overnight in brandy. Gently heat in a small saucepan. If desired, sweeten with sugar or honey. Spoon over vanilla or caramel ice cream (above).

Fresh Figs
Look for fresh figs in grocery stores from June to October. Green-skinned Calimyrna figs have a nutty flavor, and purple-skinned Mission figs are a bit sweeter. Use fresh figs within two to three days of purchase. Because figs bruise easily, place them on a plate before storing them in the refrigerator.

FAST BREAK

Chill out with these easy no-cook combinations.

BY **MAGGIE MEYER** PHOTOGRAPHS BY **KIM CORNELISON**

Vacation from the Ordinary

Pause for a little downtime with a quick, all-on-one-tray assortment of South of France flavors. This elegant plateful stimulates taste buds and impresses friends, yet the preparation couldn't be easier.

PASTIS
Serve this licorice-flavored drink from France—or your favorite sparkling water—cold or over ice for a refreshing kick.

CRACKERS
For crunch, nibble sesame or garlic crackers or pieces of toasted pepper bread.

OLIVES
From the olive stand at grocery stores and delis, select varieties such as niçoise, Alphonso, and kalamata.

ALMONDS
Be adventurous! Honey-roasted and smoked almonds are filling as well as delicious.

Seaside Flavor

Enjoy some breathing space or a quiet chat with a friend with this sophisticated yet simple fare. Pair cool, crisp radishes with a salty, buttery spread for a satisfying nibble. Complement with mineral water.

BUTTER
Spread butter on radishes so salt will stick. Any butter will work; unsalted is recommended.

SEA SALT
Set out a small bowl filled with crunchy salt crystals to dip radishes in for a mix of textures.

RADISHES
Keep radishes chilled. Butter and salt tame their peppery bite.

MINERAL WATER
Bubbly and crisp, a tall ice-cold glass refreshes.

Southern Comforts

Kick back for happy hour or a late-night snack and savor the Southern charm of these simple bites. Pair peanuts with smoked meats and a glass of bourbon or cider and enjoy the heightened flavor intensity.

SUMMER SAUSAGE
From mild to spicy, there's a sausage style for any taste. Try smoked turkey for a savory alternative.

STRONG BREW
Bourbon, stout beer, strong cider, or iced tea perfectly complements roasted peanuts and smoky sausage.

ROASTED PEANUTS
Rediscover this ballpark favorite; half the fun is cracking open the shells to find the perfect nut.

Home front

VEGGIE	THAI
olives	chicken
artichoke hearts	scallions
roasted peppers	cilantro
hummus	peanuts
lemon thyme	

In a Crunch

M's Pub in Omaha, Nebraska (above), has amassed a following of fans who crave its signature dish: pizza-style lahvosh, or Armenian cracker bread. Follow M's lead by layering a small lahvosh with Havarti cheese (a must) and your chosen ingredients. Bake at 400°F for 10 minutes. Try one of these combos inspired by the pub versions. Look for lahvosh at supermarkets. 402/342-2550; mspubomaha.com.

HOT DAYS, COOL REDS

Go ahead, open a bottle of red with those potato chips. Light, fruity reds are great partners for Labor Day picnic foods, according to Richard Swearinger, our food and wine editor and tasting panel expert for the new *Better Homes and Gardens®* Wine Club. The best news? They can be chilled slightly (about an hour in the fridge)—perfect for warm summer evenings. Try these:

Perrin Réserve, 2004, Côtes Du Rhône Smooth with a trace of sweetness that makes it ideal with salty snacks. $11; vineyardbrands.com.
Harlow Ridge, 2005, Pinot Noir Try this good value cherry-perfumed Pinot Noir with grilled lamb or chicken. $10; call 800/692-5780 for a local distributor.
Kim Crawford, 2005, Pinot Noir This wine is bold and fruity yet light. Our taste testers describe it as silky. $17; www.kimcrawfordwines.com.

Join the *Better Homes and Gardens®* Wine Club at www.bhgwineclub.com.

OCTOBER

WHEN THERE'S A NIP IN THE AIR, FEW DISHES WARM
THE SOUL LIKE A COMFORTING, SAVORY POT ROAST.
NEW TWISTS ON THE OLD CLASSIC ALSO MAKE IT THE
PERFECT FARE FOR DINNER GUESTS!

Skillet Pot Roast with Mushrooms and Cherries
page 190

POT ROAST

Plus—

Mashed Roasters
page 192

Salmon Hobo Packs
page 197

Quick-Change Chowder
page 200

Pot Roast

Wrap up a cozy fall weekend with this easy, melt-in-your-mouth classic. Dress it up with new flavors or serve more traditional fare with these tips, techniques, and recipes for delicious, no-fuss pot roast.

SLOW COOKER POT ROAST STEW
Tuck autumn fruits and vegetables into the slow cooker alongside the roast for a meal that's company special. Vinegar and red wine give this pot roast snap, while the quince and squash add a sweet note. Couscous served on the side is a quick-cook option to potatoes.

Slow Cooker Pot Roast Stew

When layering ingredients in a slow cooker, put denser vegetables, such as squash, beneath tender ones.

PREP: 40 MINUTES **COOK:** HIGH 4½ HOURS; LOW 6 HOURS PLUS 1½ HOURS ON HIGH

- 2 large onions, cut in ½-inch wedges (2 cups)
- 1 3- to 3½-lb. boneless beef chuck pot roast, cut in 1-inch cubes
- ¾ cup dry red wine or lower-sodium beef broth
- ¼ cup tomato paste
- 3 Tbsp. balsamic vinegar or cider
- 2 3-inch cinnamon sticks
- 1 tsp. dried rosemary, crushed
- 1 tsp. ground allspice
- ¾ tsp. salt
- ¼ to ½ tsp. crushed red pepper
- 1 2-lb. butternut squash, peeled, seeded, and cut in 1½-inch pieces (about 4½ cups)
- 2 large quince (see "Go Beyond Basics," page 195) or cooking apples, cored and cut in ½-inch wedges
- 4 cups hot cooked couscous

1. Place onions in a 5- to 6-quart slow cooker. Place beef on top of onions. In a bowl combine wine, tomato paste, vinegar, cinnamon, rosemary, allspice, salt, and crushed red pepper; pour over beef.

2. Cover and cook on low-heat setting for 6 hours or on high-heat setting for 3 hours. If cooking on low-heat setting, adjust to high-heat setting. Stir in squash and quince (if using). Cover and cook 1½ to 2 hours more or until squash is tender. If using apples, add to cooker the last half hour of cooking. Remove and discard cinnamon. Serve pot roast with couscous and juices. Makes 8 servings.

STOVETOP INSTRUCTIONS: Set onions aside to add later. In a 4- to 5-quart Dutch oven brown beef one-third at a time, in 2 tablespoons hot olive or cooking oil. Transfer beef to platter; drain fat and return beef to Dutch oven. Increase wine to 1½ cups and vinegar to ⅓ cup. Stir wine, tomato paste, vinegar, cinnamon, rosemary, allspice, salt, and crushed red pepper into meat. Bring to boiling. Reduce heat and simmer, covered, for 1¼ hours. Add onions, squash, and quince (if using). Return to boiling. Reduce heat. Simmer, covered, 30 minutes more or until quince and vegetables are tender. If using apples, add the last 10 minutes of cooking. Remove and discard cinnamon. Serve as above.

TEST KITCHEN TIP: If using apples instead of quince, choose a firm cooking apple such as Granny Smith, Fuji, or Gala.

LOW FAT **EACH SERVING (WITH COUSCOUS):** 398 cal, 8 g fat (2 g sat. fat), 100 mg chol, 347 mg sodium, 35 g carbo, 4 g fiber, 41 g pro. Daily Values: 21% vit. A, 27% vit. C, 6% calcium, 30% iron.

BY STEPHEN EXEL PHOTOGRAPHS BY JAMES CARRIER FOOD STYLING BY CHARLES WORTHINGTON PROP STYLING BY KAREN JOHNSON

Pot Roast Essentials

Any tips for buying pot roast? The best cuts for pot roast come from the chuck or shoulder section. Look for boneless beef chuck shoulder pot roast, boneless beef chuck arm pot roast, or boneless beef chuck blade pot roast. Some bone-in cuts are available (look for bone-in beef chuck arm or chuck blade pot roast). Select a roast that is firm to the touch and has a bright cherry red color. Avoid roasts with any grayish or brown blotches. Choose packages that are cold and do not contain excess liquid.

How do I brown the beef? Pat the pot roast dry with paper towels. To seal in the flavor of meats, brown in a small amount of hot oil, turning with kitchen tongs to brown evenly on all sides.

What is braising? This method is simply cooking food in a small amount of liquid, tightly covered, over low heat for a lengthy period of time. The long, slow cooking process tenderizes the meat and helps it develop deep flavor. Braised beef is always cooked until well done and fork-tender, about 1½ to 2 hours for a 3-pound roast. To test for doneness, insert a double-pronged meat fork into the thickest part of the beef. When the fork can be inserted without resistance and can be pulled out easily, the beef is done.

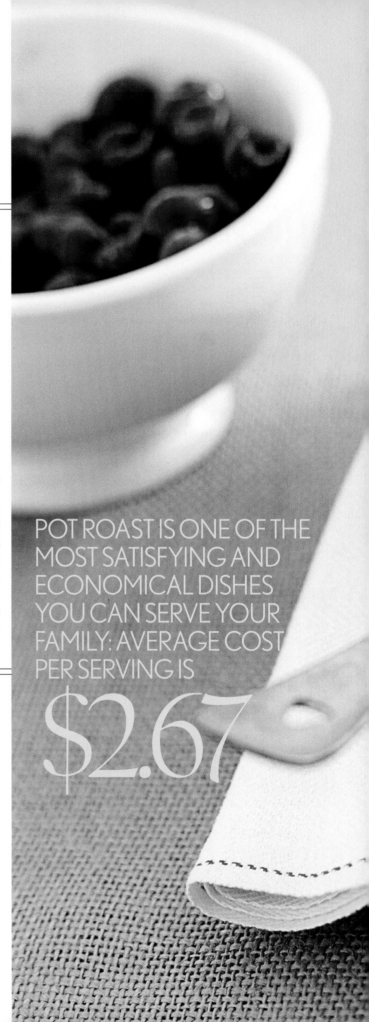

POT ROAST IS ONE OF THE MOST SATISFYING AND ECONOMICAL DISHES YOU CAN SERVE YOUR FAMILY. AVERAGE COST PER SERVING IS

$2.67

Skillet Pot Roast with Mushrooms and Cherries

Pot roast in a skillet? You bet. And it's ready to serve in only 30 minutes, just right for a weeknight meal.

START TO FINISH: 30 MINUTES

- 1 12-oz. pkg. frozen unsweetened pitted dark sweet cherries
- 8 oz. fresh button mushrooms, halved (3 cups)
- 1 medium red sweet pepper, cut in bite-size strips (3⁄4 cup)
- 1 large onion, chopped (1 cup)
- 2 Tbsp. snipped fresh herb, such as sage or thyme, or 2 tsp. dried sage or thyme, crushed
- 1 Tbsp. olive oil or cooking oil
- 2 16- to 17-oz. pkg. refrigerated cooked beef pot roast with juices
- 2 Tbsp. balsamic vinegar

1. Place frozen cherries in colander. Run cold water over cherries to partially thaw. Drain well; set aside.

2. In a 12-inch skillet cook mushrooms, sweet pepper, onion, and 1 tablespoon of the herb in hot oil until tender, about 7 minutes. Add pot roast and juices, cherries, and balsamic vinegar to skillet. Bring to boiling; reduce heat. Simmer, uncovered, for 10 minutes or until heated through and juices thicken slightly, stirring occasionally. Sprinkle with remaining herb; stir to combine. Makes 4 to 6 servings.

EACH SERVING: 420 cal, 17 g fat (5 g sat. fat), 104 mg chol, 1,174 mg sodium, 31 g carbo, 3 g fiber, 40 g pro. Daily Values: 21% vit. A, 95% vit. C, 6% calcium, 10% iron.

SKILLET POT ROAST WITH MUSHROOMS AND CHERRIES

If you're craving pot roast for a weeknight supper, here's an easy shortcut. Use one of the many delicious precooked pot roasts on the market. Most heat up in 10 minutes. Adapt a favorite recipe or try this one—cherries added to the gravy are surprisingly tasty.

The roasted potatoes mash easily with a fork.

Mashed Roasters

Want a good recipe for potatoes other than putting them in with the pot roast? Oven roast the potatoes with olive oil and fresh herbs and then mash them. Serve these potatoes with your favorite pot roast or with Skillet Pot Roast with Mushrooms and Cherries, recipe, page 190.

PREP: 20 MINUTES **ROAST:** 30 MINUTES

	Nonstick cooking spray
2½	lb. small new potatoes, halved
3	Tbsp. olive oil
2	Tbsp. snipped fresh herb such as sage or thyme or 2 tsp. dried sage or thyme, crushed
½	tsp. sea salt or ¼ tsp. salt
⅛	tsp. freshly ground black pepper
⅔	to 1 cup milk, warmed

1. Preheat oven to 450°F. Lightly coat a 15×10×1-inch baking pan with nonstick cooking spray.

2. Arrange potatoes in a single layer in pan. Cut any large potato pieces in half again. Sprinkle with olive oil, snipped herb, salt, and pepper; toss to coat. Roast potatoes, uncovered, for 30 minutes or until tender and browned, stirring twice during roasting.

3. Transfer potatoes and any drippings to a large bowl; slightly mash with a fork or potato masher. Stir in enough milk to desired consistency. Season to taste with additional salt and pepper. Makes 6 servings.

TEST KITCHEN TIP: Use two 20-oz. pkgs. refrigerated new potato wedges in place of the fresh potatoes. Prepare as above, except roast only 10 to 15 minutes.

EACH SERVING: 214 cal, 8 g fat (1 g sat. fat), 2 mg chol, 158 mg sodium, 33 g carbo, 3 g fiber, 5 g pro. Daily Values: 50% vit. C, 6% calcium, 15% iron.

Sunday Oven Pot Roast

Cover the roasting pan with a tight-fitting lid or with a double thickness of foil.

PREP: 30 MINUTES **ROAST:** 2 HOURS 5 MINUTES

1	2½- to 3-lb. boneless beef chuck pot roast
	Salt and ground black pepper
2	Tbsp. olive oil or cooking oil
1	14-oz. can beef broth
1	large onion, chopped
2	stalks celery, cut into 2-inch lengths
5	cups assorted vegetables, such as peeled Yukon gold or sweet potatoes, cut in 2-inch chunks; parsnips, peeled and cut in 2-inch chunks; whole shallots or garlic bulbs, halved horizontally; medium carrots, peeled and cut into 1½-inch pieces
¼	cup cold water
3	Tbsp. all-purpose flour

1. Preheat oven to 325°F. Trim fat from meat. Sprinkle meat with salt and pepper. In a roasting pan or large Dutch oven brown roast on all sides in hot oil over medium heat. Carefully drain fat from pan; discard. Add beef broth, onion, and celery to pan.

2. Roast, covered, for 1¼ hours. Remove celery with slotted spoon; discard. Add desired vegetables around roast. Roast, uncovered, for 50 to 60 minutes more or until meat and vegetables are tender, spooning juices over meat twice during roasting.

3. Using a slotted spoon, remove meat and vegetables to platter. For gravy, measure pan juices; skim off any fat. Discard fat. Use enough pan juice or add enough water to equal 1½ cups. In a saucepan whisk together the cold water and flour until well combined; add the 1½ cups pan juices. Cook and stir until thickened and bubbly; cook and stir for 1 minute more. Season with additional salt and pepper. Pass gravy with meat and vegetables. Makes 6 to 8 servings.

SLOW COOKER INSTRUCTIONS: Place vegetables in a 5- to 6-quart slow cooker. Trim fat from meat. Sprinkle with salt and pepper. If necessary, cut roast to fit; place on top of vegetables. Omit cooking oil. Add beef broth to cooker. Cover and cook on low-heat setting for 9 to 11 hours or on high-heat setting for 4½ to 5½ hours. Remove meat and vegetables from cooker; cover to keep warm. Using 1½ cups of the cooking juices, prepare gravy as directed in Step 3. Season to taste with salt and pepper. Pass gravy.

EACH SERVING: 419 cal, 14 g fat (4 g sat. fat), 112 mg chol, 584 mg sodium, 29 g carbo, 4 g fiber, 43 g pro. Daily Values: 21% vit. C, 5% calcium, 31% iron.

SUNDAY OVEN POT ROAST
Need a "keeper" recipe for pot roast? Here it is. This recipe has all the instructions you need for tender pot roast with vegetables and savory gravy. It's supereasy to prepare— and after you've made it once, you'll have the confidence to add new flavors with different seasonings and vegetables.

Add Unexpected Flavors

THESE TRICKS GIVE YOUR POT ROAST A WORLDLY ATTITUDE.

TRY A BOUQUET GARNI

Some pot roast recipes call for a "bouquet garni" (boo-KAY gahr-NEE). This sachet of herbs (traditionally parsley, thyme, and a bay leaf) is placed in the pot to flavor cooking juices or stews. Placing the herbs in a cheesecloth bag allows you to include other herbs and spices, such as peppercorns, or fennel or mustard seeds. To use a bouquet garni, omit any herbs or spices from the recipe and instead place the bouquet garni in the pot at the simmering step. Bring a change of pace to traditional pot roast with a Spanish- or North African-inspired bouquet garni.

WHAT YOU'LL NEED

To make a bouquet garni, you'll need double-layered 100%-cotton cheesecloth and 100%-cotton kitchen string from the kitchen supply aisle at the grocery. If you use only dried herbs, seeds, and peppercorns, you can place the ingredients in a tea ball.

WHAT'S INSIDE

For Spanish-inspired bouquet garni, tie up 6 sprigs fresh oregano or marjoram; 1 serrano pepper, halved; 2 cloves garlic, sliced; the peel from one lemon cut in long, wide strips; and 1 teaspoon whole black peppercorns.

For North African flavor, tie up 2 sprigs *each* fresh parsley and thyme; 2 bay leaves; a 1-inch piece fresh ginger, sliced; 3 inches stick cinnamon; 1/2 teaspoon *each* whole black peppercorns and coriander seeds.

PUTTING IT TOGETHER

Cut a 7-inch square of cheesecloth. Add flavor ingredients. Bring up corners of cheesecloth; tie securely with kitchen string.

Spice up the cooking liquid

Give your tried-and-true pot roast additional flavor with seasoning blends made with on-hand pantry ingredients. Add 2 to 3 tablespoons of these options when adding cooking liquid to the pot. Store the blend at room temperature, covered in an airtight container, up to 2 months.

Italian Mix
Combine 3 tablespoons dried rosemary, crushed; 3 tablespoons dried basil, crushed; 3 tablespoons dried thyme, crushed; 1 teaspoon garlic powder; 1 teaspoon salt; and 1/2 teaspoon ground black pepper.

Mexican Mix
Combine 3 tablespoons finely ground coffee beans; 3 tablespoons cocoa powder; 1 tablespoon cumin seeds, slightly crushed; 1 tablespoon chili powder; 2 teaspoons ground cinnamon; and 1 teaspoon salt.

Asian Mix Combine 1/3 cup toasted sesame seeds, 2 tablespoons dried mint, 1 teaspoon ground ginger, 1 teaspoon garlic powder, 1 teaspoon salt, and 1/2 teaspoon crushed red pepper.

PHOTOGRAPHS BY **ANDY LYONS**

Step-by-Step Pot Roast

TO PREPARE A DELICIOUS POT ROAST, JUST REMEMBER THE "3-Bs" – BUY, BROWN, AND BRAISE.

Go Beyond Basics

Our three pot roast recipes include some tasty additions beyond carrots, onions, and potatoes.

Quince This fruit has the same qualities as a green apple and a lemon: tartness and an appealing acidity. Its season is October through December. Rub the fuzzy down from the skin before slicing. Quince is hard when raw; use care when cutting.

Garlic Don't be afraid to add a whole head of garlic or garlic cloves to the pan when making pot roast. Garlic takes on a sweet flavor when roasted, and the aroma is irresistible. Remove the whole roasted head and spread the softened cloves on crusty bread.

Cherries Beef pairs well with fruit. Try orange, lemon, or lime peel; dried apricots; figs; or cranberries. Frozen cherries dress up the gravy in our precooked pot roast recipe.

3 EASY WAYS TO ROAST

Oven or Stovetop

1. You can cook pot roast in the oven or on the stovetop. Use a Dutch oven or covered roasting pan for both methods and hang a "Do Not Disturb" sign near the pot; a pot roast cooks best when it's left alone.
2. A tight-fitting lid or foil wrapping is important to prevent cooking liquids from evaporating.

Slow Cooker

1. To fill a slow cooker, place vegetables in the bottom. Top with meat. Add spices and, finally, liquid. Some recipes, such as Slow Cooker Pot Roast Stew, require adding some vegetables toward the end of the cooking time.
2. Spend the day relaxing while a rich-flavored roast cooks. The slow-cooking method needs little attention over 6 to 8 hours.

Heat 'n' Serve

1. When time is of the essence, precooked pot roast is the way to go. Most use a boil-in-bag method for quick cooking.
2. Some precooked pot roasts are available seasoned. Others allow you to adapt a favorite recipe by spicing up the gravy that's included with the roast.

GRILL ONCE DINE TWICE
(with lunch to spare)

In just a few minutes you can grill enough salmon for two dinners

plus a weekday lunch. The first night it's salmon with molasses-mustard glaze, green beans, and squash. For the next dinner, toss salmon with almonds, blue cheese, spinach, and cherry dressing. For lunch, tote Salmon and Orzo for one—just right for taking to work.

BY **LISA GADDY FREDERICK** PHOTOGRAPHS BY **KIM CORNELISON**

Salmon Hobo Packs

This recipe is a spin on a campfire classic.

PREP: 35 MINUTES **GRILL:** 12 MINUTES

- 2 lb. skinless salmon fillets, about 1 inch thick
  Salt and freshly ground pepper
- ½ cup light-colored molasses
- ¼ cup packed brown sugar
- 1 Tbsp. soy sauce
- 12 oz. green beans or haricots verts (tender young green beans), ends trimmed
- 2 small yellow summer squash, halved lengthwise and cut into ½-inch slices
- 2 Tbsp. coarse-grain mustard
- 2 Tbsp. snipped fresh parsley (optional)
- 2 tsp. finely shredded lemon peel (optional)
- ¼ tsp. freshly ground pepper (optional)

1. Sprinkle salmon lightly with salt and pepper; set aside. For glaze, in a small saucepan stir together molasses, brown sugar, and soy sauce;* heat just until sugar is dissolved, stirring occasionally. Set aside.

2. Grill salmon directly over medium coals for 6 minutes; turn. Grill for 4 minutes; brush with molasses mixture. Grill for 2 to 4 minutes more or until fish flakes easily with fork, brushing occasionally with glaze. Remove from grill. Cut salmon into 8 pieces. Cover and refrigerate 4 of the portions for use in Old-Fashioned Salmon Salad, page 198, and Salmon and Orzo, page 199.

3. Tear off four 36×18-inch sheets of heavy foil; fold in half to make 18-inch squares. In a bowl combine beans and squash; toss with mustard. Sprinkle lightly with additional salt and pepper. Divide evenly among foil sheets, placing vegetable mixture in the center. Place a salmon portion on each; spoon on any remaining glaze. Bring up two opposite edges of foil and seal with a double fold. Fold remaining edges together to completely enclose, leaving space for steam to build.

4. Grill foil packets directly over medium coals for 20 minutes.

5. To serve, transfer salmon and vegetables from packets to dinner plates. If desired, combine parsley, lemon peel, and the ¼ teaspoon pepper; sprinkle on salmon. Makes 4 servings.

*TEST KITCHEN TIP: Two-thirds cup hoisin sauce may be substituted for the glaze.

EACH SERVING WITH VEGETABLES: 334 cal, 13 g fat (3 g sat. fat), 67 mg chol, 373 mg sodium, 30 g carbo, 4 g fiber, 25 g pro. Daily Values: 41% vit. C, 11% calcium, 15% iron.

SHOPPING LIST

PRODUCE
Avocado
Green beans
Fresh parsley
Yellow summer squash
Green onions
Red onion
Spinach or arugula
Lemons and/or limes
Pear

DAIRY/DELI
2 oz. blue cheese
Kalamata olives
10-inch flour tortillas

FISH COUNTER
2 lb. skinless
  salmon fillets

PANTRY
Brown sugar
Cherry preserves
Cider vinegar
Honey-roasted almonds
Light-colored molasses
Orzo
Black pepper
Soy sauce
Yellow mustard
Coarse grain mustard

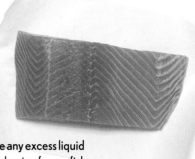

TEST KITCHEN TIP
When buying salmon, avoid fish with a strong odor or fishy smell. Packaged salmon should not have any excess liquid in the container. When buying frozen fish, look for solidly frozen packages and don't buy fish with freezer burn (patches of white ice on the surface of the fish).

Old-Fashioned Salmon Salad

START TO FINISH: 30 MINUTES

⅓ cup canola or vegetable oil

¼ cup cherry preserves

2 Tbsp. cider vinegar

2 tsp. yellow mustard

3 grilled salmon portions from Salmon Hobo Packs, chilled (recipe, page 197)

1 small pear, cored and coarsely chopped

1 avocado, peeled and chopped

½ cup sliced green onions (about 4)

½ cup honey-roasted almonds, coarsely chopped

2 oz. blue cheese, crumbled

Salt and black pepper

2 cups spinach or arugula leaves, coarsely shredded

4 10-inch flour tortillas

Lemon and lime wedges

1. In a blender combine oil, cherry preserves, vinegar, and mustard; cover and blend until combined.

2. Flake salmon into large chunks. In a large bowl combine salmon, pear, avocado, green onions, nuts, and cheese; toss with cherry preserve mixture to coat. Season to taste with salt and pepper.

3. Serve with shredded spinach, folded tortillas, and lemon and lime wedges. Makes 4 servings.

EACH SERVING: 829 cal, 50 g fat (8 g sat. fat), 60 mg chol, 704 mg sodium, 69 g carbo, 8 g fiber, 28 g pro. Daily Values: 28% vit. C, 26% calcium, 23% iron.

Think chicken salad with an attitude: Chopped pears, blue cheese, and almonds add zing to flaked salmon tossed with cherry vinaigrette.

Salmon and Orzo

START TO FINISH: 20 MINUTES

- ⅓ cup dried orzo
- 1 tsp. olive oil
- Salt
- 1 portion salmon from Salmon Hobo Packs, chilled (recipe, page 197)
- 1 to 2 Tbsp. halved or chopped, pitted kalamata olives
- 1 Tbsp. snipped fresh parsley
- ½ tsp. shredded lemon peel
- ⅛ tsp. freshly ground black pepper
- Orange slices (optional)
- Red onion slices (optional)

1. Cook orzo according to package directions. Drain; toss with olive oil and season with salt. Place on serving plate or in serving container. Top with salmon; add olives, parsley, lemon peel, and pepper. If desired, serve with orange slices and red onion. Makes 1 serving.

TEST KITCHEN TIP: While preparing parsley mixture for Salmon Hobo Packs, reserve some parsley and lemon peel for this recipe.

EACH SERVING: 458 cal, 19 g fat (3 g sat. fat), 66 mg chol, 719 mg sodium, 45 g carbo, 2 g fiber, 27 g pro. Daily Values: 17% vit. C, 8% calcium, 16% iron.

Enliven lunch with salmon, lemon, olives, parsley, and orzo, a rice-shape pasta.

QUICK-CHANGE CHOWDER
KID FRIENDLY

PREP: 20 MINUTES
COOK: 30 MINUTES

- 2 stalks celery, thinly sliced (1 cup)
- 3 Tbsp. butter
- 2 Tbsp. all-purpose flour
- 1 14-oz. can chicken or vegetable broth
- 2 cups refrigerated diced potatoes with onions (half a 1 lb. 4 oz.-pkg.)
- 1½ cups milk*
- 1 cup half-and-half*
- 4 slices bacon, crisp-cooked and crumbled (optional)
  Milk (optional)
  Salt and ground black pepper

1. In a saucepan cook celery in hot butter over medium heat about 5 minutes or until tender. Stir in flour until combined. Stir in broth; bring to boiling, stirring constantly. Add potatoes; return to boiling. Reduce heat; simmer, uncovered, 15 minutes or until tender. Slightly mash potatoes. Stir in milk, half-and-half, and bacon. Heat through. Add variation ingredients (see page 201); heat through. If desired, thin with additional milk. Season with salt and pepper. Makes 4 to 6 servings.

***TEST KITCHEN TIP:** 2½ cups whole milk may be substituted for the 1½ cups milk and 1 cup half-and-half.

EACH SERVING: 288 cal, 18 g fat (10 g sat. fat), 55 mg chol, 689 mg sodium, 24 g carbo, 2 g fiber, 8 g pro. Daily Values: 16% vit. A, 14% vit. C, 18% calcium, 4% iron.

SIMPLE CHOWDER

This basic chowder cooks in just 30 minutes.

Use stir-in ingredients to create three variations of this chunky, buttery chowder to satisfy the craving for something warm and hearty when the nip of fall is in the air. Round out the meal with rustic bread and an autumn-fresh apple or pear salad or a nutty red cabbage coleslaw.

BY **STEPHEN EXEL** PHOTOGRAPHS BY **GREG SCHEIDEMANN [N] HAUS FOTO**

Quick-Change Variations

SEAFOOD AND SWEET-AND-SPICY RED PEPPER
Cook 1 red sweet pepper, seeded and chopped, and ¼ teaspoon crushed red pepper, if desired, with the celery. Add 8 ounces poached salmon or tuna, cut into bite-size pieces, with the bacon.

CRAB, ARTICHOKE, AND BASIL
Add 12 ounces lump crabmeat, drained, flaked, and cartilage removed; one 13.75-ounce can artichoke hearts, drained and coarsely chopped; and ⅓ cup snipped fresh basil or 2 teaspoons dried basil, crushed.

CHICKEN WITH PEAS AND CARROTS
Add 1 cup frozen peas and carrots; 8 ounces chicken tenders, cooked and chopped; and 1 tablespoon snipped fresh tarragon or oregano or 1 teaspoon dried tarragon or oregano, crushed.

TEST KITCHEN TIP
Use refrigerated diced potatoes to shorten prep and cooking time for the chowder.

Chowder Bash
To feed a crowd, multiply the basic recipe to serve the number of guests. Divide into four portions and add the stir-ins to three of them.

Granny Smith and Smoked Cheddar Gratin brims with autumn flavors.

THREE GREAT GRATINS

This popular side dish becomes a versatile

dinner staple with easy additions to a basic recipe. The technique for making classic potatoes au gratin includes layering sliced potatoes and cheese in a casserole dish and baking until the top is crispy. For a gratin that's creamy and fluffy, layer deeply in a small dish. For a crispier one, use a larger dish and keep the layers thin.

BY **STEPHEN EXEL** PHOTOGRAPHS BY **GREG SCHEIDEMANN [N] HAUS FOTO**

Basic Potatoes au Gratin [KID FRIENDLY]
PREP: 40 MINUTES **BAKE:** 1 HOUR 10 MINUTES
STAND: 10 MINUTES

6	medium potatoes (2 lb.), peeled, if desired, and thinly sliced (about 6 cups)
½	cup chopped onion (1 medium)
2	large cloves garlic, minced
2	Tbsp. olive oil or cooking oil
¼	cup all-purpose flour
1	tsp. salt
¼	tsp. ground black pepper
3	cups milk
1	cup shredded Parmesan cheese (4 oz.)

1. Preheat oven to 350°F. Cook potatoes in enough lightly salted boiling water to cover for 5 minutes. Drain; set aside.

2. For sauce, in a saucepan cook onion and garlic in hot oil over medium heat until tender. Stir in flour, salt, and pepper. Add milk all at once. Cook and stir until thickened and bubbly. Remove from heat.

3. In a greased 2½- to 3-quart au gratin or rectangular baking dish or two 1½-quart au gratin dishes layer half the potatoes. Pour half the sauce over potatoes. Sprinkle with ½ cup cheese. Repeat with remaining potatoes and sauce. Cover and refrigerate remaining cheese.

4. Bake, covered, for 35 minutes for large dish and 20 minutes for small dishes. Uncover; top with remaining cheese. Bake 35 minutes more or until potatoes are tender and top is golden. Let stand 10 minutes. Makes 8 side-dish servings.

EACH SERVING: 220 cal., 8 g total fat (3 g sat. fat), 15 mg chol., 511 mg sodium, 27 g carbo., 2 g fiber, 10 g pro. Daily Values: 5% vit. A, 30% vit. C, 25% calcium, 11% iron.

> **TEST KITCHEN TIP**
> **TO MAKE AHEAD:** Gratins can be assembled and refrigerated, covered, up to 24 hours. Bake, covered, in a 350°F oven for 50 minutes for a large dish or 40 minutes for small dishes. Uncover; top with remaining cheese. Bake 40 to 50 minutes more or until potatoes are tender.

Seafood and Goat
Cheese Gratin

GRANNY SMITH AND SMOKED CHEDDAR GRATIN

Cut 2 large cored Granny Smith apples in thin wedges. Add 2 teaspoons snipped fresh thyme to sauce. Place half the apples over each layer of potatoes, then cover with sauce. Substitute smoked cheddar or Gouda for Parmesan cheese.

SEAFOOD AND GOAT CHEESE GRATIN

Add 1 tablespoon snipped fresh tarragon to sauce. Layer 8 ounces smoked salmon or whitefish, skin removed and salmon flaked, on first layer of potatoes before adding sauce. Substitute goat cheese for Parmesan cheese. Served with a green vegetable, this gratin becomes a main dish.

MUSHROOM AND BLUE CHEESE GRATIN

Cook 3 cups sliced cremini mushrooms with the onion and garlic. Add 4 teaspoons snipped fresh sage to sauce. Substitute crumbled blue cheese for Parmesan cheese.

Mushroom and Blue Cheese Gratin

TIPS FOR MAKING PERFECT GRATIN

Partner gratins with robust steaks, soups, baked fish, and roasted chicken. To achieve superior results, follow these tips.

How to Layer

Layer half the potatoes first, cover with sauce, sprinkle with cheese, and repeat.

Choosing Cheese

Just about any cheese that shreds well is suitable for gratin; Parmesan, Romano, and cheddar all work well. Crumble soft cheeses, such as goat or blue.

Potato Pointers

Russets are superb baking potatoes, so they're a good choice for gratins. Sweet potatoes are a nice holiday option. Avoid small potatoes, such as baby red, new, and Yukon gold, which are better suited to boiling.

Dish Selection

Get best results in a ceramic or glass baking dish or a cast-iron skillet.

A PIE THAT'S HANDMADE

Apple season begins soon; celebrate it with an easy-to-make pie that features a simple pat-and-fill crust.

BY **RICHARD SWEARINGER** PHOTOGRAPHS BY **JAMES CARRIER**

Easy Apple Pie KID FRIENDLY

PREP: 35 MINUTES **BAKE:** 1 HOUR 5 MINUTES
COOL: 2 HOURS

- ½ cup sugar
- 2 Tbsp. all-purpose flour
- 1 tsp. ground cinnamon
- 6 cups peeled and sliced apples
- 1 recipe No-Roll Piecrust (right)
   Sugar

1. Preheat oven to 375°F. In a large bowl stir together the ½ cup sugar, the flour, and cinnamon. Add apples. Stir to combine. Let stand while making No-Roll Piecrust.

2. For piecrust, with your hands firmly press two of the dough portions onto bottom of a 9-inch pie plate and up the sides; continue pressing to form an edge at the rim (see photos, below). Set aside.

3. Divide remaining dough portion into 6 equal parts. On waxed paper or a lightly floured work surface, pat each dough portion into 3-inch circles; set aside. Transfer apple mixture to pie shell. Top with dough circles. Sprinkle with additional sugar.

4. Place a baking sheet on oven rack; place pie plate on baking sheet. Bake pie for 65 minutes or until filling is bubbly in the center. If necessary, cover top of pie with foil the last 10 to 15 minutes of baking to prevent overbrowning. Remove pie from oven; remove foil; place on wire rack to cool completely. Makes 8 servings.

EACH SERVING: 368 cal, 14 g fat (2 g sat fat), 1 mg chol, 152 mg sodium, 57 g carbo, 3 g fiber, 4 g pro. Daily values: 1% vit. A, 5% vit. C, 3% calcium, 11% iron.

No-Roll Piecrust

This dough stays flaky when patted in the pie plate (photos, below).

- 2½ cups all-purpose flour
- 2 Tbsp. sugar
- ½ tsp. salt
- ½ cup cooking oil
- ⅓ cup milk

1. In a bowl stir together flour, sugar, and salt. In a small bowl stir together oil and milk; add all at once to flour mixture. Stir with fork until dough mixture comes together. With floured hands form in a ball. Divide in three equal balls. Continue as directed (see Step 2 of Easy Apple Pie, left).

PRESS dough to an even thickness up sides of pie plate and form a rim that will hold in bubbling juices.

PAT out palm-size circles of dough a little thicker than a quarter. Flour keeps dough from sticking.

PLACE dough circles on pie, using a spatula so they keep their shape, leaving gaps for steam to escape.

GATHER FOR TAPAS

Serving a variety of little

bites is a festive way to entertain friends. Take a cue from exuberant *tabernas* (taverns) in Spain, where afternoon gatherings for tapas—small nibbles served with wine—stave off hunger until dinner. Simple preparation and ingenious combinations of few ingredients make tapas especially appealing.

Serve these delectable finger foods as a snack or full meal on saucers and bread-and-butter plates raided from the cupboard. Accompany tapas with a glass of the sprightly fruity Spanish red wine Rioja. Play lively flamenco music—and the party is off to a good start.

The tradition of serving tapas began in the mid-1800s when Spanish tavern owners covered glasses of sherry with small plates of nuts or ham to keep flying pests from the drinks. Today it's still popular to top off a drink with a plate.

BY **STEPHEN EXEL**
PHOTOGRAPHS BY **GREG SCHEIDEMANN**

SPICY ROASTED CAULIFLOWER
In a large bowl combine ⅓ cup extra virgin olive oil, 1 teaspoon kosher salt, and ½ teaspoon crushed red pepper. Add 6 cups cauliflower florets (about 1 medium head) and toss. Roast in a preheated 400°F oven for 30 to 40 minutes, stirring once, until browned.

SMASHING BEAN DIP
In a skillet cook 1 to 2 teaspoons curry powder in 1 tablespoon extra virgin olive oil until fragrant. In a food processor blend curry mixture with one 16-ounce can butter beans; ½ cup walnuts or pecans; ½ cup olive oil; 3 tablespoons lemon juice; and 3 cloves garlic, minced, until almost smooth. Serve on yellow summer squash slices. Sprinkle with additional curry powder and sea salt.

SHRIMP WITH SPICY SAFFRON SAUCE
In a small bowl combine ⅛ teaspoon saffron threads or ground turmeric with 2 tablespoons mayonnaise. In a skillet heat 8 large peeled cooked shrimp and 1 clove garlic, minced, in hot oil until heated through. Serve shrimp with saffron sauce and small focaccia wedges. Garnish with chopped fresh cilantro.

ORANGE-ROSEMARY TUNA

Combine 1 tablespoon olive oil with 1 tablespoon orange juice. Brush over 2 fresh tuna steaks. Grill tuna 4 to 6 minutes, turning once. Chill tuna 1 hour; slice thinly. Combine $1/3$ cup mayonnaise; $1/4$ cup chopped red onion; half a peeled, seeded orange, chopped; 1 teaspoon snipped rosemary; and $1/4$ teaspoon black pepper. Serve tuna and mayonnaise mixture with crackers. Sprinkle with orange peel and fresh rosemary.

EGGPLANT ROLLS

Cut 2 medium Japanese eggplants or 1 medium eggplant into $1/2$-inch vertical slices. Brush with olive oil; sprinkle with black pepper. Roast eggplant in a preheated 425°F oven for 20 minutes or until tender; cool. Spread each slice with black olive paste or tapenade; sprinkle with feta cheese. Roll up and secure with toothpicks.

PUTTING TOGETHER A TAPAS PARTY

A small-plates party is a super way to entertain casually.

Most tapas are served at room temperature, and many can be made ahead. For a party of eight, prepare six to eight choices and serve the dishes two or three at a time. Start with light fare and consider doubling the recipe of a popular dish—a hearty eater will appreciate the effort. For in-between munching, serve olives, spiced almonds, crusty seeded bread for mopping up sauces, shards of Manchego cheese, and orange slices smothered in grated bittersweet chocolate.

NOVEMBER

DELICIOUS VARIATIONS
ON TRADITIONAL
FAVORITES MAKE THIS
THANKSGIVING SENSATIONAL!

Roast Turkey
page 212

Our Best-Ever Thanksgiving

Plus

New Sweet Potato Casserole
page 235

**Roast Turkey and
Favorite Pan Gravy**
page 212

Chocolate Harvest Cake
page 229

OUR BEST-EVER THANKSGIVING

YEAR AFTER YEAR, GOLDEN ROASTED TURKEY IS THE SPOTLIGHT DISH ON THANKSGIVING DAY. WITH A FEW SIMPLE GARNISHES, THE MAIN ATTRACTION STANDS OUT EVEN MORE.

Apple Cider Punch

START TO FINISH: 5 MINUTES

- 6 cups apple cider
- 2 cups orange juice, cranberry-raspberry juice, or orange-mango juice
- ½ cup lemon juice
- 1 750-ml bottle sparkling white grape juice or sparkling wine

1. In a punch bowl, large pitcher, or pitchers combine apple cider, orange juice, and lemon juice. Slowly add sparkling white grape juice. Serve immediately. Makes 11½ cups (about fifteen 6-oz. servings).

LOW FAT **EACH SERVING:** 99 cal., 0 g total fat, 0 mg chol., 20 mg sodium, 25 g carbo., 0 g fiber, 0 g pro. Daily Values: 1% vit. A, 34% vit. C.

Apple Cider Punch

JUST LIKE YOU, WE LOVE TO SHARE RECIPES THIS TIME OF YEAR;

and through years of testing and hours of research, we've become pretty good at putting the holiday feast on your table. This year we've searched extensively through 80 years of our books and magazines to bring you dishes you'll be proud of. Included are rediscovered gems, new creations, and a peek at the best of the new 14th edition of our Red Plaid cookbook.

BY **RICHARD SWEARINGER** PHOTOGRAPHS BY **TINA RUPP** FOOD STYLING BY **WILLIAM SMITH** PROP STYLING BY **MARINA MALCHIN** RECIPES BY **DAVID BONAM**

The cooking method is 100 percent today, although the intriguing flavor idea is from a recipe found in our 1958 cookbook. Back then, the turkey was cooked in an herb broth. We updated it by stuffing the cavity of the turkey with fresh herbs and using herb-infused drippings to make the gravy—same flavor, less fat.

Favorite Pan Gravy

You can replace the drippings with ¼ cup melted butter.

START TO FINISH: 15 MINUTES

Pan drippings from roasted turkey
¼ cup all-purpose flour
1¾ cups (approximately) reduced-sodium chicken broth
Salt and black pepper

1. After roasting, transfer turkey to platter. Pour pan drippings into a 2-cup measure. Scrape browned bits from pan into cup. Skim and reserve fat from drippings (see "Thanksgiving Answers," page 215).

2. Pour ¼ cup of fat into medium saucepan (discard any remaining fat). Stir in flour. Add enough broth to remaining drippings in measuring cup to equal 2 cups. Add broth mixture all at once to flour mixture in saucepan. Cook and stir over medium heat until thickened and bubbly. Cook and stir 1 minute more. Season to taste with salt and pepper. Makes 2 cups.

TEST KITCHEN TIP: Add a flavor twist to the gravy by stirring in 2 to 3 tablespoons pure maple syrup just before serving.

EACH ¼-CUP SERVING: 69 cal., 6 g fat (4 g sat. fat), 16 mg chol., 317 mg sodium, 3 g carbo., 0 g fiber, 1 g pro. Daily Values: 4% vit. A, 1% iron.

Roast Turkey

If you prefer turkey with stuffing, see the versatile recipe on page 223.

PREP: 15 MINUTES **ROAST:** 3 HOURS **STAND:** 15 MINUTES

1 12- to 14-lb. turkey
Salt (optional)
6 sprigs (total) of fresh flat-leaf parsley, thyme, and/or marjoram
Cooking oil
Fresh herb sprigs, halved small oranges, and/or bunches of grapes

1. Preheat oven to 325°F. Rinse inside of turkey; pat interior and exterior dry with paper towels. If desired, season body cavity with salt. Place the 6 sprigs of fresh parsley in cavity.

2. Tuck ends of drumsticks under band of skin across tail or into wire or nylon leg clamp (see "Thanksgiving Answers," page 215). If there is no skin or clamp, tie drumsticks to tail with 100%-cotton kitchen string. Twist wing tips under back.

3. Place turkey, breast side up, on rack in shallow roasting pan. Brush with oil. If using, insert meat thermometer into center of inside thigh muscle. (Thermometer should not touch bone.) Cover turkey loosely with foil.

4. Roast turkey for 2¼ hours. Remove foil; cut band of skin or string between drumsticks so thighs cook evenly. Continue roasting for 45 to 75 minutes more or until meat thermometer or instant-read thermometer registers 180°F and center of stuffing (if using) is 165°F. Juices should run clear and drumsticks should move easily in sockets.

5. Remove turkey from oven. Cover loosely with foil; let stand for 15 to 20 minutes before carving.

6. Arrange turkey, fresh herb sprigs, halved small oranges, and grapes on serving platter. (For carving instructions, see page 215.) Makes 12 to 14 servings.

TEST KITCHEN TIP: If stuffing turkey, omit herbs and loosely spoon stuffing into neck and body cavities. Continue with Step 2.

EACH SERVING: 255 cal., 12 g fat (3 g sat. fat), 101 mg chol., 83 mg sodium, 0 g carbo., 0 g fiber, 35 g pro. Daily Values: 3% calcium, 12% iron.

WHAT MAKES A RECIPE TIMELESS? SIMPLICITY, EVERYDAY INGREDIENTS USED IN FESTIVE WAYS, AND UNFORGETTABLE FLAVOR.

Roast Turkey and Favorite Pan Gravy

A BETTER WAY TO SERVE THE TURKEY

Presenting an attractive platter of turkey is easy when you follow our tips.

1. Start with evenly sliced turkey. To ensure even slices, allow the turkey to stand—covered with foil—for 15 to 20 minutes while the meat firms up. Using a sharp knife, slice with gentle pressure (if you bear down, the meat will shred).

2. Next, remove drumsticks and thighs. (See carving instructions, page 215). Then carve off half the breast meat in one piece. Place the breast portion on the platter and carve it into slices. Finally, remove the wings. Carve thigh meat from bones. If none of your guests want an entire drumstick to themselves, carve meat from drumsticks as well.

3. When putting the platter together, feel free to be creative. Add a small decorative bowl of fruit and arrange meat in simple rows.

OUR TURKEY CHECKLIST

The Tools Roast the turkey in a large sturdy roasting pan—no more than 2 inches deep—with rack. A deeper pan may prevent bottom half of bird from cooking all the way through. Also key are a meat or instant-read thermometer and pot holders or oven mitts.

How Much Buy 1 to 1½ pounds of turkey per person to allow for generous leftovers.

Thawing Allow 24 hours for every 4 pounds of turkey. Do not count roasting day as thawing time. Thawed turkeys keep for 2 days in the refrigerator. The turkey is ready for roasting when giblets and neck can be removed and no ice crystals remain in cavities.

Stuffing Allow for ¾ cup per pound of turkey (11 cups for a 15-pound bird.) Stuff the turkey just before roasting (not ahead). Loosely spoon stuffing into neck and body cavities; pull neck skin over stuffing; secure to turkey back with a short skewer or wooden pick.

Trussing After stuffing, tuck drumsticks under the band of skin across tail; reset leg clamp or tie legs to tail with kitchen string. Twist wing tips under the back.

Roasting Place turkey, breast side up, on rack of roasting pan. Brush with cooking oil. Cover loosely with foil. Place in preheated 325°F oven. After two-thirds of cooking time, cut string between drumsticks. Remove foil for the last 30 to 45 minutes.

STUFFED TURKEY ROASTING TIMES

READY-TO-COOK TURKEY WEIGHT	ROASTING TIME	TEMPERATURE
8 to 12 lb.	3 to 3¾ hours	325°F
12 to 14 lb.	3¼ to 4½ hours	325°F
14 to 18 lb.	4 to 5 hours	325°F
18 to 20 lb.	4½ to 5¼ hours	325°F
20 to 24 lb.	4¾ to 5¾ hours	325°F

UNSTUFFED TURKEYS OF THE SAME WEIGHT: REDUCE TOTAL COOKING TIME BY 15 TO 45 MINUTES.

THANKSGIVING ANSWERS

Q Which is better, a fresh or frozen turkey?
A They're about equal—base your choice on personal preference. Fresh turkeys take up shelf space in the refrigerator for a day or two. Frozen birds can be purchased further in advance but take up to a week to thaw in the refrigerator.

Q What's the most common problem you hear from readers?
A A turkey that isn't thawed enough to roast. Allow plenty of time for thawing. For a 15-pound bird, start thawing Sunday to be ready for Thursday.

Q What do I do if my turkey isn't thawed by Thanksgiving morning?
A Place the bird in a clean sink full of cold water; change the water every 30 minutes. For food safety, don't thaw the bird at room temperature, in the microwave, or in warm water. When thawed, remove giblets and neck. Rinse bird, if desired. Pat dry with paper towels.

Q How would I roast my turkey in an oven bag?
A Go to www.reynoldskitchens.com for the complete oven bag instructions.

Q How do I keep track of all the different dishes cooking Thanksgiving Day?
A Buy a dual or triple timer; they allow you to time two or three dishes at once. Find them in department stores and kitchen shops.

Q What do you mean by "band of skin" in your turkey roasting instructions?
A Turkey producers generally secure the drumsticks of the turkey with wire, nylon, or the turkey's own skin. In the skin, a wide slit is cut in the tail area; the drumsticks are then tucked under the "band" formed by the slit.

Q How do you keep the turkey from drying out when roasting?
A Don't overcook; use a meat thermometer or an instant-read thermometer, which generally cost between $10 to $20 and are widely available.

Q Where do I insert the meat thermometer?
A Push the thermometer probe into the center of an inside thigh muscle, avoiding any contact with bone.

Q When making gravy, which part of the drippings do I use?
A After pouring drippings into the measuring cup, wait a few minutes for the fat to float to the top. Use the upper layer.

Q What is standing time?
A After the bird comes out of the oven, it needs a 15- to 20-minute "rest" to make the meat easier to carve and allow the stuffing temperature to rise to a safe 165°F.

Q How long can I store turkey leftovers?
A Refrigerate meat, stuffing, and gravy separately within 2 hours after cooking. Eat or freeze within 2 days.

Q Is there a good all-purpose wine I can serve at the meal?
A Wines made from a grape called Shiraz or Syrah are a good mate for turkey. Here are three to try: Redwood Creek Syrah, $8, www.redwoodcreek.com; Ravenswood Vintner's Blend Shiraz, $10, www.ravenswood-wine.com; or Grant Burge Barossa Vines Shiraz, $14, www.wilsondaniels.com.

Q What if I still have questions?
A Call Butterball Turkey Talk-Line: 800/288-8372, the USDA Meat and Poultry Hot Line: 800/535-4555, or the Reynolds Turkey Tips Hotline: 800/745-4000.

CARVING TIPS

1. Pull one drumstick away from body. Cut through skin and meat between thigh and body. To separate thighs and drumsticks, cut through joints where drumstick and thigh bones meet.

2. With legs and thighs removed, steady the bird with a carving fork. Make a horizontal cut into the breast just above each wing and cut entire breast portion free.

3. On a cutting board, carve breast portion into slices. Carve leg and thigh meat slices; arrange meat on platter.

Pear-Blue Cheese Salad with Holiday Dijon Vinaigrette

One of our most frequent requests is for a holiday salad; here's an update to our 1953 pear-blue cheese combo that uses curly endive for flavor and texture. Why endive? The peppery leaves are practically wiltproof, so they stay crisp on the buffet table longer.

Pear-Blue Cheese Salad

Use slightly firm pears for this recipe. They should give a little under thumb pressure and be juicy when you cut into them.

START TO FINISH: 25 MINUTES

- 1 recipe Holiday Dijon Vinaigrette or ³/₄ cup favorite purchased vinaigrette
- 2 Tbsp. butter
- 1 cup pecan halves
- 1 Tbsp. sugar
- ¹/₈ tsp. salt
- 16 cups torn curly endive (chicory), romaine lettuce, or spinach
- 3 ripe pears, cored and thinly sliced
- 1 cup crumbled blue cheese

1. Prepare Holiday Dijon Vinaigrette. In a skillet melt butter over medium heat. Add pecan halves. Cook 4 to 5 minutes or until pecans are lightly toasted, stirring frequently. Sprinkle sugar and salt over pecans; cook and stir for 1 minute more. Transfer pecans to a medium bowl; cool.
2. In a 6- to 8-quart salad bowl combine curly endive, pears, blue cheese, and half of the pecans. Pour Holiday Vinaigrette over salad. Toss gently to coat. Divide among salad plates. Sprinkle with remaining pecans. Makes 10 (1¹/₂-cup) servings.

TEST KITCHEN TIP: To serve on a buffet, add only about ¹/₄ cup dressing; serve remaining dressing on the side.

EACH 1¹/₂-CUP SERVING WITH DRESSING: 265 cal., 21 g fat (6 g sat. fat), 16 mg chol., 390 mg sodium, 17 g carbo., 7 g fiber, 6 g pro. Daily Values: 5% vit. A, 11% vit. C, 12% calcium, 5% iron.

Holiday Dijon Vinaigrette

START TO FINISH: 10 MINUTES

- 5 Tbsp. extra virgin olive oil
- 3 Tbsp. chopped shallots or onions
- 2 Tbsp. white wine vinegar
- 1 Tbsp. Dijon-style mustard
- ¹/₂ tsp. salt
- ¹/₄ tsp. ground black pepper

1. In a screw-top jar combine all ingredients. Cover; shake well. Serve immediately. Or cover and store in refrigerator for up to 1 week.
2. If refrigerated, let stand at room temperature 30 minutes before serving. Shake before serving. Use for Pear-Blue Cheese Salad (right). Makes ³/₄ cup.

TEST KITCHEN TIP: To add extra zip, substitute spicy mustard for the Dijon.

EACH TABLESPOON: 81 cal., 9 g fat (1 g sat. fat), 0 mg chol., 191 mg sodium, 1 g carbo., 0 g fiber, 0 g pro. Daily Values: 1% vit. A, 1% vit. C, 1% iron.

New Cranberry Sauce

Our cookbooks and magazines have added new twists to cranberry sauce nearly every year. This easy version uses pomegranate juice and persimmon to give it a modern flavor.

New Cranberry Sauce

Persimmons and pomegranates do much more than accentuate a centerpiece. They add tropical fruit flavor and a touch of sweet-sour tang to this holiday favorite.

PREP: 10 MINUTES **COOK:** 20 MINUTES

- 1 cup chopped onion (1 medium)
- 2 cloves garlic, minced
- 1 Tbsp. olive oil or cooking oil
- 1 12-oz. bag fresh or frozen cranberries
- 1 cup pomegranate juice or cranberry juice
- 3/4 cup sugar
- 1/2 tsp. ground ginger
- 1 medium Fuyu persimmon or apple, cored and cut in 1/4-inch cubes
  Rosemary sprig (optional)

1. In large saucepan cook onion and garlic in hot oil over medium-high heat for 2 to 3 minutes or until onions begin to soften. Add cranberries, pomegranate juice, sugar, and ginger. Bring to boiling; reduce heat to medium-low. Simmer, uncovered, stirring occasionally, for 16 to 17 minutes or until mixture is just thickened. Remove from heat. Stir in persimmon. Serve warm, at room temperature, or cover and chill up to 48 hours. If desired, top sauce with a rosemary sprig. Makes 12 (1/4-cup) servings .

 EACH SERVING: 91 cal., 1 g fat, 0 mg chol., 2 mg sodium, 21 g carbo., 2 g fiber, 0 g pro. Daily Values: 1% vit. A, 14% vit. C, 1% calcium, 1% iron.

THERE ARE TWO TYPES OF PERSIMMONS: Fuyus and Hachiyas. For this recipe, use Fuyus, which are tomato shape and can be eaten when firm or slightly soft. Available October to December, the fruit should be evenly light orange, not yellow or green. Store in the refrigerator up to 14 days.

These plain rolls from our 1930 cookbook are shaped in narrow pull-apart portions. Adding milk and eggs to the dough helps the rolls bake up tender. For rolls that are even more tender, make the dough the night before and let it rest in the refrigerator overnight.

Pull-Apart Dinner Rolls

Pull-Apart Dinner Rolls

These easy-to-make rolls require only 2 to 3 minutes of kneading.
PREP: 30 MINUTES   **RISE:** 1½ HOURS   **BAKE:** 12 MINUTES

      1   cup milk
      2   Tbsp. sugar
      2   Tbsp. shortening
      1   tsp. salt
      1   pkg. active dry yeast
    ¼   cup lukewarm water (110°F to 115°F)
      1   egg, beaten
    3½   to 3¾ cups all-purpose flour

1. In a small saucepan combine milk, sugar, shortening, and salt; heat to lukewarm (110°F to 115°F). In a large bowl dissolve yeast in warm water. Add egg and the milk mixture. Gradually stir in enough flour to make a soft dough. Turn out onto lightly floured surface; knead gently 2 to 3 minutes to make a smooth ball. (Knead in just enough remaining flour so dough is no longer sticky.) Place in greased bowl, turning once to grease surface. Cover and let rise in warm place until double in size (about 1 hour). Punch dough down; turn out on lightly floured surface; allow to rest 10 minutes.

2. To shape rolls, roll or pat dough to a 10×8-inch rectangle about ¾ inch thick. Cut in 2½×1-inch strips. Lightly roll each strip and place in a greased 15×10×1-inch baking pan, leaving about ½ inch between each roll. Cover and let rise until nearly double in size (about 30 minutes).

3. Preheat oven to 400°F. Bake 12 to 15 minutes or until rolls are golden and sound hollow when lightly tapped. Remove from pan. Serve warm or cool. Makes 32 rolls.

FROZEN BREAD DOUGH OPTION: Thaw a 1-pound loaf of frozen bread dough. Roll or pat to 10×5-inch rectangle. Cut into 2½×1-inch strips. Lightly roll each strip and place almost touching in a greased 9×9×2-inch pan. Cover and let rise until nearly double in size (about 30 minutes). Preheat oven to 400°F. Bake for 12 to 15 minutes or until golden and rolls sound hollow when lightly tapped. Remove from pan. Serve warm or cool. Makes 20 rolls.

MAKE-AHEAD DIRECTIONS: Prepare through Step 1, above, except do not let dough rise. Cover dough and refrigerate up to 24 hours. Let dough stand in bowl at room temperature for 30 minutes. Continue as directed with Step 2.

 EACH ROLL (BASED ON 32 ROLLS): 63 cal., 1 g fat (0 g sat. fat), 7 mg chol., 78 mg sodium, 11 g carbo., 0 g fiber, 2 g pro. Daily Values: 1% calcium, 4% iron.

Use a pizza cutter to cut the dough into 2½×1-inch strips

Twice-Baked Sweet Potatoes

In 1976, America was celebrating its bicentennial, and we created this recipe that would be right at home on a pilgrim table. There are just six ingredients: sweet potatoes, cranberry relish, dried cranberries, butter, salt, and walnuts.

Twice-Baked Sweet Potatoes
For more sweet potato recipes, see page 235.
PREP: 20 MINUTES **BAKE:** 1 HOUR 40 MINUTES **COOL:** 30 MINUTES

  5 medium sweet potatoes (10 oz. each)
 1/2 cup cranberry relish
 1/2 cup dried cranberries or raisins, snipped or chopped
  2 Tbsp. butter, softened
 1/2 tsp. salt
 1/2 cup walnut pieces, toasted

1. Preheat oven to 325°F. Scrub sweet potatoes and pierce all over with fork. Place on oven rack. Bake for 1 1/4 to 1 1/2 hours or until tender. Set aside to cool slightly.

2. Cut each potato in half lengthwise. Using a spoon, scoop pulp from each potato half, leaving a 1/4- to 1/2-inch shell. Place pulp in medium bowl. Set aside shells.

3. Using a potato masher or fork, mash potato pulp until smooth. Stir in relish, cranberries, butter, and salt. Spoon potato mixture into each potato shell. Place, filled sides up, in a 15×10×1-inch baking pan. Sprinkle with walnut pieces.

4. Bake for 25 to 35 minutes or until heated through. Makes 10 servings.
MAKE-AHEAD DIRECTIONS: Place stuffed potato shells in baking pan. Cover and chill up to 24 hours. To serve, preheat oven to 350°F. Bake, uncovered, for 30 to 35 minutes or until heated through.
EACH POTATO HALF: 158 cal., 6 g fat (2 g sat. fat), 6 mg chol., 174 mg sodium, 25 g carbo., 3 g fiber, 2 g pro. Daily Values: 186% vit. A, 7% vit. C, 3% calcium, 4% iron.

Must-Have Mashed Potatoes

In our 2006 Red Plaid cookbook the focus is on giving cooks the confidence to adapt recipes to suit their families. That includes bringing new flavor to potatoes, such as sour cream and chives (left), pesto, or smoked cheddar and chipotle peppers. For garlic lovers, there's a variation with a 10-clove boost.

Must-Have Mashed Potatoes [KID FRIENDLY]
Try one of the flavor variations, below.
PREP: 15 MINUTES **COOK:** 20 MINUTES

- 1 5-lb. bag baking potatoes (such as russet or Yukon gold), peeled, if desired, and quartered
- 1 Tbsp. salt
- 1/3 cup butter or margarine
- 1/2 tsp. salt
- 1/4 tsp. ground black pepper
- 1/2 to 3/4 cup milk

1. In a 6-quart Dutch oven cook potatoes, covered, in enough boiling water to cover and the 1 tablespoon salt for 20 to 25 minutes or until tender; drain. Mash with potato masher or beat with an electric mixer on low speed. Add butter, the 1/2 teaspoon salt, and the pepper. Season to taste with additional salt and pepper. Gradually beat in enough milk to make mixture light and fluffy. Makes 8 to 10 servings.

TEST KITCHEN TIP: Leftovers make great potato pancakes. Stir an egg and a handful of chopped onion into leftover mashed potatoes; form into patties. In a nonstick skillet fry patties in hot butter or cooking oil over medium heat. Serve with applesauce.

EACH 3/4-CUP SERVING: 140 cal., 4 g fat (3 g sat. fat), 11 mg chol., 325 mg sodium, 22 g carbo., 3 g fiber, 4 g pro. Daily Values: 3% vit. A, 32% vit. C, 2% calcium, 6% iron.

POTATO FLAVOR VARIATIONS
Garlic Add 10 peeled garlic cloves to water while cooking potatoes and substitute 5 tablespoons olive oil for the butter.
Sour Cream and Chive Add one 8-ounce carton dairy sour cream with the butter. Stir 1/4 cup snipped fresh chives into potatoes just before serving. Sprinkle with additional snipped fresh chives.
Pesto Add 1/3 cup purchased pesto along with the butter.
Cheesy Chipotle Stir 1 cup shredded smoked cheddar (4 ounces) and 2 tablespoons finely chopped chipotle peppers in adobo sauce into potatoes just before serving.

You said you wanted Brussels sprouts. Our new version of these tiny cabbage cousins is baked in a pan with everything delicious: onion, garlic, butter, thyme, cream, nutmeg, and Parmesan cheese.

Creamy Brussels Sprouts

Creamy Brussels Sprouts

For a green bean side dish, substitute 2 pounds of trimmed green beans for the Brussels sprouts and reduce the baking time to 15 to 18 minutes.

PREP: 15 MINUTES **COOK:** 12 MINUTES **BAKE:** 20 MINUTES

   Nonstick cooking spray
 1 medium onion, quartered and thinly sliced
 3 cloves garlic, minced
 3 Tbsp. butter
 2 lb. Brussels sprouts, trimmed and halved
 1 tsp. snipped fresh thyme or ¼ tsp. dried thyme, crushed
 ¾ cup reduced-sodium chicken broth
 ¾ cup whipping cream
 ¼ tsp. ground nutmeg
 ½ cup finely shredded Parmesan cheese or Pecorino Romano cheese
 ¼ tsp. salt
 ⅛ tsp. ground black pepper

1. Preheat oven to 350°F. Lightly coat a 1½-quart oval gratin baking dish or baking dish with nonstick cooking spray.

2. In a 12-inch skillet cook onion and garlic in hot butter over medium heat for 3 minutes or until softened. Stir in Brussels sprouts and thyme. Cook for 4 minutes or until onions begin to brown. Add broth. Bring to boiling. Cook, stirring occasionally, for 3 to 4 minutes or until broth is nearly evaporated. Add whipping cream and nutmeg. Cook for 4 minutes or until mixture begins to thicken. Transfer to prepared baking dish. Stir in half of the cheese and all of the salt and pepper. Sprinkle with remaining cheese.

3. Bake, uncovered, 20 to 25 minutes or until Brussels sprouts are tender. Makes 8 to 10 servings.

EACH ⅓-CUP SERVING: 193 cal., 14 g fat (9 g sat. fat), 46 mg chol., 279 mg sodium, 13 g carbo., 5 g fiber, 7 g pro. Daily Values: 27% vit. A, 163% vit. C, 13% calcium, 9% iron.

Trim away any dry or brown leaves from base of sprout.

SIDE DISHES ARE THE REAL STARS OF
THE HOLIDAY FEAST—REMEMBER
YOUR FAVORITES BUT WORK IN
A FEW NEW DISHES TO LET YOUR
CREATIVITY SHOW.

**Old-Fashioned Bread Stuffing
and Gourmet Onions**

This stuffing is quite versatile. The basic recipe—bread cubes, celery, onion, butter, and fresh sage—can be rounded out with apples, mushrooms, chestnuts, or wild rice.

Old-Fashioned Bread Stuffing

Before stuffing the turkey, consider the flavorful additions below. This recipe makes enough for a 15-pound bird.

PREP: 15 MINUTES **BAKE:** 30 MINUTES

1½	cups chopped or sliced celery (3 stalks)
1	cup chopped onion (1 large)
½	cup butter or margarine
1	Tbsp. snipped fresh sage or 1 tsp. poultry seasoning
¼	tsp. black pepper
12	cups dry bread cubes
1	to 1¼ cups* chicken broth
	Sage leaves (optional)

1. Preheat oven to 325°F. In a large skillet cook celery and onion in hot butter over medium heat until tender but not brown. Remove from heat. Stir in sage and pepper. Place bread cubes in large bowl; add onion mixture. Drizzle with enough chicken broth to moisten; toss lightly to combine. Place stuffing in a 2-quart casserole dish. Bake, covered, for 30 to 45 minutes or until heated through. If desired, top with fresh sage. Makes 12 to 14 servings.

*TEST KITCHEN TIP: If stuffing a turkey, reduce broth to ³/₄ to 1 cup. Try a combination of whole wheat, white, and multigrain bread cubes for extra flavor.

EACH ²/₃-CUP SERVING: 181 cal., 10 g fat (5 g sat. fat), 22 mg chol., 342 mg sodium, 20 g carbo., 1 g fiber, 4 g pro. Daily Values: 6% vit. A, 2% vit. C, 5% calcium, 7% iron.

STUFFING ADDITIONS

■ Stir 2 medium cored and chopped apples into bread cubes.

■ Omit 1 cup of the celery and substitute 2 cups sliced mushrooms. Cook mushrooms with the celery in Step 1, above.

■ Stir one 15-ounce can chestnuts, drained and coarsely chopped, into bread cubes.

■ Stir 1 cup cooked wild rice into bread cubes.

Gourmet Onions

This unassuming recipe from our first cookbook has bigger flavor than its short ingredients list suggests. The recipe calls for "boiling onions," which means onions that are 1 to 1¹/₂ inches in diameter.

PREP: 30 MINUTES **COOK:** 15 MINUTES

2	lb. boiling onions, peeled
¼	cup butter
⅓	cup dry sherry or 2 Tbsp. cider vinegar
1	tsp. sugar
¼	tsp. salt
¼	tsp. ground black pepper
⅓	cup finely shredded Parmesan cheese

1. Cook onions in rapidly boiling water for 1 minute; drain and cool slightly. To peel, cut a small X in top of onion. Squeeze from the root end to slip the skin off. Trim away the roots, if necessary.

2. In a large skillet cook onions, covered, in lightly salted boiling water for 10 to 12 minutes or just until tender; drain. Set aside.

3. In same skillet melt butter over medium heat; stir in sherry, sugar, salt, and pepper. Add onions and cook over medium heat about 5 minutes or until onions start to brown and butter mixture is thickened, stirring occasionally. Turn into serving dish; sprinkle with cheese. Makes 8 servings.

TEST KITCHEN TIP: Peel onions up to 24 hours ahead. Place peeled onions in a bowl; cover and refrigerate until needed.

EACH ¹/₄-CUP SERVING: 117 cal., 7 g fat (4 g sat. fat), 18 mg chol., 179 mg sodium, 10 g carbo., 1 g fiber, 2 g pro. Daily Values: 4% vit. A, 9% vit. C, 7% calcium, 2% iron.

A jewel from the November 1955 issue, this recipe calls for twice the amount of spice and an extra egg. It makes a difference! The pie is richer and creamier.

Best Pumpkin Pie

Use the lower amount of spice for a golden, mildly spiced pie. The larger amount yields a more robust flavor.

PREP: 30 MINUTES **BAKE:** 55 MINUTES **CHILL:** 2 HOURS

    1   recipe Pastry for Single-Crust Pie
    1   15-oz. can pumpkin
  3/4   cup sugar
    1   to 1¼ tsp. ground cinnamon
  ½   to 1 tsp. ground ginger
  ½   tsp. salt
  ¼   to ½ tsp. ground nutmeg
  ¼   to ½ tsp. ground cloves
    3   slightly beaten eggs
  1¼   cups milk
    1   recipe Cranberry-Pecan Caramel Topper
        Sweetened whipped cream (optional)

1. Prepare and roll out Pastry for Single-Crust pie. Preheat oven to 375°F.

2. For filling, in a large bowl combine pumpkin, sugar, cinnamon, ginger, salt, nutmeg, and cloves. Add eggs; beat lightly with a fork until combined. Gradually add milk; stir until combined.

3. Carefully pour filling in pastry shell. To prevent overbrowning, cover edge of piecrust with foil. Bake for 30 minutes. Remove foil. Bake about 25 to 30 minutes more or until a knife inserted near center comes out clean. Cool on wire rack. Cover and refrigerate within 2 hours.

4. To serve, top with Cranberry-Pecan Caramel Topper and, if desired, whipped cream. Makes 8 slices.

PASTRY FOR SINGLE-CRUST PIE: In a medium bowl stir together 1¼ cups all-purpose flour and ¼ teaspoon salt. Using a pastry blender cut in ⅓ cup shortening until pieces are pea size. Sprinkle 1 tablespoon cold water over part of the flour mixture; gently toss with a fork. Push moistened dough to side of the bowl. Repeat moistening flour mixture, using 1 tablespoon of cold water at a time (using a total of 4 to 5 tablespoons water), until all flour mixture is moistened. Form dough in ball. On lightly floured surface, use hands to slightly flatten dough. Roll dough from center to edges into a circle about 12 inches in diameter. To transfer pastry, wrap it around rolling pin. Unroll pastry into a 9-inch pie plate. Ease pastry into plate without stretching it. Trim pastry to 1 inch beyond edge of pie plate. Fold under extra pastry. Crimp and form a high edge to keep filling from bubbling over. Do not prick pastry.

MAKE-AHEAD DIRECTIONS: Prepare pie as directed up to 2 days before serving; cover and refrigerate.

EACH SLICE: 283 cal., 12 g fat (3 g sat. fat), 82 mg chol., 263 mg sodium, 40 g carbo., 2 g fiber, 6 g pro. Daily Values: 169% vit. A, 4% vit. C, 8% calcium, 12% iron.

Cranberry-Pecan Caramel Topper

This quick sauce is also wonderful served on ice cream.

START TO FINISH: 20 MINUTES

  ⅓   cup dried cranberries
    3   Tbsp. brandy or apple juice
  1½   cups pecan halves, toasted
  ¼   cup caramel-flavored ice cream topping

1. In a medium bowl combine cranberries and brandy. Let stand for 15 minutes. Add pecan halves and ice cream topping. Toss to coat.

2. Serve immediately or cover and store in refrigerator up to 1 week. Bring to room temperature before serving. Makes eight 3-tablespoon servings.

TEST KITCHEN TIP: To toast pecans, spread nuts in single layer in shallow baking pan. Bake in a 350°F oven for 7 to 10 minutes or until nuts are light golden brown. Because pecans are already brown in color, it helps to break a nut or two in half to check for the change in color.

EACH 3-TABLESPOON SERVING: 195 cal., 15 g fat (1 g sat. fat), 0 mg chol., 36 mg sodium, 14 g carbo., 2 g fiber, 2 g pro. Daily Values: 2% calcium, 3% iron.

Crimp pastry between index fingers and thumb to form fluted edge.

Mini Sweet Potato Pies
page 226

**Best Pumpkin Pie with Cranberry-Pecan
Caramel Topper**

Gingersnap Crumble Pumpkin Parfaits
page 226

Combine a can of pumpkin with vanilla ice cream, a dash of spice, and little brown sugar for a cool after-dinner companion. These parfaits from the November 1955 magazine have easy prep and pure flavors—hallmarks of a classic.

Created especially for this holiday, these miniature pies bring together sweet potato pie—a favorite from the 1996 Red Plaid—with a billowy meringue top that's been part of the Better Homes and Gardens® recipe repertoire since the first book.

Gingersnap Crumble Pumpkin Parfaits
To make leaf pastry cutouts like the one in the photo on page 225, see tip, below.
PREP: 30 MINUTES **FREEZE:** 4 HOURS 20 MINUTES

1   recipe Gingersnap Crumble
1   quart vanilla ice cream
1   15-oz. can pumpkin
2   Tbsp. packed brown sugar
1½ tsp. pumpkin pie spice
½   tsp. salt
1   cup whipping cream, whipped
     Pumpkin pie spice (optional)

1. Prepare Gingersnap Crumble. Set aside.
2. Place ice cream in refrigerator for 20 to 30 minutes or just until softened. In a large bowl combine pumpkin, brown sugar, pumpkin pie spice, and salt. Stir ice cream to soften; fold into pumpkin mixture. Cover and freeze 20 minutes or until pumpkin mixture holds its shape when heaped with a spoon.
3. Spoon ice cream into parfait glasses; sprinkle with Gingersnap Crumble. Cover and freeze until firm (4 to 48 hours).
4. Before serving, top with whipped cream. If desired, sprinkle with additional pumpkin pie spice. Makes 10 servings.
GINGERSNAP CRUMBLE: In a small bowl stir together 1½ cups crushed gingersnaps (about 30 gingersnaps) and ¼ cup melted butter. Stir just until crumbs are coated.
TEST KITCHEN TIP: To make leaf-shape pastry cutouts, let half of a 15-ounce package of rolled refrigerated unbaked piecrust stand at room temperature according to package directions. Preheat oven to 350°F. Unroll piecrust on a lightly floured surface. Cut pastry using leaf-shape cookie cutter. Place shapes on ungreased baking sheet. If desired, brush lightly with beaten egg white. Bake 10 to 12 minutes or until golden. Cool on a wire rack. Use to garnish Gingersnap Crumble Pumpkin Parfaits.
EACH ¼-CUP SERVING: 358 cal., 25 g fat (15 g sat. fat), 100 mg chol., 294 mg sodium, 31 g carbo., 2 g fiber, 5 g pro. Daily Values: 150% vit. A, 3% vit. C, 11% calcium, 10% iron.

Mini Sweet Potato Pies
No double boiler? Use a saucepan and a heatproof bowl that fits inside the rim of the pan but doesn't touch the water.
PREP: 30 MINUTES **BAKE:** 35 MINUTES **BROIL:** 1 MINUTE

12   purchased graham cracker crumb tart shells (two 4-oz. pkg.)
1   egg white, lightly beaten
1   teaspoon water
2   23-oz. cans sweet potatoes, drained
⅔   cup whipping cream
¼   cup pure maple syrup
3   egg yolks
2   tsp. pumpkin pie spice
1   cup granulated sugar
4   egg whites
1   tsp. vanilla
⅛   tsp. salt

1. Preheat oven to 375°F. Place tart shells in a 15X10X1-inch baking pan. In a small bowl combine egg white and water. Brush beaten egg white over crusts. Bake for 5 minutes; set aside to cool.
2. For filling, in a large bowl combine sweet potatoes and whipping cream; mash and stir until smooth. Stir in maple syrup, egg yolks, and pumpkin pie spice. Spoon filling evenly in tart shells. Bake for 30 minutes. Cool on a wire rack for 2 hours.
3. Once pies are cooled, preheat broiler. For meringue, in top of double boiler combine sugar, the 4 egg whites, the vanilla, and salt. Beat with electric mixer on low speed for 30 seconds. Place over boiling water (upper pan must not touch water). Cook, beating constantly with electric mixer on high speed, for 8 to 10 minutes or until mixture is fluffy, holds soft peaks, and reaches 160°F on instant-read thermometer. Remove from heat. Beat 30 seconds more, scraping sides and bottom of pan.
4. Mound meringue mixture on baked pies, forming peaks. Broil 5 to 6 inches from heat for 1 to 2 minutes or until tops are lightly browned. Cool on wire rack for 10 minutes before serving. To store, cover with plastic wrap and chill. Makes 12 mini pies.
EACH MINI PIE: 334 cal., 11 g fat (4 g sat. fat), 69 mg chol., 231 mg sodium, 53 g carbo., 2 g fiber, 6 g pro. Daily Values: 120% vit. A, 6% vit. C, 4% calcium, 8% iron.

Turkey Frame Soup

Next-Day Turkey Panini

Any parsley or sage leaves left over from preparing stuffing make a flavorful addition to this grilled sandwich.

PREP: 20 MINUTES **COOK:** 6 MINUTES

- 4 soft French or sourdough rolls
  Olive oil
- ¼ to ½ cup cranberry relish or chutney
  Fresh baby spinach leaves, flat-leaf parsley, or fresh sage leaves
- 8 oz. sliced cooked (leftover) turkey
- 2 oz. thinly sliced country ham or prosciutto
- 8 oz. sliced smoked cheese, such as mozzarella, provolone, or cheddar

1. Split rolls horizontally. Lightly brush cut sides of rolls with olive oil. Spread 1 to 2 tablespoons cranberry relish on bottom halves of rolls. Layer the rolls with spinach, turkey, ham, and cheese. Place tops of rolls on filling.

2. Preheat covered indoor grill. Place sandwiches in grill. Cover and cook for 6 minutes or until cheese is melted and rolls are crisp. Makes 4 servings.

TEST KITCHEN TIP: If you don't have an indoor grill, heat a large heavy nonstick skillet over medium heat. Place sandwiches in skillet; weigh down top of sandwiches with a large heavy skillet. Cook for 3 to 4 minutes on each side or until cheese is melted and rolls are crisp.

EACH SERVING: 532 cal., 20 g fat (9 g sat. fat), 95 mg chol., 1,056 mg sodium, 48 g carbo., 3 g fiber, 38 g pro. Daily Values: 36% vit. A, 13% vit. C, 32% calcium, 22% iron.

Turkey Frame Soup

PREP: 30 MINUTES **COOK:** 1¾ HOURS

- 1 meaty turkey frame
- 4 cups water
- 4 cups turkey or chicken broth
- 1 large onion, quartered
- 1 clove garlic, crushed
- ½ tsp. salt
  Chopped cooked (leftover) turkey
- ¼ cups oil-packed sun-dried tomatoes, drained, cut into strips
- 1½ tsp. dried Italian seasoning
- ¼ tsp. ground black pepper
- 3 cups sliced or cubed vegetables, such as carrots, parsnips, or turnips
- 1½ cups high-fiber or whole wheat pasta, such as rotini or penne
- 1 15-oz. can Great Northern beans or white kidney beans, rinsed and drained
  Grated Parmesan cheese

1. Break turkey frame or cut in half with kitchen shears. Place in a large stockpot. Add water, broth, onion, garlic, and salt. Bring to boiling; reduce heat. Simmer, covered, for 1½ hours.

2. Remove turkey frame. Cool; cut meat off bones; coarsely chop meat. Add enough turkey to equal 2 cups. Set aside. Discard bones. Strain broth; skim off fat.

3. Return broth to pot. Stir in tomatoes, Italian seasoning, and pepper. Stir in vegetables. Return to boiling; reduce heat. Simmer, covered, for 5 minutes. Add pasta. Simmer, uncovered, for 8 to 10 minutes or until pasta is tender and still firm and vegetables are tender. Stir in turkey and beans; heat through. Serve with grated Parmesan cheese. Makes 6 main-dish servings.

LOW FAT **EACH 1¾-CUP SERVING:** 303 cal., 4 g fat (1 g sat. fat), 4 mg chol., 965 mg sodium, 42 g carbo., 8 g fiber, 26 g pro. Daily Values: 68% vit. A, 26% vit. C, 10% calcium, 20% iron.

Next-Day Turkey Panini

Easy Holiday Baking

WANT TO CREATE MOUTHWATERING HOLIDAY DESSERTS WITHOUT SPENDING ALL DAY IN THE KITCHEN? HERE'S A STEP-BY-STEP GUIDE TO MAKE THESE TEMPTING TREATS.

BY **MAGGIE MEYER** PHOTOGRAPHS BY **JAMES CARRIER** RECIPES BY **EMILY LUCHETTI** FOOD STYLING BY **POUKÉ** PROP STYLING BY **SHAZ ARASNIA**

Chocolate Harvest Cake
Simple-to-make pumpkin filling and super chocolate glaze make this moist and easy one-bowl cake a perfect fit for the holidays.

Ingredients for Chocolate Harvest Cake

See photo on front cover.

ONE-BOWL CAKE:
- 1 cup buttermilk
- 1 cup water
- 2/3 cup cooking oil
- 2 cups sugar
- 2 eggs
- 1 tsp. baking soda
- 1/2 tsp. salt
- 2 cups all-purpose flour
- 3/4 cup unsweetened cocoa powder

PUMPKIN CREAM FILLING:
- 1 8-oz. pkg. cream cheese, softened
- 1/3 cup canned pumpkin
- 1/4 cup sugar
- 1/4 tsp. ground cinnamon

CHOCOLATE GLAZE:
- 1/2 cup whipping cream
- 4 oz. semisweet chocolate, chopped

CAKE TOPPERS:
- Seedless red grapes, whole blackberries or raspberries, toasted hazelnuts, or shredded orange peel

> ❝ I made this cake again and again for these photos. It was so easy—10 minutes from start to the oven. The trick is to use a large enough bowl so the batter doesn't spill over when whisking. ❞
>
> COLLEEN WEEDEN, TEST KITCHEN HOME ECONOMIST

PREPARE OVEN AND PANS Preheat oven to 350°F. Grease and flour two 9×1½-inch round baking pans; set aside.

COMBINE INGREDIENTS In an large bowl combine buttermilk, water, oil, sugar, eggs, baking soda, and salt. Whisk until well combined. Add flour and cocoa powder; whisk vigorously until smooth. Divide batter between prepared pans.

DO THE TOUCH TEST Bake for 30 to 35 minutes until top springs back when lightly touched in center. Cool in pans on a wire rack for 10 minutes. Remove from pans and cool completely.

PREPARE PUMPKIN CREAM FILLING In a medium bowl whisk together cream cheese, pumpkin, sugar, and cinnamon until combined. Place one cake layer on plate. Spread filling over top. Top with second cake layer.

MAKE CHOCOLATE GLAZE In a saucepan bring whipping cream just to boiling over medium-high heat. Remove from heat. Add chocolate (do not stir). Let stand 5 minutes. Stir until smooth. Cool 15 minutes or until slightly thickened. Pour over cake, allowing glaze to drip down sides. Chill until set, about 30 minutes. Top with desired toppers. Makes 14 slices.

EACH SLICE: 431 cal., 23 g fat (8 g sat. fat), 60 mg chol., 254 mg sodium, 53 g carbo., 1 g fiber, 6 g pro. Daily Values: 26% vit. A, 1% vit. C, 10% calcium, 11% iron.

Banana Muffin Trifles

These delightful trifles are yummy and easy to make.
Pressed for time? Use banana muffins from the bakery
and purchased pudding.

Ingredients for Banana Muffin Trifles

BANANA MUFFINS:

- ¼ cup all-purpose flour
- ¼ cup granulated sugar
- 2 Tbsp. butter
- ⅓ cup chopped pecans
- 2 cups all-purpose flour
- ½ cup granulated sugar
- ⅓ cup packed brown sugar
- 1½ tsp. baking soda
- ½ tsp. ground cinnamon
- ¼ tsp. salt
- ½ cup butter
- 2 bananas, mashed (1 cup)
- 1 egg, beaten
- ⅓ cup milk

COCONUT PUDDING:

- 6 Tbsp. sugar
- ¼ cup cornstarch
- 1½ cups milk
- 6 egg yolks
- ¾ cup toasted coconut
- ½ tsp. vanilla
- ½ cup pineapple bits
  Toasted Coconut Curls
  (page 97)

1. Preheat oven to 375° F. Grease twelve 2½-inch muffin cups.

2. In a bowl stir together ¼ cup flour and ¼ cup sugar. Cut in 2 tablespoons butter until mixture resembles coarse crumbs. Stir in pecans; set aside.

3. To make muffins, in a large bowl, stir together remaining dry ingredients. Cut in ½ cup butter until mixture resembles crumbs.

4. Whisk together bananas, egg, and milk. Add banana mixture to flour mixture. Stir until moistened.

5. Spoon batter into cups until two-thirds full. Sprinkle with topping. Bake 18 to 20 minutes or until a pick inserted comes out clean. Cool in cups on rack 5 minutes. Remove; coo completely. Use in trifles. Makes 12 muffins.

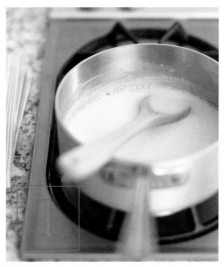

PREPARE COCONUT PUDDING In a medium saucepan combine sugar and cornstarch. Stir in milk. Cook and stir over medium heat until thickened and bubbly. Cook and stir 2 minutes more, whisking constantly. Remove from heat.

WHISK AND POUR In a mixing bowl whisk 1 cup milk mixture into 6 egg yolks. Add egg mixture to milk mixture in pan. Bring just to gentle boiling; reduce heat. Cook and stir 2 minutes more, whisking constantly. Remove from heat. Stir in toasted coconut and vanilla.

COVER PUDDING Pour pudding into bowl. Cover pudding surface with plastic wrap. Chill for about 1 hour or until cooled.

ASSEMBLE TRIFLES Vertically slice 8 Banana Muffins (save remaining muffins for another use) in three pieces. Place 1 tablespoon pudding in each serving bowl. Arrange sliced muffins on pudding in each bowl.

ADD PUDDING Spoon 1 tablespoon pineapple bits and 2 tablespoons pudding between each muffin slice. Serve immediately or cover and refrigerate up to 1 hour. Top with additional toasted coconut. Makes 8 servings.

EACH SERVING: 433 cal., 19 g fat (11 g sat. fat), 201 mg chol., 315 mg sodium, 60 g carbo., 2 g fiber, 8 g pro. Daily Values: 13% vit. A, 21% vit. C, 11% calcium, 11% iron.

Dried Fruit Tea Cakes

Chock-full of dried fruit and drizzled with a
bourbon glaze, these cakes are just right for
nibbling with a cup of tea.

Ingredients for Dried Fruit Tea Cakes

- 1 cup golden raisins
- 1 cup dried cranberries or tart dried cherries
- ½ cup bourbon or apple cider
- Nonstick cooking spray
- 1¾ cups all-purpose flour
- 1½ tsp. baking powder
- ¼ tsp. salt
- ⅔ cup butter, softened
- 1 cup sugar
- 2 eggs
- ⅔ cup milk
- 1 recipe Bourbon Drizzle
- Candied orange peel (optional)

BOURBON DRIZZLE:

Measure reserved soaking liquid; add water to equal ½ cup. In a small saucepan combine 1 teaspoon sugar and ½ teaspoon cornstarch; add liquid. Cook and stir until thickened and bubbly; cook and stir 2 minutes more. Cool 10 minutes; spoon over cakes. Makes about ⅔ cup.

> "When adding wet and dry ingredients, always start and end with the dry ingredients. Remember to check the date on the bottom of the baking powder can. Baking powder does eventually get old and lose its rising ability."
>
> MARYELLYN KRANTZ, TEST KITCHEN HOME ECONOMIST

PREPARE DRIED FRUIT In a bowl combine fruit and bourbon. Cover; let stand 1 hour. Drain fruit, reserving liquid for Bourbon Drizzle (left). Preheat oven to 350°F. Lightly coat pan(s) with cooking spray (see chart, below).

MIX DRY INGREDIENTS In a medium mixing bowl stir together flour, baking powder, and salt. In a large mixing bowl beat butter 30 seconds with electric mixer on medium to high speed. Add sugar and beat until fluffy.

COMBINE WET AND DRY INGREDIENTS Add eggs, one at a time, to butter mixture, beating well after each addition. Alternately add the dry ingredients and milk to butter mixture, beating well after each addition. Stir in drained fruit.

BAKE CAKES Spread batter in prepared pans. Bake until pick inserted in center comes out clean, about 18 minutes for mini loaf pans. Cool in pans 10 minutes; remove. If desired, spoon on Bourbon Drizzle. Top with candied orange peel. Cool on wire rack. Makes 13 mini loaves.

EACH SERVING (½ MINI LOAF): 179 cal., 6 g fat (3 g sat. fat), 32 mg chol., 87 mg sodium, 25 g carbo., 1 g fiber, 2 g pro. Daily Values: 4% vit. A, 2% calcium, 4% iron.

CHOOSE YOUR PAN

Lightly coat with nonstick cooking spray or grease and flour the bottom and ½ inch up sides of loaf pans or muffin cups.

PAN SIZE	BATTER AMOUNT	TIME	YIELD
3¼×2¼×1¼-inch	⅓ cup	18 to 20 min.	13
4½×2½×1½-inch	½ cup	18 to 20 min.	9
9×5×3-inch	Entire recipe	1 hour	1
2½-inch muffin cups	3 Tbsp.	15 min.	24

Sweet Potato Casseroles

These casseroles are as essential to Thanksgiving dinner as turkey and stuffing. Add surprising flavor to this classic with already-on-hand ingredients.

BY **STEPHEN EXEL** PHOTOGRAPHS BY **GREG SCHEIDEMANN**

PINEAPPLE AND BLUE CHEESE
Top New Sweet Potato Casserole with 1 cup pineapple chunks and ½ cup blue cheese crumbles.

New Sweet Potato Casserole

Serve this dish as is or as a starting point for your own creation.
PREP: 35 MINUTES
COOK: 25 MINUTES
BAKE: 30 MINUTES

- 4 lb. sweet potatoes, peeled and cut into quarters
- 1 cup packed brown sugar
- ½ cup butter, cut up
- ¼ cup milk
- 4 eggs, lightly beaten
- 3 to 4 Tbsp. lemon juice
  Stir-ins and/or Toppers (right)

1. In a Dutch oven cook potatoes, covered, in enough boiling salted water to cover for 25 to 30 minutes or until tender; drain and return to pan.

2. Preheat oven to 350°F. Slightly mash potatoes with a potato masher. Stir in sugar, butter, milk, eggs, lemon juice, and, if desired, one of the stir-ins; stir until well combined. Transfer sweet potato mixture to a greased 3-quart rectangular baking dish. If desired, top with one of the toppings.

3. Bake, uncovered, for 30 to 35 minutes or until heated through. Makes 8 to 12 servings.

EACH SERVING: 377 cal., 15 g fat (7 g sat. fat), 139 mg chol., 156 mg sodium, 57 g carbo., 5 g fiber, 6 g pro. Daily Values: 414% vit. A, 51% vit. C, 10% calcium, 11% iron.

MIX-AND-MATCH SWEET POTATO CASSEROLES

Suit your taste. Choose a stir-in, choose a topper—they all work together or any one can be used alone.

Stir-Ins

PEANUT BUTTER
For creaminess, add ½ cup.

ORANGE PEEL
For tart flavor, add 2 tablespoons.

RED CURRY PASTE
Add spice and heat with 2 to 4 teaspoons.

PUMPKIN OR APPLE PIE SPICE
For harvest flavor, add 4 teaspoons spice plus 1 teaspoon ground black pepper.

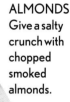

Toppers

PEANUTS AND COCONUT
Impart Far-Eastern flair with shredded coconut and chopped peanuts.

BACON AND ROSEMARY
Add smoky depth with crumbled cooked bacon tossed with snipped fresh rosemary.

ONION AND GARLIC
For earthy flavor, top with sauteed thinly sliced onion and garlic.

ALMONDS
Give a salty crunch with chopped smoked almonds.

I YAM WHAT I YAM

While sweet potatoes and yams look and taste similar, they have minor differences.

Two varieties of sweet potatoes are generally available: The familiar orange-flesh variety, and yellow-fleshed sweet potatoes that are actually not sweet are similar to white baking potatoes. Sweet potatoes are high in vitamins A and C.

Yams, on the other hand, are native to South and Central America and rarely make their way to the United States. They are similar in size and shape to sweet potatoes, and because canned sweet potatoes are erroneously labeled "yams," they are

often confused. Yams contain more natural sugar than sweet potatoes but have less vitamins A and C. If you come across true yams, they can be substituted for sweet potatoes in most recipes.

Wilted Salad Suppers

Wilted salads are greens with a warm dressing poured over. After Thanksgiving, they are a welcome change of pace.

BY **STEPHEN EXEL** PHOTOGRAPHS BY **GREG SCHEIDEMANN**

Waldorf Wilted Salad

Waldorf Wilted Salad

Bok choy substitutes for celery in this take on Waldorf salad. It has a mild flavor and substantial crunch.

START TO FINISH: 25 MINUTES

10	cups mesclun or field greens
3	cups bok choy stems cut in ½-inch pieces
½	cup walnuts, toasted and coarsely chopped
⅓	cup olive oil
⅓	cup rice vinegar
2	Tbsp. chopped shallot
1	Tbsp. Dijon-style mustard
1	tsp. sugar
⅛	tsp. *each* salt and freshly ground pepper
3	Granny Smith apples, cored, cut in wedges
3	hard cooked eggs, cut in wedges

1. In a large bowl toss greens, bok choy, and nuts. Set aside.

2. For dressing, in a small saucepan combine oil, vinegar, shallot, mustard, sugar, salt, and pepper. Bring to boiling; remove from heat. Carefully pour warm dressing over salad; toss lightly. Cover bowl with a large dinner plate for 1 to 2 minutes or just until greens begin to wilt. Remove plate. Add apples and eggs; toss lightly. Serve immediately. Makes 6 servings.

EACH SERVING: 276 cal., 21 g fat (3 g sat. fat), 106 mg chol., 174 mg sodium, 17 g carbo., 4 g fiber, 7 g pro. Daily Values: 37% vit. C, 8% calcium, 9% iron.

Grilled Chicken Wilted Salad

START TO FINISH: 30 MINUTES

- 1 lb. chicken tenderloins
- 1 medium onion, cut in thin wedges
- 3 Tbsp. olive oil
- 1 Tbsp. snipped fresh rosemary or
  ½ tsp. dried rosemary, crushed
- ¾ tsp. coarsely ground black pepper
- ½ tsp. salt
- ¼ cup cranberry or pomegranate juice
- 2 Tbsp. red wine vinegar
- 2 6-oz. pkgs. baby spinach leaves
- ¼ cup sliced, pitted kalamata olives
- ¼ cup pine nuts or slivered almonds, toasted

1. Heat indoor electric grill or grill pan over medium heat. In a bowl combine chicken and onions. Toss with 2 tablespoons of the olive oil, rosemary, and ¼ teaspoon *each* pepper and salt. Grill chicken and onions on grill rack or in grill pan for 10 minutes or until chicken is no longer pink, internal temperature reaches 170°F, and onions are tender, turning once.

2. Meanwhile, for dressing, in a saucepan combine juice, vinegar, and remaining olive oil, pepper, and salt. Bring juice mixture just to boiling; remove from heat. Place spinach, olives, pine nuts, chicken, and onions in an extra-large salad bowl; toss to combine. Pour warm dressing over salad mixture. Toss lightly. Cover salad with a large plate for 1 to 2 minutes or just until spinach is wilted. Remove plate. Serve immediately. Makes 6 servings.

EACH SERVING: 211 cal., 12 g fat (2 g sat. fat), 44 mg chol., 342 mg sodium, 7 g carbo., 2 g fiber, 21 g pro. Daily Values: 31% vit. C, 7% calcium, 16% iron.

Grilled Chicken Wilted Salad

WILTING GREENS

Gently pour warm dressing over salad ingredients.

Cover salad bowl with a dinner plate for 1 to 2 minutes until greens slightly wilt.

Scallops-Pecan Wilted Salad

Scallops-Pecan Wilted Salad

PREP: 15 MINUTES   **COOK:** 5 MINUTES

1½	lb. fresh or frozen sea scallops
½	cup pecan halves
	Salt and ground black pepper
2	Tbsp. olive oil
1	Tbsp. sesame seeds
6	cups arugula
4	medium heads endive, leaves separated and sliced crosswise (3½ to 4 cups)
½	cup maple syrup
⅓	cup reduced-sodium soy sauce
¼	tsp. cayenne pepper

1. Thaw scallops, if frozen. Halve scallops horizontally (about ½ inch thick). Rinse scallops; pat dry.

2. In a dry skillet cook and stir pecans over medium-high heat for 3 to 4 minutes or until toasted. Transfer pecans to bowl; set aside.

3. Season scallops with salt and black pepper. In the same skillet cook scallops in hot oil over medium-high heat just until golden brown, about 1 to 2 minutes per side. Transfer scallops to bowl with pecans; sprinkle with sesame seeds. Cover; keep warm.

4. In a bowl toss together arugula and endive. For dressing, in a saucepan combine syrup, soy sauce, and cayenne pepper. Bring to boiling; remove from heat. Toss greens with three-quarters of the warm dressing. Cover with plate for 30 to 60 seconds or until arugula begins to wilt. Toss remainder of dressing with scallop mixture. Divide greens among 4 plates; top with scallop mixture. Makes 4 servings.

EACH SERVING: 449 cal., 19 g fat (2 g sat. fat), 56 mg chol., 1,153 mg sodium, 37 g carbo., 2 g fiber, 33 g pro. Daily Values: 18% vit. A, 24% vit. C, 16% calcium, 14% iron.

Holiday Sangrias

Why wait for summer? These cool-weather-inspired punches liven up appetizers, desserts, even dinner.

BY **STEPHEN EXEL** PHOTOGRAPH BY **GREG SCHEIDEMANN**

Orange and Mint Sangria

Add whole kumquats on skewers to this slightly sweet accompaniment to desserts and cookies.
PREP: 10 MINUTES **CHILL:** 2 HOURS

  2 blood oranges or oranges, sliced
  8 to 12 kumquats, halved
  3 Tbsp. powdered sugar
 1/4 cup triple sec or orange-flavor
     liqueur
 1/2 cup fresh mint leaves
  1 750 ml bottle Sauvignon Blanc
  1 8 oz. bottle club soda, chilled

1. In a pitcher combine orange slices and kumquats. Add sugar and toss. Add triple sec and mint leaves; toss. Add wine; stir. Refrigerate up to 2 hours. To serve, add club soda; stir gently. Makes 6 servings.
EACH SERVING: 185 cal., 11 mg sodium, 19 g carbo., 3 g fiber, 1 g pro. Daily Values: 3% vit. A, 65% vit. C, 4% calcium, 8% iron.

Winter Fruit Sangria

To serve with a pork or turkey dinner, omit the club soda and warm slightly.
PREP: 15 MINUTES **CHILL:** UP TO 24 HOURS

  6 dried Calimyrna (light) figs, sliced
  6 dried apricots, cut in slivers
 1/2 cup *each* dried cranberries and raisins
 1/4 cup brandy
  2 Tbsp. honey
  1 750 ml bottle Rioja or Merlot
  1 10 oz. bottle club soda, chilled

1. In a saucepan stir together the dried fruits, brandy, and honey. Cook over medium-low heat until simmering. Remove from heat; cool slightly. Add wine; stir. Refrigerate up to 24 hours. To serve, strain sangria into a pitcher. Add *ice cubes* and club soda; stir gently. Makes 8 servings.
EACH SERVING: 208 cal., 8 g sodium, 32 g carbo., 3 g fiber, 1 g pro. Daily Values: 2% vit. A, 1% vit. C, 4% calcium, 6% iron.

Sparkling Sangria

This savory sangria matches well with Asian-style nibbles or smoked salmon.
PREP: 25 MINUTES **CHILL:** 2 HOURS

  1 large English (seedless) cucumber,
     thinly bias-sliced (3 1/2 cups)
  1 4- to 6-inch piece fresh ginger,
     peeled and thinly sliced
  6 large radishes, thinly sliced (1 cup)
  1 cup grapefruit juice
  1 750 ml bottle brut (dry) Champagne
     or sparkling wine, chilled

1. In a large pitcher combine cucumber, ginger, and radishes. Add grapefruit juice. Cover; chill for 2 to 24 hours. To serve, add *ice cubes* to pitcher. Add Champagne and stir gently. Makes 6 servings.
EACH SERVING: 115 cal., 3 mg sodium, 9 g carbo., 1 g pro. Daily Values: 2% vit. A, 30% vit. C, 1% calcium, 1% iron.

DECEMBER

THERE'S NO BETTER TIME THAN THE HOLIDAYS TO INDULGE IN SENSATIONAL FOOD! FROM SAVORY BEEF TENDERLOIN TO SWEET BUTTER CAKES, THIS MENU IS A SPLENDID WAY TO DO JUST THAT.

Rosemary Beef Tenderloin
page 244

On the Table in a Twinkling

Lemony Green Beans
page 249

**Pecan Cakes with
Raspberry-Cranberry Sauce**
pages 250–251

Jeweled Spaghetti Squash
page 248

Herbed Shrimp and Tomatoes
page 244

On the Table in a Twinkling

WHAT MAKES THIS
FEAST SO SPECIAL?
IT'S DELICIOUS,
GORGEOUS, AND
BRIMMING WITH
FESTIVE FLAVORS!

Basil Dipping Sauce

PREP: 10 MINUTES `FAST!`

- 1 cup mayonnaise
- 1 Tbsp. snipped fresh basil
- 2 cloves garlic, minced
- 1 tsp. lemon juice
- 1 tsp. Dijon-style mustard
- ⅛ tsp. cayenne pepper

1. In a small bowl combine mayonnaise, basil, garlic, lemon juice, mustard, and cayenne pepper. Cover and chill. Serve with Herbed Shrimp and Tomatoes. Makes 16 (1-tablespoon) servings.

MAKE-AHEAD DIRECTIONS: The dipping sauce can made and chilled up to 3 days before serving.

TEST KITCHEN TIP: Use any leftover dipping sauce as a sandwich spread.

EACH TABLESPOON: 100 cal., 11 g fat (2 g sat. fat), 5 mg chol., 86 mg sodium, 1 g carbo., 0 g fiber, 0 g pro. Daily Values: 1% vit. A, 1% vit. C.

Menu

HERBED SHRIMP AND TOMATOES

CHRISTMAS POTATO SOUP

LEMONY GREEN BEANS

ROSEMARY BEEF TENDERLOIN

JEWELED SPAGHETTI SQUASH

PECAN CAKES
RASPBERRY-CRANBERRY SAUCE

T HE NO-FUSS FEAST

From appetizer to dessert, this plan gives you all you need to prepare and serve a dazzling and delicious feast—start to finish.

UP TO ONE MONTH AHEAD:
Bake Pecan Cakes. Wrap and freeze until feast day.

3 DAYS AHEAD:
Prepare Christmas Potato Soup. Toss together Onion-Grape Marmalade for Toasted Stars. Stir together Raspberry-Cranberry Sauce for Pecan Cakes. Wrap and store all in the refrigerator.

1 DAY BEFORE:
Toss together Basil Dipping Sauce for Herbed Shrimp and Tomatoes. Choose serving bowls and platters.

THE NIGHT BEFORE CHRISTMAS:
Stir together the Dijon rub for the Rosemary Beef Tenderloin. Peel and devein shrimp for Herbed Shrimp and Tomatoes. Cover and chill. Set the feast table.

ON CHRISTMAS DAY
2 HOURS AHEAD:
Cook, cover, and chill green beans for Lemony Green Beans. Uncover soup. Transfer to slow cooker. Reheat on high-heat setting. Microwave spaghetti squash for Jeweled Spaghetti Squash. Cover and set aside.

1 HOUR AHEAD:
Remove Pecan Cakes from freezer; let thaw. Arrange on serving platter. Remove Raspberry-Cranberry Sauce from refrigerator; transfer to a serving bowl. Scrape cooked spaghetti squash into a large bowl. Roast Rosemary Beef Tenderloin. Toast bread stars for Christmas Potato Soup. Top with Onion-Grape Marmalade.

30 MINUTES AHEAD:
Finish Lemony Green Beans. Transfer to a serving bowl. Cover; keep warm. Remove tenderloin from oven; let rest 15 minutes. Meanwhile, finish Jeweled Spaghetti Squash. Slice tenderloin. Tuck in cheese and garnish platter. Serve dinner and make a toast to all!

Herbed Shrimp and Tomatoes

PREP: 20 MINUTES   **CHILL:** 10 MINUTES   **COOK:** 4 MINUTES

- 2 lb. fresh or frozen jumbo shrimp (40 to 42 shrimp)
- 2 Tbsp. snipped fresh basil and/or oregano
- 1 Tbsp. fresh lemon juice
- ¾ tsp. salt
- ¼ tsp. ground black pepper
- 2 Tbsp. extra virgin olive oil
- 2 cups grape tomatoes
- 1 recipe Basil Dipping Sauce (page 243) (optional)

1. Thaw shrimp, if frozen. Peel and devein shrimp, removing tails. Rinse shrimp; pat dry with paper towels. Set aside. In a large bowl combine basil and/or oregano, lemon juice, salt, and pepper. Add shrimp. Toss to coat. Cover and chill 10 to 30 minutes.

2. In a large skillet cook the shrimp, half at a time, in the hot olive oil over medium-high heat for 2 to 3 minutes or until shrimp are opaque, stirring often to cook evenly. Transfer shrimp to a platter. Add tomatoes to the shrimp and toss to combine. If desired, serve with Basil Dipping Sauce, *lemon wedges,* and additional *basil* and/or *oregano.* Serve warm. Makes 8 servings.

MAKE-AHEAD DIRECTIONS: This dish is also great served chilled. Cover and chill cooked shrimp mixture up to 4 hours before serving.

EACH SERVING: 162 cal., 5 g fat (1 g sat. fat), 172 mg chol., 389 mg sodium, 4 g carbo., 1 g fiber, 24 g pro. Daily Values: 13% vit. A, 32% vit. C, 7% calcium, 17% iron.

Herbed Shrimp and Tomatoes

Rosemary Beef Tenderloin

PREP: 15 MINUTES   **ROAST:** 35 MINUTES   **STAND:** 15 MINUTES

- 2 Tbsp. Dijon-style mustard
- 1 Tbsp. extra virgin olive oil
- 1 Tbsp. snipped fresh rosemary
- 3 cloves garlic, minced
- ¾ tsp. salt
- ¼ tsp. ground black pepper
- 1 2½- to 3-lb. center-cut beef tenderloin roast or boneless pork top loin roast
- 1 4- to 6-oz. log garlic and herb goat cheese (chèvre), cut crosswise into 8 slices, or ½ of an 8-oz. tub cream cheese spread with chive and onion
   Snipped fresh rosemary

1. In a bowl combine mustard, oil, rosemary, garlic, salt, and pepper. Spread on top of tenderloin or pork roast. Place meat on a rack in a shallow roasting pan.

2. To roast the beef tenderloin, preheat oven to 425°F. For medium rare, roast, uncovered, for 35 to 40 minutes or until the internal temperature reaches 135°F on an instant-read thermometer. Cover and let stand for 15 minutes. The temperature of the meat after standing should be 145°F. (For medium, roast, uncovered, for 45 to 50 minutes or until meat reaches 150°F. Cover and let stand as directed above. Temperature of the meat should reach 160°F after standing.)

3. To roast pork, preheat oven to 325°F. Roast for 1¼ to 1¾ hours or until the thermometer registers 150°F. Cover with foil and let stand for 15 minutes before slicing. The temperature of the meat will rise about 10 degrees upon standing.

4. To serve, cut 8 slices in the beef roast about 1 to 1½ inches apart, cutting to, but not through, the bottom of the meat. Tuck a slice of goat cheese into each cut (or spoon 1 tablespoon of cream cheese into each cut). Sprinkle with snipped fresh rosemary. Slice through the meat between each cheese portion to serve. For the pork roast, serve goat cheese with the roast. Makes 8 servings.

EACH SERVING: 275 cal., 14 g fat (6 g sat. fat), 101 mg chol., 440 mg sodium, 1 g carbo., 0 g fiber, 35 g pro. Daily Values: 3% vit. A, 1% vit. C, 6% calcium, 15% iron.

Rosemary Beef Tenderloin

GARNISHED WITH A DOLLOP OF CRÈME FRAÎCHE, THIS ELEGANT POTATO SOUP SERVES AS THE PERFECT STARTER TO CHRISTMAS DINNER.

Christmas Potato Soup

**Toasted Stars and
Onion-Grape Marmalade**

Christmas Potato Soup
PREP: 25 MINUTES **ROAST:** 25 MINUTES **COOK:** 15 MINUTES

- 15   cloves garlic, peeled
- ½   tsp. olive oil
- 6   slices bacon
- 4   medium leeks, sliced
- 2   14-oz. cans reduced-sodium chicken broth
- 1½   cups water
- 2   lb. round red potatoes, peeled and chopped
- ½   tsp. salt
- ¼   tsp. ground black pepper
-    Water (optional)
- ½   cup crème fraîche* or sour cream (optional)

1. Preheat oven to 425°F. Place garlic cloves in a muffin cup or custard cup. Drizzle with olive oil. Cover with foil and roast for 25 to 35 minutes or until the cloves feel soft when pressed; set aside.

2. In a Dutch oven cook the bacon over medium heat until crisp; drain on paper towels. Crumble; set aside. Reserve bacon drippings in pan.

3. In the bacon drippings cook leeks until tender but not browned, about 5 minutes. Add broth, 1½ cups water, potatoes, salt, and pepper. Bring to boiling. Reduce heat and simmer 10 to 12 minutes or until potatoes are tender. Stir in roasted garlic cloves.

4. In a large food processor or blender place half of the soup mixture. Cover and process until smooth. Return to Dutch oven. Repeat with remaining mixture. (Or use an immersion blender to blend the mixture in the Dutch oven until smooth.) Stir in crumbled bacon. Heat through. If necessary, add water to thin to desired consistency. If desired, garnish with a spoonful of crème fraîche. Makes 8 servings.

*TEST KITCHEN TIP: If you can't find crème fraîche in your supermarket, combine ¼ cup whipping cream (do not use ultrapasteurized cream) and ¼ cup dairy sour cream. Cover the mixture and let it stand at room temperature for 2 to 5 hours or until it thickens. Cover and refrigerate for up to 1 week.

MAKE-AHEAD DIRECTIONS: The garlic can be roasted up to 3 days ahead and chilled until ready to use. Prepare the soup as directed, except leave out the crumbled bacon. Transfer soup to a slow cooker on the low-heat setting and hold for up to 4 hours. Or cover and chill soup for up to 3 days. Reheat in a slow cooker on high-heat setting for 2 hours. Stir in crumbled bacon before serving.

EACH SERVING: 224 cal., 13 g fat (4 g sat. fat), 19 mg chol., 627 mg sodium, 20 g carbo., 2 g fiber, 7 g pro. Daily Values: 5% vit. A, 26% vit. C, 3% calcium, 7% iron.

Toasted Stars and Onion-Grape Marmalade
PREP: 30 MINUTES **COOK:** 16 MINUTES
BAKE: 6 MINUTES **COOL:** 20 MINUTES

- 2   Tbsp. butter
- 1¼   lb. red onions, peeled and chopped (about 4 cups)
- 2   Tbsp. sugar
- 2   Tbsp. red wine vinegar
- ½   cup chopped seedless green grapes
- ¼   tsp. salt
- 24   slices firm-textured white bread (one and one-half 16-oz. pkg.)
- 3   Tbsp. butter, melted
-    Chives (optional)

1. For marmalade, in a large skillet heat 2 tablespoons butter over medium heat. Add onions. Cook, uncovered, for 15 minutes or until tender and lightly browned, stirring occasionally. Stir in sugar and vinegar. Cook, uncovered, for 1 to 2 minutes more or until vinegar has evaporated. Remove from heat. Stir in grapes and salt. Set aside to cool slightly. (Mixture can be made up to 2 hours ahead. Cover and set aside at room temperature.)

2. Meanwhile, preheat oven to 425°F. Use a 2¾-inch star-shape cutter to cut out the centers of bread slices.* Arrange cutouts on a large baking sheet. Brush both sides of each cutout lightly with the melted butter. Bake for 6 minutes or until lightly toasted. Cool on baking sheet on a wire rack.

3. To serve, spoon about 1 tablespoon onion mixture on each toasted cutout.** Arrange on serving platters. If desired, garnish with chives. Makes 24 toasted stars and 40 (1-tablespoon) marmalade servings.

*TEST KITCHEN TIP: Use the leftover bread scraps in your holiday stuffing or cut it into small pieces and toss with butter and herbs to top your favorite vegetable casserole.

**NOTE: If you like, you can skip making the Toasted Stars and serve the Onion-Grape Marmalade on crackers.

MAKE-AHEAD DIRECTIONS: Make the Toasted Stars. Cool completely. Place in a resealable plastic freezer bag; freeze up to 1 month. Let stand at room temperature for 1 to 4 hours before serving. Make the marmalade up to 3 days ahead; cover and chill until ready to serve.

EACH TOASTED STAR + 1 TABLESPOON MARMALADE: 63 cal., 3 g fat (1 g sat. fat), 5 mg chol., 97 mg sodium, 9 g carbo., 0 g fiber, 1 g pro. Daily Values: 1% vit. A, 2% vit. C, 1% calcium, 2% iron.

Jeweled Spaghetti Squash

Jeweled Spaghetti Squash

PREP: 20 MINUTES **STAND:** 10 MINUTES

1	3- to 3½-lb. spaghetti squash, halved
¼	cup water
½	cup orange juice
¾	cup dried tart red cherries
¼	cup chopped walnuts
2	Tbsp. butter
¼	cup snipped fresh flat-leaf parsley
½	tsp. salt
⅛	tsp. ground black pepper

1. Place one of the squash halves, cut side down, in a microwave-safe baking dish with the water. Microwave, covered, on 100% power (high) for 17 to 20 minutes or until tender, rearranging once. Keep squash warm. Repeat with remaining squash half.

2. Using a fork, carefully scrape the pulp from its shell into a large serving bowl.*

3. Meanwhile, in a small saucepan bring orange juice to boiling. Remove from heat. Add cherries and let stand 10 minutes.

4. In a small skillet cook nuts in hot butter over medium heat for 2 to 3 minutes or until toasted, stirring occasionally.

5. Add cherries and juice, walnut mixture, parsley, salt, and pepper to squash pulp. Toss to coat. Serve warm. Makes 8 servings.

*TEST KITCHEN TIP: Use a hot pad holder or oven mitts to hold squash while scraping out pulp.

EACH SERVING: 135 cal., 6 g fat (2 g sat. fat), 8 mg chol., 190 mg sodium, 20 g carbo., 1 g fiber, 2 g pro. Daily Values: 14% vit. A, 21% vit. C, 4% calcium, 5% iron.

Lemony Green Beans

PREP: 15 MINUTES **COOK:** 5 MINUTES

- 1½ lb. green beans, trimmed, or three 10-oz. pkg. frozen whole green beans
- 3 Tbsp. extra virgin olive oil
- 3 large shallots, cut into thin wedges
- 6 cloves garlic, thinly sliced
- 1 Tbsp. finely shredded lemon peel
- ½ tsp. salt
- ⅛ tsp. ground black pepper
- Lemon wedges

1. In a large skillet cook beans in lightly salted boiling water for 2 to 5 minutes or until barely crisp-tender. Drain; rinse with cold water to cool quickly. Set aside.

2. In the same skillet heat oil over medium-high heat. Add shallots and garlic; cook, stirring occasionally, for 2 to 3 minutes or until softened and beginning to brown. Add green beans and cook, tossing, for 1 to 2 minutes or until heated through. Remove from heat. Stir in lemon peel, salt, and pepper. Pass with lemon wedges. Makes 8 servings.

MAKE-AHEAD DIRECTIONS: After Step 1, cover and chill beans for up to 4 hours before completing recipe as described in Step 2.

EACH SERVING: 80 cal., 5 g fat (1 g sat. fat), 0 mg chol., 152 mg sodium, 9 g carbo., 3 g fiber, 2 g pro. Daily Values: 12% vit. A, 41% vit. C, 4% calcium, 6% iron.

Lemony Green Beans

Pecan Cakes

Pecan Cakes
PREP: 25 MINUTES **BAKE:** 15 MINUTES **COOL:** 5 MINUTES

1	cup butter, softened
1½	cups granulated sugar
2½	tsp. baking powder
1	tsp. vanilla*
½	tsp. salt
3	eggs
2¼	cups all-purpose flour
½	cup pecans, toasted and ground*
1¼	cups milk
	Powdered sugar
	Fresh raspberries
	Mint leaves

1. Preheat oven to 350°F. Grease and flour twenty-four 2½-inch muffin cups; set aside.

2. In a large mixing bowl beat butter with an electric mixer on medium speed for 30 seconds. Gradually beat in granulated sugar until combined, scraping sides of bowl occasionally. Beat in baking powder, vanilla, and salt. Add eggs, one at a time, beating well after each addition.

3. In a large bowl combine flour and pecans. Add flour mixture and milk alternately to beaten mixture, beating on low speed after each addition just until combined. Spoon batter evenly into prepared muffin cups.

4. Bake for 15 to 18 minutes or until a toothpick inserted in centers comes out clean. Cool in pans on wire rack 5 minutes. Remove from pans. Cool completely on wire racks. Serve sprinkled with powdered sugar, raspberries, and mint leaves. Makes 24 cakes.

*TEST KITCHEN TIP: Ground almonds and ¼ teaspoon almond extract may be substituted for the pecans and vanilla.

MAKE-AHEAD DIRECTIONS: Bake cakes and cool completely. Place cakes in an airtight container and freeze up to 1 month. Let stand at room temperature for 1 hour or up to 24 hours before serving. Sprinkle with powdered sugar, raspberries, and mint leaves just before serving.

EACH CAKE: 190 cal, 10 g fat (5 g sat. fat), 48 mg chol, 142 mg sodium, 22 g carbo, 1 g fiber, 3 g pro. Daily Values: 6 % vit. A, 2% vit. C, 3% calcium, 4% iron.

Raspberry-Cranberry Sauce

PREP: 10 MINUTES **COOK:** 8 MINUTES

- 2 cups fresh or frozen cranberries
- ¼ cup golden raisins
- 1 cup sugar
- ¼ cup port wine or cranberry juice
- ½ tsp. ground ginger
- 1 cup fresh or frozen raspberries
- 1 tsp. finely shredded orange peel

Finely shredded orange peel (optional)

1. In a medium saucepan combine the cranberries and raisins. Stir in the sugar, port, and ginger. Cook and stir over medium heat until sugar is dissolved. Cook and stir for 5 minutes more or until the cranberries begin to pop and mixture has thickened slightly. Remove from heat. Stir in raspberries and 1 teaspoon orange peel. Serve with Pecan Cakes. If desired, top with additional orange peel. Makes about 2 cups.

MAKE-AHEAD DIRECTIONS: Prepare sauce as directed; cover and chill up to 3 days before serving.

 EACH ¼-CUP SERVING: 142 cal., 0 g fat, 0 mg chol, 2 mg sodium, 34 g carbo., 3 g fiber, 0 g pro. Daily Values: 14% vit. C, 1% calcium, 2% iron.

Raspberry-Cranberry Sauce with Pecan Cakes

Prize Tested RECIPES®

THE YEAR OF 2006 BROUGHT IN A PLETHORA OF GREAT-TASTING READER RECIPES. READ ON TO FIND THE PERFECT DISH FOR ANY OCCASION.

Citrus Breakfast Cake
page 258

Categories

Spicy Grilled Shrimp
page 280

Watermelon with Fruit Salsa
page 282

Dark Chocolate Mini Muffins
page 256

Creamy Ranch Chicken
page 262

TROPICAL FRUIT

Pork with Tropical Sauce

PREP: 15 MINUTES **BROIL:** 9 MINUTES **STAND:** 5 MINUTES

- 4 boneless pork top loin chops, cut 1 inch thick
  Salt and ground black pepper
- 2 tsp. olive oil
- 2 tsp. curry powder
- 1 tsp. ground ginger
- ¼ tsp. ground cinnamon
- 1 cup snipped assorted dried tropical fruit (such as mango, papaya, and pineapple) or tropical blend mixed dried fruit bits
- ½ cup orange juice
- 1 Tbsp. cider vinegar
- 2 Tbsp. pineapple preserves

1. Preheat broiler (if broiler has settings, use High). Sprinkle chops with salt and pepper. Brush chops with oil. In a bowl stir together curry, ginger, and cinnamon. Remove and set aside 1 teaspoon of the spice mixture. Rub remaining mixture over both sides of chops.

2. Place chops on an unheated rack of a broiler pan. Broil 4 inches from heat for 9 to 11 minutes, turning once, or until an instant-read thermometer inserted in pork chops registers 160°F.

3. Meanwhile, for sauce, in a small saucepan stir together fruit, orange juice, vinegar, and reserved spice mixture. Bring to boiling. Stir in preserves. Remove from heat and let stand, covered, for 5 minutes. Serve sauce over pork. Makes 4 servings.

LOW FAT **EACH SERVING:** 412 cal., 11 g total fat (4 g sat. fat), 77 mg chol., 257 mg sodium, 43 g carbo., 3 g fiber, 32 g pro. Daily Values: 8% vit. A, 28% vit. C, 8% calcium, 10% iron.

Mango Coffee Cake

PREP: 25 MINUTES **BAKE:** 40 MINUTES

- 2 cups all-purpose flour
- 2 cups sugar
- 1½ tsp. baking powder
- ½ tsp. baking soda
- ½ tsp. ground nutmeg
- ¼ tsp. salt
- ½ cup butter
- 1 cup buttermilk or sour milk*
- 2 eggs, beaten
- 1 tsp. vanilla
- 3 cups coarsely chopped seeded and peeled mangoes (about 3)
- ⅓ cup sugar
- ¾ tsp. ground cinnamon
  Sweetened whipped cream

1. Preheat oven to 350°F. Grease a 13×9×2-inch baking pan; set aside. In a large bowl combine flour, the 2 cups sugar, baking powder, baking soda, nutmeg, and salt. Using a pastry blender or two knives, cut in butter until mixture resembles coarse crumbs.

2. In a small bowl combine buttermilk, eggs, and vanilla. Add to flour mixture all at once; stir just until moistened. Fold in mango. Spread in prepared pan. Combine the ⅓ cup sugar and the cinnamon. Sprinkle evenly over batter. Bake for 40 to 45 minutes or until a wooden pick inserted near center comes out clean; break crust slightly when inserting pick. (Mango pieces will sink to bottom of coffee cake.) Cool slightly. Serve warm with sweetened whipped cream. Makes 12 to 16 servings.

*****SOUR MILK:** If you don't have 1 cup buttermilk on hand, substitute 1 cup sour milk by placing 1 tablespoon lemon juice or vinegar in a glass measuring cup. Add enough milk to make 1 cup total liquid. Let mixture stand for 5 minutes before using.

EACH SERVING: 387 cal., 15 g total fat (8 g sat. fat), 78 mg chol., 229 mg sodium, 61 g carbo., 1 g fiber, 4 g pro. Daily Values: 17% vit. A, 20% vit. C, 6% calcium, 7% iron.

Coconut Mango Scones

PREP: 25 MINUTES BAKE: 15 MINUTES

- 2 cups all-purpose flour
- ½ cup flaked coconut, toasted
- ¼ cup sugar
- 2 tsp. baking powder
- ¼ tsp. baking soda
- ¼ cup butter
- 1 3-oz. pkg. cream cheese, chilled
- 1 egg, beaten
- ½ cup half-and-half or light cream
- 1 medium mango, seeded, peeled, and chopped (about 1 cup)
- 2 Tbsp. half-and-half or light cream
- ¼ cup flaked coconut

1. Preheat oven to 375°F. In a large bowl combine flour, the ½ cup toasted coconut, sugar, baking powder, baking soda, and ¼ teaspoon salt. Using a pastry blender, cut in butter and cream cheese until mixture resembles coarse crumbs. Combine egg and the ½ cup half-and-half; stir into dough until combined. Stir in mango. Turn dough out onto a well floured surface. Knead dough by folding and gently pressing the dough for 10 to 12 strokes or until dough is nearly smooth. Pat or lightly roll dough into an 8-inch circle. Cut into 8 wedges.

2. Place wedges 1 inch apart on an ungreased baking sheet. Brush with the 2 tablespoons half-and-half and sprinkle with ¼ cup flaked coconut.

3. Bake for 15 to 18 minutes or until bottoms are golden brown. Serve warm. Makes 8 scones.

EACH SCONE: 315 cal., 16 g total fat (11 g sat. fat), 60 mg chol., 255 mg sodium, 37 g carbo., 2 g fiber, 6 g pro. Daily Values: 12% vit. A, 10% vit. C, 6% calcium, 9% iron.

Pacific Sunset Chicken

PREP: 20 MINUTES COOK: 9 MINUTES

- 1 medium mango, peeled, seeded, and chopped
- 1 cup chopped pineapple
- ½ cup peeled, seeded, and chopped cucumber
- 3 Tbsp. lime juice
- 2 Tbsp. snipped fresh mint
- 1 Tbsp. grated fresh ginger
- 1 Tbsp. honey
- 4 skinless, boneless chicken breast halves
- 1 Tbsp. cooking oil
- ¾ cup mango nectar
- 1 tsp. dry mustard
- ¼ tsp. crushed red pepper
- 2 cups hot cooked rice

1. In a medium bowl combine mango, pineapple, cucumber, 1 tablespoon of the lime juice, the mint, ginger, and honey; set aside.

2. In a skillet cook chicken in hot oil over medium-high heat for 3 to 4 minutes or until browned, turning once. Stir in mango nectar, remaining lime juice, the dry mustard, ½ teaspoon salt, and

crushed red pepper. Bring to boiling; reduce heat. Cover and simmer 4 to 6 minutes more or until chicken is no longer pink. Remove chicken to a platter; keep warm. Bring liquid to boiling; reduce heat. Boil gently, uncovered, for 2 to 3 minutes or until slightly thickened. Serve chicken with rice and mango mixture. Spoon cooking liquid over chicken. Makes 4 servings.

EACH SERVING: 408 cal., 6 g total fat (1 g sat. fat), 82 mg chol., 378 mg sodium, 51 g carbo., 3 g fiber, 36 g pro. Daily Values: 24% vit. A, 54% vit. C, 6% calcium, 13% iron.

Pineapple Crisp

PREP: 25 MINUTES BAKE: 30 MINUTES
COOL: 45 MINUTES

- ½ cup granulated sugar
- 1 Tbsp. all-purpose flour
- 1 tsp. ground cinnamon
- 4 cups cubed fresh pineapple
- 2 Tbsp. lemon juice
- ½ cup dried cranberries or dried tart cherries, snipped
- ½ cup packed brown sugar
- ½ cup all-purpose flour
- ½ cup rolled oats
- ¼ cup butter
- ¼ cup flaked coconut
- ¼ cup chopped macadamia nuts

1. Preheat oven to 375°F. Grease a 2-quart square baking dish; set aside. In a large mixing bowl stir together granulated sugar, the 1 tablespoon flour, cinnamon, and ¼ teasoon salt. Stir in pineapple, lemon juice, and dried fruit. Transfer mixture to prepared baking dish; set aside.

2. In a small bowl stir together brown sugar, the ½ cup flour, and rolled oats; cut in butter until mixture resembles coarse crumbs. Stir in coconut and macadamia nuts. Sprinkle over fruit.

3. Bake for 30 to 35 minutes or until topping is golden. Cool for 45 minutes; serve warm. Makes 6 to 8 servings.

EACH SERVING: 419 cal., 14 g total fat (7 g sat. fat), 20 mg chol., 179 mg sodium, 72 g carbo., 4 g fiber, 3 g pro. Daily Values: 5% vit. A, 29% vit. C, 4% calcium, 10% iron.

Tropical Fruit-Topped Spice Cake

PREP: 30 MINUTES BAKE: 30 MINUTES

- 2 cups all-purpose flour
- 1¼ tsp. ground nutmeg
- 1 tsp. baking powder
- 1 tsp. baking soda
- ¼ tsp. ground allspice
- ½ cup butter, softened
- 1½ cups sugar
- ½ tsp. vanilla
- 3 eggs
- 1 cup buttermilk
- ½ cup orange marmalade
- 3 cups peeled and chopped tropical fruits

1. Preheat oven to 350°F. Grease and lightly flour a 13×9×2-inch baking pan; set aside. Stir together flour, 1 teaspoon of the nutmeg, the baking powder, baking soda, ¼ teasoon salt, and allspice. In a bowl beat butter with an electric mixer on medium speed about 30 seconds. Add sugar and vanilla; beat until combined. Add eggs, 1 at a time, beating on medium speed for 1 minute after each.

2. Add dry ingredients and buttermilk alternately to beaten mixture, beating on low speed after each addition. Pour batter into prepared pan. Bake about 30 minutes or until a wooden toothpick inserted in center comes out clean and top springs back when lightly touched. Cool on wire rack.

3. In a medium saucepan heat orange marmalade until just melted. Remove from heat, stir in remaining nutmeg and the fruit. Serve over cake squares. Makes 16 squares.

EACH SQUARE: 233 cal., 7 g total fat (4 g sat. fat), 56 mg chol., 208 mg sodium, 40 g carbo., 1 g fiber, 3 g pro. Daily Values: 6% vit. A, 30% vit. C, 4% calcium, 5% iron.

Tropical Pavlova

PREP: 40 MINUTES BAKE: 35 MINUTES
STAND: 1 HOUR

- 4 egg whites
- 1⅓ cups sugar
- 2 tsp. ground ginger
- 1 tsp. vanilla
- ¼ tsp. cream of tartar
- 1 cup whipping cream
- ¼ cup ginger preserves
- 1½ cups chopped fresh pineapple
- 2 medium kiwifruits, peeled and sliced
- 1 medium carambola (star fruit), sliced

1. Allow egg whites to stand at room temperature for 30 minutes. In a small bowl combine sugar and ground ginger; set aside. Cover a large baking sheet with parchment paper; set aside.

2. Preheat oven to 300°F. Combine egg whites, vanilla, and cream of tartar. Beat with an electric mixer on medium speed until soft peaks form (tips curl). Gradually add sugar mixture, 1 tablespoon at a time, beating about 4 minutes on high speed or until stiff peaks form (tips stand straight) and sugar is almost dissolved.

3. Spoon meringue mixture onto prepared baking sheet, forming it into a 10-inch shell. Bake for 35 minutes. Turn oven off. Let meringue dry in oven for 1 hour. Remove from oven; cool completely on baking sheet. Transfer to a serving platter.

4. Beat cream on medium speed until soft peaks form. Fold in the ginger preserves and half of the pineapple, kiwifruit, and carambola. Spoon fruit mixture over shell. Top with remaining fruit. Makes 10 servings.

EACH SERVING: 238 cal., 9 g total fat (6 g sat. fat), 33 mg chol., 35 mg sodium, 38 g carbo., 1 g fiber, 2 g pro. Daily Values: 8% vit. A, 45% vit. C, 3% calcium, 1% iron.

SNACKS FOR SUCCESSFUL DIETING

Dark Chocolate Mini Muffins

PREP: 25 MINUTES **BAKE:** 8 MINUTES **COOL:** 5 MINUTES

1¼	cups all-purpose flour
¾	cup whole wheat flour
¼	cup granulated sugar
¼	cup packed brown sugar
3	Tbsp. unsweetened cocoa powder
1½	tsp. baking soda
¾	cup fat-free milk
¾	cup unsweetened applesauce
1	Tbsp. cooking oil
1	Tbsp. molasses
2	tsp. balsamic vinegar
1	tsp. vanilla
⅓	cup miniature semisweet chocolate pieces

1. Preheat oven to 350°F. Coat about forty-eight* 1¾-inch or eighteen 2½-inch muffin cups with nonstick cooking spray; set aside. In a bowl combine flours, sugars, cocoa powder, baking soda, and ¼ teaspoon salt. Make a well in center of flour mixture; set aside. In another bowl combine milk, applesauce, oil, molasses, vinegar, and vanilla. Add to flour mixture. Stir just until moistened (batter should be lumpy). Stir in half the chocolate pieces.
2. Spoon batter into prepared muffin cups, filling each mini pan cup about two-thirds full or regular cups just over half full. Sprinkle with remaining chocolate pieces. Bake for 8 to 10 minutes for mini or about 15 minutes for regular muffins or until a wooden pick inserted near centers comes out clean. Cool in pan on rack for 5 minutes. Remove from muffin cups; serve warm. Or cool completely; wrap tightly and freeze up to 3 months. Reheat to serve. Makes 48 mini or 18 regular muffins.
*NOTE: If you don't have enough muffin cups, bake in batches. Cover and refrigerate muffin batter no longer than 30 minutes. Wash and prepare pans between batches.
EACH MINI MUFFIN: 39 cal., 1 g total fat (0 g sat. fat), 0 mg chol., 54 mg sodium, 8 g carbo., 0 g fiber, 1 g pro. Daily Values: 1% calcium, 2% iron.

Reduced-Fat Blue Cheese Spread

PREP: 10 MINUTES

¼	cup light mayonnaise or salad dressing
3	Tbsp. fat-free dairy sour cream
1	Tbsp. buttermilk
1	tsp. Dijon-style mustard
¼	tsp. Worcestershire sauce
½	cup crumbled blue cheese (2 ounces)
	Salt and ground black pepper
	Celery sticks, apple slices, and/or pear slices

1. In a small bowl stir together mayonnaise, sour cream, buttermilk, mustard, and Worcestershire sauce. Stir in blue cheese until mixture is almost smooth. Season to taste with salt and pepper. If desired, cover and refrigerate up to 3 days. Serve with celery sticks and apple and/or pear slices. Makes 6 (2-tablespoon) servings.
EACH 2-TABLESPOON SERVING: 76 cal., 6 g total fat (2 g sat. fat), 11 mg chol., 245 mg sodium, 3 g carbo., 0 g fiber, 3 g pro. Daily Values: 2% vit. A, 6% calcium.

Chilled Tomato Soup for 4

START TO FINISH: 15 MINUTES

- 1   11.5-oz. can tomato juice, chilled
- 2   6-oz. cartons plain low-fat yogurt
- 4   green onions, thinly sliced
- 1   Tbsp. lemon juice
     Several dashes bottled hot pepper sauce
- ½   of a small cucumber, seeded and chopped (½ cup)
- ¼   cup shredded carrot
- ⅛   tsp. celery seeds

1. In a blender combine tomato juice, 1½ cartons (about 1 cup) of the yogurt, half of the green onion, the lemon juice, and hot pepper sauce; cover and blend until smooth. Divide mixture among 4 serving bowls; top with cucumber, carrot, and remaining green onion. Top each serving with some of the remaining yogurt and sprinkle lightly with celery seeds. Makes 4 servings.

 EACH ⅔-CUP SERVING: 79 cal., 1 g total fat (1 g sat. fat), 5 mg chol., 287 mg sodium, 12 g carbo., 1 g fiber, 6 g pro. Daily Values: 30% vit. A, 35% vit. C, 18% calcium, 4% iron.

Creamy Kiwi Bites KID FRIENDLY

PREP: 25 MINUTES **FREEZE:** 2 HOURS

- 32   reduced-fat vanilla wafers
- 2   Tbsp. low-sugar orange marmalade
- ½   cup frozen fat-free whipped dessert topping, thawed
- 1   kiwifruit, peeled and finely chopped
- ½   tsp. finely shredded lime peel

1. Spread the flat sides of half of the vanilla wafers lightly with orange marmalade; set aside, spread sides up.
2. In a small bowl stir together dessert topping, kiwifruit, and lime peel. Spoon mixture on the wafers with marmalade. Top with remaining wafers, flat sides down. Wrap each in a small piece of plastic wrap. Freeze at least 2 hours or for up to 1 month. Serve frozen. Makes 16 snacks.

 EACH SNACK: 45 cal., 1 g total fat (0 g sat. fat), 4 mg chol., 26 mg sodium, 8 g carbo., 0 g fiber, 0 g pro. Daily Values: 8% vit. C, 1% calcium, 1% iron.

Less-Guilt Oatmeal Raisin Cookies

PREP: 30 MINUTES **BAKE:** 12 MINUTES PER BATCH **COOL:** 2 MINUTES PER BATCH

-      Nonstick cooking spray
- 2½   cups regular rolled oats
- ½   cup pecans
- ¾   cup whole wheat flour
- ¾   cup golden raisins
- 1½   tsp. ground cinnamon
- 5   egg whites
- 2   tsp. vanilla
- ½   tsp. salt
- ⅔   cup packed brown sugar
- ⅓   cup granulated sugar

1. Preheat oven to 325°F. Lightly coat several large cookie sheets with nonstick cooking spray. In a blender or food processor blend or process oats and pecans, a portion at a time, until coarsely ground. Transfer to a very large bowl. Add whole wheat flour, raisins, and cinnamon; set aside.
2. In a large mixing bowl combine egg whites, vanilla, and salt; beat with an electric mixer on medium to high speed just until stiff peaks begin to form. Combine sugars; add to egg white mixture, ⅓ cup at a time, beating until sugar is almost dissolved.
3. Fold beaten egg white mixture into oat mixture. Drop from a teaspoon onto prepared cookie sheets.
4. Bake for 12 to 15 minutes or until set. Cool on cookie sheets for 2 minutes. Transfer to wire racks; cool completely. Serve cookies the day they are prepared. For longer storage, pack in freezer containers; seal, label, and freeze. Makes about 40 cookies.

 EACH COOKIE: 69 cal., 1 g total fat (0 g sat. fat), 0 mg chol., 38 mg sodium, 13 g carbo., 1 g fiber, 2 g pro. Daily Values: 1% calcium, 3% iron.

Maple and Peanut Dip KID FRIENDLY

PREP: 5 MINUTES

- 1   6-oz. carton vanilla low-fat yogurt
- ½   cup reduced-fat peanut butter spread
- ⅓   cup sugar-free maple-flavor pancake and waffle syrup product
     Apple or pear slices and/or celery sticks

1. In a medium bowl stir together yogurt, peanut butter, and syrup until well combined. Serve immediately or cover and chill for up to 3 days. Serve with apples, pears, and/or celery. Makes 10 servings.

EACH 2-TABLESPOON SERVING (DIP ONLY): 90 cal., 5 g total fat (1 g sat. fat), 1 mg chol., 121 mg sodium, 8 g carbo., 1 g fiber, 4 g pro. Daily Values: 1% vit. A, 1% vit. C, 3% calcium, 2% iron.

Spicy Chicken Salad Wraps

PREP: 30 MINUTES **CHILL:** 1 HOUR

- 8   oz. uncooked ground chicken
- ¼   cup chopped red onion
- 1¼   cups packaged shredded broccoli (broccoli slaw)
- 2   green onions, thinly sliced
- ¼   cup reduced-fat mayonnaise
- 2   Tbsp. reduced-sodium soy sauce or fish sauce
- 2   Tbsp. snipped fresh cilantro
- 2   Tbsp. snipped fresh mint
- ¼   tsp. crushed red pepper
- 8   large butterhead lettuce leaves

1. In a medium nonstick skillet cook chicken and onion until chicken is brown and onion is tender; drain mixture.
2. In a large bowl combine chicken mixture, broccoli, green onion, mayonnaise, soy sauce, cilantro, mint, crushed red pepper, and ¼ teaspoon *salt*. Cover and chill for 1 to 24 hours.
3. Divide mixture evenly among 8 lettuce leaves. Bring all sides of each lettuce leaf up to the center to form a bundle. Makes 8 wraps.

EACH WRAP: 75 cal., 4 g total fat (0 g sat. fat), 3 mg chol., 281 mg sodium, 3 g carbo., 1 g fiber, 6 g pro. Daily Values: 15% vit. A, 23% vit. C, 2% calcium, 5% iron.

Blueberry Raspberry Bites

START TO FINISH: 20 MINUTES

- 3   tablespoons low-sugar red raspberry preserves
- ½   cup blueberries
- ¼   teaspoon ground ginger
     Dash ground black pepper
- 12   miniature cinnamon rice cakes
- ¼   cup tub-style light cream cheese

1. To make blueberry raspberry topper, in a small bowl combine preserves, blueberries, ginger, and pepper. Use immediately or cover and chill for up to 2 days.
2. To serve, spread each rice cake with 1 teaspoon of cream cheese. Add a rounded teaspoon of blueberry raspberry topper. Serve immediately. Makes 12 snacks.

EACH SNACK: 26 cal., 1 g total fat (1 g sat. fat), 3 mg chol., 26 mg sodium, 4 g carbo., 0 g fiber, 1 g pro. Daily Values: 2% vit. A, 3% vit. C, 1% calcium.

Very Berry Tarts

PREP: 20 MINUTES

- ⅓   cup tub-style light cream cheese spread with strawberries, softened
- 2   Tbsp. low-sugar strawberries preserves
- ½   cup blueberries
- ½   cup chopped strawberries
- 1   2.1-oz. pkg. baked miniature phyllo dough shells, thawed
- ¼   cup vanilla low-fat yogurt
- 2   tsp. finely snipped crystallized ginger

1. In a small bowl stir together cream cheese and low-sugar preserves until well combined. Fold in berries. Spoon mixture evenly into miniature phyllo shell using a rounded 1 tablespoon filling per shell. Serve immediately or cover and chill up to 8 hours.
2. To serve, combine yogurt and ginger in a bowl; spoon mixture on top of tarts. Make 15 tarts.

EACH TART: 47 cal., 2 g total fat (0 g sat. fat), 3 mg chol., 34 mg sodium, 6 g carbo., 1 g fiber, 1 g pro. Daily Values: 1% vit. A, 7% vit. C, 3% calcium, 1% iron.

EASY COFFEE CAKES

Citrus Breakfast Cake

PREP: 20 MINUTES **BAKE:** 45 MINUTES **COOL:** 15 MINUTES

      Nonstick cooking spray
    3 cups all-purpose flour
 1½ cups granulated sugar
  ¾ cup packed brown sugar
    3 Tbsp. finely shredded orange peel
    4 tsp. finely shredded lemon peel
    4 tsp. snipped fresh rosemary
 1½ tsp. baking soda
  ½ tsp. salt
    2 eggs, lightly beaten
    1 cup buttermilk
  ¾ cup butter, melted
    1 cup powdered sugar
    3 to 4 tsp. orange juice
    2 Tbsp. toasted pine nuts or slivered almonds, chopped
      Rosemary sprigs (optional)

1. Preheat oven to 350°F. Lightly coat a 10-inch fluted tube pan with nonstick cooking spray; set aside. In a large bowl combine flour, granulated sugar, brown sugar, orange peel, lemon peel, snipped rosemary, baking soda, and salt.
2. In a medium bowl combine eggs, buttermilk, and butter. Add to flour mixture and stir just until combined. Spoon batter into prepared pan. Bake for 45 to 50 minutes or until a wooden toothpick inserted near the center comes out clean.
3. Cool in pan on wire rack for 15 minutes. Invert onto a serving platter. In a small bowl combine powdered sugar and enough orange juice to make a drizzling consistency. Drizzle over warm cake. Sprinkle with nuts. Serve warm. If desired, top with rosemary sprigs. Makes 12 servings.
EACH SERVING: 421 cal., 14 g total fat (7 g sat. fat), 68 mg chol., 380 mg sodium, 70 g carbo., 1 g fiber, 5 g pro. Daily Values: 9% vit. A, 6% vit. C, 5% calcium, 11% iron.

Overnight Coffee Cake

PREP: 25 MINUTES **BAKE:** 35 MINUTES

    3 cups all-purpose flour
 1½ tsp. baking powder
 1½ tsp. baking soda
    1 cup butter, softened
 1¼ cups granulated sugar
    3 eggs
    1 15-oz. carton ricotta cheese
  ¾ cup chopped nuts
  ½ cup packed dark brown sugar
    2 Tbsp. toasted wheat germ
    1 Tbsp. ground cinnamon
    1 tsp. ground nutmeg

1. Grease bottom and ½ inch up sides of a 13×9×2-inch baking pan; set aside. In a 3-quart bowl combine flour, baking powder, baking soda, and 1 teaspoon *salt*; set aside. In a 4-quart mixing bowl beat butter on medium speed for 30 seconds. Add granulated sugar; beat until combined. Add eggs, 1 at a time, beating well after each. Beat in cheese. Beat in as much of the flour mixture as you can. Stir in any remaining flour mixture with a spoon. Spread batter in prepared pan. In a bowl combine nuts, brown sugar, wheat germ, cinnamon, and nutmeg. Sprinkle evenly over batter in pan.*
2. Preheat oven to 350°F. Uncover coffee cake and bake for 35 to 40 minutes or until a wooden toothpick inserted near center comes out clean. Cool slightly in pan on a wire rack. Serve warm. Makes 15 servings.
***MAKE-AHEAD DIRECTIONS:** After spreading batter in the pan in Step 1, cover and refrigerate up to 24 hours.
EACH SERVING: 397 cal., 22 g total fat (10 g sat. fat), 91 mg chol., 438 mg sodium, 43 g carbo., 1 g fiber, 8 g pro. Daily Values: 12% vit. A, 10% calcium, 11% iron.

Blueberry Coffee Cake with Walnut Sticky Topping

PREP: 35 MINUTES **BAKE:** 45 MINUTES
COOL: 50 MINUTES

- ⅓ cup packed brown sugar
- ¼ cup butter
- ¼ cup dark-colored corn syrup
- ¼ tsp. ground cinnamon
- ½ cup chopped walnuts
- 2 cups all-purpose flour
- 1¼ cups granulated sugar
- 2 tsp. baking powder
- ½ tsp. salt
- ¼ tsp. ground cinnamon
- ⅔ cup milk
- ¼ cup cooking oil
- 1 egg, slightly beaten
- 2 cups blueberries

1. Preheat oven to 350°F. Grease a 9×9×2-inch baking pan; set aside. In a small saucepan combine brown sugar, butter, corn syrup, and ¼ teaspoon cinnamon. Heat over medium-low heat until butter is melted and mixture is combined, stirring occasionally. Remove from heat; stir in walnuts. Spread mixture evenly into the prepared pan.
2. Meanwhile, in a large bowl combine flour, granulated sugar, baking powder, salt, and ¼ teaspoon cinnamon. Make a well in the center of the flour mixture. In a medium bowl whisk together milk, oil, and egg until combined. Add milk mixture all at once to flour mixture. Using a wooden spoon, stir just until combined. Gently stir in blueberries.
3. Spoon blueberry mixture over walnut mixture in pan; spread evenly. Bake for 45 to 50 minutes or until a wooden toothpick inserted near center comes out clean (avoid sticking the toothpick into a blueberry). Cool cake in pan on wire rack for 5 minutes. Carefully invert cake onto a serving platter. Cool 45 minutes. Serve warm. Makes 9 servings.
EACH SERVING: 428 cal., 17 g total fat (5 g sat. fat), 39 mg chol., 252 mg sodium, 66 g carbo., 3 g fiber, 5 g pro. Daily Values: 5% vit. A, 5% vit. C, 7% calcium, 10% iron.

Cranberry-Almond Coffee Cake

PREP: 30 MINUTES **BAKE:** 40 MINUTES
COOL: 30 MINUTES

- 1 Tbsp. butter
- 2 Tbsp. all-purpose flour
- 2 Tbsp. sugar
- 1 tsp. ground cinnamon
- ½ cup butter, softened
- 1 cup sugar
- 1 tsp. baking powder
- 1 tsp. baking soda
- ½ tsp. salt
- 2 eggs
- 1 8-oz. carton dairy sour cream
- 1 tsp. almond extract
- ½ tsp. vanilla
- 2 cups all-purpose flour
- 1 8-oz. can or ½ of a 16-oz. can whole cranberry sauce (¾ cup)
- ½ cup sliced almonds, toasted
- ¼ cup sliced almonds

1. Preheat oven to 350°F. Lightly grease a 9×9×2-inch baking pan; set aside. For crumb mixture, in a small microwave-safe bowl or custard cup microwave 1 tablespoon butter on 100% power (high) for 20 to 30 seconds or until melted. Stir in the 2 tablespoons flour, 2 tablespoons sugar, and cinnamon; set aside.
2. In a large bowl stir together softened butter, the 1 cup sugar, baking powder, baking soda, and salt until combined. Stir in eggs, sour cream, almond extract, and vanilla until combined. Stir in 2 cups flour until moistened.
3. Spoon half of the batter into prepared pan. Spoon cranberry sauce over batter in pan; spread evenly. Sprinkle with toasted almonds. Top with remaining batter; spread evenly. Sprinkle with crumb mixture and the ¼ cup almonds.
4. Bake for 40 to 45 minutes or until a wooden toothpick inserted near the center comes out clean. Cool in pan on a wire rack about 30 minutes before serving. Serve warm. Makes 12 servings.
EACH SERVING: 354 cal., 18 g total fat (9 g sat. fat), 66 mg chol., 315 mg sodium, 44 g carbo., 2 g fiber, 6 g pro. Daily Values: 9% vit. A, 6% calcium, 9% iron.

Poppy Seed Coffee Cake

PREP: 15 MINUTES **BAKE:** 30 MINUTES

- 1½ cups all-purpose flour
- 1 Tbsp. poppy seeds
- 2 tsp. baking powder
- 1 egg, slightly beaten
- ¾ cup buttermilk
- ⅓ cup butter, melted
- ¼ cup honey
- ½ tsp. almond extract
- ¼ cup packed brown sugar
- ¼ cup chopped walnuts or almonds
- ½ cup cherry, peach, or raspberry spreadable fruit
- 1 cup powdered sugar
- 1 to 2 Tbsp. orange juice

1. Preheat oven to 350°F. Grease bottom and ½ inch up sides of 8×8×2-inch baking pan; set aside. In a bowl combine flour, poppy seeds, and baking powder. In a bowl combine egg, buttermilk, butter, honey, and almond extract. Add buttermilk mixture all at once to flour mixture. Stir just until combined. Spoon batter into prepared pan.
2. In a bowl combine brown sugar and walnuts. Sprinkle evenly over the batter in the pan. Spoon spreadable fruit in 9 mounds on top of the batter. Bake for 30 to 35 minutes or until a wooden toothpick inserted near the center of the cake comes out clean. Cool slightly on a wire rack.

3. Meanwhile, in another small bowl combine powdered sugar and 1 tablespoon orange juice. Stir in additional orange juice, 1 teaspoon at a time, to make a drizzling consistency. Drizzle over cake. Makes 9 servings.
EACH SERVING: 319 cal., 10 g total fat (5 g sat. fat), 42 mg chol., 134 mg sodium, 55 g carbo., 1 g fiber, 4 g pro. Daily Values: 5% vit. A, 2% vit. C, 7% calcium, 8% iron.

Tropical Crumb Cake

PREP: 25 MINUTES **BAKE:** 50 MINUTES
COOL: 30 MINUTES

- Nonstick cooking spray
- 2 cups all-purpose flour
- 1 Tbsp. baking powder
- 1 Tbsp. ground cinnamon
- 1 tsp. ground ginger
- ½ tsp. salt
- 1 cup milk
- ½ cup granulated sugar
- ½ cup packed brown sugar
- ½ cup dairy sour cream
- 2 eggs, slightly beaten
- 1 Tbsp. cooking oil
- 2 cups tropical blend mixed dried fruit bits
- 1 recipe Crumb Topping

1. Preheat oven to 350°F. Lightly coat a 9-inch springform pan with nonstick cooking spray; set aside.
2. In a large bowl combine flour, baking powder, cinnamon, ginger, and salt; set aside. In a medium bowl whisk together milk, granulated sugar, brown sugar, sour cream, eggs, and oil. Add milk mixture all at once to the flour mixture. Stir just until moistened. Gently stir in fruit bits. Pour batter into the prepared pan. Sprinkle with Crumb Topping.
3. Bake for 50 to 55 minutes or until a wooden toothpick inserted near center comes out clean. If necessary, cover with foil the last 5 to 10 minutes to prevent overbrowning. Remove to a wire rack. Remove sides of pan. Cool on a wire rack about 30 minutes. Remove from bottom of pan to a serving plate. Cut into wedges and serve warm. Makes 10 to 12 servings.
CRUMB TOPPING: In a small bowl combine ½ cup packed brown sugar and ¼ cup all-purpose flour. Stir in 2 tablespoons melted butter until combined. Stir in ½ cup pecan pieces.
EACH SERVING: 449 cal., 12 g total fat (5 g sat. fat), 55 mg chol., 283 mg sodium, 80 g carbo., 3 g fiber, 6 g pro. Daily Values: 9% vit. A, 1% vit. C, 14% calcium, 14% iron.

Tarragon Tuna Melts

PREP: 25 MINUTES **COOK:** 6 MINUTES

- ⅓ cup mayonnaise or salad dressing
- 3 Tbsp. snipped fresh flat-leaf parsley
- 2 Tbsp. snipped fresh chives
- 1 to 2 Tbsp. snipped fresh tarragon or 2 tsp. dried tarragon, crushed
- 1 tsp. finely shredded lemon peel
- 2 tsp. lemon juice
- 1 tsp. Dijon-style mustard
- ⅛ tsp. ground black pepper
- 1 12-oz. can solid white tuna (water pack), drained and flaked
- 8 ½-inch slices sourdough bread
- 8 to 12 thin tomato slices (optional)
- 4 oz. sharp white cheddar cheese, shredded (1 cup)
- 2 Tbsp. butter, softened

1. In a medium bowl combine mayonnaise, parsley, chives, tarragon, lemon peel, lemon juice, mustard, and pepper; stir until well combined. Stir in tuna, breaking up any large pieces with a fork.

2. Place 4 bread slices on work surface; evenly divide tuna mixture on bread slices. Top each with tomato, if desired, and cheese. Spread one side of remaining bread slices with half the butter. Place bread slices, buttered sides up, on top of cheese. Place sandwiches, buttered sides down, on a large nonstick griddle over medium heat. (Or cook sandwiches, half at a time, in a large nonstick skillet.) Carefully butter top bread slices. Cook sandwiches for 6 to 8 minutes or until cheese is melted and bread is golden, carefully turning once halfway through cooking. Serve warm. Makes 4 sandwiches.

EACH SANDWICH: 550 cal., 34 g total fat (12 g sat. fat), 95 mg chol., 988 mg sodium, 27 g carbo., 2 g fiber, 32 g pro. Daily Values: 16% vit. A, 11% vit. C, 26% calcium, 14% iron.

Tuna-Stuffed Avocados

START TO FINISH: 25 MINUTES **FAST!**

- 2 medium mangoes, peeled, seeded, and chopped
- 3 Tbsp. chopped red onion
- 2 Tbsp. snipped fresh cilantro
- 1 Tbsp. olive oil
- ¼ to ½ tsp. ground cumin
- ½ tsp. salt
- ⅛ tsp. cayenne pepper
- 1 12-oz. can solid white tuna (water pack), drained
- 2 large avocados, halved and pitted
  Lemon wedges

1. In a medium bowl stir together the mangoes, onion, cilantro, oil, cumin, salt, and cayenne. Add tuna; stir gently to break up slightly. If desired, cover and refrigerate up to 4 hours. To serve, spoon tuna mixture into the center of each avocado half. Serve immediately with lemon wedges. Makes 4 servings (half an avocado plus a generous ½ cup filling).

EACH SERVING: 355 cal., 19 g total fat (3 g sat. fat), 36 mg chol., 622 mg sodium, 27 g carbo., 8 g fiber, 22 g pro. Daily Values: 22% vit. A, 71% vit. C, 4% calcium, 9% iron.

Nutty Tuna Bundles

PREP: 45 MINUTES **BAKE:** 15 MINUTES

- 1 5.2- to 6.5-oz. container semisoft cheese with garlic and herb
- 1/3 cup finely shredded Parmesan cheese
- 1/2 cup chopped walnuts, toasted
- 1/4 cup finely chopped red onion
- 4 teaspoons Dijon-style mustard
- 1 12-oz. can chunk white tuna (water pack), drained and flaked
- 20 sheets frozen phyllo dough (14×9-inch rectangles), thawed
- 1/2 cup butter, melted
- 1/4 cup crème fraîche

1. Preheat oven to 375°F. In a medium bowl combine semisoft cheese, 1/4 cup of the Parmesan cheese, the walnuts, red onion, and 2 teaspoons of the mustard. Gently stir in tuna.

2. Place 1 sheet of phyllo dough on a cutting board or other flat surface. Lightly brush entire surface of dough with some of the melted butter. Place another sheet of phyllo on top; brush with butter. (Keep remaining phyllo sheets covered with plastic wrap until needed.)

3. Cut the layered phyllo sheets lengthwise into 3 equal 14-inch strips. Spoon about 1 tablespoon of tuna mixture about 1 inch from an end of each dough strip.

4. To fold, bring a corner over the filling so the short edge lines up with the side edge. Continue folding the triangular shape along the strip until the end is reached. Repeat with remaining phyllo and tuna mixture. Place triangles on a baking sheet; brush with any remaining butter. Sprinkle with remaining Parmesan cheese. Bake for 15 minutes or until golden brown.

5. Combine crème fraîche and remaining mustard; drizzle over triangles. Serve warm. Makes 30 appetizers.

EACH APPETIZER: 105 cal., 8 g total fat (4 g sat. fat), 20 mg chol., 132 mg sodium, 5 g carbo., 0 g fiber, 4 g pro. Daily Values: 2% vit. A, 2% calcium, 2% iron.

Salsa-Sauced Tuna Tortilla Rolls

PREP: 30 MINUTES **BAKE:** 40 MINUTES

- Nonstick cooking spray
- 1 12-oz. can solid white tuna (water pack), drained and flaked
- 2 Granny Smith apples, cored and finely chopped (2 cups)
- 2 green onions, chopped
- 3/4 cup red or green seedless grapes, halved
- 1/2 cup mayonnaise or salad dressing
- 1/4 tsp. seasoned salt
- 1/4 tsp. freshly ground black pepper
- 12 7-inch flour tortillas
- 1 16-oz. jar pineapple-flavor salsa
- 1/2 cup sliced almonds, toasted
- 1 Tbsp. snipped fresh cilantro

1. Preheat oven to 350°F. Coat a 3-quart rectangular baking dish with nonstick cooking spray.

2. In a large bowl combine tuna, apples, green onions, grapes, mayonnaise, seasoned salt, and pepper; mix well. Spoon tuna mixture along one edge of each tortilla. Roll up, starting from the edge with the tuna mixture. Arrange rolls, seam side down, in the prepared dish.

3. Spoon salsa evenly over tortillas. Cover and bake for 35 minutes. Uncover and sprinkle with almonds. Bake 5 minutes more or until heated through. Sprinkle with cilantro. Makes 6 servings.

EACH 2-ROLL SERVING: 500 cal., 27 g total fat (5 g sat. fat), 30 mg chol., 679 mg sodium, 45 g carbo., 4 g fiber, 20 g pro. Daily Values: 3% vit. A, 8% vit. C, 11% calcium, 17% iron.

Tuna Appetizer Cheesecake

PREP: 40 MINUTES **BAKE:** 43 MINUTES
COOL: 45 MINUTES **CHILL:** OVERNIGHT

- 2/3 cup seasoned fine dry bread crumbs
- 8 oz. smoked Gouda cheese, shredded
- 2 Tbsp. butter, melted
- 2 8-oz. pkg. cream cheese, softened
- 1/2 cup dairy sour cream
- 1 Tbsp. milk
- 5 green onions, thinly sliced
- 2 chipotle chile peppers in adobo sauce, finely chopped
- 2 cloves garlic, minced
- 2 eggs
- 2 3-oz. pkg. chunk white albacore tuna (water pack), drained and flaked
- Toasted baguette slices or assorted crackers

1. Preheat oven to 325°F. Grease the bottom of a 9-inch springform pan. In a medium bowl stir together bread crumbs, 1/2 cup of the Gouda cheese, and the butter. Press mixture onto bottom of prepared pan. Bake for 8 minutes; cool on wire rack while preparing filling.

2. For filling, in a large bowl beat cream cheese, remaining Gouda cheese, sour cream, and milk with an electric mixer on medium speed until combined. Add green onions, chile peppers, and garlic. Beat until combined. Add eggs; beat on low speed just until combined. Gently stir in tuna. Pour mixture into prepared pan.

3. Bake for 35 to 40 minutes or until center is set. Cool in pan on a wire rack for 15 minutes. Using a sharp small knife, loosen the cheesecake from sides of pan; cool 30 minutes more. Remove the sides of the pan. Cover and chill overnight. To serve, cut into wedges and serve with baguette slices or crackers. Makes 16 appetizer servings.

EACH SERVING: 214 cal., 17 g total fat (11 g sat. fat), 81 mg chol., 513 mg sodium, 6 g carbo., 0 g fiber, 9 g pro. Daily Values: 11% vit. A, 2% vit. C, 14% calcium, 4% iron.

Tuna Cakes with Roasted Pepper Aïoli

PREP: 30 MINUTES **CHILL:** 1 HOUR
BAKE: 15 MINUTES

- 2 1/4 cups soft bread crumbs (3 slices)
- 1/2 cup finely chopped red and/or yellow sweet pepper
- 1/3 cup finely chopped onion
- 2/3 cup mayonnaise
- 1 egg, slightly beaten
- 1/4 cup snipped fresh basil
- 2 tsp. Dijon-style mustard
- 2 tsp. Worcestershire sauce
- 1/4 tsp. salt
- 1/4 tsp. ground black pepper
- 3 6-oz. cans chunk white tuna (water pack), drained and flaked
- 1 Tbsp. olive oil
- 1/3 cup chopped roasted red sweet pepper, drained
- 2 tsp. red wine vinegar

1. In a large bowl combine bread crumbs, sweet pepper, onion, 1/4 cup of the mayonnaise, the egg, 2 tablespoons of the basil, 1 teaspoon of the mustard, the Worcestershire sauce, salt, and black pepper. Gently stir in tuna. Using about 1/4 cup of the mixture, shape into 12 patties about 3 inches in diameter. Cover and chill for 1 hour (patties will be soft).

2. Preheat oven to 350°F. In a very large skillet cook the patties, half at a time, in the hot oil for 1 to 2 minutes per side or until golden. Place on a baking sheet. Bake for 15 minutes.

3. Meanwhile, for the aïoli, in a small bowl combine remaining mayonnaise, the roasted red sweet pepper, remaining basil, the vinegar, and remaining mustard. Serve with tuna cakes. Makes 6 servings.

EACH 2-CAKE SERVING: 378 cal., 26 g total fat (5 g sat. fat), 80 mg chol., 741 mg sodium, 12 g carbo., 1 g fiber, 23 g pro. Daily Values: 11% vit. A, 78% vit. C, 5% calcium, 11% iron.

Creamy Ranch Chicken

START TO FINISH: 30 MINUTES **FAST!**

- 6 slices bacon
- 4 skinless, boneless chicken breast halves, cut into bite-size pieces
- 2 Tbsp. all-purpose flour
- 2 Tbsp. ranch dry salad dressing mix
- 1¼ cups whole milk
- 3 cups dried medium noodles
- 1 Tbsp. finely shredded Parmesan cheese

1. Cut bacon into narrow strips. In a large skillet cook bacon over medium heat until crisp. Drain bacon on paper towels; reserve 2 tablespoons drippings.
2. In the same skillet cook chicken in reserved drippings until tender and no longer pink, turning to brown evenly. Sprinkle flour and salad dressing mix over the chicken in the skillet; stir well. Stir in milk. Cook and stir until thickened and bubbly. Cook and stir for 1 minute more. Stir in bacon. Meanwhile, cook noodles according to package directions. Serve chicken with noodles; sprinkle with Parmesan. Makes 4 servings.
EACH SERVING: 488 cal., 18 g total fat (7 g sat. fat), 137 mg chol., 574 mg sodium, 27 g carbo., 1 g fiber, 45 g pro. Daily Values: 4% vit. A, 16% calcium, 13% iron.

Chicken 'n' Pineapple Rice KID FRIENDLY

PREP: 15 MINUTES **COOK:** 18 MINUTES
STAND: 5 MINUTES **BAKE:** 15 MINUTES

- 1 15¼-oz. or two 8-oz. cans pineapple tidbits (juice pack)
- ¾ cup uncooked long grain rice
- ½ tsp. salt
- ½ cup coarsely chopped green sweet pepper
  Nonstick cooking spray
- 1 cup finely crushed gingersnaps (about 20 cookies)
- ¼ tsp. salt
- 1 egg
- 1 Tbsp. water
- 4 skinless, boneless chicken breast halves (1 to 1¼ lb.), cut into halves lengthwise

1. Preheat oven to 400°F. Drain pineapple, reserving juice. Set pineapple aside. Add enough water to reserved juice to equal 1¾ cups. In a medium saucepan stir together juice mixture, rice, and the ½ teaspoon salt. Bring to boiling; reduce heat. Simmer, covered, for 18 minutes. Remove from heat. Stir in pineapple and green sweet pepper. Let stand, covered, for 5 minutes.
2. Meanwhile, lightly coat a 15×10×1-inch baking pan with nonstick cooking spray; set aside. In a shallow dish combine gingersnaps and the ¼ teaspoon salt. In another shallow dish use a fork or whisk to combine egg and 1 tablespoon water. Dip chicken pieces, one at a time, into egg mixture, then into gingersnap mixture to coat. Arrange chicken in a single layer in prepared baking pan. Lightly coat chicken with nonstick cooking spray. Bake, uncovered, for 15 to 18 minutes or until chicken is no longer pink. Serve chicken strips with rice mixture. Makes 4 servings.
LOW FAT EACH SERVING: 481 cal., 6 g total fat (2 g sat. fat), 119 mg chol., 769 mg sodium, 71 g carbo., 2 g fiber, 32 g pro. Daily Values: 3% vit. A, 45% vit. C, 6% calcium, 28% iron.

Chicken Lo Mein

START TO FINISH: 30 MINUTES

- 6 oz. dried Chinese egg noodles, dried spaghetti, or dried angel hair pasta
- ¼ cup bottled hoisin sauce
- ¼ cup rice vinegar or lemon juice
- 1 Tbsp. cooking oil
- 12 oz. skinless, boneless chicken breast halves, cut into bite-size strips
- 2 tsp. bottled minced garlic
- 2 cups frozen stir-fry vegetables
- 1 8-oz. can sliced water chestnuts, drained
- 1 11-oz. can mandarin orange sections, drained, and/or ¼ cup dry-roasted cashews or peanuts (optional)

1. Cook noodles according to package directions; drain and set aside. Meanwhile, in a small bowl combine hoisin sauce and vinegar; set aside.

2. In a very large skillet heat oil over medium-high heat; add chicken and garlic. Stir-fry about 4 minutes or until chicken is no longer pink. Stir in vegetables and water chestnuts. Cover and cook for 2 minutes, stirring once. Stir vinegar mixture; add to skillet along with cooked egg noodles. Heat through, tossing to combine. Divide mixture among serving plates. If desired, top with orange sections and/or cashews. Makes 4 servings.

EACH SERVING: 415 cal., 10 g total fat (1 g sat. fat), 90 mg chol., 286 mg sodium, 54 g carbo., 2 g fiber, 28 g pro. Daily Values: 15% vit. A, 26% vit. C, 22% calcium, 12% iron.

Chicken Tacos with a Twist

START TO FINISH: 30 MINUTES **FAST!**

- 16 oz. uncooked ground chicken
- ¾ cup bottled peach salsa
- ½ cup mixed dried fruit bits
- 2 Tbsp. peach or apricot preserves
- 8 7- to 8-inch flour tortillas, warmed,* or 8 taco shells
- 2 cups shredded spinach or lettuce
- ½ cup shredded Monterey Jack cheese (2 oz.)
- ⅓ cup light dairy sour cream

1. In a large skillet cook ground chicken over medium heat until no longer pink, stirring to break up chicken as it cooks. Stir in salsa, fruit bits, and preserves. Cover and cook over medium-low heat for 5 minutes, stirring occasionally.

2. Serve chicken mixture in flour tortillas or taco shells; top with spinach, cheese, and sour cream. Makes 4 servings.

*****NOTE:** To warm tortillas, wrap in foil and heat in a 350°F oven for 10 minutes.

EACH SERVING: 592 cal., 26 g total fat (5 g sat. fat), 19 mg chol., 560 mg sodium, 59 g carbo., 2 g fiber, 29 g pro. Daily Values: 55% vit. A, 9% vit. C, 25% calcium, 21% iron.

Chuck Wagon Chicken Shepherd's Pie

PREP: 30 MINUTES **BAKE:** 30 MINUTES

- 2¼ cups milk
- 1 22-oz. pkg. frozen mashed potatoes
- ¼ cup snipped fresh parsley
- ½ tsp. salt
- 1 2- to 2½-lb. purchased roasted chicken
- 1 28-oz. can baked beans
- 1 11-oz. can whole kernel corn with sweet peppers, drained
- ½ cup bottled salsa

1. Preheat oven to 350°F. In a large saucepan heat milk over medium heat until simmering. Stir in frozen mashed potatoes. Cook over medium-low heat for 5 to 8 minutes or until heated through and smooth, stirring often. Stir in 2 tablespoons of the parsley and the salt; set aside.

2. Remove skin and bones from chicken. Using 2 forks, shred chicken. In a large bowl stir together chicken, undrained beans, corn, salsa, and remaining 2 tablespoons parsley. Spoon into a 3-quart rectangular baking dish. Spoon potatoes over chicken mixture and spread evenly.

3. Bake, uncovered, for 30 to 35 minutes or until heated through. Makes 6 servings.

EACH SERVING: 645 cal., 22 g total fat (7 g sat. fat), 106 mg chol., 1,200 mg sodium, 70 g carbo., 11 g fiber, 42 g pro. Daily Values: 14% vit. A, 14% vit. C, 19% calcium, 21% iron.

Nacho Chicken Legs

PREP: 30 MINUTES **BAKE:** 1 HOUR

- 1½ cups bottled mild taco sauce
- 2 cups crushed tortilla chips
- 12 chicken drumsticks (about 3 pounds)
- 1 recipe Sweet Ranch Dipping Sauce, Sweet Barbecue Dipping Sauce, and/or Cheese & Salsa Dipping Sauce (optional)

1. Preheat oven to 350°F. Line a large baking sheet with foil. Grease foil. Place taco sauce in a shallow dish. Place tortilla chips in another shallow dish. Dip drumsticks into the taco sauce and then into the crushed chips to cover. Place drumsticks on the prepared baking sheet. Bake for 1 hour or until chicken is no longer pink (180°F). Do not turn chicken pieces while baking.

2. If desired, prepare one or more of the dipping sauces; serve with drumsticks. Makes 6 servings.

EACH SERVING (CHICKEN ONLY): 418 cal., 21 g total fat (5 g sat. fat), 118 mg chol., 612 mg sodium, 25 g carbo., 2 g fiber, 30 g pro. Daily Values: 3% vit. A, 5% vit. C, 7% calcium, 10% iron.

SWEET RANCH DIPPING SAUCE: In a bowl combine ½ cup bottled Parmesan or cheddar-Parmesan ranch salad dressing, 2 tablespoons honey, and a dash of black pepper. Makes ⅔ cup.

SWEET BARBECUE DIPPING SAUCE: In a small microwave-safe bowl combine ⅓ cup barbecue sauce, ⅓ cup strawberry jelly, and 1 tablespoon lemon juice. Microwave on 100% power (high) for 30 seconds. Stir. Microwave 30 seconds more or until jelly is melted. Makes ⅔ cup.

CHEESE & SALSA DIPPING SAUCE: In a small microwave-safe bowl combine ⅓ cup salsa, ⅓ cup process cheese spread, and, if desired, 1 tablespoon snipped fresh cilantro. Microwave on 100% power (high) for 30 seconds. Stir. Microwave 30 seconds more or until melted. Makes ⅔ cup.

Peanut & Chicken Rolls

PREP: 25 MINUTES **BAKE:** 12 MINUTES

- Nonstick cooking spray
- 8 oz. skinless, boneless chicken breast halves, cut into bite-size pieces
- Ground black pepper
- 1 Tbsp. olive oil or cooking oil
- 3 Tbsp. peanut butter
- 2 Tbsp. apricot or strawberry jam
- ¼ cup honey-roasted peanuts, chopped
- 1 8-oz. pkg. (8) refrigerated crescent rolls
- 1 Tbsp. milk

1. Preheat oven to 400°F. Line a baking sheet with foil. Lightly coat foil with nonstick cooking spray; set aside. Sprinkle chicken with pepper. In a large skillet cook chicken in hot oil over medium-high heat for 3 minutes or until no longer pink. Stir in peanut butter, jam, and 2 tablespoons of the peanuts. Remove from heat and set aside.

2. Unroll crescent rolls and divide into 8 triangles. Divide chicken mixture among triangles, placing it along the bottom edges. Roll up dough to enclose filling. Pinch dough to seal. Place rolls on prepared baking sheet. Brush lightly with milk and sprinkle with remaining peanuts.

3. Bake for 12 to 15 minutes or until rolls are golden brown. Serve warm. Makes 8 rolls (4 servings).

EACH SERVING: 217 cal., 13 g total fat (2 g sat. fat), 17 mg chol., 290 mg sodium, 17 g carbo., 1 g fiber, 11 g pro. Daily Values: 1% vit. C, 1% calcium, 4% iron.

HEALTHY BREAKFAST TREATS

Whole Grain Berry Biscuits

PREP: 20 MINUTES **BAKE:** 18 MINUTES

- ½ cup all-purpose flour
- ½ cup whole wheat flour
- ¼ cup rolled oats
- 2 Tbsp. whole bran cereal
- 2 Tbsp. sugar
- 1 tsp. baking powder
- ¼ tsp. salt
- ⅓ cup milk
- ¼ cup water
- 3 Tbsp. cooking oil
- ⅓ cup fresh or frozen blueberries, thawed
- Favorite fruit jam (optional)

1. Preheat oven to 400°F. Lightly grease a baking sheet; set aside. In a medium bowl combine all-purpose flour, whole wheat flour, rolled oats, bran cereal, sugar, baking powder, and salt.

2. In a small bowl combine milk, water, and oil. Stir milk mixture into the flour mixture until just combined. Gently stir in the blueberries.

3. Spoon the batter into 6 mounds (about ⅓ cup each) on prepared baking sheet. Bake for 18 to 20 minutes or until lightly browned. If desired, serve with fruit jam. Makes 6 biscuits.

EACH BISCUIT: 175 cal., 8 g total fat (1 g sat. fat), 1 mg chol., 156 mg sodium, 24 g carbo., 3 g fiber, 4 g pro. Daily Values: 1% vit. A, 2% vit. C, 4% calcium, 7% iron.

Hawaiian Hotcakes

PREP: 20 MINUTES **COOK:** 4 MINUTES PER BATCH

- ⅓ cup unbleached all-purpose flour
- ⅓ cup whole wheat flour
- ½ tsp. baking powder
- ¼ tsp. baking soda
- ½ cup fat-free cottage cheese
- ½ cup refrigerated or frozen egg product, thawed, or 2 eggs, beaten
- 1 small banana, mashed (¼ cup)
- 1 15¼-oz. can pineapple tidbits (juice pack), drained
- 1 6-oz. carton plain low-fat yogurt
- 2 Tbsp. fat-free milk
- 1 Tbsp. canola oil
- 2 Tbsp. shredded coconut, toasted if desired
- 1 tsp. packed brown sugar (optional)
- Dry roasted macadamia nuts, chopped (optional)
- Warm maple syrup (optional)

1. In a bowl combine flours, baking powder, baking soda, and ¼ teaspoon *salt*. Make a well in center of mixture; set aside. In food processor combine cottage cheese, egg product, banana, ½ cup of the pineapple tidbits, 2 tablespoons of the yogurt, the milk, and oil. Cover; process until combined. Add egg mixture all at once to flour mixture. Stir just until moistened.

2. Fold in coconut. For each hotcake, pour a rounded tablespoon of batter into a 2-inch circle onto a hot, lightly greased griddle. Cook over medium heat for 2 minutes on each side or until golden brown, turning to second sides when surfaces are bubbly and edges are slightly dry. If desired, stir brown sugar into remaining yogurt. Top warm hotcakes with yogurt, remaining pineapple tidbits, and, if desired, nuts and/or warm maple syrup. (Cover and refrigerate any remaining pineapple for another use.) Makes about 24 pancakes (6 servings).

EACH 4 HOTCAKES + 1 TABLESPOON YOGURT + 1 TABLESPOON PINEAPPLE: 313 cal., 7 g total fat (4 g sat. fat), 16 mg chol., 463 mg sodium, 44 g carbo., 2 g fiber, 19 g pro. Daily Values: 3% vit. A, 17% vit. C, 53% calcium, 6% iron.

Dried Apple Scramble

START TO FINISH: 25 MINUTES

- 1 cup refrigerated or frozen egg product, thawed, or 4 eggs, beaten
- 1 6-oz. carton plain low-fat yogurt
- ¾ cup snipped dried apples
- ½ cup regular rolled oats
- ¼ cup slivered almonds, toasted

1. In a medium bowl combine egg product and yogurt. Stir in dried apples and oats. Let stand for 15 minutes.
2. Lightly coat a large nonstick skillet with cooking spray. Heat skillet over medium heat; pour in egg mixture. Cook over medium heat, without stirring, until mixture begins to set on the bottom and around edge.
3. With a spatula or large spoon, lift and fold the egg mixture for 2 to 3 minutes or until egg mixture is cooked through but is still glossy and moist. Remove from heat immediately. To serve, sprinkle with toasted almonds. Makes 4 servings.

EACH SERVING: 182 cal., 6 g total fat (1 g sat. fat), 3 mg chol., 159 mg sodium, 23 g carbo., 3 g fiber, 11 g pro. Daily Values: 15% vit. A, 2% vit. C, 12% calcium, 12% iron.

Spicy Breakfast Muffins

PREP: 10 MINUTES BAKE: 18 MINUTES

- Nonstick cooking spray
- 1¼ cups reduced-fat packaged biscuit mix
- ½ cup refrigerated or frozen egg product, thawed
- ¼ cup bottled green salsa
- ¼ cup finely shredded reduced-fat cheddar cheese
- 2 Tbsp. canola oil or cooking oil
- Honey

1. Preheat oven to 350°F. Lightly coat six 2½-inch muffin cups with nonstick cooking spray; set aside.
2. In a medium bowl combine biscuit mix, egg product, salsa, cheese, and oil; stir to combine. Spoon mixture into muffin cups, filling each about ⅔ full. Bake about 18 minutes or until golden.
3. To serve, split warm muffins and drizzle with a little honey. Makes 6 muffins.

EACH MUFFIN: 183 cal., 7 g total fat (1 g sat. fat), 3 mg chol., 403 mg sodium, 24 g carbo., 0 g fiber, 5 g pro. Daily Values: 6% vit. A, 1% vit. C, 8% calcium, 6% iron.

Everything Breakfast Bars

PREP: 25 MINUTES BAKE: 22 MINUTES

- Nonstick cooking spray
- ½ cup refrigerated egg product
- ¼ cup cooking oil
- ¼ cup water
- 1 14-oz. pkg. fat-free banana muffin mix
- 1¾ cups crisp rice cereal
- 1½ cups low-fat granola
- ⅔ cup cinnamon-flavor pieces
- ½ cup dried cranberries
- ½ cup sliced almonds, toasted

1. Preheat oven to 350°F. Line a 13×9×2-inch baking pan with foil, allowing foil to hang over edges of pan. Lightly coat foil with nonstick cooking spray; set aside.
2. In a large bowl stir together egg product, oil, and water. Add muffin mix, cereal, granola, cinnamon pieces, cranberries, and almonds; stir to combine. Transfer mixture to prepared pan. Use the back of a spoon to press mixture evenly into the pan.
3. Bake for 22 to 25 minutes or until edges start to brown. Cool in pan on a wire rack. When cool, use foil to lift bars from pan. Remove foil and cut into bars.
4. Store bars in a covered container at room temperature for up to 3 days. For longer storage, wrap, label, and freeze for up to 3 months. Makes 24 bars.

EACH BAR: 171 cal., 6 g total fat (1 g sat. fat), 0 mg chol., 196 mg sodium, 27 g carbo., 2 g fiber, 3 g pro. Daily Values: 5% vit. A, 1% vit. C, 15% calcium, 5% iron.

Sweet Breakfast Couscous

START TO FINISH: 10 MINUTES

- ¾ cup couscous
- ¼ cup raisins
- 1 Tbsp. packed brown sugar
- ¼ tsp. ground cinnamon
- 1 cup fat-free milk
- 1 Tbsp. maple syrup or honey
- Fat-free milk (optional)

1. In a 1- to 1½-quart casserole combine couscous, raisins, brown sugar, and cinnamon. Stir in the 1 cup milk. Microwave, covered, on 100% power (high) for 3 to 4 minutes or until milk is absorbed, stirring once. Let stand, covered, for 3 minutes.
2. Spoon into bowls and drizzle with maple syrup or honey. If desired, pass additional fat-free milk. Makes 4 servings.

LOW FAT — EACH SERVING: 204 cal., 0 g total fat, 1 mg chol., 32 mg sodium, 44 g carbo., 2 g fiber, 7 g pro. Daily Values: 3% vit. A, 10% calcium, 4% iron.

Whole Grain Scones with Warm Fruit

PREP: 30 MINUTES BAKE: 12 MINUTES

- ½ cup rolled oats
- 1 cup all-purpose flour
- ¾ cup whole wheat flour
- 2 Tbsp. sugar
- 2 tsp. baking powder
- ½ tsp. salt
- ¼ tsp. baking soda
- ¼ tsp. ground cinnamon
- 2 Tbsp. cold butter, cut up
- 1 cup fat-free dairy sour cream
- 1 egg, beaten
- 1 tsp. vanilla
- 1 Tbsp. fat-free milk
- 2 Tbsp. rolled oats
- 1 recipe Warm Fruit Topping

1. Preheat oven to 400°F. Grease a baking sheet; set aside. Place the ½ cup rolled oats in a food processor.* Cover and process until coarsely ground. Add all-purpose flour, whole wheat flour, sugar, baking powder, salt, baking soda, and cinnamon. Cover and process until combined. Add butter; cover and process with on/off turns until combined (some small pieces of butter may remain).
2. In a small bowl combine sour cream, egg, and vanilla. Add to flour mixture in food processor. Cover and process with on/off turns just until combined (mixture will be sticky). Turn dough out onto a floured surface. Knead by folding and gently pressing dough for 6 to 8 strokes or until dough is nearly smooth.
3. Pat or lightly roll dough into an 8-inch circle. Cut into 8 wedges. Place wedges 1 inch apart on prepared baking sheet. Brush tops with fat-free milk. Sprinkle with the 2 tablespoons rolled oats. Bake about 12 to 15 minutes or until lightly browned on top; serve warm with Warm Fruit Topping. Makes 8 scones.

WARM FRUIT TOPPING: Thaw one 16-ounce package unsweetened frozen fruit (such as whole strawberries, peach slices, raspberries, blueberries, or mixed berries). Drain fruit, reserving liquid. Measure liquid. If necessary, add enough orange juice to equal ⅔ cup. In a medium saucepan combine 2 to 4 tablespoons sugar and 1 tablespoon cornstarch. Add orange juice mixture and fruit. Cook and stir over medium heat until thickened and bubbly. Cook and stir for 2 minutes more.

*NOTE: To use a blender instead of a food processor, place the ½ cup rolled oats in a blender. Cover and blend until coarsely ground. In a large bowl combine blended oats, all-purpose flour, whole wheat flour, sugar, baking powder, salt, baking soda, and cinnamon. Using a pastry blender, cut in butter until mixture resembles coarse crumbs. Make a well in the center of flour mixture; set aside. In a medium bowl combine sour cream, egg, and vanilla. Add egg mixture all at once to flour mixture. Using a fork, stir just until moistened. Knead mixture as directed above.

EACH SCONE: 221 cal., 4 g total fat (2 g sat. fat), 37 mg chol., 322 mg sodium, 41 g carbo., 4 g fiber, 6 g pro. Daily Values: 7% vit. A, 39% vit. C, 8% calcium, 11% iron.

QUICK SANDWICHES

PRIZE TESTED RECIPES® $400 WINNER

AMRA ALIHODZIC, PHOENIX, ARIZ..

PRIZE TESTED RECIPES® $200 WINNER

KATHLEEN BOLANOS, MERRITT ISLAND, FLA.

Crostini a la Mia

PREP: 15 MINUTES **BAKE:** 15 MINUTES

- 1 4½- to 5-oz. round Brie cheese
- 1 16-oz. loaf French bread
- 1½ cups coarsely chopped roma tomatoes
- 6 oz. cooked ham or prosciutto, coarsely chopped (about 1 cup)
- 2 Tbsp. olive oil
- 1 tsp. bottled minced garlic or 2 cloves garlic, minced
- 1 tsp. dried oregano, crushed
- ½ cup finely shredded Italian blend cheese (2 ounces)
- 2 Tbsp. balsamic vinegar

1. Preheat oven to 350°F. If desired, remove edible rind from Brie cheese using a vegetable peeler. Cube cheese; set aside.
2. Split French bread in half horizontally. Hollow out one of the bread halves, leaving a ½-inch shell. Place hollowed bread half, cut side up, on a large baking sheet; set aside. (Save remaining bread for another use.)
3. In a medium bowl combine tomatoes, ham, Brie, oil, garlic, and oregano. Toss to combine. Spoon into hollowed bread half. Sprinkle with finely shredded cheese. Bake about 15 minutes or until heated through. Drizzle with vinegar. To serve, cut crosswise into 4 portions. Makes 4 servings.
EACH SERVING: 618 cal., 26 g total fat (10 g sat. fat), 66 mg chol., 1,541 mg sodium, 66 g carbo., 5 g fiber, 28 g pro. Daily Values: 15% vit. A, 18% vit. C, 25% calcium, 22% iron.

Classy Cuban Sandwiches

START TO FINISH: 25 MINUTES

- 8 oz. thin asparagus spears, trimmed
- 4 hoagie buns or torpedo rolls, split
- 2 to 3 Tbsp. coarse-grain mustard
- 8 oz. sliced Swiss cheese
- 6 oz. thinly sliced Serrano ham or any cooked ham
- 6 oz. thinly sliced cooked turkey breast
-   Dill pickle slices
- 1 Tbsp. olive oil

1. Place asparagus in a microwave-safe 9-inch pie plate or shallow baking dish with 2 tablespoons *water*; cover with vented plastic wrap. Microwave on high (100% power) for 3 minutes; drain and set aside.
2. Spread bottom halves of rolls with mustard. Top with cheese, asparagus, ham, turkey, and pickle slices. Add roll tops. Heat oil in a very large skillet or grill pan over medium heat (or preheat a covered electric indoor grill and brush with oil). Place sandwiches in skillet or grill pan or on electric grill (may need to cook in batches); cover sandwiches in skillet or grill pan with a large heavy plate and press gently (or close electric grill lid). Cook for 2 to 3 minutes per side (3 to 4 minutes total in covered grill) or until bread is toasted and cheese is melted. Makes 4 sandwiches.
EACH SANDWICH: 799 cal., 35 g total fat (15 g sat. fat), 109 mg chol., 2,224 mg sodium, 79 g carbo., 5 g fiber, 42 g pro. Daily Values: 18% vit. A, 8% vit. C, 60% calcium, 35% iron.

Beef Sandwiches with Horseradish and Onion

START TO FINISH: 20 MINUTES

    1 large red onion, thinly sliced
    1 Tbsp. olive oil
    3 Tbsp. white wine vinegar
    1 tsp. honey
  ¼ cup dairy sour cream
    2 Tbsp. prepared horseradish
    1 Tbsp. white wine vinegar
  ¼ tsp. salt
  ¼ tsp. ground black pepper
  12 slices dark rye bread, toasted
  ¼ cup creamy Dijon-style mustard blend
  16 oz. thinly sliced cooked roast beef

1. In a large skillet cook onion in hot oil, covered, over medium heat for 5 to 10 minutes or until nearly tender, stirring occasionally. Add the 3 tablespoons vinegar and the honey. Bring to boiling; cook, uncovered, for 5 to 10 minutes or until liquid has evaporated.

2. Meanwhile, in a small bowl combine sour cream, horseradish, 1 tablespoon vinegar, the salt, and pepper; set aside.

3. To assemble, spread one side of 6 bread slices with mustard blend. Top with roast beef and onion mixture. Spoon sour cream mixture over all. Add remaining bread slices. Cut in half to serve. Makes 6 sandwiches.

EACH SANDWICH: 417 cal., 17 g total fat (5 g sat. fat), 63 mg chol., 735 mg sodium, 39 g carbo., 4 g fiber, 26 g pro. Daily Values: 1% vit. A, 7% vit. C, 8% calcium, 23% iron.

Crunchy Curried Chicken Salad Wraps

START TO FINISH: 20 MINUTES

    4 10-inch flour tortillas
    1 9-oz. pkg. frozen cooked chicken breast strips, thawed
  ⅓ cup mayonnaise or salad dressing
  1½ tsp. curry powder
  ⅛ tsp. ground black pepper
  1½ cups shredded cabbage with carrot (coleslaw mix)
    1 medium apple, cored and chopped
  ½ cup pine nuts or slivered almonds, toasted (optional)
  ⅓ cup fresh mint leaves, finely shredded

1. Place tortillas on a flat surface; divide chicken among tortillas, placing near edge.

2. In a large bowl combine mayonnaise, curry powder, and pepper. Add cabbage mixture, apple, pine nuts (if desired), and mint. Stir until well mixed.

3. Spoon over chicken. Roll up tortillas around filling; secure with wooden toothpicks, if necessary. Serve immediately or, if desired, wrap and chill for up to 24 hours. Makes 4 wraps.

EACH WRAP: 366 cal., 19 g total fat (4 g sat. fat), 44 mg chol., 329 mg sodium, 29 g carbo., 2 g fiber, 18 g pro. Daily Values: 8% vit. A, 25% vit. C, 8% calcium, 19% iron.

Island Reuben

PREP: 10 MINUTES **BROIL:** 5 MINUTES

    8 slices dark rye bread, toasted
  ½ cup bottled Thousand Island salad dressing
    6 oz. sliced cooked turkey
    6 oz. sliced cooked ham
    4 slices Swiss cheese
    1 cup canned sauerkraut, well drained
  ½ cup canned crushed pineapple, well drained
    4 slices sharp cheddar cheese
    4 slices red onion

1. Place bread slices on an extra-large baking sheet. Spread one side of each slice with Thousand Island salad dressing. Top half of the bread slices with turkey, ham, and Swiss cheese. Top the remaining bread slices with sauerkraut, crushed pineapple, cheddar cheese, and sliced onion.

2. Broil 5 inches from the heat for 5 minutes or until cheese is melted. Carefully top turkey-topped bread slices with the sauerkraut-topped slices, onion sides down. Makes 4 sandwiches.

EACH SANDWICH: 677 cal., 36 g total fat (15 g sat. fat), 120 mg chol., 2,948 mg sodium, 44 g carbo., 9 g fiber, 40 g pro. Daily Values: 12% vit. A, 75% vit. C, 50% calcium, 22% iron.

Mariachi Turkey Sandwich

START TO FINISH: 25 MINUTES

    4 hoagie buns, split
    3 Tbsp. cooking oil
  1½ teaspoons chili powder
    1 8-oz. container refrigerated guacamole
  ¼ cup snipped fresh cilantro
  ¼ to ½ tsp. chipotle-flavor bottled hot pepper sauce or bottled hot pepper sauce
  12 oz. thinly sliced cooked turkey
    2 medium roma tomatoes, thinly sliced
    1 cup shredded Mexican cheese blend (4 oz.)

1. Preheat broiler. Place hoagie buns, cut sides up, on 1 very large or 2 large baking sheets. In a small bowl combine oil and chili powder; lightly brush mixture on cut sides of hoagie buns. Broil, 1 sheet at a time if necessary, 3 to 4 inches from the heat for 2 to 3 minutes or until toasted.

2. Meanwhile, in a medium bowl combine guacamole, cilantro, and bottled hot pepper sauce; set aside.

3. Divide turkey among bottom halves of toasted buns. Top with tomatoes and cheese. If desired, broil 3 to 4 inches from heat for 1 to 2 minutes or until cheese is melted. Top with guacamole and bun tops. Makes 4 sandwiches.

EACH SANDWICH: 851 cal., 39 g total fat (11 g sat. fat), 90 mg chol., 1,141 mg sodium, 79 g carbo., 9 g fiber, 44 g pro. Daily Values: 26% vit. A, 20% vit. C, 29% calcium, 35% iron.

Open-Face Chicken and Basil Sandwiches

START TO FINISH: 30 MINUTES

    1 8-oz. container whipped cream cheese
  ½ cup snipped fresh basil
    3 Tbsp. bottled ranch salad dressing
    2 6-oz. pkgs. refrigerated chopped cooked chicken
    1 cup diced roma tomatoes
    2 Tbsp. snipped fresh basil
    8 ½-inch-thick slices French or Italian bread, toasted
  ½ cup finely shredded Parmesan cheese

1. In a small bowl combine cream cheese, the ½ cup basil, and salad dressing. Stir well to combine; set aside. In a medium bowl combine chicken, tomatoes, and the 2 tablespoons basil.

2. Spread one side of each bread slice with cream cheese mixture. Top with chicken mixture; sprinkle with cheese. Broil 3 to 4 inches from heat for 1 to 2 minutes or until Parmesan melts. Makes 8 sandwiches.

EACH SANDWICH: 268 cal., 15 g total fat (7 g sat. fat), 62 mg chol., 795 mg sodium, 17 g carbo., 1 g fiber, 17 g pro. Daily Values: 13% vit. A, 6% vit. C, 9% calcium, 7% iron.

SIMPLY GORGEOUS DESSERTS

GLORIA PLEASANTS, WILLIAMSBURG, VA.

MARGIE TYLER, MURFREESBORO, TENN.

Panna Cotta Di Casa

PREP: 30 MINUTES **CHILL:** 4 HOURS

- 1¼ cups regular or fat-free half-and-half or light cream
- 1 envelope unflavored gelatin
- 2 6-oz. cartons thick and creamy lemon low-fat yogurt
- 1 10- to 12-oz. jar lemon curd
- 1 8-oz. carton mascarpone cheese or one 8-oz. package cream cheese, softened
- ¾ cup half-and-half
- 1 recipe Berry Sauce

1. Lightly coat eight 6-ounce custard cups with *nonstick cooking spray*; set aside. Place ½ cup of the half-and-half in a 2-cup glass measure. Sprinkle in gelatin; let stand for 5 minutes. Microwave, uncovered, on 50% power (medium) for 1 to 2 minutes or until gelatin is dissolved; stir every 30 seconds. Set aside.

2. In a bowl combine yogurt, lemon curd, and mascarpone cheese. Beat on medium speed until smooth. Beat in the remaining ¾ cup half-and-half on low speed. Slowly pour in warm gelatin mixture; beat on low speed until combined. Divide evenly among prepared cups. Cover; chill at least 4 hours or up to 24 hours. Meanwhile, prepare 1 recipe Berry Sauce. To serve, remove panna cotta by running a spatula around inside edges of cups. Dip bottoms of cups briefly in warm water. Invert onto plates. Top with Berry Sauce. If desired, garnish with *mint leaves*. Makes 8 servings.

BERRY SAUCE: In a saucepan combine ¼ cup each Marsala or red grape juice, water, and sugar; ½ teaspoon whole black peppercorns; two 6-inch sprigs fresh rosemary; and 1½ teaspoons balsamic vinegar. Bring to boiling; reduce heat. Simmer, uncovered, 10 minutes. Strain through a fine sieve. Discard peppercorns and rosemary. Return mixture to saucepan. Stir 1 teaspoon cornstarch into 1½ teaspoons water. Add to saucepan. Cook and stir over medium heat until slightly thickened and bubbly; cook and stir 2 minutes more. Remove from heat. Stir in ¼ teaspoon each lemon juice and balsamic vinegar and 1 cup fresh blueberries. Cover and chill sauce until serving time.

EACH SERVING: 376 cal., 20 g total fat (11 g sat. fat), 79 mg chol., 89 mg sodium, 46 g carbo., 4 g fiber, 10 g pro. Daily Values: 3% vit. A, 4% vit. C, 11% calcium, 1% iron.

Chocolate Mousse with Raspberry Sauce

PREP: 20 MINUTES **CHILL:** 1 HOUR

- ¾ cup raspberry jam
- 1 Tbsp. raspberry liqueur or orange juice
- 3 oz. semisweet chocolate
- 1 oz. bittersweet chocolate
- 2 Tbsp. honey
- 1 Tbsp. brandy or orange juice
- 2½ cups whipping cream
  Chocolate curls* or grated chocolate

1. In a small saucepan heat jam over low heat until melted, stirring occasionally. Remove from heat. Stir in raspberry liqueur; set aside to cool completely.

2. In another small saucepan heat chocolates over low heat until melted and smooth. Remove from heat. Stir in honey, brandy, and 1 tablespoon of the whipping cream until well combined. Transfer mixture to a large bowl; set aside to cool completely.

3. In a chilled large mixing bowl beat remaining cream until stiff peaks form. Remove 1 cup of the whipped cream; set aside. Stir ½ cup whipped cream into the chocolate mixture to lighten. Fold remaining whipped cream into chocolate mixture.

4. Spoon chocolate mixture into 6 wineglasses or dessert dishes. Top with reserved whipped cream. Spoon cooled raspberry sauce over whipped cream and top with chocolate curls. Cover and chill for 1 to 6 hours. Makes 6 servings.

***NOTE:** For chocolate curls, slowly draw a vegetable peeler across the edge of a bar of semisweet or milk chocolate. It works best if chocolate is at room temperature.

EACH SERVING: 584 cal., 43 g total fat (27 g sat. fat), 137 mg chol., 51 mg sodium, 47 g carbo., 2 g fiber, 4 g pro. Daily Values: 29% vit. A, 7% vit. C, 8% calcium, 6% iron.

Cherry Cassata Torte

PREP: 45 MINUTES **BAKE:** 35 MINUTES
COOL: 1½ HOURS **CHILL:** OVERNIGHT

 1 10.75-oz. frozen pound cake, thawed and
   sliced ½ inch thick
 3 Tbsp. Kirsch or cherry brandy
 2 8-oz. pkgs. cream cheese, softened
 1 cup whole milk ricotta cheese
 ¾ cup sugar
 3 Tbsp. all-purpose flour
 3 eggs
 ⅔ cup dried tart cherries, snipped
 1 cup sliced almonds, toasted
 2 5-oz. bars milk chocolate, chopped
 1 cup whipping cream
 1 Tbsp. sugar
 1 cup fresh cherries or maraschino cherries

1. Preheat oven to 350°F. Drizzle cake slices with Kirsch. Arrange some cake slices around sides of a 9-inch springform pan; arrange remaining cake on bottom of pan, cutting to fit. Set aside.
2. In a bowl beat cream cheese, ricotta, ¾ cup sugar, and flour with an electric mixer on medium speed until smooth. Beat in eggs just until combined. Stir in cherries, ⅓ cup of the almonds, and ¼ cup of the chocolate. Pour into prepared pan. Bake for 35 to 40 minutes or until outer 1½ inches of filling is set. Cool in pan on a wire rack for 30 minutes. Remove sides of pan. Cool for 1 hour.
3. Finely chop 2 tablespoons of the remaining chocolate and reserve for garnish. In a medium microwave-safe bowl heat ⅓ cup of the whipping cream on 100% power (high) for 30 to 60 seconds or until bubbly. Add remaining chocolate, stirring until melted. Spread over top and sides of torte. Press remaining almonds onto sides. Cover loosely and chill overnight.
4. To serve, in a chilled mixing bowl beat remaining whipping cream and 1 tablespoon sugar with an electric mixer on medium to high speed until soft peaks form. Pipe whipped cream around edges of torte. Place fresh cherries on top of the whipped cream; sprinkle with the reserved chocolate. Makes 12 servings.
EACH SERVING: 624 cal., 43 g total fat (23 g sat. fat), 174 mg chol., 217 mg sodium, 50 g carbo., 3 g fiber, 12 g pro. Daily Values: 25% vit. A, 13% vit. C, 15% calcium, 12% iron.

Caramel Apple Trifle Parfaits

PREP: 45 MINUTES

 1 pkg. 2-layer-size spice cake mix
 1 8-oz. pkg. cream cheese, softened
 1 12.25-oz. jar caramel ice cream topping
 1½ cups whipping cream
 1 21-oz. can apple pie filling
 ⅔ cup chopped walnuts, toasted

1. Prepare cake mix according to package directions using the 13×9×2-inch pan option. Cool cake completely in pan on a wire rack. Cut

half of the cake into 1-inch cubes (you should have 8 cups). Set aside. Reserve remaining cake for another use.
2. In a large mixing bowl beat cream cheese with an electric mixer on medium speed until light and fluffy. Slowly add ice cream topping, beating on low speed until just combined. In a medium mixing bowl beat whipping cream until stiff peaks form. Fold whipped cream into cream cheese mixture.
3. In each of eight 14-ounce glasses, spoon 2 tablespoons of whipped cream mixture. Top with ½ cup cake cubes. Top with 2 tablespoons whipped cream mixture. Top each with ¼ cup apple pie filling. Sprinkle walnuts over pie filling. Top with ½ cup cake and remaining whipped cream. Serve immediately or cover and chill for up to 4 hours. Makes 8 servings.
EACH SERVING: 803 cal., 38 g total fat (19 g sat. fat), 93 mg chol., 670 mg sodium, 108 g carbo., 2 g fiber, 6 g pro. Daily Values: 21% vit. A, 1% vit. C, 21% calcium, 11% iron.

Chocolate-Banana Cheese Pie

PREP: 20 MINUTES **BAKE:** 13 MINUTES
COOL: 1 HOUR **CHILL:** 3 HOURS

 ½ of a 15-oz. pkg. rolled refrigerated
   unbaked piecrust (1 crust)
 1 cup semisweet chocolate pieces
 1 8-oz. container mascarpone cheese
 ½ cup powdered sugar
 1 cup whipping cream
 3 medium bananas, sliced
 ¼ cup semisweet chocolate pieces
 ⅓ cup coarsely chopped pistachio nuts

1. Preheat oven to 450°F. Let piecrust stand according to package directions. Unroll piecrust. Line a 9-inch pie plate with piecrust; trim and crimp edge as desired. Prick crust all over with a fork. Line with a double thickness of foil. Bake for 8 minutes. Remove foil. Bake 5 to 6 minutes more or until golden. Cool on a wire rack for 1 hour.
2. In a saucepan combine 1 cup chocolate pieces, mascarpone cheese, and powdered sugar. Cook over medium-low heat until chocolate is melted and mixture is smooth, stirring gently. Remove from heat. If desired, stir in 2 tablespoons *banana liqueur*. Set aside to cool to room temperature.
3. Remove 2 tablespoons of the whipping cream and place in a small microwave-safe bowl; cover and chill. In a chilled large bowl beat remaining whipping cream with an electric mixer on medium speed until soft peaks form. Stir about ½ cup of the whipped cream into cooled chocolate mixture to lighten. Fold chocolate mixture into remaining whipped cream until just combined. Arrange half of the banana slices on the bottom of the baked pastry shell. Carefully spoon in half of the filling; spread evenly. Arrange remaining banana slices over filling. Top with remaining filling; spread evenly. Cover; chill for 3 to 24 hours or until set.
4. Before serving, add the ¼ cup chocolate pieces to reserved cream. Microwave, uncovered, on 100% power (high) for 30 seconds; stir until

melted and smooth. Cool slightly. Drizzle over top of pie. Sprinkle with pistachio nuts. Makes 8 to 10 servings.
EACH SERVING: 504 cal., 34 g total fat (18 g sat. fat), 77 mg chol., 240 mg sodium, 51 g carbo., 4 g fiber, 12 g pro. Daily Values: 10% vit. A, 7% vit. C, 3% calcium, 9% iron.

Sweet Potato Torte with Candied Pecans

PREP: 45 MINUTES **BAKE:** 10 MINUTES
FREEZE: 8 HOURS **STAND:** 20 MINUTES

 1½ cups finely crushed gingersnaps (about 28)
 ½ cup finely chopped pecans
 3 Tbsp. packed brown sugar
 ¼ tsp. ground cinnamon
 ½ cup butter, melted
 1 cup whipping cream
 2 8-oz. pkgs. cream cheese, softened
 1 cup packed brown sugar
 1 tsp. ground cinnamon
 1 tsp. ground nutmeg
 1 15-oz. can sweet potatoes, drained
   and mashed
 1 cup whipping cream
 ⅓ cup packed brown sugar
 1 recipe Candied Pecans

1. Preheat oven to 350°F. Line the bottom of a 9-inch springform pan with parchment paper. Combine crushed gingersnaps, pecans, 3 tablespoons brown sugar, and ¼ teaspoon ground cinnamon; add melted butter, stirring until combined. Press in the springform pan. Bake for 10 minutes. Cool on a wire rack.
2. Meanwhile, in a chilled medium mixing bowl beat 1 cup whipping cream with an electric mixer on high speed until soft peaks form; set aside.
3. In a large mixing bowl beat cream cheese, 1 cup brown sugar, 1 teaspoon cinnamon, and nutmeg with an electric mixer on medium speed until fluffy. Beat in sweet potatoes. Fold in whipped cream. Pour over crust, spreading evenly. Set aside.
4. In a chilled medium mixing bowl beat 1 cup whipping cream and ⅓ cup brown sugar until soft peaks form; spread over sweet potato mixture. Cover and freeze for 8 to 24 hours.
5. Remove torte from freezer about 20 minutes before serving; loosen sides and remove. Transfer torte to serving platter. Coarsely crush the Candied Pecans and sprinkle over top of torte. Makes 12 to 16 servings.
CANDIED PECANS: Line a baking sheet with foil. Butter foil. In a heavy skillet cook ¼ cup sugar over medium-high heat until sugar begins to melt. Do not stir. Reduce heat to low. Continue cooking until sugar is golden brown, stirring occasionally. Stir in ¾ cup pecan halves, 1 tablespoon butter, and ½ teaspoon vanilla just until combined. Pour nut mixture onto baking sheet. Cool completely.
EACH SERVING: 650 cal., 46 g total fat (24 g sat. fat), 119 mg chol., 333 mg sodium, 56 g carbo., 2 g fiber, 6 g pro. Daily Values: 27% vit. A, 4% vit. C, 12% calcium, 16% iron.

Steaks with Tomato Salsa

START TO FINISH: 25 MINUTES FAST!

- ¾ tsp. kosher salt or ½ tsp. salt
- ½ tsp. ground cumin
- ½ tsp. chili powder
- ½ tsp. dried oregano, crushed
- ½ tsp. packed brown sugar
- 2 8-oz. boneless beef ribeye steaks, cut ½ to ¾ inch thick
  Nonstick cooking spray
- ½ cup chopped onion
- 2 cloves garlic, minced
- 2 Tbsp. olive oil
- 2 cups red and/or yellow cherry or pear tomatoes, halved
- 1 canned chipotle pepper in adobo sauce, drained and finely chopped
- 2 Tbsp. lime juice
- ¼ cup snipped fresh cilantro

1. In a bowl stir together ½ teaspoon of the kosher salt (or ¼ teaspoon salt), the cumin, chili powder, oregano, and brown sugar. Rub into both sides of steaks. Lightly coat a grill pan with nonstick cooking spray. Preheat pan over medium-high heat. Add steaks. Reduce heat to medium. Cook for 8 to 10 minutes or until desired doneness, turning occasionally. (Or for a charcoal grill, place steaks on rack of uncovered grill directly over medium coals. Grill for 9 to 11 minutes or until desired doneness; turn once. For gas grill, preheat grill. Reduce heat to medium. Place steak on grill rack over heat. Cover; grill as above.)

2. For salsa, in large skillet cook and stir onion and garlic in hot oil over medium heat until tender. Stir in tomatoes, chipotle, lime juice, and ¼ teaspoon kosher salt. Cook and stir 1 minute. Transfer to a bowl; stir in cilantro. Cut each steak in half; serve with salsa. Makes 4 servings.

EACH SERVING: 257 cal., 14 g total fat (4 g sat. fat), 54 mg chol., 451 mg sodium, 8 g carbo., 2 g fiber, 25 g pro. Daily Values: 24% vit. A, 29% vit. C, 3% calcium, 15% iron.

Cheese-Topped Steaks

PREP: 20 MINUTES **GRILL:** 11 MINUTES

- 2 oz. Gorgonzola cheese or other blue cheese, crumbled (½ cup)
- ¼ cup cooked bacon pieces
- ¼ cup pine nuts or slivered almonds, toasted
- 2 Tbsp. fresh thyme leaves
- 2 cloves garlic, minced
- ¼ tsp. freshly ground black pepper
- 4 boneless beef top loin steaks, cut 1 inch thick (about 3 lb. total)
  Coarse salt or salt

1. In a small bowl combine cheese, bacon, nuts, thyme, garlic, and pepper; set aside.

2. Sprinkle steaks lightly with coarse salt. For a charcoal grill, place steaks on rack of an uncovered grill directly over medium coals. Grill to desired doneness, turning once halfway through grilling. Allow 10 to 12 minutes for medium-rare (145°F) or 12 to 15 minutes for medium doneness (160°F). (For a gas grill, preheat grill. Reduce heat to medium. Place steaks on grill rack over heat. Cover and grill as above.)

3. To serve, top steaks with cheese mixture. Grill 1 to 2 minutes longer to soften cheese slightly. Makes 4 servings.

TO BROIL: Place steaks on the unheated rack of a broiler pan. Broil 3 to 4 inches from heat until desired doneness, turning once. Allow 12 to 14 minutes for medium-rare and 15 to 18 minutes for medium doneness. Top steaks with cheese mixture. Broil 1 to 2 minutes more to soften cheese slightly.

EACH SERVING: 640 cal., 30 g total fat (11 g sat. fat), 181 mg chol., 616 mg sodium, 3 g carbo., 0 g fiber, 86 g pro. Daily Values: 3% vit. A, 4% vit. C, 11% calcium, 40% iron.

Brandy Steak

START TO FINISH: 30 MINUTES

- 1 small sweet onion (such as Vidalia or Walla Walla), thinly sliced and separated into rings
- 2 Tbsp. chopped shallot
- 2 tsp. packed brown sugar
- ½ tsp. dried thyme, crushed
- 1 Tbsp. butter
- ¼ cup whipping cream
- 2 Tbsp. brandy or beef broth
- 2 beef tenderloin steaks (10 oz. total) or one 10- to 12-oz. ribeye steak, cut ¾ inch thick
  Salt and freshly ground black pepper
- 1 Tbsp. butter
  Fresh chives (optional)

1. In a small skillet cook onion, shallot, brown sugar, and thyme, covered, in 1 tablespoon hot butter over medium-low heat for 13 to 15 minutes or until onions are tender, stirring occasionally. Uncover; cook and stir over medium-high heat for 3 to 5 minutes more or until onions are golden. Stir in whipping cream and brandy. Cook and stir for 3 to 5 minutes more or until slightly thickened.
2. Meanwhile, sprinkle steaks with salt and pepper. In a medium skillet melt 1 tablespoon butter over medium-high heat. Add steaks. Reduce heat to medium. Cook for 7 to 10 minutes or until desired doneness (145°F for medium rare or 160°F for medium), turning once halfway through cooking. Transfer steaks to plates; cover to keep warm.
3. Spoon sauce over steaks. If desired, top with fresh chives. Makes 2 servings.
EACH SERVING: 507 cal., 33 g total fat (18 g sat. fat), 159 mg chol., 308 mg sodium, 11 g carbo., 1 g fiber, 31 g pro. Daily Values: 20% vit. A, 6% vit. C, 5% calcium, 24% iron.

Cuban Steak Sandwiches

START TO FINISH: 20 MINUTES

- 12 oz. boneless beef sirloin steak
- ½ tsp. ground coriander
- 2 Tbsp. cooking oil
- 1 cup canned black beans, rinsed and drained
- ½ cup purchased lime and garlic salsa
- ¼ cup snipped fresh cilantro
- 4 French rolls, split and toasted
- ½ cup purchased guacamole

1. Trim fat from steak. Thinly slice steak across the grain into bite-size strips. In a medium bowl toss steak strips with coriander.
2. In a large skillet heat oil over medium-high heat. Add steak strips. Cook and stir for 5 minutes or until desired doneness. Drain off fat. Stir beans, salsa, and cilantro into skillet; heat through.
3. Spread cut sides of rolls with guacamole. Divide beef mixture among rolls. Makes 4 sandwiches.
EACH SANDWICH: 504 cal., 18 g total fat (3 g sat. fat), 52 mg chol., 999 mg sodium, 55 g carbo., 8 g fiber, 30 g pro. Daily Values: 12% vit. A, 9% vit. C, 11% calcium, 30% iron.

Ginger Flank Steak

PREP: 20 MINUTES **MARINATE:** OVERNIGHT
GRILL: 17 MINUTES

- 1½ lb. beef flank steak
- ¾ cup reduced-sodium soy sauce
- ½ cup sweet rice wine (mirin)
- 2 Tbsp. toasted sesame oil
- 2 green onions, chopped
- 4 tsp. grated fresh ginger
- 1 Tbsp. bottled minced garlic
- 1 tsp. crushed red pepper
- 4 oz. dried rice noodles

1. Score steak on both sides by making shallow cuts at 1-inch intervals in a diamond pattern. Place steak in a plastic bag set in a shallow dish.
2. For marinade, in a small bowl combine soy sauce, rice wine, sesame oil, chopped green onions, ginger, garlic, and crushed red pepper. Pour 1 cup marinade over steak; seal bag. Marinate in the refrigerator overnight. Cover and chill remaining marinade to use as dressing.
3. Cook rice noodles according to package directions. Drain steak; discard marinade. For a charcoal grill, place steak on the rack of an uncovered grill directly over medium coals. Grill for 17 to 21 minutes for medium doneness (160°F), turning once halfway through grilling. (For a gas grill, preheat grill. Reduce heat to medium. Place steak on rack over heat. Cover; grill as above.)
4. To serve, thinly slice steak diagonally across the grain. Serve over cooked noodles. Drizzle with reserved dressing and, if desired, sprinkle with *green onion.* Makes 6 servings.
 EACH SERVING: 271 cal., 8 g total fat (3 g sat. fat), 47 mg chol., 447 mg sodium, 22 g carbo., 0 g fiber, 25 g pro. Daily Values: 2% vit. A, 2% vit. C, 5% calcium, 13% iron.

Glazed Beef Tenderloin with Onion Chutney

PREP: 25 MINUTES **COOK:** 21 MINUTES
GRILL: 11 MINUTES

- ⅓ cup raspberry vinegar
- ⅓ cup balsamic vinegar
- ¼ cup seedless raspberry preserves
- 2 large sweet onions, halved lengthwise and thinly sliced
- 2 cloves garlic, minced
- ½ tsp. sugar
- 3 Tbsp. olive oil
- ½ cup coarsely chopped walnuts, toasted
- 6 beef tenderloin steaks or ribeye steaks, cut 1 inch thick

1. For glaze, in a small saucepan combine raspberry vinegar and balsamic vinegar. Bring to boiling; reduce heat and boil gently, uncovered, about 5 minutes until reduced to ⅓ cup. Set aside 3 tablespoons of mixture. Stir jam into remaining mixture for glaze.
2. Meanwhile, for chutney, in a very large skillet cook onions, garlic, sugar, ¼ teaspoon *salt,* and ¼ teaspoon *ground black pepper* in hot oil over medium heat for 15 to 20 minutes or until onions are very tender and evenly browned, stirring occasionally (turn heat to medium-low to prevent overbrowning, if necessary). Stir in reserved vinegar mixture. Bring to boiling; boil gently for 1 to 2 minutes or until most of the liquid is evaporated. Remove from heat; stir in walnuts.
3. Lightly season steaks with *salt* and *pepper.* For a charcoal grill, grill steaks on rack of an uncovered grill directly over medium coals until desired doneness, turning once halfway through grilling and brushing with glaze the last 3 to 4 minutes of grilling. Allow 11 to 15 minutes for medium-rare (145°F) or 14 to 18 minutes for medium doneness (160°F). (For a gas grill, preheat grill. Reduce heat to medium. Place steaks on grill rack over heat. Cover; grill as above.) Drizzle with any remaining glaze; top with onion chutney. Makes 6 servings.
EACH SERVING: 483 cal., 27 g total fat (7 g sat. fat), 105 mg chol., 199 mg sodium, 21 g carbo., 2 g fiber, 37 g pro. Daily Values: 8% vit. C, 4% calcium, 30% iron.

Italian Cube Steaks

PREP: 10 MINUTES **COOK:** 35 MINUTES

- 4 beef cubed steaks (about 1¼ lb.)
- 1 Tbsp. olive oil
- 1 14½-oz. can diced tomatoes
- ¼ cup dry white wine or beef broth
- ¼ cup purchased basil pesto
- 1 Tbsp. cornstarch
- 1 Tbsp. dry white wine or beef broth
- ¼ cup shredded Parmesan cheese

1. In a very large skillet brown steaks on both sides in hot oil over medium-high heat. Add undrained tomatoes and ¼ cup wine to skillet. Bring to boiling; reduce heat. Cover and simmer about 30 minutes or until steak is tender.
2. Transfer steaks to a serving platter; spread pesto over steaks. Cover to keep warm. In a small bowl stir together cornstarch and 1 tablespoon wine until well combined. Add to tomato mixture in skillet. Cook and stir until thickened and bubbly; cook and stir 2 minutes more. Spoon tomato mixture over steaks. Sprinkle with cheese. If desired, serve with hot cooked *noodles.* Makes 4 servings.
EACH SERVING: 399 cal., 22 g total fat (4 g sat. fat), 73 mg chol., 442 mg sodium, 10 g carbo., 0 g fiber, 36 g pro. Daily Values: 1% vit. A, 21% vit. C, 11% calcium, 17% iron.

SPRING VEGETABLES

Roasted Asparagus

PREP: 10 MINUTES **ROAST:** 15 MINUTES

    2 lb. fresh asparagus, trimmed
    2 Tbsp. olive oil
   ¼ cup grated Parmesan cheese
   ¼ cup butter, softened
   ¼ cup finely chopped radishes
    2 Tbsp. snipped fresh chives
    1 Tbsp. lemon juice

1. Preheat oven to 450°F. Place asparagus in a 3-quart rectangular baking dish. Drizzle with olive oil and sprinkle with cheese. Roast, uncovered, about 15 minutes or until crisp-tender, using tongs to lightly toss twice.
2. Meanwhile, in a small bowl combine butter, radishes, chives, and lemon juice. Transfer asparagus to a warm serving platter. Serve with butter mixture. Makes 8 servings.

EACH SERVING: 105 cal., 10 g total fat (5 g sat. fat), 17 mg chol., 82 mg sodium, 3 g carbo., 1 g fiber, 2 g pro. Daily Values: 13% vit. A, 8% vit. C, 5% calcium, 8% iron.

Glazed Pearl Onions

PREP: 25 MINUTES **COOK:** 15 MINUTES

    1 lb. pearl onions*
    1 Tbsp. cooking oil
    1 clove garlic, thinly sliced
   ½ cup orange marmalade
   ½ tsp. salt
   ⅛ tsp. ground black pepper
    1 Tbsp. snipped fresh chives or parsley

1. In a medium saucepan cook onions in enough boiling water to cover for 1 minute; drain well. Cool onions slightly and peel. In the same saucepan cook peeled onions, covered, in a small amount of boiling lightly salted water for 10 minutes or until tender; drain well and set aside.
2. In a large skillet heat oil over medium-high heat. Add garlic; cook and stir about 30 seconds or until golden. Stir in marmalade until melted. Stir in onions, salt, and pepper; cook and stir for 3 to 5 minutes or until marmalade is slightly thickened and coats onions. Stir in chives. Makes 4 to 6 servings.

*NOTE: If desired, omit fresh onions and Step 1; substitute one 16-ounce package frozen small whole onions and cook according to package directions until tender. Drain well and set aside. Proceed with Step 2. Serve with a slotted spoon.

EACH SERVING: 173 cal., 3 g total fat (1 g sat. fat), 0 mg chol., 315 mg sodium, 37 g carbo., 2 g fiber, 1 g pro. Daily Values: 1% vit. A, 14% vit. C, 4% calcium, 2% iron.

Artichokes and Asparagus with Tomato Topper

PREP: 25 MINUTES **ROAST:** 10 MINUTES

    1 large tomato, seeded and chopped
    1 large shallot, finely chopped
    2 to 3 tsp. snipped fresh tarragon
    1 tsp. finely shredded lemon peel
    3 Tbsp. olive oil
    ½ tsp. kosher salt or salt
    12 oz. fresh asparagus spears, trimmed
    1 9-oz. pkg. frozen artichoke hearts, thawed
    ¼ tsp. freshly ground black pepper

1. Preheat oven to 425°F. In a medium bowl combine tomato, shallot, tarragon, lemon peel, 2 tablespoons of the olive oil, and ¼ teaspoon of the salt; set aside.
2. In a 15×10×1-inch pan toss asparagus and artichoke hearts with remaining olive oil, remaining salt, and the pepper. Roast, uncovered, for 10 to 12 minutes or until asparagus is crisp-tender. Transfer to a dish. Spoon tomato mixture over. Makes 6 servings.

EACH SERVING: 116 cal., 9 g total fat (1 g sat. fat), 0 mg chol., 191 mg sodium, 7 g carbo., 4 g fiber, 2 g pro. Daily Values: 11% vit. A, 15% vit. C, 3% calcium, 6% iron.

Roasted Asparagus-Cannellini Bean Salad

PREP: 20 MINUTES **ROAST:** 12 MINUTES
CHILL: 2 HOURS

    12 oz. fresh asparagus spears, trimmed and cut into 1½-inch pieces
    3 Tbsp. extra virgin olive oil
    1 clove garlic, minced
    1 19-oz. can cannellini beans (white kidney beans), rinsed and drained
    1 medium red sweet pepper, seeded and chopped
    ¼ cup chopped red onion
    2 Tbsp. snipped fresh basil
    3 Tbsp. balsamic vinegar
    4 tsp. toasted sesame oil
    1 Tbsp. Dijon-style mustard
    ¼ tsp. salt
    ¼ tsp. ground black pepper
    4 cups mixed baby greens or mesclun
    1 Tbsp. sesame seeds, toasted

1. Preheat oven to 400°F. Spread asparagus in a shallow baking pan. Drizzle with 1 tablespoon of the olive oil and the garlic; toss to coat. Roast for 12 minutes, stirring halfway through roasting.
2. In a large bowl combine asparagus, cannellini beans, sweet pepper, onion, and basil.
3. In a screw-top jar combine vinegar, remaining olive oil, the sesame oil, mustard, salt, and black pepper. Cover and shake well to combine. Add to asparagus mixture; toss to coat. Cover and chill for 2 hours or until well chilled. To serve, spread greens on a serving platter. Top with asparagus mixture. Sprinkle with toasted sesame seeds. Makes 4 to 6 servings.

EACH SERVING: 271 cal., 16 g total fat (2 g sat. fat), 0 mg chol., 452 mg sodium, 29 g carbo., 9 g fiber, 11 g pro. Daily Values: 32% vit. A, 102% vit. C, 9% calcium, 19% iron.

Spring Green on Greens

PREP: 30 MINUTES **CHILL:** 2 HOURS

    1 medium zucchini, chopped (1¼ cups)
    8 oz. fresh asparagus spears, trimmed and cut into ½- to 1-inch slices (1 cup)
    4 green onions, thinly sliced (¼ cup)
    ½ cup frozen peas
    1 Tbsp. olive oil
    2 cups fresh arugula or spinach
    2 cups watercress
    ¼ cup bottled mild or medium green salsa or green taco sauce
    1 Tbsp. white balsamic vinegar
    1 hard-cooked egg, peeled and chopped

1. In a large skillet cook zucchini, asparagus, green onion, and peas in hot oil over medium heat for 3 to 5 minutes or until asparagus is just crisp tender, stirring occasionally. Transfer to a medium bowl; cover and chill for 2 to 24 hours.
2. In a large bowl toss together arugula and watercress. Arrange on a serving platter. Stir salsa and vinegar into chilled vegetables; spoon over greens. Sprinkle with hard-cooked egg. Makes 6 servings.

EACH SERVING: 64 cal., 3 g total fat (1 g sat. fat), 35 mg chol., 73 mg sodium, 6 g carbo., 2 g fiber, 3 g pro. Daily Values: 26% vit. A, 29% vit. C, 5% calcium, 1% iron.

Spring Vegetable Soup with Pesto Croutons

PREP: 25 MINUTES **COOK:** 20 MINUTES

    1 large onion, chopped (1 cup)
    ½ cup chopped fennel
    3 cloves garlic, minced
    ¼ cup olive oil
    3 14-ounce cans vegetable broth
    1½ lb. fresh asparagus spears, trimmed and cut into 1-inch pieces
    2 medium zucchini, quartered lengthwise and sliced
    3 medium roma tomatoes, chopped
    ½ teaspoon kosher salt or salt
    ¼ teaspoon freshly ground black pepper
    2 tablespoons chopped fresh basil
    1 recipe Pesto Croutons

1. In a 4-quart Dutch oven cook onion, fennel, and garlic in hot oil for 10 minutes or until onions are tender and start to caramelize. Stir in vegetable broth. Bring to boiling; reduce heat. Simmer, covered, for 5 minutes. Stir in asparagus, zucchini, and tomatoes. Return to boiling; reduce heat and simmer 5 minutes more or until zucchini is just tender. Season with salt and pepper. Sprinkle with basil. Serve with Pesto Croutons. Makes 8 side-dish servings.

PESTO CROUTONS: Preheat broiler. Lightly spread sixteen ¼-inch-thick baguette slices with ¼ cup purchased basil pesto. Place, spread sides up, on a baking sheet. Top with 2 tablespoons finely shredded Parmesan cheese. Broil 3 to 4 inches from heat for 1 to 2 minutes or until toasted.

EACH SERVING: 171 cal., 12 g total fat (1 g sat. fat), 2 mg chol., 813 mg sodium, 12 g carbo., 2 g fiber, 4 g pro. Daily Values: 20% vit. A, 27% vit. C, 5% calcium, 9% iron.

Vegetable Egg Drop Soup with Spring Onion Relish

PREP: 10 MINUTES **COOK:** 10 MINUTES

    1 32-oz. box chicken broth (4 cups)
    2 tsp. hoisin or oyster sauce
    ¼ tsp. ground white pepper
    ⅛ tsp. sea salt or salt
    8 oz. fresh asparagus spears, trimmed and cut into 1-inch pieces
    1 cup packaged fresh julienned carrots
    2 eggs, lightly beaten
    1 recipe Spring Onion Relish (optional)

1. In a large saucepan combine broth, hoisin sauce, pepper, and salt. Bring mixture to boiling; add asparagus and carrots. Return to boiling; reduce heat. Simmer, covered, for 4 to 5 minutes or until asparagus is crisp-tender.
2. Pour eggs into soup in a steady stream, stirring a few times to create shreds. Remove from heat. Ladle soup into bowls. If desired, spoon about 1 tablespoon Spring Onion Relish on each serving of soup. Makes 4 servings.

 PER 1¼-CUP SERVING: 75 cal., 3 g total fat (1 g sat. fat), 108 mg chol., 1,101 mg sodium, 6 g carbo., 2 g fiber, 5 g pro. Daily Values: 80% vit. A, 5% vit. C, 3% calcium, 7% iron.

SPRING ONION RELISH: In a small bowl combine ⅓ cup sliced green onions, 2 teaspoons finely snipped fresh cilantro, 2 teaspoons rice vinegar, ½ teaspoon bottled hoisin or oyster sauce, and several dashes toasted sesame oil. Makes about ½ cup relish.

PRIZE TESTED RECIPES® $400 WINNER

BEV JONES, BRUNSWICK, MO.

PRIZE TESTED RECIPES® $200 WINNER

BOBBIE HARMS, ERIE, COLO.

Open-Face Crab Ciabatta

START TO FINISH: 15 MINUTES **FAST!**

1 ½-pint container purchased deli crab salad
½ cup smoked almonds, chopped, or dried fruit-and-nut trail mix, chopped
1 tsp. snipped fresh rosemary
6 ½-inch-thick slices ciabatta or French bread, toasted

1. In a small bowl combine crab salad, almonds, and rosemary. Spread on toasted ciabatta or French bread slices. Makes 6 servings.
EACH SERVING: 192 cal., 11 g total fat (1 g sat. fat), 24 mg chol., 373 mg sodium, 15 g carbo., 2 g fiber, 9 g pro. Daily Values: 1% vit. A, 2% vit. C, 8% calcium, 7% iron.

Tomato-Tortellini Soup KID FRIENDLY

START TO FINISH: 15 MINUTES **FAST!**

2 14-oz. cans reduced-sodium chicken broth or vegetable broth
1 9-oz. pkg. refrigerated tortellini
½ of an 8-oz. tub cream cheese spread with chive and onion
1 10¾- or 11-oz. can condensed tomato or tomato bisque soup
Snipped fresh chives (optional)

1. In a medium saucepan bring broth to boiling. Add tortellini; reduce heat. Simmer, uncovered, for 5 minutes. In a bowl whisk ⅓ cup of the hot broth into the cheese spread until smooth. Stir cheese mixture into saucepan along with tomato soup; heat through. If desired, sprinkle with chives. Makes 4 servings.
EACH SERVING: 363 cal., 14 g total fat (8 g sat. fat), 57 mg chol., 1,264 mg sodium, 44 g carbo., 1 g fiber, 14 g pro. Daily Values: 13% vit. A, 6% vit. C, 15% calcium, 10% iron.

Alfredo Beef Sandwiches

PREP: 10 MINUTES **BAKE:** 5 MINUTES

- 1 16-oz. jar Alfredo pasta sauce (about 1¾ cups)
- 6 hoagie buns, split
- 12 oz. thinly sliced roast beef
- 6 slices provolone cheese (about 6 oz.)

1. Preheat oven to 350°F. Spread 1 tablespoon Alfredo sauce over the bottom halves of buns. Place roast beef and cheese over spread sides of buns. Replace bun tops. Place on a large baking sheet. Bake for 5 to 7 minutes or until buns are toasted and cheese melts. Heat remaining Alfredo sauce and pass for dipping. Makes 6 servings.

EACH SERVING: 774 cal., 36 g total fat (16 g sat. fat), 108 mg chol., 1,493 mg sodium, 76 g carbo., 4 g fiber, 36 g pro. Daily Values: 12% vit. A, 37% calcium, 31% iron.

ITALIAN HAM SANDWICH: Prepare as above, except substitute marinara sauce for Alfredo sauce and thinly sliced ham or turkey for roast beef. Makes 6 servings.

EACH SERVING: 629 cal., 21 g total fat (8 g sat. fat), 52 mg chol., 1,994 mg sodium, 82 g carbo., 6 g fiber, 28 g pro. Daily Values: 5% vit. A, 22% vit. C, 36% calcium, 28% iron.

Asian Tuna Wraps

START TO FINISH: 10 MINUTES

- 1 12-oz. can solid white tuna (in water), drained and broken into chunks
- ⅓ cup bottled Asian sesame-ginger salad dressing
- 4 7- to 8-inch flour tortillas
- 1 small red or green sweet pepper, seeded and cut into thin strips

1. In a medium bowl stir together tuna and dressing. Divide mixture among tortillas. Top with pepper strips and roll up. Makes 4 wraps.

ASIAN CHICKEN WRAPS: Prepare as above, except substitute one 10-ounce can chunk-style chicken, drained, for tuna. Makes 4 wraps.

EACH WRAP TUNA AND CHICKEN VARIATION: 208 cal., 9 g total fat (2 g sat. fat), 17 mg chol., 543 mg sodium, 21 g carbo., 1 g fiber, 11 g pro. Daily Values: 12% vit. A, 63% vit. C, 3% calcium, 6% iron.

Italian Meatball Stew

START TO FINISH: 25 MINUTES

- 1 16-oz. pkg. frozen cooked Italian-style meatballs (32)
- 2 14½-oz. cans Italian-style stewed tomatoes, cut up
- 1 15- to 19-oz. can white kidney (cannellini) beans, rinsed and drained
- ¾ cup water
- ¼ cup purchased basil pesto

1. In a large saucepan combine all ingredients. Bring to boiling; reduce heat. Simmer, covered, for 15 minutes. Makes 6 servings.

ITALIAN SAUSAGE STEW: Prepare as above, except omit meatballs. In a large saucepan cook 1 pound bulk Italian sausage over medium heat until brown. Drain fat. Stir in remaining ingredients; heat through. Makes 6 servings.

EACH SERVING MEATBALL AND SAUSAGE VARIATION: 391 cal., 25 g total fat (8 g sat. fat), 50 mg chol., 1,031 mg sodium, 25 g carbo., 7 g fiber, 19 g pro. Daily Values: 2% vit. C, 9% calcium, 17% iron.

Salsa Beef Sandwiches

PREP: 10 MINUTES **COOK:** 15 MINUTES

- 1 lb. lean ground beef
- 1 cup bottled chunky salsa
- ¼ cup water
- 1½ tsp. chili powder
- 6 hamburger buns, split and toasted

1. In a large skillet cook beef until brown. Drain fat; discard. Stir in salsa, water, and chili powder. Bring to boiling. Reduce heat. Simmer, uncovered, for 5 to 10 minutes or until desired consistency is reached. Divide mixture among hamburger buns. Makes 6 servings.

 **EACH SERVING:** 257 cal., 9 g total fat (3 g sat. fat), 48 mg chol., 466 mg sodium, 24 g carbo., 1 g fiber, 18 g pro. Daily Values: 4% vit. A, 6% vit. C, 7% calcium, 16% iron.

Taco Soup

PREP: 10 MINUTES **COOK:** 10 MINUTES

- 1 lb. lean ground beef
- 2 cups water
- 1 15-oz. can black beans, rinsed and drained
- 1 14½-oz. can Mexican-style stewed tomatoes, cut up
- 1 10¾-oz. can fiesta nacho cheese soup Broken tortilla chips (optional)

1. In a large saucepan cook ground beef until brown, breaking up beef as it cooks. Drain fat; discard. Stir in water, beans, undrained tomatoes, and cheese soup. If necessary, use a whisk to stir mixture until smooth. Bring to boiling; reduce heat. Simmer, covered, for 10 minutes. If desired, top with tortilla chips. Makes 4 to 6 servings.

EACH SERVING: 355 cal., 16 g total fat (7 g sat. fat), 78 mg chol., 1,148 mg sodium, 27 g carbo., 5 g fiber, 30 g pro. Daily Values:: 6% vit. A, 26% vit. C, 11% calcium, 19% iron.

VEGETARIAN TACO SOUP: Prepare as above, except omit ground beef. Stir in one 16-ounce can refried beans before cooking. Makes 4 to 6 servings.

EACH SERVING: 266 cal., 6 g total fat (2 g sat. fat), 6 mg chol., 1,646 mg sodium, 43 g carbo., 11 g fiber, 15 g pro. Daily Values: 6% vit. A, 26% vit. C, 14% calcium, 17% iron.

Cranberry-Blue Cheese Burgers

PREP: 15 MINUTES

- 6 4-oz. frozen ground beef patties
- 1 8-oz. dairy sour cream blue cheese-flavor dip
- ½ cup dried cranberries
- 6 Kaiser rolls or hamburger buns, split and toasted Lettuce leaves, tomato slices, onion slices (optional)

1. Cook patties according to package directions. Meanwhile, stir together blue cheese-flavor dip and dried cranberries.

2. Place each patty on top of the bottom of a bun. Top with blue cheese-flavor dip mixture and, if desired, lettuce, tomato, and/or onion slices. Top each burger with a bun top. Makes 6 burgers.

EACH BURGER: 698 cal., 49 g total fat (20 g sat. fat), 95 mg chol., 702 mg sodium, 39 g carbo., 2 g fiber, 24 g pro. Daily Values: 6% calcium, 22% iron.

MEXICAN-STYLE BURGERS: Prepare as directed above, except substitute Mexican-style dip for the blue cheese-flavor dip and 2 to 3 tablespoons chopped sliced pickled jalapeños for the dried cranberries. Makes 6 burgers.

EACH BURGER: 554 cal., 36 g total fat (20 g sat. fat), 103 mg chol., 644 mg sodium, 33 g carbo., 1 g fiber, 23 g pro. Daily Values: 6% vit. A, 6% vit. C, 12% calcium, 22% iron.

BROCCOLI SLAW BURGERS: Prepare as directed above, except substitute chive-style or chive and onion-style dip for the blue cheese-flavor dip and ½ cup packaged shredded broccoli (broccoli slaw mix) for the dried cranberries. Makes 6 burgers.

EACH BURGER: 568 cal., 36 g total fat (20 g sat. fat), 103 mg chol., 552 mg sodium, 33 g carbo., 1 g fiber, 24 g pro. Daily Values: 10% vit. A, 10% vit. C, 11% calcium, 22% iron.

DOUBLE ONION BURGERS: Prepare as directed above, except substitute French-onion dip for the blue cheese-flavor dip and ½ cup sliced green onion for the dried cranberries. Makes 6 burgers.

EACH BURGER: 560 cal., 35 g total fat (20 g sat. fat), 76 mg chol., 632 mg sodium, 34 g carbo., 2 g fiber, 24 g pro. Daily Values: 2% vit. A, 3% vit. C, 6% calcium, 22% iron.

SPREADS FOR MUFFINS, TOAST & BAGELS

PRIZE TESTED RECIPES® $400 WINNER

MARGARET B. FRENCH, WINSTON-SALEM, N.C.

PRIZE TESTED RECIPES® $200 WINNER

REBECCA WALCH, ORLAND, CALIF.

Cherry Pecan Spread

START TO FINISH: 15 MINUTES FAST!

- 2 cups cream-style cottage cheese
- 2 Tbsp. dairy sour cream
- 1 Tbsp. packed brown sugar
- ½ cup chopped pecans, toasted*
- ½ cup dried tart cherries, halved
- 1 tsp. finely shredded lemon peel
  Muffins, toasted English muffins, toast, or bagels

1. Place cottage cheese in a blender or food processor. Cover and blend or process until smooth, stopping blender and scraping down sides as needed (food processor results will be slightly less smooth than blender). Transfer mixture to a serving bowl. Stir in sour cream, brown sugar, pecans, cherries, and lemon peel until combined. Serve immediately or cover and chill for up to 8 hours before serving. Spread on muffins, toasted English muffins, toast, or bagels. Makes 2⅓ cups spread.

*NOTE: To toast nuts, preheat oven to 350°F. Spread nuts in a single layer in a shallow baking pan. Bake for 5 to 7 minutes or until lightly toasted.

EACH 2 TABLESPOONS SPREAD: 62 cal., 3 g total fat (1 g sat. fat), 4 mg chol., 96 mg sodium, 5 g carbo., 0 g fiber, 3 g pro. Daily Values: 3% vit. A, 2% calcium, 1% iron.

Fabulous Bagel Spread

PREP: 15 MINUTES **CHILL:** 6 HOURS

- 3 green onions
- ½ of a small cucumber, seeded and cut into chunks (about ½ cup)
- 1 8-oz. pkg. cream cheese, softened
- 1 tsp. Worcestershire sauce
- ⅛ tsp. salt
  Toasted bagel halves

1. Trim the green onions; remove white bottom portions and place in a food processor.* Thinly slice green tops of onions; reserve for garnish. Place cucumber in food processor with onions. Cover and process until coarsely chopped. Add cream cheese, Worcestershire sauce, and salt. Cover and process until almost smooth. Transfer to a medium bowl. Cover and chill for 6 hours or overnight. Top with sliced green onion tops. Spread on toasted bagel halves. Makes 1⅓ cups spread.

*NOTE: If you don't have a food processor, finely chop the cucumber and white parts of green onions. In a medium bowl combine cucumber, green onion, cream cheese, Worcestershire sauce, and salt. Beat with an electric mixer on medium speed until smooth. Cover, chill, and serve as directed.

EACH 1 TABLESPOON SPREAD: 39 cal., 4 g total fat (2 g sat. fat), 12 mg chol., 49 mg sodium, 1 g carbo., 0 g fiber, 1 g pro. Daily Values: 3% vit. A, 1% vit. C, 1% calcium, 1% iron.

Avocado Cilantro Spread

PREP: 20 MINUTES **CHILL:** OVERNIGHT

- 1½ cups plain low-fat yogurt*
- 1 8-oz. pkg. reduced-fat cream cheese (Neufchâtel), softened
- 1 ripe avocado, halved, seeded, peeled, and cut up
- 4 green onions, cut up
- 1 clove garlic, quartered
- 2 tsp. ground cumin
- 2 tsp. lemon juice or lime juice
- ¼ tsp. bottled hot pepper sauce
- ½ tsp. salt
- ½ cup snipped fresh cilantro
  Sourdough bread slices, toasted

1. Place a coffee filter in a fine-mesh sieve set over a bowl or line sieve with a double thickness of cheesecloth. Place yogurt in lined sieve. Cover and chill overnight.
2. Discard liquid in bowl. Place yogurt in a food processor or blender. Add cream cheese, avocado, green onions, garlic, cumin, lemon juice, hot pepper sauce, and salt. Cover and process or blend until smooth. Stir in cilantro. Transfer to a serving bowl. Serve immediately or cover and chill for up to 1 week. Spread on toasted sourdough bread slices. Makes 3 cups.
*NOTE: Use a brand of yogurt that contains no gums, gelatin, or fillers. These ingredients may prevent the whey from separating from the curd to make cheese.
EACH ¼ CUP SPREAD: 94 cal., 7 g total fat (3 g sat. fat), 15 mg chol., 204 mg sodium, 5 g carbo., 1 g fiber, 4 g pro. Daily Values: 10% vit. A, 7% vit. C, 8% calcium, 2% iron.

Chai Chutney Schmear

PREP: 15 MINUTES **CHILL:** 2 HOURS

- 1 8-oz. pkg. cream cheese, softened
- ⅓ cup chai tea latte concentrate (any flavor)
- ⅓ cup dried cranberries, chopped
- ¼ cup golden raisins, chopped
- 2 Tbsp. finely chopped almonds, toasted
  Muffins, toast, and/or bagels

1. In a large bowl beat cream cheese with an electric mixer on medium speed until smooth. Gradually beat in chai tea latte concentrate until well combined. Stir in cranberries, raisins, and almonds. Cover and chill for 2 to 24 hours before serving. Spread on muffins, toast, and bagels. Makes 1½ cups spread.
EACH 1 TABLESPOON SPREAD: 53 cal., 4 g total fat (2 g sat. fat), 10 mg chol., 29 mg sodium, 4 g carbo., 0 g fiber, 1 g pro. Daily Values: 3% vit. A, 1% calcium, 1% iron.

Ginger and Citrus Spread

PREP: 15 MINUTES

- 1 8-oz. pkg. cream cheese, softened
- 1 Tbsp. finely shredded orange peel
- 1 Tbsp. orange juice
- 1 Tbsp. finely shredded lemon peel
- 1 Tbsp. lemon juice
- ¾ cup ginger preserves or ¾ cup apricot preserves plus ½ teaspoon ground ginger
  Toasted English muffins

1. In a small bowl beat the cream cheese, orange peel, orange juice, lemon peel, and lemon juice with an electric mixer on medium speed until smooth. Stir in preserves. Spread on toasted English muffins. Makes 1½ cups spread.
EACH 2 TABLESPOONS SPREAD: 123 cal., 7 g total fat (4 g sat. fat), 21 mg chol., 62 mg sodium, 15 g carbo., 0 g fiber, 2 g pro. Daily Values: 5% vit. A, 7% vit. C, 2% calcium, 2% iron.

Gingered Pineapple Spread

PREP: 15 MINUTES

- 1 8-oz. pkg. cream cheese, softened
- ½ cup pineapple preserves
- 2 Tbsp. finely chopped crystallized ginger or ½ teaspoon ground ginger
- 2 Tbsp. raisins, chopped
- 2 Tbsp. finely chopped pecans, toasted
  Toasted English muffin halves

1. In a small bowl beat the cream cheese with an electric mixer on medium speed until smooth. Beat in preserves. Stir in ginger, raisins, and pecans. Serve at once or cover and chill overnight. Let chilled spread stand at room temperature about 30 minutes before serving. Spread on toasted English muffin halves. Makes 2 cups spread.
EACH 2 TABLESPOONS SPREAD: 90 cal., 6 g total fat (3 g sat. fat), 16 mg chol., 46 mg sodium, 9 g carbo., 0 g fiber, 1 g pro. Daily Values: 4% vit. A, 2% vit. C, 1% calcium, 2% iron.

Italian Spread

PREP: 15 MINUTES **BROIL:** 1 MINUTE

- ¼ cup purchased dried tomato pesto
- ¼ cup finely chopped bottled roasted red sweet peppers
- ¼ cup mayonnaise
- 2 Tbsp. snipped fresh basil
- ⅛ tsp. cayenne pepper
- 8 slices French or sourdough bread, toasted
- ¼ cup finely shredded Parmesan cheese or Italian cheese blend

1. Preheat broiler. In a small bowl combine pesto, sweet peppers, mayonnaise, basil, and cayenne pepper. Spread on bread slices; sprinkle with cheese. Arrange on a baking sheet.
2. Broil 3 to 4 inches from heat for 1 to 1½ minutes or until cheese melts. Makes 8 servings.
EACH SERVING: 158 cal., 9 g total fat (2 g sat. fat), 5 mg chol., 289 mg sodium, 15 g carbo., 1 g fiber, 4 g pro. Daily Values: 2% vit. A, 23% vit. C, 7% calcium, 7% iron.

Tuscanini Spread

START TO FINISH: 10 MINUTES

- 2 5-oz. containers semisoft cheese with garlic and fine herbes
- 2 Tbsp. milk
- ½ tsp. garlic powder
- ¼ cup pepperoncini salad peppers, drained and finely chopped
- ¼ cup bottled roasted red sweet peppers, drained and finely chopped
- ¼ cup finely chopped hard salami
  Toasted baguette slices

1. In a medium bowl combine cheese, milk, and garlic powder. Stir until well combined. Stir in pepperoncini, sweet peppers, and salami. Spread on toasted baguette slices. Makes 1¾ cups spread.
EACH 2 TABLESPOONS SPREAD: 94 cal., 8 g total fat (5 g sat. fat), 22 mg chol., 155 mg sodium, 1 g carbo., 0 g fiber, 3 g pro. Daily Values: 12% vit. C, 2% calcium.

Orange Ambrosia Spread

PREP: 15 MINUTES **STAND:** 5 MINUTES

- 1 cup mixed dried fruit bits
- 1 8-oz. tub cream cheese, softened
- ¼ cup dairy sour cream
- ¼ cup orange marmalade
- ⅛ tsp. ground nutmeg
- ¼ cup flaked or shredded coconut, toasted
  Muffins or toasted bagel halves

1. Place dried fruit bits in a bowl; cover with boiling water. Let stand 5 minutes; drain.
2. In a medium mixing bowl beat cream cheese, sour cream, marmalade, and nutmeg with an electric mixer until smooth. Stir in fruit bits and coconut.
3. Serve with muffins or bagels. Make 2 cups (sixteen 2-tablespoon servings).
EACH 2 TABLESPOONS SPREAD: 100 cal., 6 g total fat (4 g sat. fat), 17 mg chol., 57 mg sodium, 10 g carbo., 0 g fiber, 2 g pro. Daily Values: 4% vit. A, 1% vit. C, 2% calcium, 1% iron.

QUICK, NO-COOK APPETIZERS

PATRICIA GRIFT, BOTHELL, WASH.

MARY SHIELDS, PACIFICA, CALIF.

Sonoma Harvest Salsa

PREP: 25 MINUTES **CHILL:** 1 HOUR

- 3 roma tomatoes, halved, seeded, and cut up
- ½ small red onion, cut up
- ¼ of a small cantaloupe, seeded, peeled, and cut up
- 1 Gravenstein or pink lady apple, cored and cut up
- ½ of a medium green sweet pepper, seeded and cut up
- 1 or 2 fresh jalapeño chile peppers, seeded and cut up (see note, page 49)
- 1 Tbsp. sugar
- 1 Tbsp. lime juice
- ¼ tsp. salt
- ¼ tsp. ground cumin
  Tortilla chips or orange or red sweet pepper wedges

1. In a food processor combine tomatoes, onion, cantaloupe, apple, sweet pepper, jalapeño pepper, sugar, lime juice, salt, and cumin. Cover and process with several on/off turns until chopped. (Or coarsely chop with a knife.) Cover and chill for 1 to 6 hours. Stir well before serving. Serve with chips or sweet pepper wedges. Makes 3 cups salsa.

LOW FAT EACH ¼ CUP SALSA: 20 cal., 0 g total fat, 0 mg chol., 51 mg sodium, 5 g carbo., 1 g fiber, 0 g pro. Daily Values: 9% vit. A, 18% vit. C, 1% calcium, 1% iron.

Arugula-Cannellini Dip

PREP: 10 MINUTES

- 3 cups lightly packed arugula leaves
- ¼ cup olive oil
- 2 Tbsp. lemon juice
- 2 cloves garlic, halved
- ½ tsp. salt
- 1 15-oz. can cannellini beans (white kidney beans), rinsed and drained
- 1 medium tomato, seeded and chopped
  Assorted crackers, toasted baguette slices, or cut-up vegetables

1. In a food processor or blender combine arugula, oil, lemon juice, garlic, and salt. Cover and process or blend until nearly smooth. Add cannellini beans. Cover and process or blend until beans are coarsely chopped and mixture is combined (mixture should be slightly chunky). Transfer mixture to a serving bowl. Gently stir in chopped tomato. Serve immediately or cover and chill for up to 24 hours. Serve with crackers, baguette slices, or vegetable dippers. Makes 1½ cups dip.

EACH 2 TABLESPOONS DIP: 64 cal., 5 g total fat (1 g sat. fat), 0 mg chol., 154 mg sodium, 6 g carbo., 2 g fiber, 2 g pro. Daily Values: 4% vit. A, 6% vit. C, 2% calcium, 3% iron.

Artichoke-Water Chestnut Spread

PREP: 15 MINUTES **CHILL:** 1 HOUR

- 1 13¾-oz. can artichoke bottoms, drained and cut up
- 1 8-oz. can sliced water chestnuts, drained
- 2 cloves garlic, minced
- ½ cup mayonnaise
- ¼ cup tahini (sesame seed paste)
- ¼ tsp. salt
- 2 Tbsp. thinly sliced green onion
  Sesame seed crackers and/or assorted vegetable dippers

1. In a food processor combine artichoke bottoms and water chestnuts. Process with on/off turns until finely chopped. Add garlic, mayonnaise, tahini, and salt; process until combined. Cover and chill for 1 to 24 hours.
2. Sprinkle with green onions. Serve with crackers and/or vegetable dippers. Makes 2¼ cups spread.

EACH 2 TABLESPOONS SPREAD: 88 cal., 7 g total fat (1 g sat. fat), 2 mg chol., 142 mg sodium, 5 g carbo., 1 g fiber, 1 g pro. Daily Values: 1% vit. A, 3% vit. C, 5% calcium, 3% iron.

Black Bean and Ginger Lettuce Wraps

PREP: 25 MINUTES **CHILL:** 1 HOUR

- 1 16-oz. jar black bean and corn salsa
- 1½ cups shredded cooked chicken or pork
- ½ cup chopped red sweet pepper
- ¼ cup snipped fresh cilantro
- 2 tsp. grated fresh ginger
- 12 large butterhead lettuce leaves
  Honey-roasted peanuts and/or shredded carrot (optional)

1. Drain salsa in a sieve for 5 minutes. Discard drained juice. In a medium bowl combine drained salsa, chicken, sweet pepper, cilantro, and ginger. Cover and chill for 1 to 24 hours.
2. Spoon about 3 tablespoons of the chicken mixture into each lettuce leaf. If desired, top with peanuts and/or carrot. Roll up leaves. Makes 12 wraps.

 EACH WRAP: 62 cal., 1 g total fat (0 g sat. fat), 16 mg chol., 130 mg sodium, 6 g carbo., 1 g fiber, 6 g pro. Daily Values: 11% vit. A, 21% vit. C, 1% calcium, 2% iron.

Chipotle Roll-Ups

START TO FINISH: 25 MINUTES

- 2 8-oz. tubs cream cheese spread with chive and onion
- 3 Tbsp. finely chopped canned chipotle peppers in adobo sauce
- 6 10-inch flour tortillas
- 8 oz. thinly sliced salami
- ⅓ cup sliced pepperoncini salad peppers
- 1 medium red, yellow, or orange sweet pepper, cut into thin bite-size strips
- ½ cup snipped fresh cilantro

1. In a medium bowl stir together cream cheese and chipotle peppers. Spread over tortillas. Top each with salami, pepperoncini, sweet pepper strips, and half of the cilantro. Roll up tightly. If desired, wrap and chill for up to 24 hours.
2. To serve, trim ends of rolls. Cut each crosswise into 1-inch slices. Arrange slices, cut sides up, on serving platters. Sprinkle with remaining cilantro. Makes about 45 appetizers.

EACH APPETIZER: 75 cal., 5 g total fat (3 g sat. fat), 15 mg chol., 194 mg sodium, 4 g carbo., 0 g fiber, 2 g pro. Daily Values: 6% vit. A, 9% vit. C, 2% calcium, 2% iron.

Fruit-and-Nut Cheese Balls

PREP: 15 MINUTES **CHILL:** 4 HOURS
STAND: 15 MINUTES

- 2 8-oz. pkg. cream cheese, softened
- 1 8-oz. can crushed pineapple (juice pack), well drained
- 2 3.75 oz. pkg. honey roasted-flavor sliced almonds
- ⅔ cup dried cranberries
- ¼ cup finely chopped green onion
- 1 tsp. seasoned salt
- 3 or 4 drops bottled hot pepper sauce
  Assorted crackers

1. In a large mixing bowl beat cream cheese with an electric mixer until fluffy. Beat in drained pineapple, one package of the almonds, dried cranberries, green onion, seasoned salt, and hot pepper sauce. Cover and chill for 4 to 24 hours.
2. Shape mixture into two balls; roll each ball in remaining nuts. Let stand for 15 minutes before serving. Serve with crackers. Cover and chill any remaining cheese ball for up to 24 hours. Makes 3⅓ cups.

EACH 2 TABLESPOONS: 108 cal., 9 g total fat (4 g sat. fat), 17 mg chol., 105 mg sodium, 6 g carbo., 1 g fiber, 2 g pro. Daily Values: 4% vit. A, 2% vit. C, 3% calcium, 2% iron.

Quick Apple Carrot Cheese Balls

PREP: 30 MINUTES **CHILL:** 2 HOURS

- 1 8-oz. pkg. reduced-fat cream cheese (Neufchâtel), softened
- ⅓ cup light mayonnaise or salad dressing
- 2 tsp. lemon juice
  Dash salt
  Dash ground black pepper
- ¾ cup purchased shredded carrot
- ½ cup finely chopped apple
- 1 Tbsp. finely chopped onion
- 1 cup finely chopped pecans, toasted
  Assorted crackers

1. In a large bowl stir together cream cheese, mayonnaise, lemon juice, salt, and pepper until smooth. Stir in carrot, apple, and onion. Cover and chill for 1 hour.
2. Spread pecans on waxed paper. Drop dough by well rounded teaspoons onto nuts. Roll gently to coat and form balls. Transfer to a serving plate. Cover and chill for 1 to 4 hours. Serve with assorted crackers. Makes 24 servings.

EACH SERVING: 144 cal., 10 g total fat (2 g sat. fat), 8 mg chol., 193 mg sodium, 11 g carbo., 1 g fiber, 3 g pro. Daily Values: 10% vit. A, 1% vit. C, 3% calcium, 4% iron.

Ham Bites with Cilantro-Corn Cream

START TO FINISH: 25 MINUTES

- ¾ cup frozen corn, thawed
- 1 8-oz. carton dairy sour cream
- ⅓ cup snipped fresh cilantro
- 1 teaspoon bottled minced garlic
- 1 teaspoon Dijon-style mustard
- ¼ teaspoon salt
- ⅛ teaspoon cayenne pepper
- 4 to 6 ounces thinly sliced cooked ham
- 36 ¼-inch-thick diagonally sliced baguette slices, toasted

1. Drain corn; pat dry with paper towels. In a medium bowl combine the corn, sour cream, cilantro, garlic, mustard, salt, and cayenne pepper. Use immediately or cover and chill up to 6 hours.
2. To make ham bites, cut ham slices to fit baguette slices. Place ham on baguette slices; top with the sour cream mixture. Serve immediately. Makes 36 slices.

EACH SLICE: 39 cal., 2 g total fat (1 g sat. fat), 5 mg chol., 102 mg sodium, 4 g carbo., 0 g fiber, 1 g pro. Daily Values: 2% vit. A, 1% vit. C, 1% calcium, 1% iron.

HOT & SPICY ENTRÉES FROM THE GRILL

PATRICIA A. HARMON, BADEN, PA.

ELIZABETH LLODRA, LONGMEADOW, MASS.

Lime Jerked Pork with Banana Salsa

PREP: 30 MINUTES **MARINATE:** 1 HOUR
GRILL: 30 MINUTES **STAND:** 10 MINUTES

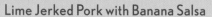

    2 Tbsp. finely shredded lime peel
  1/3 cup lime juice
    2 Tbsp. packed brown sugar
    1 Tbsp. canola oil or cooking oil
    1 Tbsp. Jamaican jerk seasoning
    2 cloves garlic, minced
  1/4 tsp. cayenne pepper
    2 pork tenderloins (about 3/4 lb. each)
    1 recipe Banana Salsa

1. For marinade, in a bowl combine lime peel, lime juice, brown sugar, oil, jerk seasoning, garlic, and cayenne pepper. Place pork tenderloins in a large resealable plastic bag set in a shallow dish. Pour marinade over pork. Seal bag. Marinate in the refrigerator for 1 hour, turning bag occasionally. Drain pork, discarding marinade. Prepare Banana Salsa.

2. For a charcoal grill, arrange hot coals around a drip pan. Test for medium-high heat above pan. Place pork on grill rack over the drip pan. Cover and grill for 30 to 35 minutes or until an instant-read thermometer inserted in pork registers 155°F. (For a gas grill, preheat grill. Reduce heat to medium-high. Adjust for indirect cooking. Place pork on rack in a roasting pan, place on grill rack, and grill as above.) Let pork stand for 10 minutes. Slice and serve with Banana Salsa. Makes 8 servings.

BANANA SALSA: In a small bowl combine 1 cup chopped banana; 1/3 cup raisins; 2 medium fresh jalapeño chile peppers, seeded and finely chopped (see note, page 49); 3 tablespoons lime juice; 2 tablespoons finely chopped red onion; 1 tablespoon canola oil or cooking oil; 1 tablespoon frozen orange juice concentrate, thawed; 2 teaspoons snipped fresh cilantro; 1 teaspoon ground coriander; 1 teaspoon honey; and 1 teaspoon grated fresh ginger.

LOW FAT **EACH SERVING:** 167 cal., 5 g total fat (1 g sat. fat), 55 mg chol., 64 mg sodium, 13 g carbo., 1 g fiber, 18 g pro. Daily Values: 2% vit. A, 18% vit. C, 1% calcium, 7% iron.

Spicy Grilled Shrimp

PREP: 15 MINUTES **GRILL:** 7 MINUTES **MARINATE:** 1 HOUR

  1 1/2 lb. fresh or frozen peeled and deveined extra-large shrimp
  1/4 cup orange marmalade
  1/4 cup honey
    2 to 3 tsp. Cajun seasoning
    1 Tbsp. olive oil
    2 cups hot cooked rice

1. Thaw shrimp, if frozen. If using wooden skewers, soak in water for 1 hour. Rinse shrimp; pat dry. In a small saucepan stir together marmalade, honey, and 1/2 teaspoon of the Cajun seasoning; set aside.

2. Place shrimp in a resealable plastic bag set in a shallow bowl. For marinade, in a small bowl combine oil and remaining Cajun seasoning. Pour marinade over shrimp. Seal bag. Marinate in the refrigerator for 1 hour, turning bag occasionally.

3. Drain shrimp, discarding marinade. Thread shrimp onto skewers. For a charcoal grill, place skewers on the greased rack of an uncovered grill directly over medium coals. Grill for 7 to 9 minutes or until shrimp are opaque, turning halfway through grilling. (For a gas grill, preheat grill. Reduce heat to medium. Place skewers on greased grill rack over heat. Cover; grill as above.)

4. Cook and stir marmalade mixture over low heat for 2 to 3 minutes or until melted. Transfer shrimp to plates; drizzle with marmalade mixture. Serve with hot cooked rice. Makes 4 servings.

LOW FAT **EACH SERVING:** 430 cal., 7 g total fat (1 g sat. fat), 259 mg chol., 357 mg sodium, 55 g carbo., 1 g fiber, 37 g pro. Daily Values: 6% vit. A, 8% vit. C, 11% calcium, 30% iron.

Honey-Banana Baby Back Ribs

PREP: 25 MINUTES **BAKE:** 1½ HOURS
GRILL: 10 MINUTES

- 2 Tbsp. paprika
- 1 Tbsp. ground chipotle pepper
- 1 Tbsp. ground cumin
- 2 tsp. packed brown sugar
- ½ tsp. garlic powder
- ½ to 1 tsp. cayenne pepper
- 4 lb. pork loin back ribs
- 1 recipe Honey-Banana Barbecue Sauce

1. Preheat oven to 350°F. For rub, combine paprika, chipotle pepper, cumin, brown sugar, 1 teaspoon *salt*, garlic powder, and cayenne pepper.
2. Cut ribs into serving-size pieces. Rub mixture onto both sides. Place in a roasting pan. Bake, covered, about 1½ hours or until ribs are tender.
3. For a charcoal grill, place ribs, bone sides down, on grill rack directly over medium coals. (Or place ribs in a rib rack; place on grill rack.) Grill for 5 minutes. Brush with Honey-Banana Barbecue Sauce and grill 5 minutes more or until glazed and heated through. Heat and pass sauce with ribs. Makes 6 servings.

HONEY-BANANA BARBECUE SAUCE: In a medium saucepan cook ½ cup finely chopped onion and 2 cloves garlic, minced, in 1 tablespoon hot cooking oil until tender. Stir in 1 cup chili sauce, ½ cup mashed ripe banana (1 large), ⅓ cup honey, and ¼ cup orange juice. Bring to boiling; reduce heat. Simmer, uncovered, about 10 minutes or until desired consistency, stirring occasionally.

EACH SERVING: 601 cal., 39 g total fat (13 g sat. fat), 122 mg chol., 1,116 mg sodium, 36 g carbo., 5 g fiber, 27 g pro. Daily Values: 31% vit. A, 29% vit. C, 9% calcium, 15% iron.

Chorizo Burgers

PREP: 25 MINUTES **GRILL:** 20 MINUTES

- 1 egg, slightly beaten
- ¼ cup fine dry bread crumbs
- 1 tsp. dried oregano, crushed
- 1 tsp. dried thyme, crushed
- 8 oz. lean ground beef
- 8 oz. chorizo sausage
- 4 slices Monterey Jack cheese with jalapeño peppers
- 4 kaiser rolls, split and toasted
- 1 recipe Chile Pepper Salsa (optional)

1. In a bowl combine egg, bread crumbs, oregano, thyme, and ¼ teaspoon *salt*. Add beef and chorizo; mix well. Shape into four ¾-inch-thick patties.
2. For a charcoal grill, arrange medium-hot coals around a drip pan. Test for medium heat. Place patties on grill rack over drip pan. Cover and grill for 20 to 24 minutes or until an instant-read thermometer inserted into the side of a patty registers 160°F, turning halfway through grilling and adding cheese the last 1 minute. Serve on kaiser rolls with Chile Pepper Salsa. Makes 4 servings.

CHILE PEPPER SALSA: Combine 2 medium tomatoes, seeded and chopped; half of a 4-oz. can diced green chile peppers, drained; ¼ cup finely chopped onion; ¼ cup snipped fresh cilantro; 1 tablespoon lime juice; and ¼ teaspoon garlic salt.

EACH SERVING: 671 cal., 40 g total fat (16 g sat. fat), 164 mg chol., 1,526 mg sodium, 37 g carbo., 2 g fiber, 39 g pro. Daily Values: 8% vit. A, 31% calcium, 27% iron.

Glazed Chicken with Three-Pepper Salsa

PREP: 30 MINUTES **GRILL:** 12 MINUTES

- ⅓ cup red jalapeño pepper jelly
- 1 teaspoon finely shredded lime peel
- 1 tablespoon lime juice
- 1 tablespoon chopped chipotle pepper in adobo sauce
- ½ teaspoon bottled minced garlic (1 clove)
- 4 skinless, boneless chicken breast halves
- 1 recipe Three-Pepper Salsa

1. For glaze, in a small bowl combine jelly, lime peel, lime juice, chipotle peppers, ½ teaspoon *salt*, and garlic. Stir until combined.
2. Sprinkle chicken lightly with *salt* and *ground black pepper*. For a charcoal grill, grill chicken on the rack of an uncovered grill directly over medium coals for 12 to 15 minutes or until chicken is no longer pink (170°F), turning once halfway through grilling and brushing with sauce during the last 5 minutes of grilling. (For a gas grill, preheat grill. Reduce heat to medium. Place chicken on grill rack over heat. Cover and grill as above.) Serve with Three-Pepper Salsa and, if desired, *lime wedges*. Makes 4 servings.

THREE-PEPPER SALSA: In a medium bowl combine 1 large tomato, seeded and chopped; 4 cherry peppers, seeded and chopped; 1 jalapeño pepper, seeded and chopped (see note, page 49); ¼ cup finely chopped onion; 2 tablespoons snipped fresh cilantro; 1 tablespoon lime juice; 1 to 2 teaspoons finely chopped chipotle chile peppers in adobo sauce; 1 teaspoon bottled minced garlic; and ¼ teaspoon salt.

 EACH SERVING: 259 cal., 3 g total fat (1 g sat. fat), 82 mg chol., 698 mg sodium, 24 g carbo., 2 g fiber, 34 g pro. Daily Values: 16% vit. A, 20% vit. C, 3% calcium, 7% iron.

Ribeye Steaks with Chipotle-Cherry Butter

PREP: 25 MINUTES **GRILL:** 10 MINUTES

- 3 Tbsp. olive oil
- 1 Tbsp. chili powder
- 1 Tbsp. paprika
- 1 tsp. ground cumin
- 1 tsp. ground chipotle pepper
- ¾ tsp. garlic salt
- 4 beef ribeye steaks, cut 1 inch thick
- 1 recipe Chipotle-Cherry Butter

1. In a small bowl combine oil, chili powder, paprika, cumin, chipotle pepper, and garlic salt. Brush mixture evenly over both sides of steaks.
2. For a charcoal grill, grill steaks on the rack of an uncovered grill directly over medium coals until desired doneness, turning halfway through grilling. Allow 10 to 12 minutes for medium-rare (145°) or 12 to 15 minutes for medium doneness (160°F). Serve with Chipotle-Cherry Butter. Makes 4 servings.

CHIPOTLE-CHERRY BUTTER: In a small bowl combine ⅓ cup butter, softened; 2 tablespoons snipped dried tart cherries; 1 tablespoon finely chopped green onion; and 1 to 2 teaspoons finely chopped chipotle peppers in adobo sauce. Stir until combined.

EACH SERVING: 697 cal., 48 g total fat (19 g sat. fat), 206 mg chol., 476 mg sodium, 6 g carbo., 2 g fiber, 58 g pro. Daily Values: 42% vit. A, 4% vit. C, 5% calcium, 38% iron.

Salsa Verde Pork Salad

PREP: 20 MINUTES **MARINATE:** 2 HOURS
GRILL: 30 MINUTES **STAND:** 10 MINUTES

- 1¼ cups salsa verde
- 6 green onions, sliced (¾ cup)
- 1 cup fresh cilantro, snipped
  - Several dashes bottled hot pepper sauce
- ½ cup cooking oil
- 1 1- to 1¼-lb. pork tenderloin
- 1 10-oz. pkg. torn mixed salad greens
- 2 medium red sweet peppers, cut into strips
- ½ cup cucumber slices, halved
- ½ cup sliced radishes

1. Combine salsa verde, half of the green onions, half of the cilantro, ½ teaspoon *salt*, ¼ teaspoon *black pepper*, and hot pepper sauce. Whisk in oil until combined. Reserve ¾ cup of the salsa for dressing; cover and chill.
2. Trim fat from pork. Place pork in a resealable plastic bag set in a dish. Pour remaining salsa mixture over pork; seal bag. Marinate pork in the refrigerator for 2 to 4 hours, turning bag occasionally.
3. Drain pork, discarding marinade. For a charcoal grill, arrange hot coals around a drip pan. Test for medium-high heat above pan. Place meat on grill rack over pan. Cover and grill for 30 to 35 minutes or until an instant-read thermometer inserted in the pork registers 155°F. Let pork stand for 10 minutes before slicing.
4. In a very large salad bowl place greens, remaining onions, remaining cilantro, sweet pepper strips, cucumber, and radishes. Toss to combine. Stir reserved salsa mixture and add to the greens mixture, tossing to coat. Divide greens mixture equally among 4 to 6 dinner plates. Arrange pork slices on top of greens. Makes 4 to 6 servings.

EACH SERVING: 440 cal., 31 g total fat (5 g sat. fat), 73 mg chol., 464 mg sodium, 14 g carbo., 3 g fiber, 26 g pro. Daily Values: 76% vit. A, 217% vit. C, 7% calcium, 13% iron.

SIMPLE FRUIT DESSERTS

Watermelon with Fruit Salsa

START TO FINISH: 25 MINUTES **FAST!**

  2 kiwifruits, peeled and chopped
  2 mangoes, seeded, peeled, and chopped (2 cups)
  2 cups chopped fresh strawberries
  1 small fresh jalapeño pepper, seeded and finely chopped
     (about 1 tablespoon) (see note, page 49)
  ¼ cup snipped fresh mint
  2 Tbsp. lime juice
  2 Tbsp. honey
  ½ cup fresh raspberries
  8 1-inch-thick slices quartered watermelon
  1 pint lemon or lime sorbet or sherbet

1. In a large bowl combine kiwifruits, mangoes, strawberries, jalapeño pepper, mint, lime juice, and honey. Gently stir in raspberries. Serve immediately or cover and chill for up to 4 hours. Serve over watermelon quarters with sorbet. Makes 8 servings.

LOW FAT **EACH SERVING:** 220 cal., 1 g total fat (0 g sat. fat), 0 mg chol., 10 mg sodium, 55 g carbo., 4 g fiber, 3 g pro. Daily Values: 42% vit. A, 141% vit. C, 4% calcium, 8% iron.

Ginger Peach Freeze

PREP: 10 MINUTES **STAND:** 30 MINUTES **FREEZE:** 3 HOURS

  1 cup water
  1 cup sugar
  3 Tbsp. lemon juice
  ¼ tsp. ground ginger
  1 16-oz. pkg. frozen unsweetened peach slices
     Fresh peach slices (optional)

1. In a medium saucepan combine water, sugar, lemon juice, and ginger. Bring to boiling. Remove from heat and add frozen peaches. Let stand about 30 minutes or until peaches are thawed and mixture has cooled.

2. Transfer peach mixture, half at a time, to a blender. Cover and blend until smooth. Pour mixture into a 2-quart rectangular baking dish. Cover and freeze for 3 to 4 hours. Break up mixture with a fork and serve. If desired, garnish with fresh peach slices. Make 8 (½-cup) servings.

LOW FAT **EACH SERVING:** 119 cal., 0 g total fat, 0 mg chol., 1 mg sodium, 31 g carbo., 1 g fiber, 0 g pro. Daily Values: 6% vit. A, 11% vit. C.

Apple-Pear Pizza Pie

PREP: 20 MINUTES **BAKE:** 30 MINUTES

½ of a 15-oz. pkg. rolled refrigerated
  unbaked piecrust (1 crust)
½ cup packed brown sugar
½ cup regular or quick-cooking rolled oats
¼ cup all-purpose flour
½ tsp. apple pie spice or pumpkin pie spice
¼ cup butter
1 cup shredded sharp cheddar cheese
2 medium cooking apples, peeled, cored,
  and thinly sliced (2 cups)
1 medium pear, peeled, cored, and
  thinly sliced

1. Preheat oven to 400°F. Let piecrust stand according to package directions. Meanwhile, for topping, in a medium bowl combine brown sugar, oats, flour, and pie spice. Using a pastry blender, cut in butter until mixture resembles coarse crumbs; set aside.
2. Unroll piecrust. On a lightly floured surface, roll piecrust into a 13-inch circle. Transfer piecrust to a 12-inch round pizza pan. Build up edges slightly and crimp as desired. Sprinkle piecrust with cheese. Arrange apple and pear slices on top. Sprinkle with topping mixture.
3. Bake for 30 to 35 minutes or until top is golden brown and apples are tender. Cool about 30 minutes. Cut into wedges and serve warm. Makes 12 servings.
EACH SERVING: 224 cal., 12 g total fat (6 g sat. fat), 23 mg chol., 162 mg sodium, 26 g carbo., 1 g fiber, 3 g pro. Daily Values: 4% vit. A, 2% vit. C, 8% calcium, 3% iron.

Strawberry Ricotta Crostini

START TO FINISH: 30 MINUTES

1 8-oz. loaf baguette-style French bread
1 cup part-skim ricotta cheese, drained
¼ cup powdered sugar
1 tsp. finely shredded lime peel
1 tsp. vanilla
2 cups sliced fresh strawberries
2 Tbsp. lime juice
1 Tbsp. powdered sugar
2 Tbsp. honey

1. Preheat oven to 350°F. For crostini, slice baguette into ¼-inch slices and place on a baking sheet. Bake for 10 minutes, turning once halfway through baking time.
2. In a medium bowl stir together ricotta, the ¼ cup powdered sugar, the lime peel, and vanilla; set aside. In another medium bowl stir together strawberries, lime juice, and remaining 1 tablespoon powdered sugar. Spread ricotta mixture onto each crostini; top each piece with a few strawberry slices.

3. In a small bowl, microwave honey on high (100% power) for 20 seconds. Drizzle crostini with honey. Serve immediately. Makes 36 crostini.
PER CROSTINI: 37 cal., 1 g total fat (0 g sat. fat), 2 mg chol., 47 mg sodium, 6 g carbo., 0 g fiber, 1 g pro. Daily Values: 1% vit. A, 8% vit. C, 2% calcium, 1% iron.

Blueberry Tortilla Pizza

START TO FINISH: 20 MINUTES

1 10-inch flour tortilla
1 Tbsp. butter, melted
2 tsp. granulated sugar
¼ tsp. ground cinnamon
½ cup ricotta cheese or whipped
  cream cheese
1 Tbsp. powdered sugar
½ tsp. finely shredded lemon peel or
  orange peel
½ cup fresh blueberries
½ cup sliced fresh strawberries
¼ cup shredded or flaked coconut, toasted

1. Preheat broiler. Brush both sides of tortilla with butter. Place tortilla on a baking sheet. Broil 5 to 6 inches from the heat for 2 to 3 minutes or until lightly browned. Turn tortilla over. In a small bowl stir together granulated sugar and cinnamon. Sprinkle over tortilla. Broil 2 to 3 minutes more or until light brown. Remove and cool several minutes.
2. To serve, in a small bowl stir together cheese, powdered sugar, and lemon peel. Spread over tortilla. Top with berries. Sprinkle with coconut. Cut into wedges to serve. Makes 4 servings.
EACH SERVING: 179 cal., 10 g total fat (7 g sat. fat), 23 mg chol., 111 mg sodium, 17 g carbo., 2 g fiber, 5 g pro. Daily Values: 5% vit. A, 21% vit. C, 8% calcium, 4% iron.

Tropical Fruit Brûlée

PREP: 20 MINUTES **BROIL:** 4 MINUTES

1 3-oz. pkg. cream cheese, softened
⅓ cup dairy sour cream
¼ cup packed brown sugar
2 Tbsp. butter
1 20-oz. can pineapple chunks, drained
½ of a 24-oz. jar refrigerated mango slices,
  drained and cut into chunks (1 cup)
2 medium-ripe, firm bananas, peeled and
  cut into ½-inch slices
¼ cup granulated sugar
¼ cup shredded coconut

1. Preheat broiler. In a small bowl stir together cream cheese, sour cream, and 2 tablespoons of the brown sugar until combined (mixture may be lumpy); set aside.

2. In a large skillet cook and stir butter and remaining 2 tablespoons brown sugar over medium heat until melted and combined. Add pineapple, mango, and bananas. Cook and stir for 2 to 4 minutes or until fruit is just heated through.
3. Transfer fruit mixture to a 1½-quart broiler-proof shallow baking dish or au gratin dish. Spoon cream cheese mixture over the fruit mixture in small mounds; spread to an even layer. Sprinkle with granulated sugar. Broil 3 to 4 inches from the heat for 3 to 5 minutes or until sugar is light brown and bubbly. Remove dish from broiler and sprinkle with coconut. Broil about 1 minute more or until coconut is light brown (watch closely to prevent coconut from burning). Serve warm. Makes 6 servings.
EACH SERVING: 304 cal., 12 g total fat (8 g sat. fat), 30 mg chol., 87 mg sodium, 50 g carbo., 2 g fiber, 2 g pro. Daily Values: 15% vit. A, 46% vit. C, 5% calcium, 4% iron.

Pears with Walnut Streusel

PREP: 15 MINUTES **BAKE:** 15 MINUTES

1 29-oz. can pear slices, drained
¼ cup tub-style cream cheese
¼ cup dried cranberries
¼ cup all-purpose flour
¼ cup quick-cooking rolled oats
3 Tbsp. packed brown sugar
¼ tsp. ground nutmeg
¼ cup butter
¼ cup walnuts, coarsely chopped

1. Preheat oven to 375°F. Place sliced pears, cut sides up, in a 2-quart square baking dish. Combine cream cheese and cranberries; spoon into pear core openings. Set aside.
2. In a small bowl combine flour, rolled oats, brown sugar, and nutmeg; cut in butter until mixture resembles coarse crumbs. Stir in walnuts. Sprinkle over pears.
3. Bake, uncovered, for 15 minutes. Serve warm. Makes 6 servings.
EACH SERVING: 307 cal., 15 g total fat (7 g sat. fat), 31 mg chol., 94 mg sodium, 44 g carbo., 3 g fiber, 3 g pro. Daily Values: 7% vit. A, 3% vit. C, 3% calcium, 6% iron.

NOODLE BOWLS

Rice Noodles with Shrimp

START TO FINISH: 35 MINUTES

 1 Tbsp. green curry paste or Homemade Curry Paste
 2 Tbsp. olive oil
 1 14-oz. can unsweetened coconut milk
 1 14-oz. can chicken broth
¼ cup lemon juice
 2 Tbsp. fish sauce
 1 14-oz. pkg. wide rice stick noodles
 1 lb. large shrimp, peeled, deveined, and cut in half lengthwise
 1 large red sweet pepper, cut into thin strips
 1 cup fresh snow pea pods, trimmed
¼ cup chopped fresh cilantro leaves
 2 hard-cooked eggs, quartered

1. For sauce, in a large saucepan cook curry paste in hot oil until fragrant and beginning to stick to pan. Add coconut milk, broth, lemon juice and fish sauce. Bring to boiling; reduce heat. Simmer, uncovered, for 8 to 10 minutes or until reduced to 3⅔ cups.

2. Cook noodles in boiling salted *water* for 4 to 6 minutes or until tender; drain. Rinse noodles under cold water; drain. Divide noodles among 4 bowls. Add shrimp, sweet pepper, and snow peas to sauce. Return to boiling; reduce heat. Simmer, uncovered, for 1 to 3 minutes or until shrimp are opaque and vegetables are crisp-tender. Stir in cilantro. Spoon sauce mixture over noodles. Garnish with eggs. Makes 4 servings.

HOMEMADE CURRY PASTE: In a food processor or blender combine 1 large onion, chopped; 2 stalks lemongrass, thinly sliced (tender white portion only); ¼ cup water; a 2-inch piece of peeled fresh ginger, cut up; a handful of cilantro stems; 2 to 3 fresh serrano chile peppers, seeded (see note, page 49); 4 cloves garlic, minced; 1 to 2 teaspoons curry powder; 1 teaspoon five-spice powder; and ¾ teaspoon salt. Cover and process or blend until smooth.

EACH SERVING: 781 cal., 32 g total fat (19 g sat. fat), 236 mg chol., 1,402 mg sodium, 96 g carbo., 3 g fiber, 24 g pro. Daily Values: 35% vit. A, 120% vit. C, 12% calcium, 34% iron.

Peanut-Chicken Bowl

START TO FINISH: 25 MINUTES **FAST!**

 2 3-oz. pkg. Oriental-flavor ramen noodles
 3 cups cut-up vegetables, such as broccoli florets, red sweet pepper strips, halved pea pods, and/or thinly sliced carrots
1¼ cups water
¼ cup peanut butter
¼ cup soy sauce
 2 Tbsp. packed brown sugar
 1 Tbsp. cornstarch
½ tsp. crushed red pepper
 2 cups chopped cooked chicken
 1 8-oz. can sliced water chestnuts, drained
 1 8-oz. can bamboo shoots, drained
¼ cup chopped peanuts
¼ cup sliced green onions (about 2)

1. In a large saucepan bring 2 quarts *water* to boiling. Break up noodles slightly and add to water along with cut-up vegetables. Set aside 1 seasoning packet from noodles to use in recipe and save remaining packet for another use. Return mixture to boiling; reduce heat. Boil gently, uncovered, for 3 minutes. Drain mixture and return to saucepan.

2. Meanwhile, for sauce, in a medium saucepan whisk together the 1¼ cups water, the peanut butter, soy sauce, brown sugar, cornstarch, crushed red pepper, and reserved seasoning packet until smooth. Cook and stir over medium heat until thickened and bubbly. Cook and stir for 2 minutes more. Add chicken, water chestnuts, and bamboo shoots to sauce; heat through. Add to noodle mixture in saucepan. Toss to combine. Serve immediately in bowls; top with peanuts and green onions. Makes 4 servings.

EACH SERVING: 646 cal., 30 g total fat (4 g sat. fat), 82 mg chol., 1,511 mg sodium, 64 g carbo., 6 g fiber, 38 g pro. Daily Values: 37% vit. A, 113% vit. C, 27% calcium, 21% iron.

Chicken with Pickled Ginger Noodle Bowl

START TO FINISH: 40 MINUTES

- 6 oz. rice stick noodles
- 1 Tbsp. wasabi powder
- 3 Tbsp. cooking oil
- 1 medium red sweet pepper, cut into bite-size strips
- 1 medium yellow sweet pepper, cut into bite-size strips
- 1 lb. skinless, boneless chicken breasts, cut into thin bite-size strips
- ¼ cup chopped pickled ginger
- 1 14-oz. can reduced-sodium chicken broth
- ¼ cup soy sauce
- 2 Tbsp. lemon juice
- 2 cups pea pods, halved

1. Prepare noodles according to package directions; set aside. Combine ¼ cup water and wasabi powder; set aside. In a 12-inch skillet heat oil over medium-high heat. Cook and stir sweet pepper strips for 3 to 4 minutes or until crisp-tender; remove and set aside.

2. Add chicken and pickled ginger to skillet. Cook and stir for 4 to 5 minutes or until chicken is no longer pink. Stir in chicken broth, wasabi mixture, soy sauce, and lemon juice. Bring to boiling; reduce heat. Stir in pepper strips, pea pods, and cooked noodles; heat through. Makes 6 servings.

 EACH SERVING: 296 cal., 8 g total fat (1 g sat. fat), 44 mg chol., 968 mg sodium, 33 g carbo., 2 g fiber, 20 g pro. Daily Values: 15% vit. A, 166% vit. C, 3% calcium, 11% iron.

Pork and Asparagus Char Siu

PREP: 25 MINUTES MARINATE: 30 MINUTES
COOK: 10 MINUTES

- ⅓ cup char siu* (Chinese barbecue sauce)
- 3 Tbsp. cooking oil
- ½ tsp. grated fresh ginger or ⅛ teaspoon ground ginger
- 8 oz. pork tenderloin, cut into bite-size pieces
- 6 oz. dried linguine
- 2 cloves garlic, minced
- ½ tsp. grated fresh ginger
- 12 oz. asparagus, trimmed and cut into 1-inch pieces
- 4 green onions, sliced diagonally
- ½ of a 16-oz. pkg. shredded broccoli (broccoli slaw mix) (3⅓ cups)
- 1 14-oz. can reduced-sodium chicken broth

1. In a resealable plastic bag combine 2 tablespoons of the char siu, 1 tablespoon of the oil, and the ½ teaspoon ginger. Add pork; seal bag and turn to coat with marinade. Marinate in the refrigerator for 30 minutes to 1 hour. Drain.

2. Cook linguine according to package directions; drain and set aside.

3. Meanwhile, in a wok or an extra-large skillet heat 1 tablespoon of the oil over medium-high heat; add pork. Cook and stir for 2 to 3 minutes or until no longer pink. Remove from pan; set aside. Add remaining oil, the garlic, and the ½ teaspoon ginger; cook for 30 seconds. Add asparagus. Cook and stir over medium-high heat for 2 to 4 minutes or until crisp-tender.

4. Add green onions and broccoli slaw mix; cook and stir for 2 to 3 minutes more. Add drained linguine, pork, the remaining char siu, and broth. Heat through. If desired, top with additional green onions. Makes 4 servings.

*NOTE: If desired, substitute 3 tablespoons hoisin sauce and 3 tablespoons barbecue sauce for the ⅓ cup char siu.

EACH SERVING: 434 cal., 13 g total fat (2 g sat. fat), 37 mg chol., 1,566 mg sodium, 57 g carbo., 4 g fiber, 22 g pro. Daily Values: 43% vit. A, 90% vit. C, 6% calcium, 20% iron.

Green Curry Chicken

START TO FINISH: 30 MINUTES

- 8 oz. rice vermicelli noodles or dried vermicelli pasta
- 12 oz. skinless, boneless chicken breast halves, cut into bite-size strips
- 1 Tbsp. cooking oil
- 1 14-oz. can unsweetened coconut milk
- 2 Tbsp. soy sauce
- 1 to 2 tsp. green curry paste
- 2 cups cauliflower florets
- 1 medium red sweet pepper, cut into strips
- ½ cup packaged shredded fresh carrot

1. Cook vermicelli according to package directions; drain and keep warm.

2. Meanwhile, in a large skillet cook chicken in hot oil over medium heat for 3 to 4 minutes or until no longer pink; remove from skillet. Stir in coconut milk, soy sauce, and curry paste. Bring to boiling; reduce heat. Boil gently, uncovered, for 5 minutes. Add cauliflower; simmer, uncovered, for 5 minutes. Add sweet pepper, carrot, and chicken. Return to boiling; reduce heat and simmer about 3 minutes more or until vegetables are crisp-tender.

3. Divide noodles among 4 bowls; top with chicken mixture. Makes 4 servings.

EACH SERVING: 538 cal., 26 g total fat (20 g sat. fat), 49 mg chol., 633 mg sodium, 56 g carbo., 4 g fiber, 24 g pro. Daily Values: 66% vit. A, 138% vit. C, 8% calcium, 30% iron.

Plum-Sauced Chicken Pasta Bowls

START TO FINISH: 30 MINUTES

- 8 oz. dried spaghetti, broken
- 1 lb. skinless, boneless chicken breasts, cut into 1-inch pieces
- ½ tsp. ground black pepper
- 1 Tbsp. cooking oil
- 1 cup broccoli florets
- ½ cup chopped green sweet pepper
- ¼ cup finely chopped onion
- 1 14-oz. can reduced-sodium chicken broth
- ½ cup plum sauce
- 2 Tbsp. rice vinegar or cider vinegar
- 2 Tbsp. soy sauce
    Snipped fresh parsley

1. In a large saucepan cook spaghetti according to package directions. Drain and return to saucepan. Cover and keep warm.

2. Meanwhile, in a medium bowl toss chicken with black pepper. In a large skillet heat oil over medium-high heat. Add half of the chicken; cook and stir for 5 minutes or until chicken is no longer pink. Remove from skillet. Add remaining chicken, broccoli, sweet pepper, and onion. Cook and stir for 5 minutes or until chicken is no longer pink. Stir into pasta with remaining chicken. Stir in chicken broth, plum sauce, vinegar, and soy sauce. Heat through. Ladle into bowls and sprinkle with parsley. Makes 4 servings.

 EACH SERVING: 459 cal., 6 g total fat (1 g sat. fat), 65 mg chol., 947 mg sodium, 62 g carbo., 3 g fiber, 38 g pro. Daily Values: 9% vit. A, 63% vit. C, 5% calcium, 15% iron.

Seafood and Garlic Noodle Bowl

START TO FINISH: 30 MINUTES

- 2 Tbsp. minced garlic (12 cloves)
- 2 Tbsp. cooking oil
- 1 pound bok choy, trimmed and coarsely chopped (4 cups)
- 1 15-oz. can straw mushrooms, drained
- 1 14-oz. can chicken broth
- 2 cups water
- 1 3-oz. pkg. shrimp-flavor ramen noodles
- 12 oz. peeled and deveined shrimp and/or ¾-inch pieces firm-textured white fish
- ¼ cup snipped fresh cilantro
- 1 Tbsp. toasted sesame oil
    Fresh cilantro sprigs and lime wedges

1. In a 4-quart Dutch oven cook garlic in hot oil for 30 seconds. Add bok choy and mushrooms; cook and stir for 1 minute. Add broth and water; bring to boiling. Stir in noodles, seasoning packet, and shrimp. Return to boiling; reduce heat.

2. Simmer, uncovered, for 3 minutes or until shrimp are opaque (or fish flakes), stirring occasionally to break up noodles.

3. Add snipped cilantro and sesame oil. Serve in bowls. Garnish with cilantro sprigs and lime wedges. Makes 4 servings.

EACH SERVING: 285 cal., 15 g total fat (2 g sat. fat), 130 mg chol., 1,067 mg sodium, 16 g carbo., 3 g fiber, 24 g pro. Daily Values: 71% vit. A, 62% vit. C, 15% calcium, 23% iron.

AFTER-SCHOOL SNACKS

Nutty Cereal Cookies

PREP: 30 MINUTES **BAKE:** 12 MINUTES PER BATCH **STAND:** 2 MINUTES

> 1 cup all-purpose flour
> ½ cup flaxseed meal
> 1 tsp. baking powder
> 1 tsp. baking soda
> 1 tsp. ground cinnamon
> 1 cup butter, softened
> 1 cup granulated sugar
> 1 cup packed brown sugar
> 2 eggs
> 1 tsp. vanilla
> 2 cups wheat cereal flakes
> 2 cups rolled oats
> 1½ cups chopped walnuts, toasted
> 1½ cups dried cranberries, raisins, dried cherries, or dried blueberries

1. Preheat oven to 325°F. In a medium bowl combine flour, flaxseed meal, baking powder, baking soda, and cinnamon; set aside.

2. In a large bowl beat butter with an electric mixer on medium to high speed for 30 seconds. Add granulated sugar and brown sugar. Beat until combined, scraping sides of bowl occasionally. Beat in eggs and vanilla until combined. Beat in as much of the flour mixture as you can with the mixer. Stir in any remaining flour mixture. Stir in wheat cereal, oats, walnuts, and dried fruit.

3. Drop by well-rounded teaspoons 2 inches apart onto cookie sheets lined with parchment paper. Bake for 12 to 14 minutes or until golden and set. Let cool on cookie sheets 2 minutes. Transfer cookies to a wire rack and cool. Makes about 60 cookies.

EACH COOKIE: 110 cal., 6 g total fat (2 g sat. fat), 15 mg chol., 58 mg sodium, 14 g carbo., 1 g fiber, 2 g pro. Daily Values: 2% vit. A, 1% calcium, 4% iron.

Tutti-Fruity Smoothie

START TO FINISH: 10 MINUTES FAST!

> 1 banana, peeled and cut up
> ¼ cup fresh or frozen blueberries
> ¼ cup sliced fresh or frozen strawberries
> ¾ cup light vanilla soymilk or milk
> ½ cup pomegranate-blueberry juice, pomegranate juice, grape juice, or cranberry juice, chilled
> ½ cup vanilla frozen yogurt or pineapple sherbet

1. In a blender combine banana, berries, soymilk, juice, and yogurt. Cover and blend until smooth. Pour into glasses. Makes 2 servings.

EACH SERVING: 209 cal., 4 g total fat (2 g sat. fat), 5 mg chol., 80 mg sodium, 42 g carbo., 3 g fiber, 4 g pro. Daily Values: 5% vit. A, 30% vit. C, 19% calcium, 3% iron.

Banana Oatmeal Cookies

PREP: 30 MINUTES
CHILL: 1 HOUR
BAKE: 8 MINUTES PER BATCH

½ cup butter, softened
1 cup sugar
¾ tsp. ground cinnamon
½ tsp. baking soda
¼ tsp. ground nutmeg
1 cup mashed banana (about 3 medium)
1 egg
1 tsp. vanilla
1¼ cups all-purpose flour
1¾ cups quick-cooking rolled oats
¾ cup raisins
½ cup coarsely chopped dried cherries
½ cup chopped pecans, toasted

1. Beat butter with an electric mixer on medium to high speed for 30 seconds. Add sugar, cinnamon, ½ teaspoon *salt*, baking soda, and nutmeg. Beat until well combined, scraping sides of bowl occasionally. Beat in mashed banana, egg, and vanilla until combined (mixture will be lumpy). Beat in flour. Stir in oats, raisins, cherries, and pecans. Cover and chill dough for 1 to 24 hours.
2. Preheat oven to 375°F. Form dough into 1-inch balls and place 2 inches apart on greased cookie sheets. Flatten balls by hand to ½-inch thickness. Bake for 8 to 10 minutes or until edges are light brown and centers are set. Transfer cookies to a wire rack to cool. Makes 4½ dozen cookies.

EACH COOKIE: 73 cal., 3 g total fat (1 g sat. fat), 8 mg chol., 47 mg sodium, 12 g carbo., 1 g fiber, 1 g pro. Daily Values: 2% vit. A, 1% vit. C, 2% iron.

Fruit 'n' Popcorn Bites

PREP: 25 MINUTES **STAND:** 30 MINUTES

6 cups popped popcorn
1 cup dried cranberries
1 cup shredded coconut, toasted
¾ cup slivered almonds, toasted
Butter
1 10-oz. pkg. marshmallows
3 Tbsp. butter

1. Combine popcorn, cranberries, coconut, and almonds. Toss to combine. Line a very large baking sheet with foil; butter the foil and set aside.
2. In a saucepan combine marshmallows and 3 tablespoons butter. Cook and stir over medium heat until melted. Pour over popcorn mixture; stir to coat completely. Drop by large spoonfuls onto prepared baking sheet, using spoons to shape into mounds. Flatten slightly with the spoon. Cover with waxed paper; let stand for 30 minutes. Wrap each in plastic wrap. Store at room temperature for up to 2 days. Makes 16 pieces.

EACH PIECE: 164 cal., 7 g total fat (3 g sat. fat), 6 mg chol., 32 mg sodium, 25 g carbo., 2 g fiber, 2 g pro. Daily Values: 1% vit. A, 2% calcium, 3% iron.

Roasted Snack Mix

PREP: 10 MINUTES **BAKE:** 24 MINUTES

3 cups bite-size shredded wheat biscuits
1½ cups tiny pretzel twists
1 cup oyster crackers
½ cup peanuts
¼ cup extra virgin olive oil
2 tsp. dried Italian seasoning, crushed
½ tsp. seasoned salt
¼ tsp. ground black pepper

1. Preheat oven to 300°F. In a large roasting pan combine shredded wheat biscuits, pretzels, crackers, and peanuts; set aside.
2. In a small bowl combine olive oil, Italian seasoning, salt, and pepper. Microwave on high (100% power) for 30 seconds. Drizzle oil mixture over cereal mixture, stirring to coat.
3. Bake for 24 to 30 minutes or until lightly toasted, stirring every 8 minutes. Spread cereal mixture on a large sheet of foil to cool. Store in an airtight container. Makes 12 (½-cup) servings.

EACH SERVING: 141 cal., 8 g total fat (1 g sat. fat), 0 mg chol., 222 mg sodium, 15 g carbo., 2 g fiber, 3 g pro. Daily Values: 1% calcium, 14% iron.

Sweet Potato Bread Snacks

PREP: 25 MINUTES **BAKE:** 55 MINUTES
STAND: OVERNIGHT

2 cups all-purpose flour
¾ cup whole wheat flour
1½ tsp. baking powder
½ tsp. baking soda
½ tsp. salt
½ tsp. ground cinnamon
1 cup mashed cooked or canned sweet potato
1 cup mashed banana (3 medium)
2 Tbsp. milk
2 tsp. vanilla
1 cup butter-flavor shortening
1 cup granulated sugar
1 cup packed dark brown sugar
4 eggs
Peanut butter (optional)
Sliced bananas or miniature semisweet chocolate pieces (optional)

1. Preheat oven to 350°F. Grease bottom and ½ inch up the sides of two 8×4×2- or 9×5×3-inch loaf pans; set aside. In a medium bowl stir together flours, baking powder, baking soda, salt, and cinnamon; set aside. In another bowl stir together sweet potato, banana, milk, and vanilla; set aside.
2. In a large mixing bowl beat shortening and sugars until combined. Add eggs, 1 at a time, beating until combined. Alternately add flour mixture and banana mixture, beating well after each addition. Spread batter in prepared pans.
3. Bake for 55 to 65 minutes for the 8×4-inch pan or 45 to 55 minutes for the 9×5-inch pan or until a wooden toothpick inserted in centers comes

out clean. Cool in pans for 10 minutes; remove from pans. Cool on wire racks. Wrap and store overnight before slicing.
4. If desired, spread each slice with peanut butter; top with banana slices or miniature chocolate pieces. Makes 2 loaves (32 servings).

EACH SERVING: 168 cal., 7 g total fat (2 g sat. fat), 27 mg chol., 82 mg sodium, 25 g carbo., 1 g fiber, 2 g pro. Daily Values: 35% vit. A, 4% vit. C, 2% calcium, 5% iron.

Whole Wheat Graham Cookies

PREP: 45 MINUTES
BAKE: 10 MINUTES PER BATCH

⅔ cup milk
½ cup honey
2 cups whole wheat flour
2 cups all-purpose flour
1 cup quick-cooking rolled oats
½ cup packed brown sugar
2 tsp. baking powder
½ tsp. baking soda
½ tsp. salt
⅔ cup butter
½ cup shortening
3 Tbsp. granulated sugar
½ tsp. ground cinnamon

1. Preheat oven to 375°F. In a small bowl stir together milk and honey until well combined. Set aside. In a large bowl stir together whole wheat flour, all-purpose flour, oats, brown sugar, baking powder, baking soda, and salt. Using a pastry blender, cut in butter and shortening until mixture resembles coarse crumbs. Make a well in center of flour mixture. Add milk mixture all at once. Using a fork, stir until mixture can be gathered into a ball.
2. Turn dough out onto a lightly floured surface. Knead dough by gently folding and pressing for 12 to 15 strokes or until dough is nearly smooth. Divide dough into thirds.
3. Sprinkle surface with additional whole wheat flour. Roll each third of dough into a 12×12-inch square. Using a pastry wheel or pizza cutter, cut dough lengthwise into six strips. Cut strips crosswise into six strips to make thirty-six 2-inch squares. Place on ungreased baking sheets. If desired, prick cookies in several places with the tines of a fork. Combine granulated sugar and cinnamon; sprinkle on top of cookies.
4. Bake for 10 to 12 minutes or until tops are light brown. Transfer to wire racks to cool. Store in an airtight container at room temperature for up to 3 days or freeze for up to 3 months. Makes 108 cookies.

ANIMAL CRACKERS: Instead of cutting with a pastry wheel, use 2-inch animal-shape cookie cutters.
EACH COOKIE: 47 cal., 2 g total fat (1 g sat. fat), 3 mg chol., 30 mg sodium, 6 g carbo., 0 g fiber, 1 g pro. Daily Values: 1% vit. A, 1% calcium, 1% iron.

SAUSAGE SUPPERS

PRIZE TESTED RECIPES® $400 WINNER

CANDACE McMENAMIN, LEXINGTON, S.C.

PRIZE TESTED RECIPES® $200 WINNER

CHRISTINE WOOD, SANTA CRUZ, CALIF.

Picadillo Sandwiches

PREP: 10 MINUTES **COOK:** 20 MINUTES

- 1 lb. bulk pork sausage
- 1 large onion, chopped (1 cup)
- 1 14½-oz. can petite diced tomatoes, undrained
- ½ cup golden raisins
- ¼ cup chopped green olives
- 2 Tbsp. tomato paste
- 1 Tbsp. balsamic vinegar
- ½ tsp. ground cumin
- ½ tsp. dried oregano, crushed
- ⅛ tsp. crushed red pepper (optional)
- 6 hoagie buns, split and toasted
- 1 cup shredded Monterey Jack cheese (4 oz.)

1. In a 12-inch skillet cook sausage and onion for 10 minutes or until sausage is brown and onion is tender. Drain off fat. Stir in undrained tomatoes, raisins, olives, tomato paste, vinegar, cumin, oregano, and, if desired, crushed red pepper. Bring to boiling; reduce heat. Simmer, uncovered, for 10 minutes or until sauce is thickened. Serve mixture on toasted buns. Top with cheese and add bun tops. Makes 6 sandwiches.

EACH SANDWICH: 750 cal., 29 g total fat (11 g sat. fat), 66 mg chol., 1,399 mg sodium, 91 g carbo., 6 g fiber, 28 g pro. Daily Values: 4% vit. A, 19% vit. C, 29% calcium, 30% iron.

Baked Spaghetti Squash

PREP: 30 MINUTES **COOK:** 13 MINUTES
BAKE: 35 MINUTES **STAND:** 10 MINUTES

- 1 medium spaghetti squash (2¼ lb.)
- 12 oz. bulk Italian sausage
- 1½ cups sliced fresh mushrooms
- 1 medium green or red sweet pepper, chopped
- ⅓ cup finely chopped onion
- 3 cloves garlic, minced
  Nonstick cooking spray
- 1 4¼-oz. can chopped, pitted ripe olives (optional)
- ½ tsp. dried Italian seasoning, crushed
- ⅛ tsp. ground black pepper
- 1½ cups purchased red pasta sauce
- 1½ cups shredded Monterey Jack, mozzarella, or Italian blend cheese (6 oz.)
- ¼ cup snipped fresh flat-leaf parsley

1. Halve squash crosswise; remove seeds and strings. Place squash, cut sides down, in a 2-quart rectangular baking dish. Add ¼ cup *water.* Cover with vented plastic wrap. Microwave on high (100% power) for 13 to 15 minutes or until squash is tender, carefully rearranging squash once during cooking.
2. Meanwhile, in a large skillet cook sausage, mushrooms, sweet pepper, onion, and garlic over medium heat until sausage is brown, stirring to break up sausage. Drain off fat; set sausage mixture aside.
3. Preheat oven to 350°F. Hold squash with a pot holder and scrape the stringy pulp from the shell (you should have about 3 cups). Wipe out the baking dish; lightly coat with cooking spray. Evenly spread half of the squash in the dish. Top with half of the sausage mixture and, if desired, half of the olives. Sprinkle with Italian seasoning and black pepper. Top with half of the sauce and half of the cheese. Top with remaining squash, remaining sausage mixture, remaining olives (if desired), and remaining sauce.
4. Bake, uncovered, for 30 minutes. Sprinkle with remaining cheese. Bake, uncovered, 5 minutes more or until heated through and cheese is melted. Let stand on a wire rack for 10 minutes. Sprinkle with parsley. Makes 6 servings.
EACH SERVING: 351 cal., 24 g total fat (11 g sat. fat), 64 mg chol., 941 mg sodium, 13 g carbo., 4 g fiber, 18 g pro. Daily Values: 16% vit. A, 42% vit. C, 27% calcium, 16% iron.

Savory Sausage and Bow Ties

PREP: 25 MINUTES **COOK:** 20 MINUTES

8 oz. dried bow tie pasta
1 lb. uncooked hot-style Italian sausage links, cut into ½-inch slices
2 cloves garlic, minced
1 medium onion, cut into thin wedges
1 medium fennel, cored and cut into thin wedges
⅛ to ¼ tsp. crushed red pepper
⅛ tsp. ground black pepper
1 cup whipping cream
⅓ cup purchased dried tomato pesto
4 ounces Asiago or Parmesan cheese, finely shredded (1 cup)
Salt
¼ cup chopped fresh flat-leaf parsley

1. Cook pasta according to package directions; drain and set aside.
2. Meanwhile, in a 12-inch skillet cook sausage over medium heat until brown. Drain fat. Add garlic, onion, fennel, crushed red pepper, and black pepper, Cook, uncovered, over medium heat for 10 minutes or until vegetables are just tender, stirring occasionally. Stir in whipping cream and tomato pesto. Bring to boiling; reduce heat. Simmer, uncovered, for 2 to 3 minutes or until cream is slightly thickened. Stir in ½ cup of the cheese until melted. Stir in cooked pasta and heat through. Season to taste with salt.
3. Transfer pasta mixture to a serving platter and sprinkle with remaining cheese and the parsley. Makes 6 servings.
EACH SERVING: 642 cal., 44 g total fat (21 g sat. fat), 127 mg chol., 735 mg sodium, 35 g carbo., 2 g fiber, 22 g pro. Daily Values: 18% vit. A, 12% vit. C, 24% calcium, 10% iron.

Sausage and Radicchio in Vodka Sauce

PREP: 15 MINUTES **STAND:** 30 MINUTES
COOK: 15 MINUTES

1 small radicchio, cored and coarsely chopped (about 2½ cups)
1 lb. bulk mild Italian sausage
1 medium onion, cut into thin wedges
3 cloves garlic, minced
4 tsp. all-purpose flour
¾ cup whipping cream
3 roma tomatoes, coarsely chopped
2 Tbsp. snipped fresh flat-leaf parsley
¼ tsp. ground black pepper
Dash salt
2 Tbsp. vodka
8 oz. dried penne pasta (2½ cups)
2 Tbsp. freshly shredded Parmesan cheese

1. In a large bowl soak radicchio in lightly salted cold water to cover for 30 minutes. Drain well.
2. In a 12-inch skillet cook sausage, onion, and garlic until meat is brown and onion is tender; drain off fat. Add radicchio; cook and stir for 2 to 3 minutes or until wilted. Stir in flour. Add cream, tomatoes, parsley, pepper, and salt. Cook and stir until bubbly; cook and stir for 2 to 3 minutes more or until slightly thickened. Stir in vodka.
3. Meanwhile, cook penne according to package directions; drain. Serve sausage mixture over penne; sprinkle with Parmesan cheese. Makes 4 to 5 servings.
EACH SERVING: 759 cal., 44 g total fat (21 g sat. fat), 140 mg chol., 728 mg sodium, 53 g carbo., 3 g fiber, 27 g pro. Daily Values: 27% vit. A, 26% vit. C, 11% calcium, 16% iron.

Sausage with Horseradish-and-Mustard Potatoes

PREP: 15 MINUTES **BAKE:** 30 MINUTES
COOK: 10 MINUTES

Nonstick cooking spray
2 lb. potatoes, peeled and cut into ¼-inch slices (about 4 large potatoes)
1 cup dairy sour cream horseradish-flavor dip
2 Tbsp. all-purpose flour
2 Tbsp. Dijon-style mustard
⅓ cup milk
⅓ cup chopped green onions (2 to 3)
Dash cayenne pepper
1 lb. cooked smoked sausage, halved lengthwise and cut into ½-inch slices
6 oz. Gouda or Gruyère cheese, shredded (1½ cups)

1. Preheat oven to 350°F. Coat a 2-quart square baking dish with cooking spray; set aside. In a large saucepan cook potato slices in enough lightly salted boiling water to cover for 10 minutes or until potatoes are just tender. Drain.
2. In a medium bowl combine sour cream dip, flour, mustard, milk, green onions, and cayenne pepper; set aside.
3. Layer half of the potato slices and sausage slices in the prepared baking dish. Spoon half of the sour cream mixture over the potato slices; sprinkle with half of the cheese. Repeat with remaining potato slices, sausage slices, sour cream mixture, and cheese. Bake, uncovered, for 30 to 40 minutes or until heated through. Makes 6 servings.
EACH SERVING: 684 cal., 47 g total fat (18 g sat. fat), 105 mg chol., 1,755 mg sodium, 37 g carbo., 2 g fiber, 30 g pro. Daily Values: 5% vit. A, 42% vit. C, 26% calcium, 13% iron.

Zuppa Toscana

START TO FINISH: 30 MINUTES

12 oz. bulk mild or hot Italian sausage
1 medium onion, chopped (½ cup)
2 cloves garlic, minced
2 14-oz. cans reduced-sodium beef broth
1 14-oz. can diced tomatoes with Italian herbs
¼ cup chopped prosciutto (about 1½ oz.)
¼ cup tomato paste
1 lb. potatoes, unpeeled and cut into ½-inch pieces
3 cups chopped fresh kale
½ cup whipping cream
Black pepper

1. In a 4-quart Dutch oven cook sausage until brown; drain well in a colander. Return to Dutch oven. Add onion and garlic; cook for 2 minutes. Stir in broth, undrained tomatoes, prosciutto, and tomato paste; bring to boiling. Add potatoes; return to boiling. Reduce heat; simmer, covered, for 8 to 10 minutes or until potatoes are tender.
2. Stir in kale. Cook for 2 to 4 minutes more or until kale is just tender. Add whipping cream; heat through. Season to taste with pepper. Makes 6 servings.
EACH SERVING: 399 cal., 26 g total fat (11 g sat. fat), 75 mg chol., 1,044 mg sodium, 26 g carbo., 3 g fiber, 16 g pro. Daily Values: 104% vit. A, 80% vit. C, 11% calcium, 16% iron.

Sausage Penne with Cheese

PREP: 20 MINUTES **COOK:** 15 MINUTES

1 lb. bulk pork sausage
6 oz. dried penne pasta (2 cups)
1 lb. asparagus, trimmed and cut into bite-size pieces
1 medium yellow sweet pepper, cut into bite-size strips
1 pint cherry or grape tomatoes, halved
1 5.2-oz. container semisoft cheese with garlic and herb
¼ cup milk

1. In a large skillet cook sausage until brown; remove from skillet. Drain in a colander. Meanwhile, cook penne according to package directions; drain. Keep warm.
2. In the same skillet cook asparagus and sweet pepper for 3 minutes or until almost crisp-tender. Stir in sausage, tomatoes, cheese, and milk; cook and stir until bubbly. Serve over hot cooked penne. Makes 6 servings.
EACH SERVING: 422 cal., 23 g total fat (11 g sat. fat), 73 mg chol., 370 mg sodium, 28 g carbo., 3 g fiber, 19 g pro. Daily Values: 18% vit. A, 111% vit. C, 6% calcium, 13% iron.

PRIZE TESTED RECIPES® $400 WINNER
CHRISTOPHER DOAN, SAN JOSE, CALIF.

PRIZE TESTED RECIPES® $200 WINNER
AMANDA KRUNIC, SAN JOSE, CALIF.

Topped Coconut Waffles [KID FRIENDLY]
PREP: 15 MINUTES **BAKE:** 3 MINUTES PER WAFFLE

1¾ cups all-purpose flour
2 Tbsp. sugar
1 Tbsp. baking powder
    Dash salt
3 eggs
1 14-oz. can unsweetened coconut milk
6 Tbsp. butter, melted
¾ cup coconut
½ cup chocolate-flavored ice cream topping
½ cup chopped almonds, toasted
    Sweetened whipped cream or powdered sugar (optional)

1. In a medium bowl combine flour, sugar, baking powder, and salt. Make a well in center of flour mixture; set aside. In another medium bowl beat eggs lightly; stir in coconut milk and butter. Stir in coconut. Add egg mixture all at once to flour mixture. Stir just until moistened (batter should be slightly lumpy).
2. Pour ½ cup of batter onto grids of a preheated, lightly greased waffle baker. Close lid quickly and do not open until done. Bake according to manufacturer's directions (about 3 minutes or until golden brown). When done, use a fork to lift waffle off grid. Repeat with remaining batter.
3. Drizzle waffles with ice cream topping, sprinkle with almonds, and, if desired, top with whipped cream or dust with powdered sugar. Serve warm. Makes 8 waffles.
EACH WAFFLE: 453 cal., 28 g total fat (18 g sat. fat), 102 mg chol., 253 mg sodium, 43 g carbo., 3 g fiber, 9 g pro. Daily Values: 7% vit. A, 8% calcium, 14% iron.

Italian Breakfast Burrito
START TO FINISH: 25 MINUTES [FAST!]

2 Tbsp. extra virgin olive oil
2 cups fresh baby spinach, chopped
3 oz. prosciutto, chopped
½ cup fresh basil, snipped
1 6-oz. jar marinated artichoke hearts, drained
3 shallots, finely chopped
2 cloves garlic, minced
8 eggs
    Dash salt
    Dash ground black pepper
6 10-inch flour tortillas
½ cup purchased basil pesto
1½ cups shredded mozzarella cheese (6 oz.)
1 15-oz. container refrigerated marinara sauce, heated

1. In a large skillet heat olive oil over medium heat. Add spinach, prosciutto, basil, artichoke hearts, shallots, and garlic. Cook and stir until spinach is wilted.
2. In a medium mixing bowl whisk together eggs, salt, and pepper. Pour over cooked vegetables in skillet. Cook over medium heat, without stirring, until mixture begins to set on the bottom and around edge. With a spatula or a large spoon, lift and fold the partially cooked egg mixture so that the uncooked portion flows underneath. Continue cooking for 2 to 3 minutes or until egg mixture is cooked through but is still glossy and moist. Remove from heat.
3. Wrap tortillas in white paper towels; heat in the microwave on 100% power (high) for 30 to 60 seconds or just until warm. Spread each tortilla with some of the pesto to within 1 inch of the edge. Sprinkle cheese over pesto. Evenly divide egg mixture among tortillas and roll up, tucking in the ends. Serve with warm marinara sauce. Makes 6 servings.
EACH SERVING: 538 cal., 32 g total fat (9 g sat. fat), 317 mg chol., 1,371 mg sodium, 35 g carbo., 2 g fiber, 27 g pro. Daily Values: 36% vit. A, 18% vit. C, 40% calcium, 20% iron.

Apple-Almond Cinnamon Strata

PREP: 20 MINUTES **CHILL:** 2 HOURS
BAKE: 50 MINUTES **STAND:** 15 MINUTES

    1 1-lb. loaf cinnamon-raisin bread,
       cut into 1-inch pieces
    8 eggs, lightly beaten
    2 cups milk
   ¼ tsp. salt
   ¼ tsp. almond extract
    1 21-oz. can apple pie filling
   ½ cup slivered almonds, toasted
       Powdered sugar

1. Place bread pieces in a greased 3-quart rectangular baking dish; set aside. In a large mixing bowl whisk together eggs, milk, salt, and almond extract. Stir in apple pie filling and half of the almonds. Carefully pour mixture over the bread in the baking dish. Press down lightly with a rubber spatula or the back of a large spoon to moisten all of the bread. Sprinkle with remaining almonds. Cover and chill for 2 to 24 hours.
2. Bake, uncovered, in a 325°F oven about 50 minutes or until a knife inserted near the center comes out clean. Let stand for 15 minutes. Sift powdered sugar over the top before serving. Makes 8 servings.
EACH SERVING: 387 cal., 13 g total fat (3 g sat. fat), 216 mg chol., 422 mg sodium, 55 g carbo., 4 g fiber, 15 g pro. Daily Values: 7% vit. A, 16% calcium, 14% iron.

Chocolate Oven Pancake FAST!

PREP: 15 MINUTES **BAKE:** 15 MINUTES

   ¾ cup all-purpose flour
   ¼ cup unsweetened cocoa powder
    3 Tbsp. sugar
    1 Tbsp. baking powder
   ¾ cup milk
    1 egg, lightly beaten
    3 Tbsp. butter, melted
    2 tsp. vanilla
   ⅓ cup miniature semisweet chocolate
       pieces
   ¼ cup sliced almonds, toasted
       Maple syrup

1. Preheat oven to 425°F. In a large bowl combine flour, cocoa powder, sugar, baking powder, and ¼ teaspoon *salt*. In a small bowl combine milk, egg, butter, and vanilla. Add egg mixture all at once to flour mixture. Stir just until moistened.
2. Pour batter into a greased and floured 15×10×1-inch baking pan. Sprinkle with chocolate pieces and almonds. Bake for 15 minutes or until surface is dry and edges pull away from pan. Cut into 12 squares. Pass maple syrup. Makes 6 servings.
EACH SERVING: 279 cal., 14 g total fat (7 g sat. fat), 53 mg chol., 282 mg sodium, 31 g carbo., 1 g fiber, 7 g pro. Daily Values: 6% vit. A, 14% calcium, 11% iron.

Easy Huevos Rancheros Casserole

PREP: 15 MINUTES **BAKE:** 38 MINUTES
STAND: 10 MINUTES

       Nonstick cooking spray
    1 32-oz. pkg. frozen fried potato nuggets
   12 eggs
    1 cup milk
   1½ tsp. dried oregano, crushed
   1½ tsp. ground cumin
   ½ tsp. chili powder
   ¼ tsp. garlic powder
    1 8-oz. pkg. Mexican cheese blend
    1 16-oz. jar thick and chunky salsa
    1 8-oz. carton dairy sour cream
       Snipped fresh cilantro leaves

1. Preheat oven to 375°F. Lightly coat a 3-quart rectangular baking dish with nonstick cooking spray. Place potato nuggets in baking dish. In a large mixing bowl combine eggs, milk, oregano, cumin, chili powder, and garlic powder. Beat with a rotary beater or whisk until well combined. Pour egg mixture over potato nuggets. Bake for 35 to 40 minutes or until a knife inserted near center comes out clean.
2. Sprinkle cheese evenly over egg mixture. Bake about 3 minutes more or until cheese melts. Let stand on a wire rack for 10 minutes before serving. Top each serving with salsa, sour cream, and cilantro. Makes 12 servings.
EACH SERVING: 343 cal., 21 g total fat (9 g sat. fat), 238 mg chol., 823 mg sodium, 26 g carbo., 2 g fiber, 14 g pro. Daily Values: 13% vit. A, 12% vit. C, 21% calcium, 10% iron.

Spinach Artichoke Frittata

PREP: 10 MINUTES **COOK:** 12 MINUTES
BAKE: 4 MINUTES FAST!

    6 eggs
    3 cups frozen loose-pack diced hash brown
       potatoes, thawed
    2 to 3 Tbsp. butter
    1 8-oz. pkg. frozen spinach artichoke dip,
       thawed
   ¼ cup finely shredded Parmesan cheese
    1 large tomato, chopped
    1 Tbsp. snipped flat-leaf parsley (optional)

1. Preheat oven to 450°F. In a medium bowl combine eggs, ¼ cup *water*, ⅛ teaspoon *salt*, and ⅛ teaspoon *pepper*; set aside.
2. In a 10-inch oven-going skillet cook potatoes in 2 tablespoons hot butter over medium heat about 10 minutes or until lightly browned, turning occasionally. Stir in spinach artichoke dip. If pan is dry, add an additional tablespoon butter. Pour egg mixture over potato mixture. As egg mixture sets, run a spatula around edge of skillet, lifting egg mixture so the uncooked portion flows underneath. Continue cooking and lifting edges for 2 to 3 minutes or until the egg mixture is almost set.

3. Remove from heat; sprinkle with cheese, tomato, and, if desired, parsley. Bake for 4 to 5 minutes or until set. Makes 6 servings.
EACH SERVING: 258 cal., 13 g total fat (6 g sat. fat), 230 mg chol., 381 mg sodium, 22 g carbo., 2 g fiber, 12 g pro. Daily Values: 20% vit. A, 21% vit. C, 15% calcium, 11% iron.

Super Pancakes KID FRIENDLY

PREP: 15 MINUTES
STAND: 10 MINUTES
COOK: 3 MINUTES PER BATCH

    2 cups packaged complete whole wheat
       pancake mix*
   ¼ cup soy flour
   ¼ cup flaxseed meal
   ¼ cup toasted wheat germ
   ¼ cup finely ground almonds
   ½ tsp. baking powder
   2½ cups fat-free milk
    2 tsp. vanilla
    1 cup fresh blueberries
       Butter
       Maple syrup

1. In a large bowl stir together pancake mix, soy flour, flaxseed meal, wheat germ, almonds, and baking powder. Add milk and vanilla; stir just until combined. Stir in blueberries. Cover loosely and let stand for 10 minutes (batter will thicken as it stands).
2. For each pancake, pour about ¼ cup of the batter onto a hot, lightly greased griddle or heavy skillet. If necessary, spread batter to a 4-inch circle. Cook over medium heat for 3 to 4 minutes or until pancakes are lightly browned, turning to second sides when edges start to bubble and bottoms are golden brown. If pancakes get too dark, turn heat down. Serve warm with butter and maple syrup. Makes about 18 pancakes.
*NOTE: If your pancake mix is not a complete mix, add 1 lightly beaten egg to the dry mixture with the milk.
EACH PANCAKE: 179 cal., 5 g total fat (2 g sat. fat), 7 mg chol., 317 mg sodium, 31 g carbo., 2 g fiber, 5 g pro. Daily Values: 3% vit. A, 1% vit. C, 10% calcium, 10% iron.

FASTEST AFTER-WORK DINNERS

PRIZE TESTED RECIPES® $400 WINNER

MARIA BOTOULAS, LAKE PLACID, N.Y.

PRIZE TESTED RECIPES® $200 WINNER

MEGAN M. BARTH, BOUNTIFUL, UTAH

Salmon au Poivre

START TO FINISH: 25 MINUTES

    4 6-oz. salmon fillets, skin removed
    ¼ tsp. salt
    2 to 3 tsp. cracked black pepper
    2 Tbsp. olive oil
    ½ cup chicken broth
    1 5- or 6-oz. pkg. torn mixed salad greens
    1 cup halved fresh strawberries
    ¼ cup bottled balsamic vinaigrette salad dressing
    2 Tbsp. honey

1. Sprinkle salmon fillets with salt. Lightly coat each side of salmon with cracked black pepper. In a large skillet cook salmon fillets for 1 minute in hot oil. Turn salmon over and carefully add chicken broth. Bring to boiling; reduce heat. Simmer, covered, for 5 minutes or until salmon flakes when tested with a fork.
2. Meanwhile, divide salad greens and strawberries among 4 plates. Drizzle greens with vinaigrette salad dressing. Remove salmon from cooking liquid and place on greens; drizzle salmon with honey. Makes 4 servings.
EACH SERVING: 467 cal., 30 g total fat (5 g sat. fat), 100 mg chol., 546 mg sodium, 15 g carbo., 1 g fiber, 35 g pro. Daily Values: 5% vit. A, 46% vit. C, 4% calcium, 7% iron.

Wasatch Mountain Chili

START TO FINISH: 15 MINUTES

    1 medium onion, chopped
    1 Tbsp. cooking oil
    1 15- to 16-oz. can hominy, rinsed and drained
    1 15- to 16-oz. can Great Northern beans, rinsed and drained
    1 14-oz. can reduced-sodium chicken broth
    1 9-oz. pkg. frozen cooked chicken breast strips
    ¼ cup lime juice
    2 Tbsp. chopped fresh cilantro
    ¼ tsp. ground cumin
    ¼ tsp. ground black pepper
    ½ cup shredded Colby and Monterey Jack cheese, Monterey Jack, or cheddar cheese (2 oz.)
       Bottled green salsa
       White corn tortilla chips

1. In a large saucepan cook onion in hot oil over medium heat for 3 minutes. Stir in hominy, beans, chicken broth, frozen chicken, lime juice, cilantro, cumin, and pepper. Cover and bring to boiling over high heat, stirring occasionally. Top with cheese, salsa, and tortilla chips. Makes 4 (1¼-cup) servings.
EACH SERVING: 434 cal., 14 g total fat (5 g sat. fat), 58 mg chol., 1,001 mg sodium, 48 g carbo., 9 g fiber, 31 g pro. Daily Values: 9% vit. A, 17% vit. C, 20% calcium, 17% iron.

Creamy Chicken Casserole
PREP: 15 MINUTES **BAKE:** 30 MINUTES

- 1 9-oz. pkg. refrigerated fettuccine or linguine
- 1 10¾-oz. can condensed cream of chicken and herbs soup
- 1 6-oz. pkg. refrigerated cooked chicken breast strips, coarsely chopped
- ½ of a 9-oz. pkg. frozen artichoke hearts, thawed
- ⅓ cup milk
- ½ cup finely shredded Parmesan cheese
- ¼ cup purchased basil pesto
- ¼ cup oil-packed sun-dried tomatoes, drained and chopped
  Shredded Parmesan cheese (optional)

1. Preheat oven to 375°F. Prepare fettuccine according to package directions. Drain pasta and keep warm.
2. Meanwhile, in a large bowl combine soup, chicken, artichoke hearts, milk, ¼ cup of the Parmesan cheese, pesto, and dried tomatoes. Fold in cooked pasta. Spoon into a 2-quart rectangular baking dish. Sprinkle with remaining Parmesan cheese.
3. Bake, uncovered, for 30 to 35 minutes or until bubbly and heated through. If desired, sprinkle with additional cheese. Makes 4 to 5 servings.
EACH SERVING: 480 cal., 21 g total fat (4 g sat. fat), 88 mg chol., 1,239 mg sodium, 48 g carbo., 3 g fiber, 26 g pro. Daily Values: 8% vit. A, 15% vit. C, 18% calcium, 16% iron.

Fiesta Casserole
PREP: 15 MINUTES **BAKE:** 35 MINUTES
STAND: 5 MINUTES

- 1 18.8-oz. can ready-to-serve thick and chunky vegetable soup
- 12 oz. cooked smoked sausage, sliced
- 1 8.5-oz. pkg. corn muffin mix
- ⅓ cup milk
- 1 egg, lightly beaten
- 1 4-oz. can diced green chiles, drained
- 1 cup shredded taco cheese
- 2 Tbsp. snipped fresh cilantro
  Dairy sour cream and/or refrigerated guacamole

1. Preheat oven to 350°F. In a 2-quart square microwave-safe baking dish combine soup and sausage. Cover with vented plastic wrap and microwave on 100% power (high) for 5 minutes, stirring once.
2. Meanwhile combine corn muffin mix, milk, egg, drained green chiles, ½ cup of the cheese, and the cilantro. Spoon on top of soup mixture.
3. Bake, uncovered, for 35 to 40 minutes or until a toothpick inserted into corn bread comes out clean. Remove from oven; sprinkle with remaining

cheese. Cool for 5 minutes. Spoon onto serving plates. Top with sour cream and/or guacamole. Makes 6 servings.
EACH SERVING: 502 cal., 31 g total fat (14 g sat. fat), 81 mg chol., 1,334 mg sodium, 40 g carbo., 1 g fiber, 16 g pro. Daily Values: 52% vit. A, 18% vit. C, 16% calcium, 12% iron.

Hearty Italian Stew
START TO FINISH: 15 MINUTES

- 1 tsp. bottled minced garlic
- 1 Tbsp. olive oil
- 2 14½-oz. cans diced tomatoes with basil, garlic, and oregano, undrained
- 1 14-oz. can beef broth
- 1¾ cups water
- 1 16-oz. pkg. frozen cooked Italian-style meatballs (16)
- ½ of a 16-oz. pkg. frozen (yellow, green, and red) sweet peppers and onion stir-fry vegetables (about 2½ cups)
- 1 9-oz. pkg. refrigerated three-cheese tortellini
- ½ of a 10-oz. pkg. shredded cabbage (about 3 cups)
  Grated Parmesan cheese

1. In a 4- to 5-quart Dutch oven cook garlic in hot oil over medium heat for 30 seconds.
2. Stir in undrained tomatoes, beef broth, and water. Add meatballs and frozen pepper blend. Bring mixture to boiling over medium-high heat. Stir in tortellini and cabbage. Cook, covered, for 5 minutes more. Ladle soup into bowls and sprinkle with Parmesan cheese. Makes 6 servings.
EACH SERVING: 459 cal., 23 g total fat (10 g sat. fat), 71 mg chol., 1,705 mg sodium, 40 g carbo., 4 g fiber, 23 g pro. Daily Values: 22% vit. A, 52% vit. C, 24% calcium, 27% iron.

Ravioli with Spinach Cream Sauce
START TO FINISH: 15 MINUTES

- 1 9-oz. pkg. refrigerated cheese- or meat-filled ravioli
- 1 tsp. bottled minced garlic
- 1 Tbsp. butter
- 1 9- to 10-oz. pkg. frozen creamed spinach, thawed
- ¼ cup half-and-half or milk
- ¼ tsp. salt
- ¼ tsp. ground black pepper
- ⅛ tsp. ground sage
- ⅓ cup roasted red sweet pepper strips (optional)
  Grated Parmesan cheese

1. In a large saucepan cook pasta according to package directions. Drain pasta.
2. Meanwhile, in a medium saucepan cook garlic in hot butter over medium heat for 30 seconds. Stir in creamed spinach, half-and-half, salt, black pepper, and sage. Heat through.

3. Gently stir in cooked pasta and, if desired, roasted sweet pepper strips. Transfer to serving bowl. Sprinkle with Parmesan. Makes 3 servings.
EACH SERVING: 461 cal., 27 g total fat (13 g sat. fat), 107 mg chol., 869 mg sodium, 38 g carbo., 2 g fiber, 17 g pro. Daily Values: 66% vit. A, 1% vit. C, 36% calcium, 9% iron.

Shredded Pork Roast and Tomato Tacos
PREP: 10 MINUTES **COOK:** 5 MINUTES

- 1 17-oz. pkg. refrigerated cooked pork roast
- 1 10-oz. can diced tomatoes and green chiles, undrained
- 2 tsp. taco seasoning
- 8 taco shells
- ½ cup shredded lettuce
- ½ cup shredded cheddar cheese
  Dairy sour cream
  Bottled salsa

1. In a large skillet combine refrigerated pork, undrained tomatoes, and taco seasoning; bring to boiling. Reduce heat and boil gently, uncovered, for 5 minutes. Remove from heat; using two forks, carefully shred pork.
2. To serve, remove meat and tomatoes from skillet with a slotted spoon. Spoon meat mixture into taco shells. Top with shredded lettuce and cheddar cheese. Serve with sour cream and salsa. Makes 8 tacos.
EACH TACO: 206 cal., 11 g total fat (5 g sat. fat), 49 mg chol., 529 mg sodium, 12 g carbo., 2 g fiber, 16 g pro. Daily Values: 7% vit. A, 5% vit. C, 10% calcium, 7% iron.

LEFTOVER TURKEY IDEAS

Cranberry Turkey Enchiladas

PREP: 30 MINUTES **BAKE:** 50 MINUTES

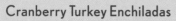

    Nonstick cooking spray
 2 to 2½ cups shredded cooked turkey
 1 16-oz. can whole cranberry sauce
 1 15-oz. can black beans, rinsed and drained
1½ cups bottled salsa
 1 cup shredded Colby and Monterey Jack cheese (4 oz.)
 ½ cup dairy sour cream
 3 green onions, sliced
 ¼ cup snipped fresh cilantro
 1 tsp. ground cumin
 ½ tsp. salt
 ½ tsp. ground black pepper
 8 7- to 8-inch whole wheat or regular flour tortillas
 1 tsp. bottled hot pepper sauce

1. Preheat oven to 350°F. Lightly coat a 3-quart rectangular baking dish with cooking spray; set aside. For filling, in a large bowl stir together turkey, half of the cranberry sauce, the beans, ½ cup of the salsa, ¾ cup of the cheese, the sour cream, green onions, cilantro, cumin, salt, and pepper. Spoon about ⅔ cup filling on each tortilla. Roll up tortillas around filling. Place, seam sides down, in prepared dish; set aside.
2. For sauce, in a medium bowl stir together remaining cranberry sauce, remaining salsa, and the hot pepper sauce. Spoon over filled tortillas. Cover with foil. Bake for 45 minutes. Uncover; top with remaining cheese. Bake, uncovered, for 5 to 10 minutes more or until heated through and cheese melts. If desired, sprinkle with additional snipped cilantro and sliced green onion. Makes 8 servings.
EACH SERVING: 406 cal., 12 g total fat (6 g sat. fat), 45 mg chol., 963 mg sodium, 57 g carbo., 6 g fiber, 22 g pro. Daily Values: 10% vit. A, 4% vit. C, 18% calcium, 15% iron.

Turkey Paella Salad

PREP: 40 MINUTES **CHILL:** 2 HOURS

 1 8-oz. pkg. saffron-flavored yellow rice mix
 2 to 3 cups chopped cooked turkey
 1 cup chopped tomato
 1 cup broccoli florets or frozen baby sweet peas
 1 medium red or yellow sweet pepper, chopped
 ⅓ cup dried cranberries or golden raisins
 ¼ cup sliced green onion
 2 oz. prosciutto, crisp-cooked,* or cooked ham, cut into thin strips
 ¾ cup bottled vinaigrette salad dressing
 ⅓ cup sliced almonds, toasted
 2 Tbsp. snipped fresh basil

1. Prepare rice according to package directions. Spread on a baking sheet; cover and refrigerate about 20 minutes or until cool.
2. In a very large bowl combine turkey, tomato, broccoli, sweet pepper, cranberries, green onion, and prosciutto. Add rice and salad dressing; toss to coat. Cover and refrigerate for 2 to 24 hours. Sprinkle with almonds and basil before serving. Makes 6 servings.
*NOTE: To crisp-cook prosciutto, arrange slices in a single layer on a baking sheet lined with parchment paper. Bake in a 450°F oven for 6 to 8 minutes or until browned and crisp. Remove and cool on the baking sheet.
EACH SERVING: 433 cal., 24 g total fat (4 g sat. fat), 25 mg chol., 846 mg sodium, 42 g carbo., 6 g fiber, 15 g pro. Daily Values: 26% vit. A, 103% vit. C, 4% calcium, 17% iron.

Baked Turkey Pockets

PREP: 20 MINUTES **BAKE:** 15 MINUTES
COOL: 5 MINUTES

- 12 oz. cooked turkey, chopped
- 1 9-oz. pkg. frozen artichoke hearts, thawed, drained, and coarsely chopped
- ¾ cup purchased dried tomato pesto
- ¾ cup finely shredded Parmesan or Romano cheese
- ¼ tsp. ground black pepper
- 2 13.8-oz. pkgs. refrigerated pizza dough
  Milk
- 1 8-oz. can pizza sauce, warmed

1. Preheat oven to 375°F. Lightly grease a very large baking sheet; set aside. For filling, in a large bowl combine turkey, artichokes, pesto, ½ cup of the cheese, and the pepper.
2. On a lightly floured surface, gently stretch or roll one package of pizza dough into a 15×10-inch rectangle. Using a pizza cutter or sharp knife, cut crosswise into three 10×5-inch rectangles.
3. Place about ⅔ cup of the turkey mixture on half of each rectangle; spread to within about 1 inch of edges. Fold dough over filling, forming a square. Pinch or press with a fork to seal edges. Prick tops with a fork. Brush with milk and sprinkle with half of the remaining cheese. Repeat with remaining pizza crust, filling, and cheese.
4. Bake for 15 to 18 minutes or until golden. Cool 5 minutes before serving. Serve with pizza sauce for dipping. Makes 6 (½-pocket) servings.
EACH SERVING: 553 cal., 20 g total fat (5 g sat. fat), 53 mg chol., 1,059 mg sodium, 60 g carbo., 6 g fiber, 31 g pro. Daily Values: 10% vit. A, 11% vit. C, 24% calcium, 27% iron.

Cheesy Turkey and Spinach Pie

PREP: 30 MINUTES **BAKE:** 45 MINUTES
STAND: 10 MINUTES

- Nonstick cooking spray
- 4 oz. dried fine noodles (1¾ cups)
- 3 eggs
- 1 8-oz. carton mascarpone cheese or cream cheese, softened
- ⅓ cup dairy sour cream
- ⅓ cup mayonnaise
- ¼ cup snipped fresh basil or 1 tablespoon dried basil, crushed
- ½ tsp. garlic salt
- ¼ tsp. crushed red pepper
- 2 cups chopped cooked turkey
- 1 10-oz. pkg. frozen chopped spinach, thawed and well drained
- 1 cup shredded Monterey Jack cheese (4 oz.)
- ⅓ cup chopped roasted red sweet pepper

1. Preheat oven to 350°F. Coat a 9-inch deep-dish pie plate or a 2-quart square baking dish with cooking spray; set plate or dish on a baking sheet. Set aside. Cook noodles according to package directions; drain well.

2. Meanwhile, in a large bowl whisk together eggs, mascarpone cheese, sour cream, mayonnaise, basil, garlic salt, and crushed red pepper until well combined. Stir in cooked noodles, turkey, spinach, Monterey Jack cheese, and roasted sweet pepper. Spread mixture in prepared plate or dish.
3. Bake, uncovered, for 45 to 50 minutes or until edges are slightly puffed and golden. Let stand on a wire rack for 10 minutes before serving. Makes 6 to 8 servings.
EACH SERVING: 549 cal., 40 g total fat (18 g sat. fat), 231 mg chol., 412 mg sodium, 18 g carbo., 2 g fiber, 33 g pro. Daily Values: 78% vit. A, 44% vit. C, 22% calcium, 14% iron.

Curried Cranberry Turkey Skillet

PREP: 20 MINUTES **COOK:** 20 MINUTES
STAND: 5 MINUTES

- 2 medium carrots, thinly sliced
- 1 medium onion, finely chopped
- 1 clove garlic, minced
- 1 Tbsp. cooking oil
- ¾ cup long grain white rice
- 2 tsp. curry powder
- 1 14-oz. can chicken broth
- ½ of a 16-oz. can whole cranberry sauce (about 1 cup)
- 1 teaspoon lemon peel (optional)
- 1 Tbsp. lemon juice or cider vinegar
- 3 cups cubed cooked turkey
- 1 cup snow pea pods, trimmed and halved diagonally

1. In a large skillet cook carrots, onion, and garlic in hot oil over medium heat about 5 minutes until onion is tender. Stir in rice and curry powder; cook and stir 1 minute more.
2. Stir in broth, cranberry sauce, lemon peel (if desired), lemon juice, and ¼ teaspoon salt. Bring to boiling. Reduce heat; simmer, covered, for 20 to 25 minutes or until rice is tender and liquid is absorbed. Stir in turkey and pea pods; heat through. Remove from heat. Cover; let stand 5 minutes before serving. Makes 4 to 5 servings.
EACH SERVING: 480 cal., 9 g total fat (2 g sat. fat), 81 mg chol., 677 mg sodium, 62 g carbo., 3 g fiber, 35 g pro. Daily Values: 93% vit. A, 10% vit. C, 7% calcium, 22% iron.

Tex-Mex Turkey Pasta Salad

START TO FINISH: 30 MINUTES

- 8 oz. dried bow tie pasta (3 cups)
- 2 cups frozen whole kernel corn
- 3 cups coarsely chopped cooked turkey (about 12 oz.)
- 1 2.25-oz. can sliced, pitted ripe olives, drained
- ½ cup snipped fresh cilantro
- 2 medium orange, red, and/or yellow sweet peppers, chopped
- ½ cup dairy sour cream
- ½ cup mayonnaise

- 1 1.25-oz. envelope taco seasoning mix
- 2 Tbsp. lime juice
- 1 Tbsp. olive oil
- ¼ cup sliced almonds, toasted

1. Cook pasta according to package directions, adding corn the last 1 minute of cooking; drain. Rinse with cold water; drain again and set aside.
2. Meanwhile, in a large bowl combine turkey, olives, cilantro, and sweet pepper. Add pasta mixture and toss gently to combine.
3. In a small bowl combine sour cream, mayonnaise, taco seasoning, lime juice, and olive oil. Add to pasta mixture. Toss gently to combine. Serve immediately or, if desired, cover and chill for up to 24 hours. Sprinkle with almonds just before serving. Makes 6 servings.
EACH SERVING: 567 cal., 30 g total fat (7 g sat. fat), 67 mg chol., 52 mg sodium, 47 g carbo., 4 g fiber, 31 g pro. Daily Values: 38% vit. A, 138% vit. C, 8% calcium, 19% iron.

Turkey, Asparagus, and Pasta

PREP: 25 MINUTES **BAKE:** 40 MINUTES
STAND: 10 MINUTES

- 6 oz. dried spaghetti, broken
- 1 9- or 10-oz. pkg. frozen cut asparagus
  Nonstick cooking spray
- 3 eggs
- 1 5.2- to 6-oz. container semisoft cheese with garlic and herbs
- 3 cups chopped cooked turkey
- ¾ cup freshly grated Parmesan cheese
- ¾ cup thinly sliced green onions
- ¾ cup chicken broth
- 1 Tbsp. snipped fresh sage or ½ tsp. dried leaf sage, crushed
- ¼ tsp. ground black pepper
- 1 8-oz. carton dairy sour cream
- 2 Tbsp. honey mustard (optional)

1. Preheat oven to 350°F. Cook spaghetti according to package directions, adding asparagus during the last 2 minutes of cooking time; drain and set aside. Lightly coat a 2-quart rectangular baking dish with nonstick cooking spray; set aside.
2. In a large mixing bowl lightly beat eggs. Whisk in semisoft cheese until well combined. Stir in turkey, ½ cup of the Parmesan cheese, ½ cup of the green onions, the broth, cooked pasta mixture, sage, and pepper. Spread mixture in prepared dish. Cover with foil.
3. Bake about 40 minutes or until heated through. Meanwhile, in a small bowl combine sour cream, honey mustard (if desired), remaining ¼ cup Parmesan cheese, and remaining ¼ cup green onions. Spread mixture over hot pasta mixture. Let stand, uncovered, 10 minutes before serving. Makes 6 servings.
EACH SERVING: 491 cal., 25 g total fat (14 g sat. fat), 206 mg chol., 400 mg sodium, 27 g carbo., 2 g fiber, 36 g pro. Daily Values: 19% vit. A, 27% vit. C, 24% calcium, 17% iron.

LOOKS-LIKE-YOU-FUSSED APPETIZERS

Cilantro Canapés

START TO FINISH: 30 MINUTES

- 2 cups lightly packed fresh cilantro leaves
- ¼ cup lightly packed fresh mint leaves
- 1 fresh jalapeño chile pepper, seeded and cut up (see note, page 49)
- 1 Tbsp. lime juice
- 1 tsp. sugar
- ½ tsp. grated fresh ginger
- ¼ cup salted peanuts
- 1 to 2 Tbsp. water
- 20 ¼-inch-thick baguette slices, toasted*
- ¾ cup chopped cucumber
- 5 cherry tomatoes, quartered
  Mint sprigs (optional)

1. In a food processor combine cilantro, mint, jalapeño pepper, lime juice, sugar, and ginger. Cover and process until nearly smooth. Add peanuts; cover and process until combined. Add the water to reach spreading consistency. (If desired, cover and refrigerate mixture for up to 6 hours.)

2. Spread one side of each toasted baguette slice with some of the cilantro mixture. Top with cucumber, a tomato quarter, and, if desired, a mint sprig. Makes 20 appetizers.

*TIP: To toast bread slices, brush slices lightly with olive oil (3 to 4 tablespoons total). Arrange in a single layer on a large baking sheet. Broil 4 to 5 inches from the heat for 1 to 2 minutes or until lightly browned. Turn over bread slices. Broil 1 to 2 minutes more or until lightly browned. Transfer to a wire rack to cool.

LOW FAT EACH APPETIZER: 50 cal., 1 g total fat (0 g sat. fat), 0 mg chol., 86 mg sodium, 8 g carbo., 1 g fiber, 2 g pro. Daily Values: 10% vit. A, 7% vit. C, 2% calcium, 3% iron.

Apple Anise Pizza

PREP: 20 MINUTES **BAKE:** 13 MINUTES

- 1 12-inch Italian bread shell
- 2 shallots, thinly sliced
- 1 Tbsp. olive oil
- 2 medium Granny Smith apples, cored and thinly sliced (about 3 cups)
- ¼ cup coarsely chopped walnuts
- 2 Tbsp. honey
- 1 Tbsp. anise seeds
  Dash ground black pepper
- 1 cup shredded Swiss cheese or Gruyère cheese (4 oz.)
  Honey (optional)

1. Preheat oven to 450°F. Place bread shell on a pizza pan. Bake for 8 minutes or until hot. Meanwhile, in a large skillet cook shallots in hot oil for 3 minutes or until tender. Stir in apple slices. Cook and stir for 5 minutes or until apples are crisp-tender. Stir in walnuts, 2 tablespoons honey, the anise seeds, and pepper.

2. Spoon apple mixture evenly over bread shell. Sprinkle with cheese. Bake for 5 to 8 minutes more or until cheese melts. If desired, drizzle with additional honey. Cut into thin wedges to serve. Makes 16 appetizer servings.

EACH SERVING: 135 cal., 6 g total fat (2 g sat. fat), 8 mg chol., 150 mg sodium, 17 g carbo., 1 g fiber, 5 g pro. Daily Values: 2% vit. A, 2% vit. C, 9% calcium, 4% iron.

Artichoke-and-Mushroom-Topped Camembert

START TO FINISH: 20 MINUTES

- 1 4½-oz. pkg. Camembert or Brie cheese
- 1 6-oz. jar marinated artichokes
- 2 cups cremini or button mushrooms, quartered
- ¼ cup bottled roasted red sweet pepper, chopped
- ¼ cup finely shredded Parmesan cheese
- 12 ¼-inch-thick baguette slices, toasted (see tip, page 296)

1. Cut cheese into six wedges. Place one wedge on each of six small plates; set aside.

2. Drain artichoke hearts, reserving liquid. Cut artichokes into thin slivers and set aside. In a large skillet heat reserved liquid. Add mushrooms and cook until just tender; stir in artichokes and roasted red pepper. Heat through. Spoon mixture on top of cheese wedges. Sprinkle with Parmesan cheese. Add two baguette slices to each plate. Serve immediately. Makes 6 appetizer servings.

EACH SERVING: 142 cal., 8 g total fat (4 g sat. fat), 18 mg chol., 401 mg sodium, 11 g carbo., 1 g fiber, 8 g pro. Daily Values: 4% vit. A, 40% vit. C, 14% calcium, 4% iron.

Focaccia Sweet Squares

PREP: 20 MINUTES **BAKE:** 10 MINUTES

- 1 Italian flatbread (focaccia), about 16×12 inches
- 1 cup chopped red onion (2 medium)
- 1 medium red sweet pepper, chopped
- 1 medium green sweet pepper, chopped
- 1 tsp. bottled minced garlic
- 1 Tbsp. olive oil
- 2 Tbsp. seasoned fine dry bread crumbs
- 2 Tbsp. purchased basil pesto
- 1 Tbsp. honey
- 1 Tbsp. balsamic vinegar
- ¼ cup finely shredded Parmesan cheese

1. Preheat oven to 350°F. If focaccia is thicker than 2 inches, split focaccia in half horizontally. Cut into twenty-four 1½- to 2-inch pieces. Place on a large baking sheet. Bake, uncovered, for 10 minutes.

2. Meanwhile, in a large skillet cook red onion, sweet peppers, and garlic in hot oil until just tender. Stir in bread crumbs, pesto, honey, and vinegar.

3. Place about 1 tablespoon of vegetable mixture on each bread square. Sprinkle with cheese. Serve warm. Makes 24 appetizers.

EACH APPETIZER: 34 cal., 2 g total fat (0 g sat. fat), 1 mg chol., 50 mg sodium, 4 g carbo., 0 g fiber, 1 g pro. Daily Values: 3% vit. A, 20% vit. C, 2% calcium, 1% iron.

Layered Olive Appetizers

PREP: 25 MINUTES **CHILL:** 1 HOUR

- 1 8-oz. tub cream cheese spread with garden vegetables
- ¼ cup pitted kalamata or ripe olives, chopped
- ¼ cup pimiento-stuffed green olives, chopped
- 2 Tbsp. capers, drained
- 2 8-inch flour tortillas
- 2 9- to 10-inch spinach-flavored flour tortillas

1. In a medium bowl stir together half of the cream cheese and the black olives; set aside. In another bowl combine remaining cream cheese, green olives, and capers.

2. Spread plain flour tortillas with the black olive mixture. Spread spinach tortillas with the green olive mixture. Place one plain tortilla, spread side up, on top of one spinach tortilla. Roll up; trim ends. Secure at 1-inch intervals with wooden picks. Slice between picks. Repeat with remaining tortillas and spread. Cover and chill for 1 to 8 hours. Makes 14 servings.

EACH SERVING: 107 cal., 7 g total fat (3 g sat. fat), 14 mg chol., 261 mg sodium, 8 g carbo., 1 g fiber, 2 g pro. Daily Values: 1% vit. C, 4% calcium, 2% iron.

Savory Shrimp Pâté

PREP: 20 MINUTES **CHILL:** 2 HOURS

- ⅓ cup plain yogurt
- 1 3-oz. pkg. cream cheese, cut into cubes
- ⅓ cup chopped green onion
- 1 Tbsp. horseradish mustard
- 1½ tsp. finely shredded lemon peel
- 1 tsp. dried dillweed
- ½ tsp. sugar
- ½ tsp. bottled hot pepper sauce
- ¼ tsp. salt
- 12 oz. cooked peeled and deveined shrimp
- 36 crackers and/or 2-inch pieces of celery
  Sliced green onion (optional)

1. In a food processor place yogurt and cream cheese; cover and process until combined. Add ⅓ cup green onion, horseradish mustard, lemon peel, dillweed, sugar, hot pepper sauce, and salt. Cover and process until nearly smooth. Add shrimp; cover and process with on/off turns until shrimp are finely chopped. Transfer to a medium bowl. Cover and chill for 2 to 24 hours.

2. To serve, place shrimp mixture in a heavy resealable plastic bag; snip off one corner. Pipe shrimp mixture onto crackers and/or celery pieces. If desired, top with sliced green onion. Makes 36 appetizers.

EACH APPETIZER (PÂTÉ ONLY): 34 cal., 2 g total fat (1 g sat. fat), 21 mg chol., 74 mg sodium, 2 g carbo., 0 g fiber, 3 g pro. Daily Values: 1% vit. A, 1% vit. C, 1% calcium, 3% iron.

MIXER METHOD. In a large mixing bowl beat yogurt and cream cheese with an electric mixer on medium speed until combined. Add onion, horseradish mustard, lemon peel, dillweed, sugar, hot pepper sauce, and salt; beat until almost smooth. Finely chop the shrimp and stir into mixture. Proceed with Step 2.

Sensational Portobellos

PREP: 20 MINUTES **BROIL:** 5 MINUTES

- 6 medium portobello mushrooms (about 4½ inches in diameter)
- ¼ cup purchased basil pesto
- ¾ cup bottled roasted red sweet pepper, cut into strips
- 1½ oz. sliced pepperoni, coarsely chopped
- ⅓ cup walnuts, toasted and chopped
- ⅛ to ¼ tsp. crushed red pepper
- 1 cup shredded Italian cheese blend (4 oz.)

1. Preheat broiler. If desired, remove stems and gills from mushrooms. Place mushrooms, gills sides up, in a 15×10×1-inch baking pan. Broil 3 to 4 inches from the heat for 4 minutes.

2. Meanwhile, in a medium bowl combine pesto, roasted red sweet pepper, pepperoni, walnuts, and crushed red peppers. Divide evenly among mushrooms; sprinkle with cheese.

3. Broil for 1 to 2 minutes or until heated through and cheese is bubbly. Halve to serve. Makes 12 appetizer servings.

EACH SERVING: 132 cal., 11 g total fat (2 g sat. fat), 12 mg chol., 166 mg sodium, 5 g carbo., 1 g fiber, 7 g pro. Daily Values: 2% vit. A, 43% vit. C, 6% calcium, 4% iron.

SANTA-PLEASING COOKIES

Toasty Three-Seed Crescents
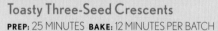
PREP: 25 MINUTES **BAKE:** 12 MINUTES PER BATCH

- ¼ cup raw sunflower kernels, coarsely chopped
- ¼ cup raw pumpkin seeds (pepitas), coarsely chopped
- 2 Tbsp. sesame seeds
- 1 cup butter, softened
- ½ cup powdered sugar
- 1 tsp. vanilla
- 2 cups all-purpose flour
- 1 cup powdered sugar

1. In a medium skillet combine sunflower kernels, pumpkin seeds, and sesame seeds. Cook and stir over medium heat for 3 to 5 minutes or until seeds are toasted. Remove from skillet; cool.
2. In a medium mixing bowl beat butter with electric mixer on medium to high speed for 30 seconds. Add ½ cup powdered sugar and vanilla. Beat until combined, scraping sides of bowl occasionally. Beat in as much of the flour as you can with the mixer. Stir in any remaining flour. Stir in toasted seeds. If necessary, cover and chill for 1 hour or until dough is easy to handle.
3. Preheat oven to 350°F. Shape dough into 2½-inch-long ropes, then into crescents. Place 2 inches apart on an ungreased cookie sheet. Bake for 12 to 15 minutes or until bottoms are lightly browned. Cool on cookie sheet for 1 minute. Transfer cookies to wire racks and let cool. Gently shake cooled cookies, a few at a time, in a plastic bag with the 1 cup powdered sugar. Makes about 36 cookies.
EACH COOKIE: 104 cal., 6 g total fat (3 g sat. fat), 14 mg chol., 37 mg sodium, 11 g carbo., 0 g fiber, 1 g pro. Daily Values: 3% vit. A, 1% calcium, 3% iron.

Almond Butter Blossoms
PREP: 30 MINUTES **BAKE:** 8 MINUTES PER BATCH

- ½ cup butter, softened
- ½ cup almond butter
- ½ cup granulated sugar
- ½ cup packed brown sugar
- ¾ tsp. baking soda
- ½ tsp. cream of tartar
- ¼ tsp. salt
- 1 egg
- 2 Tbsp. milk
- ½ tsp. vanilla
- 1 cup whole wheat flour
- 1 cup all-purpose flour
- 3 Tbsp. granulated sugar
- 2 Tbsp. finely ground almonds
- 48 to 60 milk chocolate kisses with almonds

1. Preheat oven to 350°F. In a large mixing bowl beat butter and almond butter with an electric mixer on medium to high speed for 30 seconds. Add ½ cup granulated sugar, brown sugar, baking soda, cream of tartar, and salt. Beat until combined, scraping sides of bowl occasionally. Beat in egg, milk, and vanilla until combined. Beat in whole wheat flour and as much of the all-purpose flour as you can with the mixer. Stir in any remaining flour.
2. In a shallow dish combine 3 tablespoons granulated sugar and ground almonds. Shape dough into 1-inch balls. Roll balls in sugar mixture to coat. Place balls 2 inches apart on an ungreased cookie sheet. Bake for 8 to 10 minutes or until edges are firm and tops are cracked. Remove from oven and immediately press a chocolate kiss into the center of each cookie. Transfer cookies to a wire rack and let cool. Makes 48 to 60 cookies.
EACH COOKIE: 101 cal., 5 g total fat (2 g sat. fat), 11 mg chol., 52 mg sodium, 12 g carbo., 1 g fiber, 2 g pro. Daily Values: 1% vit. A, 2% calcium, 2% iron.

Coconut Lime Cookies

PREP: 25 MINUTES
BAKE: 9 MINUTES PER BATCH

- ½ cup butter, softened
- ¾ cup packed brown sugar
- ⅓ cup granulated sugar
- ¾ tsp. baking powder
- ½ tsp. baking soda
- 1 egg
- 1 Tbsp. finely shredded lime peel
- 2 Tbsp. lime juice
- 1 tsp. vanilla
- 1 tsp. coconut extract
- 1¾ cups all-purpose flour
- 1 12-oz. pkg. white baking pieces and/or semisweet chocolate pieces
- 1 cup flaked coconut, toasted

1. Preheat oven to 375°F. In a bowl beat butter with an electric mixer on medium to high speed for 30 seconds. Add brown sugar, granulated sugar, baking powder, baking soda, and ½ teaspoon *salt*. Beat until mixture is combined, scraping bowl. Beat in egg, lime peel, lime juice, vanilla, and coconut extract until combined. Beat in flour. Stir in baking pieces and coconut.

2. Drop dough by rounded teaspoons 2 inches apart onto ungreased cookie sheets. Bake for 9 to 10 minutes or until cookies are lightly browned. Transfer cookies to a wire rack and let cool. Makes about 36 cookies.

EACH COOKIE: 140 cal., 7 g total fat (5 g sat. fat), 13 mg chol., 100 mg sodium, 18 g carbo., 0 g fiber, 1 g pro. Daily Values: 2% vit. A, 1% vit. C, 1% calcium, 2% iron.

Red Velvet Shortbread Cookies

PREP: 30 MINUTES **BAKE:** 20 MINUTES

- 1¼ cups all-purpose flour
- ⅓ cup sugar
- 2 Tbsp. unsweetened cocoa powder
- ½ cup butter, cut up
- 1 Tbsp. red food coloring
- ½ cup semisweet chocolate pieces
- 1 tsp. shortening

1. Preheat oven to 325°F. In a food processor combine flour, sugar, cocoa powder, and ¼ teaspoon *salt*. Cover and process with on/off turns until combined. Add butter and red food coloring. Process with on/off turns until mixture resembles fine crumbs. Process until mixture forms a ball.

2. On a lightly floured surface, knead dough until smooth. Roll dough to a ½-inch thickness. Using a floured 1½-inch round cutter, cut out dough. Place 1 inch apart on an ungreased cookie sheet.

3. Bake for 20 to 25 minutes or until centers are set. Transfer cookies to a wire rack and let cool.

4. In a heavy saucepan melt chocolate pieces and shortening over low heat, stirring constantly. Dip half of each cookie into melted chocolate; if desired, sprinkle with finely chopped toasted nuts or nonpareils. Let stand until set. Store undipped cookies in an airtight container at room temperature for up to 3 days or freeze dipped or undipped cookies in an airtight container for up to 3 months. Makes about 28 cookies.

EACH COOKIE: 74 cal., 4 g total fat (3 g sat. fat), 9 mg chol., 45 mg sodium, 8 g carbo., 0 g fiber, 1 g pro. Daily Values: 2% vit. A, 1% calcium, 2% iron.

Cranberry Oatmeal Cookies

PREP: 30 MINUTES
BAKE: 12 MINUTES PER BATCH

- 1½ cups butter, softened
- 1¾ cups packed brown sugar
- 1 cup granulated sugar
- 1½ tsp. baking soda
- 1½ tsp. ground nutmeg
- 3 eggs
- ¼ cup apple butter
- 1 4-serving-size pkg. French vanilla instant pudding and pie filling mix
- 3 cups all-purpose flour
- 4 cups rolled oats
- 1½ cups dried cranberries
- 1½ cups coarsely chopped pecans

1. Preheat oven to 350°F. In a large mixing bowl beat butter with an electric mixer on medium to high speed for 30 seconds. Add brown sugar, granulated sugar, soda, nutmeg, and 1 teaspoon *salt*. Beat until combined, scraping bowl occasionally. Beat in eggs and apple butter until combined. Beat in pudding mix and as much of the flour as you can with the mixer. Stir in any remaining flour, oats, cranberries, and pecans.

2. Drop dough by rounded measuring tablespoons 1½ inches apart onto ungreased cookie sheets. Bake about 12 minutes or until browned. Transfer to wire racks; cool. Makes about 60 cookies.

EACH COOKIE: 163 cal., 7 g total fat (3 g sat. fat), 23 mg chol., 133 mg sodium, 23 g carbo., 1 g fiber, 2 g pro. Daily Values: 3% vit. A, 1% calcium, 4% iron.

Streusel Cookies

PREP: 35 MINUTES
CHILL: 2 HOURS
BAKE: 10 MINUTES PER BATCH

- 1 cup butter, softened
- 1 cup granulated sugar
- 2 tsp. baking powder
- 2 eggs
- ½ tsp. almond extract
- 2½ cups all-purpose flour
- ⅔ cup all-purpose flour
- ¼ cup packed brown sugar
- 1½ tsp. ground cinnamon
- ¼ tsp. ground nutmeg
- ¼ cup butter

1. In a large mixing bowl beat 1 cup butter with an electric mixer on medium to high speed for 30 seconds. Add 1 cup granulated sugar, baking powder, and ½ teaspoon *salt*. Beat until combined, scraping bowl occasionally. Beat in eggs and almond extract. Beat in 2½ cups flour with the mixer. Divide dough in half. Cover and chill for 2 hours or until dough is easy to handle.

2. Preheat oven to 375°F. In a bowl combine ⅔ cup flour, ¼ cup brown sugar, cinnamon, nutmeg, and dash *salt*. Using a pastry blender, cut in ¼ cup butter until mixture resembles coarse cornmeal.

3. On a lightly floured surface, roll half the dough at a time to a ¼-inch thickness. Using a 3-inch round cookie cutter, cut dough into rounds. Place cutouts 1 inch apart on an ungreased cookie sheet. Spoon about 2 teaspoons of the cinnamon-crumb mixture over each cookie, pressing mixture lightly into the cookies.

4. Bake about 10 minutes or until edges are firm and bottoms are lightly browned. Transfer cookies to wire racks; cool. Makes about 24 cookies.

EACH COOKIE: 187 cal., 10 g total fat (6 g sat. fat), 43 mg chol., 150 mg sodium, 22 g carbo., 0 g fiber, 2 g pro. Daily Values: 6% vit. A, 2% calcium, 5% iron.

Tropical Vacation Cookies

PREP: 25 MINUTES
BAKE: 10 MINUTES PER BATCH
STAND: 1 MINUTE

- 1 8-oz. can crushed pineapple
- ½ cup butter, softened
- ¾ cup granulated sugar
- ¼ cup packed brown sugar
- 1 tsp. baking powder
- ¼ tsp. baking soda
- 1 egg
- 1 teaspoon vanilla
- 1 teaspoon rum flavoring
- 2 cups all-purpose flour
- ½ cup chopped macadamia nuts
- ⅔ cup shredded coconut, toasted
- 2 cups powdered sugar

1. Preheat oven to 375°F. Drain pineapple well, reserving liquid. In a large mixing bowl beat butter with an electric mixer on medium speed for 30 seconds. Add granulated sugar and brown sugar. Beat until combined, scraping bowl occasionally. Beat in baking powder, baking soda, and ¼ teaspoon *salt*. Add egg, drained pineapple, vanilla, and rum flavoring; beat until combined. Beat in flour. Stir in nuts and ⅓ cup of the coconut.

2. Drop dough by rounded teaspoons 2 inches apart onto an ungreased cookie sheet. Bake for 10 to 12 minutes or until tops are golden. Cool on cookie sheet for 1 minute. Transfer cookies to wire racks and cool completely.

3. Beat together powdered sugar and enough pineapple liquid to make a drizzling consistency (2 to 3 tablespoons). Drizzle over cookies and sprinkle with coconut. Makes about 48 cookies.

EACH COOKIE: 90 cal., 4 g total fat (2 g sat. fat), 9 mg chol., 42 mg sodium, 14 g carbo., 0 g fiber, 1 g pro. Daily Values 1% vit. A, 1% vit. C, 1% calcium, 2% iron.

FAMILY PARTY DRINKS

Pomegranate Tea

PREP: 10 MINUTES **STAND:** 30 MINUTES

      3 cups water
      3 Tbsp. sugar
      1 family-size tea bag
      1 cup pomegranate juice
    ¼ tsp. almond extract
         Raw sugar or brown sugar (optional)
         Lemon wedges (optional)

1. In a medium saucepan bring water and sugar to boiling. Remove saucepan from heat. Add tea bag. Allow to stand, covered, for 30 minutes; remove tea bag.

2. Add pomegranate juice and almond extract. Reheat, if necessary. If desired, sweeten to taste with raw sugar. Serve the tea warm or cold; if desired, garnish with lemon wedges. Makes 4 (8-ounce) servings.

LOW FAT **EACH SERVING:** 75 cal., 0 g total fat (0 g sat. fat), 0 mg chol., 8 mg sodium, 19 g carbo., 0 g fiber, 0 g pro. Daily Values: 11% vit. C, 2% iron.

Eggnog Punch

START TO FINISH: 15 MINUTES **FAST!**

    1¾ to 2 qt. French vanilla or cinnamon ice cream
      2 qt. dairy eggnog or canned eggnog, chilled (8 cups)
      1 1-liter bottle cream soda, chilled
         Peppermint sticks, cinnamon sticks, and/or candy canes (optional)
    ⅛ tsp. ground cinnamon

1. Place ice cream in a large punch bowl. Add half of the eggnog. Using a potato masher, stir and mash mixture until ice cream is melted and mixture is well combined. Stir in remaining eggnog. Slowly pour in cream soda, stirring to combine. Serve in punch cups or small glasses. If desired, garnish each glass with a peppermint stick. Sprinkle lightly with cinnamon. Makes about 24 (6-ounce) servings.

EACH SERVING: 224 cal., 11 g total fat (7 g sat. fat), 79 mg chol., 77 mg sodium, 26 g carbo., 0 g fiber, 5 g pro. Daily Values: 6% vit. A, 2% vit. C, 17% calcium, 1% iron.

Creamy Fruit Punch with Lime

START TO FINISH: 15 MINUTES

1 1¾-qt. carton strawberry ice cream
1 1¾-qt. carton peach ice cream
2 12-oz. cans evaporated milk, chilled
1 Tbsp. finely shredded lime peel
¾ cup lime juice
1 2-liter bottle ginger ale, chilled
  Lime wedge (optional)
⅓ cup sugar (optional)
  Fresh pineapple wedges (optional)
  Whole fresh strawberries (optional)

1. Stir ice creams to soften; transfer to a very large punch bowl. Gradually stir in evaporated milk; stir in lime peel and lime juice. Carefully stir in ginger ale.

2. If desired, wet rims of glasses with lime wedge. Spread sugar in a small saucer. Dip rims of glasses in sugar to coat. If desired, garnish glasses with pineapple wedges and strawberries. Fill glasses with punch. Makes 32 (6-ounce) servings.

EACH SERVING: 209 cal., 9 g total fat (6 g sat. fat), 46 mg chol., 64 mg sodium, 28 g carbo., 0 g fiber, 4 g pro. Daily Values: 6% vit. A, 9% vit. C, 12% calcium, 2% iron.

Pumpkin Pie Sipper

START TO FINISH: 10 MINUTES

4 cups milk or vanilla soymilk
1 cup canned pumpkin
¼ cup sugar
1 tsp. ground nutmeg
1 tsp. vanilla
  Cinnamon sticks

1. In a large saucepan combine milk, pumpkin, sugar, and nutmeg. Heat through (do not boil). Remove from heat. Stir in vanilla. Garnish with cinnamon sticks. Makes 6 (7-ounce) servings.

EACH SERVING: 130 cal., 3 g total fat (2 g sat. fat), 13 mg chol., 69 mg sodium, 19 g carbo., 1 g fiber, 6 g pro. Daily Values: 133% vit. A, 3% vit. C, 20% calcium, 3% iron.

Hot Cider Surprise Punch

PREP: 10 MINUTES **COOK:** 20 MINUTES

4 cups apple cider
4 cups cranberry juice
2 cups pomegranate juice
6 inches stick cinnamon
3 pieces whole star anise
2 2- to 3-inch strips orange peel*
1 2- to 3-inch strip lemon peel*
  Orange slices

1. In a 4- to 5-quart Dutch oven combine cider, cranberry juice, pomegranate juice, stick cinnamon, star anise, orange peel, and lemon peel. Bring to boiling; reduce heat. Simmer, covered, for 20 minutes. Using a slotted spoon, remove stick cinnamon, star anise, orange peel, and lemon peel. Serve warm in mugs and garnish with orange slices. Makes 10 (8-ounce) servings.

***TIP:** When removing citrus peel, avoid using the white pith, which will add bitterness.

EACH SERVING: 122 cal., 0 g total fat, 0 mg chol., 20 mg sodium, 31 g carbo., 0 g fiber, 0 g pro. Daily Values: 49% vit. C, 1% iron.

Hazelnut Chocolate Cooler

PREP: 10 MINUTES **STAND:** 4 MINUTES
COOL: 30 MINUTES

¾ cup boiling water
2 vanilla-hazelnut- or French vanilla-flavored tea bags
⅓ cup chocolate-hazelnut spread
2 cups milk
2 6-oz. cartons vanilla yogurt
  Small ice cubes or crushed ice
  Whipped cream
  Chocolate-flavored syrup

1. Place the water in a 2-cup glass measure. Add tea bags; steep for 4 minutes. Remove and discard tea bags. Stir in chocolate-hazelnut spread until smooth. Cool completely, about 30 minutes.

2. In a blender combine tea mixture, milk, and yogurt. Cover and blend until frothy. To serve, pour mixture over ice in glasses. Garnish drinks with whipped cream and chocolate syrup. Makes 5 (12-ounce) servings.

EACH SERVING: 159 cal., 6 g total fat (1 g sat. fat), 10 mg chol., 85 mg sodium, 20 g carbo., 0 g fiber, 6 g pro. Daily Values: 4% vit. A, 1% vit. C, 19% calcium.

Frosty Mint Cocktail

PREP: 20 MINUTES **FREEZE:** 12 HOURS
STAND: 30 MINUTES

1 cup water
⅔ cup sugar
½ cup loosely packed mint leaves
3 cups orange juice
1 6-ounce can unsweetened pineapple juice
⅓ cup lemon juice
1 1-liter bottle lemon-lime carbonated beverage, chilled

1. In a small saucepan combine water, sugar, and mint leaves. Bring to boiling. Reduce heat and simmer, uncovered, for 2 minutes. Remove from heat; strain. Discard mint leaves. Pour sugar mixture into a 2-quart square baking dish. Stir in orange juice, pineapple juice, and lemon juice. Cover and freeze at least 12 hours or until completely frozen.

2. To serve, let frozen mixture stand at room temperature for 30 minutes. Scrape the top of the mixture with a large metal spoon to form slush. Spoon slush into 12-ounce glasses, filling glasses half full. Fill glass with carbonated beverage. Makes 10 to 12 (12-ounce) servings.

EACH SERVING: 134 cal., 0 g total fat, 0 mg chol., 23 mg sodium, 34 g carbo., 0 g fiber, 1 g pro. Daily Values: 3% vit. A, 71% vit. C, 1% calcium, 1% iron.

MENUS

FOOD IS AN ESSENTIAL ELEMENT IN OUR EVERYDAY LIVES, WHETHER IT IS ENJOYED AS A QUICK LUNCH-ON-THE-RUN OR A PULL-OUT-THE-STOPS ELEGANT DINNER PARTY. HERE ARE SOME MENU IDEAS TO GET YOU STARTED ON YOUR NEXT CELEBRATION—BIG OR SMALL. BON APPÉTIT!

Classy Cuban Sandwiches
page 266

Menus for Many Occasions

Flip through the following 28 menus for a variety of different occasions. Use them—all carefully chosen from our Prize Tested Recipes® collection from 2006—to create memorable and tasty breakfasts, brunches, lunches, snacks, and dinners.

Overnight Coffee Cake
page 258

Cheese-Topped Steaks
page 270

Panna Cotta Di Casa
page 268

make it healthful

YOU DON'T HAVE TO SACRIFICE FLAVOR TO EAT HEALTHFULLY, AND THESE RECIPES WILL PROVE THAT. SERVE THESE DISHES TO YOUR FAMILY OR INVITE YOUR FRIENDS OVER TO SHARE—THEY'LL NEVER GUESS THEY'RE EATING GOOD-FOR-YOU FOOD—AND THERE'S NO REASON TO TELL THEM!

LUNCH ON THE DECK
Reduced-Fat Blue Cheese Spread (page 256)
Spicy Chicken Salad Wraps (page 257)
Fruit salad drizzled with purchased raspberry yogurt
Banana Oatmeal Cookies (page 287)
Iced tea with lemon

SOME LIKE IT HOT
Cilantro Canapés (page 296)
Glazed Chicken with Three-Pepper Salsa (page 281)
Hot cooked rice
Strawberries drizzled with balsamic vinegar
Ice water with lime slices

SOUP AND SANDWICH LUNCH
Chilled Tomato Soup for 4 (page 257)
Asian Tuna Wraps (page 275)
Cut-up melon
Less-Guilt Oatmeal Raisin Cookies (page 257)
Iced green tea

SOUTH-OF-THE BORDER SUPPER
Fat-free tortilla chips
Sonoma Harvest Salsa (page 278)
Salsa Beef Sandwiches (page 275)
Taco Soup (page 275)
Very Berry Tarts (page 257)
Iced tea with lemon

Sonoma Harvest Salsa
page 278

Reduced-Fat Blue Cheese Spread
page 256

30 minutes or less

LET'S FACE IT ... WE'RE ALL BUSY THESE DAYS. FROM WORKING LONG HOURS TO TAKING KIDS TO SOCCER PRACTICE, LIFE CAN SEEM OVERWHELMING. IT DOESN'T HAVE TO BE WHEN IT COMES TO GETTING A TASTY MEAL ON THE TABLE. THE RECIPES IN THESE MENUS WILL PROVE TO YOU THAT QUICK DOESN'T MEAN DULL—IN THESE CASES, IT MEANS DELICIOUS!

MAKE IT ITALIAN
Hearty Italian Stew (page 293)
Green salad with purchased balsamic vinaigrette
Purchased foccacia bread with olive oil for dipping
Strawberry Ricotta Crostini (page 283)
Dry red wine or sparkling water

KID FAVORITES
Creamy Ranch Chicken (page 262)
Steamed broccoli with cheese sauce
Corn bread with honey and butter
Watermelon with Fruit Salsa (page 282)
Milk or chocolate milk

NOODLE NIGHT
Purchased deli egg rolls
Peanut-Chicken Bowl (page 284)
Purchased ginger ice cream
Imported beer

MEXICAN MARVELS
Chipotle Roll-Ups (page 279)
Chicken Tacos with a Twist (page 263)
Packaged Spanish-flavored rice
Canned refried beans
Vanilla ice cream
Margaritas or lemonade

Watermelon with Fruit Salsa
page 282

Peanut-Chicken Bowl
page 284

Creamy Ranch Chicken
page 262

morning meals

BREAKFAST AND BRUNCH CAN BE REALLY SPECIAL MEALS WHETHER YOU'RE CELEBRATING A HOLIDAY BEFORE OPENING GIFTS (IF YOU CAN GET THE KIDS TO WAIT THAT LONG!) OR A SIMPLE WEDNESDAY MORNING MEAL BEFORE WORK. TURN TO THESE MENUS AND RECIPES AND MAKE SURE THAT THE FIRST MEAL OF THE DAY IS ONE OF THE BEST.

GRADUATION BRUNCH
Spinach Artichoke Frittata (page 291)
Strawberries dipped in chocolate
Overnight Coffee Cake (page 258)
Coffee and hot tea
Mimosas

ON-THE-GO BREAKFAST
Fabulous Bagel Spread (page 276)
Chai Chutney Schmear (page 277)
Assorted bagels
Cut-up bananas
Tutti-Fruity Smoothie (page 286)
Coffee or milk

LAZY SUNDAY BRUNCH
Super Pancakes (page 291)
Scrambled eggs with Monterey Jack cheese
Bacon or sausage patties
Hash brown potatoes
Pomegranate Tea (page 300)

HOLIDAY MORNING MEAL
Cranberry-Almond Coffee Cake (page 259)
Italian Breakfast Burrito (page 290)
Cut-up pear and apple salad
Eggnog Punch (page 300)

Tutti-Fruitty Smoothie
page 286

Fabulous Bagel Spread
page 276

sandwich meals

SOMETIMES THERE'S NOTHING MORE COMFORTING OR SATISFYING THAN A SANDWICH. THEY'RE EASY ON THE COOK, EVERYONE LOVES THEM, AND CLEANUP IS A SNAP. PAIR WITH SOUPS, SALADS, OR YUMMY SIDES AND DESSERTS AND YOU'LL FORGET THAT IT IS "JUST" A SANDWICH MEAL.

AFTER THE GAME
Tuna Appetizer Cheesecake (page 261)
Picadillo Sandwiches (page 288)
Purchased potato chips and dip
Tropical Fruit-Topped Spice Cake (page 255)
Cold beer or assorted soft drinks

GEAR UP FOR SHOPPING
Quick Apple Carrot Cheese Balls (page 279)
Open-Face Chicken and Basil Sandwiches (page 267)
Deli pasta salad
Hot fudge sundaes
Raspberry lemonade

FRIDAY NIGHT BEFORE THE MOVIE
Island Reuben (page 267)
Baked french fries with ketchup
Pickles and olives
Apple-Pear Pizza Pie (page 283)
Assorted soft drinks

PICNIC IN THE PARK
Crunchy Curried Chicken Salad Wraps (page 267)
Carrot and celery sticks with ranch dip
Deli mustard potato salad
Nutty Cereal Cookies (page 286)
Iced tea

Nutty Cereal Cookies
page 286

Picadillo Sandwiches
page 288

exotic endeavors

TANTALIZE THOSE TASTE BUDS WITH SOME EXOTIC FLAVORS. EXPLORE DIFFERENT REGIONS OF THE WORLD THROUGH FOOD—AND PERHAPS COOK WITH INGREDIENTS YOU'VE NEVER USED BEFORE. TRYING TO GET KIDS TO EAT WITH YOU? FIND BOOKS ABOUT THE DIFFERENT REGIONS AND TALK ABOUT THE FOOD AND EACH AREA'S CULTURE. THE WHOLE FAMILY WILL ENJOY AN INTERNATIONAL FOOD QUEST.

ORIENTAL FEAST
Black Bean and Ginger Lettuce Wraps (page 279)
Vegetable Egg Drop Soup with Spring Onion Relish (page 273)
Purchased vegetable fried rice
Ginger Peach Freeze (page 282)
Saké or sparkling lemon-flavored water

CRAZY FOR CUBAN
Pita chips with black bean salsa
Classy Cuban Sandwiches (page 266)
Fried plantains
Purchased flan
Mojitos

A TASTE OF TUSCANY
Tuscanini Spread (page 277)
Sensational Portobellos (page 297)
Zuppa Toscana (page 289)
Mixed greens with Italian dressing and cooked calamari slices
Panna Cotta Di Casa (page 268)
Chianti

TIME FOR TAPAS
Open-Face Crab Ciabatta (page 274)
Artichoke-and-Mushroom-Topped Camembert (page 297)
Savory Shrimp Pâté (page 297)
Crostini a la Mia (page 266)
Arugula-Canellini Dip (page 278)
Assorted premium chocolates
Spanish or French red wine or water with lemon slices

Open-Face Crab Ciabatta
page 274

Ginger Peach Freeze
page 282

Arugula-Canellini Dip
page 278

simply awesome

THERE ARE OCCASIONS THAT CALL FOR PULLING OUT ALL THE STOPS AND SPLURGING A LITTLE ON THE FOOD AND DRINK YOU SERVE. TURN TO THESE MENUS WHEN SUCH SITUATIONS ARISE—THE LUCKY HONOREE WILL DEFINITELY FEEL SPECIAL AFTER EATING THESE AWE-INSPIRING MEALS.

ANNIVERSARY CELEBRATION
Layered Olive Appetizers (page 297)
Brandy Steak (page 271)
Roasted Asparagus-Cannellini Bean Salad (page 273)
French bread and butter
Chocolate Mousse with Raspberry Sauce (page 268)
Red wine

START-OF-SUMMER SOIRÉE
Artichoke-Water Chestnut Spread (page 279)
Pacific Sunset Chicken (page 255)
Mesclun salad with raspberry vinaigrette and blue cheese crumbles
Tropical Pavlova (page 255)
Semisweet white wine or sparkling raspberry water

BIRTHDAY PARTY BASH
Purchased smoked salmon and sturdy crackers
Cheese-Topped Steaks (page 270)
Glazed Pearl Onions (page 272)
Steamed broccoli with hollandaise sauce
Caramel Apple Trifle Parfaits (page 269)
Red wine sangria or red wine

FATHER'S DAY FETE
Purchased cooked shrimp with cocktail sauce and lemons
Glazed Beef Tenderloin with Onion Chutney (page 271)
Fresh mozzarella and tomato salad with balsamic vinaigrette and snipped basil
Chocolate-Banana Cheese Pie (page 269)
Red wine or dark beer

Glazed Pearl Onions
page 272

Chocolate Mousse with Raspberry Sauce
page 268

grill it right

TIME TO FIRE UP THE GRILL! SOMETIMES THERE'S NOTHING BETTER THAN A MEAL COOKED OVER FIRE TO TANTALIZE THOSE TASTE BUDS AND SATISFY THE APPETITE. WHILE WE ALL LOVE TO GRILL IN THE SUMMER, DON'T FORGET IT'S A METHOD OF COOKING THAT YOU CAN ENJOY ALL YEAR LONG!

GUYS GAME NIGHT
Roasted Snack Mix (page 287)
Chorizo Burgers (page 281)
Deli potato salad
Deli baked beans
Streusel Cookies (page 299)
Cold beer

INVITE THE NEIGHBORS
Ham Bites with Cilantro-Corn Cream (page 279)
Steaks with Tomato Salsa (page 270)
Deli scalloped potatoes
Soft breadsticks and butter
Pears with Walnut Streusel (page 283)
Red or blush wine and lemonade

SHRIMP ON THE BARBIE
Sliced cheese and salami platter with crackers
Spicy Grilled Shrimp (page 280)
Artichokes and Asparagus with Tomato Topper (page 273)
Baked potatoes with sour cream and butter
Ciabatta bread and butter
Deli cheesecake topped with thawed frozen strawberries
Riesling or lemonade

SATURDAY NIGHT SUPPER
Fruit-and-Nut Cheese Balls (page 279)
Salsa Verde Pork Salad (page 281)
Warmed whole wheat rolls
Banana splits
Iced tea with lemon or dry white wine

Spicy Grilled Shrimp
page 280

Steaks with Tomato Salsa
page 270

ANNUAL Recipes INDEX

A

B

M

serving, 214
Tex-Mex Turkey Pasta Salad, 295
trussing, 214
Turkey, Asparagus, and Pasta, 295
Turkey Frame Soup, 227
Turkey Paella Salad, 294
whole, yield from, 214

V

VEGETABLES. *See also specific vegetables*
Chicken Lo Mein, 263
Grilled Garden Pasta, 41
Hearty Italian Stew, 293
Peanut-Chicken Bowl, 284
Pizza Bar for a Crowd, 110
roasting times, 29
Summer Vegetables and Herb
  Dressing, 152
Turkey Frame Soup, 227

W

Waffles, Topped Coconut, 290
WALNUTS
Blueberry Coffee Cake with Walnut
  Sticky Topping, 259
Breakfast in Bread, 57
Caramel Apple Trifle Parfaits, 269
Nutty Cereal Cookies, 286
Nutty Tuna Bundles, 261
Pears with Walnut Streusel, 283
Toasted Walnuts, 46
Waldorf Wilted Salad, 236
Water Chestnut Spread, Artichoke-, 279
WATERMELON
Lemon-Watermelon Bites, 162
Melon Salad with Lime Syrup, 179
Watermelon with Fruit Salsa, 282
WINE
Orange and Mint Sangria, 239
Sparkling Sangria, 239
Winter Fruit Sangria, 239

Z

ZUCCHINI
Grilled Garden Pasta, 41
Spring Green on Greens, 273

Spring Vegetable Soup with Pesto
  Croutons, 273
Steak with Squash and Arugula, 144
Summer Vegetable Pasta Salad, 173
Tomato-Squash Salad, 74

TIPS
artichokes, buying and storing, 70
artichokes, preparing and eating, 71
artichokes, steaming, 70
Asian dressings, cooking with, 94
asparagus vinegar, buying, 52
baking powder, freshness of, 233
beef pot roast, preparing, 195
bouquet garni, preparing, 194
cedar papers, grilling in, 163
cheese, artisanal, buying, 163
cheese and beer, pairing, 17
chile peppers, working with, 49
chives, cooking with, 84
chives, cutting, 84
chocolate, buying, 77
chutney, buying, 52
clams, buying and storing, 100
clams, varieties of, 101
clementines, serving ideas, 17
coconut, cooking with, 96
coconut, cracking open, 96
coconut, varieties of, 98
coconut, young, preparing, 99
coconut curls, creating, 99
coffee, adding to recipes, 64
coffee, fair trade, buying, 120
coffee machines, cleaning, 120
cranberry dessert sauce, buying, 35
edible flowers, serving ideas, 118–119
figs, buying and storing, 181
flavored syrups, serving ideas, 136
gratins, preparing, 203
greens, wilting, 237
guava cactus sauce, buying, 35
healthy food choices, 50–51
herbs, preserving, 158–159
hot dogs, topping ideas, 138
lemon verbena, cooking with, 89
lemon verbena, growing, 89
marigolds, handling, 156
marshmallows, buying, 53
marshmallows, toasting, 53
mayonnaise, flavoring ideas, 121
peanut butter dessert, preparing, 76
peppers, buying and storing, 90

persimmons, buying and storing, 217
pink pesto, buying, 35
pizza, healthful, preparing, 68–69
pizza-style lahvosh, 185
rosemary, cooking with, 83
salmon, buying, 197
side dishes, for grilled entrées, 45
snack gift packs, assembling, 17
soaps, odor-neutralizing, 163
spinach, buying and washing, 66
sweet potatoes, varieties of, 235
tarragon, cooking with, 92
tarragon, growing, 92
tomatoes, mini, growing, 72
tomatoes, mini, varieties of, 73
traveling, packing food for, 179
turkey questions and answers, 215
Valentine's Day shaped cookies, 34
wine, matching with food, 185

MENUS
After the Game, 310
Anniversary Celebration, 314
Birthday Party Bash, 314
Crazy for Cuban, 312
Father's Day Fete, 314
Friday Night Before the Movie, 310
Gear Up for Shopping, 310
Graduation Brunch, 308
Guys Game Night, 316
Holiday Morning Meal, 308
Invite the Neighbors, 316
Kid Favorites, 306
Lazy Sunday Brunch, 308
Lunch on the Deck, 304
Make It Italian, 306
Mexican Marvels, 306
Noodle Night, 306
On-the-Go Breakfast, 308
Oriental Feast, 312
Picnic in the Park, 310
Saturday Night Supper, 316
Shrimp on the Barbie, 316
Some Like It Hot, 304
Soup and Sandwich Lunch, 304
South-of-the-Border Supper, 304
Start-of-Summer Soirée, 314
A Taste of Tuscany, 312
Time for Tapas, 312

Nutrition information.
With each recipe, we give important nutrition information you easily can apply to your own needs. You'll find the calorie count of each serving and the amount, in grams, of fat, saturated fat, cholesterol, sodium, carbohydrates, fiber, and protein to help you keep tabs on what you eat. You can check the levels of each recipe serving for vitamin A, vitamin C, calcium, and iron, if they are present. These are noted in percentages of the Daily Values. The Daily Values are dietary standards determined by the Food and Drug Administration (FDA). To stay in line with the nutrition breakdown of each recipe, follow the suggested number of servings.

How we analyze.
The Better Homes and Gardens® Test Kitchen computer analyzes each recipe for the nutritional value of a single serving.
- The analysis does not include optional ingredients.
- We use the first serving size listed when a range is given. For example: If we say a recipe "Makes 4 to 6 servings," the nutrition information is based on 4 servings.
- When ingredient choices (such as butter or margarine) appear in a recipe, we use the first one mentioned for analysis. The ingredient order does not mean we prefer one ingredient over another.
- When milk and eggs are recipe ingredients, the analysis is calculated using 2 percent (reduced-fat) milk and large eggs.

What you need.
The dietary guidelines below suggest nutrient levels that moderately active adults should strive to eat each day. There is no real harm in going over or under these guidelines in any single day, but it is a good idea to aim for a balanced diet over time.

Calories: About 2,000
Total fat: Less than 65 grams
Saturated fat: Less than 20 grams
Cholesterol: Less than 300 milligrams
Carbohydrates: About 300 grams
Sodium: Less than 2,400 milligrams
Dietary fiber: 20 to 30 grams

Low Fat icon.
Certain recipes throughout the book have an icon next to the nutrition information that indicates the recipe is low fat. For a recipe to earn this icon, it must meet certain nutritional requirements. For a main dish, one serving should have 12 grams of fat per serving or less, one serving of a side dish should have 5 grams of fat or less, an appetizer serving should have 2 grams of fat or less, and cookies and desserts should have 2 grams of fat or less per serving. Occasionally, the fat level will slightly exceed one of the recommended numbers, but typically they remain below the listed amounts.

Emergency substitutions.

If you don't have:	Substitute:
Bacon, 1 slice, crisp-cooked, crumbled	1 tablespoon cooked bacon pieces
Baking powder, 1 teaspoon	$^1/_2$ teaspoon cream of tartar plus $^1/_4$ teaspoon baking soda
Balsamic vinegar, 1 tablespoon	1 tablespoon cider vinegar or red wine vinegar plus $^1/_2$ teaspoon sugar
Bread crumbs, fine dry, $^1/_4$ cup	$^3/_4$ cup soft bread crumbs, or $^1/_4$ cup cracker crumbs, or $^1/_4$ cup cornflake crumbs
Broth, beef or chicken, 1 cup	1 teaspoon or 1 cube instant beef or chicken bouillon plus 1 cup hot water
Butter, 1 cup	1 cup shortening plus $^1/_4$ teaspoon salt, if desired
Buttermilk, 1 cup	1 tablespoon lemon juice or vinegar plus enough milk to make 1 cup (let stand 5 minutes before using), or 1 cup plain yogurt
Chocolate, semisweet, 1 ounce	3 tablespoons semisweet chocolate pieces, or 1 ounce unsweetened chocolate plus 1 tablespoon granulated sugar, or 1 tablespoon unsweetened cocoa powder plus 2 teaspoons sugar and 2 teaspoons shortening
Chocolate, sweet baking, 4 ounces	$^1/_4$ cup unsweetened cocoa powder plus $^1/_3$ cup granulated sugar and 3 tablespoons shortening
Chocolate, unsweetened, 1 ounce	3 tablespoons unsweetened cocoa powder plus 1 tablespoon cooking oil or shortening, melted
Cornstarch, 1 tablespoon (for thickening)	2 tablespoons all-purpose flour
Corn syrup (light-colored), 1 cup	1 cup granulated sugar plus $^1/_4$ cup water
Egg, 1 whole	2 egg whites, or 2 egg yolks, or $^1/_4$ cup refrigerated or frozen egg product, thawed
Flour, cake, 1 cup	1 cup minus 2 tablespoons all-purpose flour
Flour, self-rising, 1 cup	1 cup all-purpose flour plus 1 teaspoon baking powder, $^1/_2$ teaspoon salt, and $^1/_4$ teaspoon baking soda
Garlic, 1 clove	$^1/_2$ teaspoon bottled minced garlic or $^1/_8$ teaspoon garlic powder
Ginger, grated fresh, 1 teaspoon	$^1/_4$ teaspoon ground ginger
Half-and-half or light cream, 1 cup	1 tablespoon melted butter or margarine plus enough whole milk to make 1 cup
Molasses, 1 cup	1 cup honey
Mustard, dry, 1 teaspoon	1 tablespoon prepared mustard (in cooked mixtures)
Mustard, prepared, 1 tablespoon	$^1/_2$ teaspoon dry mustard plus 2 teaspoons vinegar
Onion, chopped, $^1/_2$ cup	2 tablespoons dried minced onion or $^1/_2$ teaspoon onion powder
Sour cream, dairy, 1 cup	1 cup plain yogurt
Sugar, brown, 1 cup packed	1 cup granulated sugar plus 2 tablespoons molasses
Sugar, granulated, 1 cup	1 cup packed brown sugar or 2 cups sifted powdered sugar
Tomato juice, 1 cup	$^1/_2$ cup tomato sauce plus $^1/_2$ cup water
Tomato sauce, 2 cups	$^3/_4$ cup tomato paste plus 1 cup water
Vanilla bean, 1 whole	2 teaspoons vanilla
Wine, red, 1 cup	1 cup beef or chicken broth in savory recipes; cranberry juice in desserts
Wine, white, 1 cup	1 cup chicken broth in savory recipes; apple juice or white grape juice in desserts
Yeast, active dry, 1 package	about $2^1/_4$ teaspoons active dry yeast

Seasonings

Apple pie spice, 1 teaspoon	$^1/_2$ teaspoon ground cinnamon plus $^1/_4$ teaspoon ground nutmeg, $^1/_8$ teaspoon ground allspice, and dash ground cloves or ginger
Cajun seasoning, 1 tablespoon	$^1/_2$ teaspoon white pepper, $^1/_2$ teaspoon garlic powder, $^1/_2$ teaspoon onion powder, $^1/_2$ teaspoon cayenne pepper, $^1/_2$ teaspoon paprika, and $^1/_2$ teaspoon black pepper
Herbs, snipped fresh, 1 tablespoon	$^1/_2$ to 1 teaspoon dried herb, crushed, or $^1/_2$ teaspoon ground herb
Poultry seasoning, 1 teaspoon	$^3/_4$ teaspoon dried sage, crushed, plus $^1/_4$ teaspoon dried thyme or marjoram, crushed
Pumpkin pie spice, 1 teaspoon	$^1/_2$ teaspoon ground cinnamon plus $^1/_4$ teaspoon ground ginger, $^1/_4$ teaspoon ground allspice, and $^1/_8$ teaspoon ground nutmeg

Metric Information

The charts on this page provide a guide for converting measurements from the U.S. customary system, which is used throughout this book, to the metric system.

Product Differences

Most of the ingredients called for in the recipes in this book are available in most countries. However, some are known by different names. Here are some common American ingredients and their possible counterparts:

- Sugar (white) is granulated, fine granulated, or castor sugar.
- Powdered sugar is icing sugar.
- All-purpose flour is enriched, bleached or unbleached white household flour. When self-rising flour is used in place of all-purpose flour in a recipe that calls for leavening, omit the leavening agent (baking soda or baking powder) and salt.
- Light-colored corn syrup is golden syrup.
- Cornstarch is cornflour.
- Baking soda is bicarbonate of soda.
- Vanilla or vanilla extract is vanilla essence.
- Green, red, or yellow sweet peppers are capsicums or bell peppers.
- Golden raisins are sultanas.

Volume and Weight

The United States traditionally uses cup measures for liquid and solid ingredients. The chart below shows the approximate imperial and metric equivalents. If you are accustomed to weighing solid ingredients, the following approximate equivalents will be helpful.

- 1 cup butter, castor sugar, or rice = 8 ounces = $1/2$ pound = 250 grams
- 1 cup flour = 4 ounces = $1/4$ pound = 125 grams
- 1 cup icing sugar = 5 ounces = 150 grams

Canadian and U.S. volume for a cup measure is 8 fluid ounces (237 ml), but the standard metric equivalent is 250 ml.

1 British imperial cup is 10 fluid ounces.

In Australia, 1 tablespoon equals 20 ml, and there are 4 teaspoons in the Australian tablespoon.

Spoon measures are used for smaller amounts of ingredients. Although the size of the tablespoon varies slightly in different countries, for practical purposes and for recipes in this book, a straight substitution is all that's necessary. Measurements made using cups or spoons always should be level unless stated otherwise.

Common Weight Range Replacements

Imperial / U.S.	Metric
$1/2$ ounce	15 g
1 ounce	25 g or 30 g
4 ounces ($1/4$ pound)	115 g or 125 g
8 ounces ($1/2$ pound)	225 g or 250 g
16 ounces (1 pound)	450 g or 500 g
$1 1/4$ pounds	625 g
$1 1/2$ pounds	750 g
2 pounds or $2 1/4$ pounds	1,000 g or 1 Kg

Oven Temperature Equivalents

Fahrenheit Setting	Celsius Setting*	Gas Setting
300°F	150°C	Gas Mark 2 (very low)
325°F	160°C	Gas Mark 3 (low)
350°F	180°C	Gas Mark 4 (moderate)
375°F	190°C	Gas Mark 5 (moderate)
400°F	200°C	Gas Mark 6 (hot)
425°F	220°C	Gas Mark 7 (hot)
450°F	230°C	Gas Mark 8 (very hot)
475°F	240°C	Gas Mark 9 (very hot)
500°F	260°C	Gas Mark 10 (extremely hot)
Broil	Broil	Grill

*Electric and gas ovens may be calibrated using celsius. However, for an electric oven, increase celsius setting 10 to 20 degrees when cooking above 160°C. For convection or forced air ovens (gas or electric) lower the temperature setting 25°F/10°C when cooking at all heat levels.

Baking Pan Sizes

Imperial / U.S.	Metric
9×$1 1/2$-inch round cake pan	22- or 23×4-cm (1.5 L)
9×$1 1/2$-inch pie plate	22- or 23×4-cm (1 L)
8×8×2-inch square cake pan	20×5-cm (2 L)
9×9×2-inch square cake pan	22- or 23×4.5-cm (2.5 L)
11×7×$1 1/2$-inch baking pan	28×17×4-cm (2 L)
2-quart rectangular baking pan	30×19×4.5-cm (3 L)
13×9×2-inch baking pan	34×22×4.5-cm (3.5 L)
15×10×1-inch jelly roll pan	40×25×2-cm
9×5×3-inch loaf pan	23×13×8-cm (2 L)
2-quart casserole	2 L

U.S. / Standard Metric Equivalents

$1/8$ teaspoon = 0.5 ml

$1/4$ teaspoon = 1 ml

$1/2$ teaspoon = 2 ml

1 teaspoon = 5 ml

1 tablespoon = 15 ml

2 tablespoons = 25 ml

$1/4$ cup = 2 fluid ounces = 50 ml

$1/3$ cup = 3 fluid ounces = 75 ml

$1/2$ cup = 4 fluid ounces = 125 ml

$2/3$ cup = 5 fluid ounces = 150 ml

$3/4$ cup = 6 fluid ounces = 175 ml

1 cup = 8 fluid ounces = 250 ml

2 cups = 1 pint = 500 ml

1 quart = 1 litre